Old Testament Theology

4/22/98

OTHER FORTRESS PRESS BOOKS
BY WALTER BRUEGGEMANN

The Land: Place as Gift, Promise, and Challenge
in the Biblical Faith (1977)

The Prophetic Imagination (1978)

The Creative Word: Canon as a Model for
Biblical Education (1982)

David's Truth in Israel's Imagination and Memory (1985)

Hopeful Imagination: Prophetic Voices in Exile (1986)

Israel's Praise: Doxology against Idolatry and Ideology (1988)

Finally Comes the Poet: Daring Speech
for Proclamation (1989)

Interpretation and Obedience:
From Faithful Reading to Faithful Living (1991)

Texts under Negotiation:
The Bible and Postmodern Imagination (1993)

Old Testament Theology

Essays on Structure, Theme, and Text

Walter Brueggemann

Edited by Patrick D. Miller

FORTRESS PRESS   MINNEAPOLIS

OLD TESTAMENT THEOLOGY
Essays on Structure, Theme, and Text

Library of Congress Cataloging-in-Publication Data

Brueggemann, Walter.
    Old Testament theology : essays on structure, theme, and text
/ Walter Brueggemann ; edited by Patrick D. Miller
      p.   cm.
    Includes bibliographical references and index.
    ISBN 0-8006-2537-4 (alk. paper)
    1. Bible.   O.T.—theology.   I. Miller, Patrick D.   II. Title.
BS1192.5.B78   1992
230—dc20   91-37202
                                    CIP

Manufactured in the U.S.A.   AF 1-2537
96   95   94   93   2   3   4   5   6   7   8   9   10

Contents

Acknowledgments

I AM GLAD TO EXPRESS my appreciation to four people: Marshall Johnson at Fortress Press was willing to take on the manuscript and bring it to print; Tempie Alexander has maintained good order in my work and kept the paper moving in her efficient way; Donna Lograsso has retyped the entire manuscript in speedy fashion, even the small print notes from previously printed copy; Patrick D. Miller thought up the whole idea of republication, and without his initiative and nerve the book would not have happened. My appreciation is genuine and my debts great.

Walter Brueggemann
Columbia Theological Seminary

Abbreviations

AASF	*Annales Academiae Scientiarum Fennicae*
AB	Anchor Bible
AnBib	Analecta biblica
ARW	*Archiv für Religionswissenschaft*
ATD	Das Alte Testament Deutsch
BA	*Biblical Archeologist*
BASOR	*Bulletin of the American Schools of Oriental Research*
BBB	Bonner biblische Beiträge
Bib	*Biblica*
BibOr	Biblica et orientalia
BR	*Biblical Research*
BWANT	Beiträge zur Wissenschaft vom Alten und Neuen Testament
BZ	*Biblische Zeitschrift*
BZAW	Beihefte zur *ZAW*
CBQ	*Catholic Biblical Quarterly*
ConBOT	Coniectanea Biblica, Old Testament
CTM	*Concordia Theological Monthly*

CurTM	*Currents in Theology and Mission*
EvT	*Evangelische Theologie*
FRLANT	Forschungen zur Religion und Literatur des Alten und Neuen Testaments
GAT	Grundrisse zum Alten Testament
HAT	Handbuch zum Alten Testament
HBT	*Horizons in Biblical Theology*
HUCA	*Hebrew Union College Annual*
IDB	*Interpreter's Dictionary of the Bible* (G. A. Buttrick, ed.)
IDBSup	Supplementary volume to *IDB*
Int	*Interpretation*
IRT	Issues in Religion and Theology
JAAR	*Journal of the American Academy of Religion*
JBL	*Journal of Biblical Literature*
JJS	*Journal of Jewish Studies*
JSOT	*Journal for the Study of the Old Testament*
JSOTSup	Journal for the Study of the Old Testament—Supplement Series
JTC	*Journal for Theology and the Church*
KAT	Kommentar zum Alten Testament
LXX	Septuagint
MT	Masoretic Text
NKZ	*Neue kirchliche Zeitschrift*
NovT	*Novum Testamentum*
OBT	Overtures to Biblical Theology
OTL	Old Testament Library
RSV	Revised Standard Version
SBT	Studies in Biblical Theology
SJT	*Scottish Journal of Theology*
SOTSMS	Society for Old Testament Study Monograph Series

ST	*Studia theologica*
SWBA	Social World of Biblical Antiquity
TBü	*Theologische Bücherei*
TD	*Theology Digest*
ThStud	Theologische Studien
TToday	*Theology Today*
TynBul	*Tyndale Bulletin*
TZ	*Theologische Zeitschrift*
UF	*Ugarit-Forschungen*
USQR	*Union Seminary Quarterly Review*
VT	*Vetus Testamentum*
VTSup	Vetus Testamentum, Supplements
WD	*Wort und Dienst*
WMANT	Wissenschaftliche Monographien zum Alten und Neuen Testament
ZAW	*Zeitschrift für die alttestamentliche Wissenschaft*
ZTK	*Zeitschrift für Theologie und Kirche*

Introduction

Patrick D. Miller

EVEN THOUGH HIS INTERESTS and writings are many and diverse, Walter Brueggemann is first and foremost an Old Testament theologian. The chapters that follow, most of which have appeared in print previously but as essays scattered throughout various books and journals, demonstrate this in different ways. They show his work as an Old Testament theologian in the narrow—although no less important—sense in that he explicitly addresses the issues of what a theology of the Old Testament should look like and engages other Old Testament theologians around the methodological issues. The essays and articles collected here, however, reveal that he is an Old Testament theologian also in a broader—although no more important—sense in that he believes that the Old Testament is a *theological* document in every sense of the word. Its subject matter is theological and its appropriation is theological. Brueggemann moves freely back and forth from scholarly and academic writing to the general and popular. In neither case, however, does he ever fail to lift up theological issues in the text or texts before him.

And there are always texts before him. This volume presents some of Brueggemann's more important theoretical or methodological essays, but concern for theory and method does not represent his primary approach to the Bible. Perhaps more accurately stated, his theoretical conclusions are worked out on the basis of text. He is most at home with texts, and he acknowledges openly both his reticence to write about things in general and his preference for a careful analysis of a text and reflection on its meaning and significance. The primary text before him frequently resonates with other texts so that he discerns a trajectory or creates a conversation out of them. Long before intratextuality or intertextuality became a phenomenon of much discussion in contemporary biblical interpretation, Brueggemann was articulating the resonances among texts and uncovering the richness of that dialogue.

The critical questions under constant debate in the work of Old Testament theologians receive answers in Brueggemann's work. With regard to the debate about whether Old Testament theology is essentially a descriptive task or has a normative function as well, he clearly assumes the responsibility of the theologian to set forth, in as careful a fashion as possible, what the texts are about. Exegesis is Brueggemann's forte. Some readers, impatient that he does not touch every text-critical and philological base, may miss the fact that detailed reading of the text is the only ground for the larger and often weighty conclusions that are drawn from it. Brueggemann's work, however, does not reflect an indifference to the technical issues of text and language. Indeed, they are his tools. It does reflect a serious impatience with technical exegetical and literary skill that issues forth in sterile and nontheological results. The influence of James Muilenburg, his teacher, and the contemporary focus on literary analysis of texts have served to sharpen his own literary instincts and sensitivities, as the essays on specific texts in the last half of this volume will indicate, particularly the ones on the beginning and the end of the books of Samuel. What is crucial at this point is that literary and rhetorical study is, in Brueggemann's approach, a tool for a theological reading of the text and not a replacement of it, which it is in some contemporary literary studies of the Bible.[1]

In the effort to set forth the theological meaning of texts, Brueggemann reveals an openness to different approaches to that enterprise in his increasing attention to the directions suggested by

---

1. See, for example, his comment in chap. 15, "The 'Uncared For' Now Cared For": "Thus the newer critical methods, especially rhetorical criticism, have important theological implications." For the move away from theology in narrative criticism, see Stephen Moore, *Literary Criticism and the Gospels* (New Haven: Yale University Press, 1989). George Steiner has criticized the widely acclaimed *Literary Guide to the Bible* (Cambridge: Harvard University Press, 1987), edited by Robert Alter and Frank Kermode, for its "separation...between a theological-religious experiencing of Biblical texts and a literary one" ("The Good Books," *The New Yorker*, 11 January 1988, 97); cf. his own *Real Presences: Is There Anything in What We Say?* (Chicago: University of Chicago Press, 1989).

Brevard Childs. Although he is hardly a disciple of Childs, his attention to the theological character of books in their present form (see the essays on the books of Samuel and Isaiah) receives significant impulse from Childs's work. He is also aligned with Childs in understanding the meaning of the canonical character of the Bible as having to do with its character as Scripture, as text about which one confesses its authority and claim on the lives of those whose communities receive it as Scripture. This means, as is everywhere evident in his writing, that the normative function of Old Testament theology is not simply a matter that one decides methodologically but is inherent in the character of the text and the relation to it of those who read and study. Such a perspective is implicit in his programmatic essays at the beginning of this volume and explicitly articulated in the chapter "Futures in Old Testament Theology."

Brueggemann is also sharply aware that a description of the theology of the Old Testament as well as the way in which it exercises its authority upon the interpreter is shaped and affected by the *social location* of the reader. His theological work, however, is an argument against facile notions that reading of texts is *controlled* by one's context and experience. One of the most notable things about his interpretation generally, and certainly about his proposals for Old Testament theology, is that they are sensitive to the way the text speaks out of, about, and to human experience that is not his own directly. He is able to read texts from and in the light of the social location of others. Furthermore, the critical dismantling of existing edifices built upon the Bible is as much or more a part of the normative or norming function of Old Testament theology as is the constructive function.

The importance of this critical function is evident in the way in which Brueggemann has taken his place among a number of Old Testament theologians (for example, Claus Westermann, Paul Hanson, and Samuel Terrien) who understand that the theology of the Old Testament develops not out of a particular central or foundational point but in various kinds of tensions and dialectics. His own analysis of this approach and its relation to previous developments in Old Testament theology is set forth in the essays "A Convergence in Recent Old Testament Theologies" and "Futures in Old Testament Theology." Brueggemann first set forth such a perspective in his small book *The Prophetic Imagination*, which is still one of the best-selling of all his works. He talks therein about the prophetic tasks of criticizing and energizing—the radical critique of the way things

are and the powerful imagination of new possibilities. Such dialectic is carried through in various forms in these chapters and often
signaled in their very titles: "The *Crisis* and *Promise* of Presence in
Israel," "The Rhetoric of *Hurt* and *Hope*." A somewhat different but
related dialectic is found in his proposed structure for understanding Old Testament theology—the dialectic between the *majority* voice
that is creation-oriented, a voice that assumes an ordered world
under the governance of a sovereign God and so serves to legitimate the structures of the universe, and a *minority* voice that is in
tension with the legitimation of structure, a voice embracing the pain
that is present in the world and protesting against an order that allows such to be. Brueggemann's dialectical approach, which assumes
an ongoing tension between voices "above the fray" and those "in
the fray," is fundamental to his reading of the Old Testament. In all
its formulations—the critical and the constructive, the hurt and the
hope, the protest and the possibility—this approach manifests not
only an interpretation *of* the Old Testament but an interpretation
from within the Old Testament, an interpretation of the way things
are in the world, then and now, of the way God is at work in the
world, not just the way God was at work in Israel. What is described
in the process becomes address as well.

The brief essay entitled "The 'Uncared For' Now Cared For" is
an example of Brueggemann's bringing together various aspects of
the dimensions mentioned above and developing method out of example. In this essay, he works with the tension he sees in Jeremiah's
message, the tension between "plucking up" and "tearing down" and
"planting" and "building"; but he does so via the modes of rhetorical
analysis that lead to important theological conclusions. Here, as in
all the chapters, the subject matter with which he is always wrestling
is the reality of God in and through the text and what that reality
means for human existence.

The necessity for thinking about the shape and structure of Old
Testament theology is thus addressed directly by Brueggemann in
this dialectic and programmatically so in the first two essays, both
chapters entitled "A Shape for Old Testament Theology," in which he
has laid the groundwork for a comprehensive—and probably con-
troversial—Old Testament theology. (Should controversy appear, it
will be, as all the essays in this volume indicate, very much "in the
fray.") How such an approach is applicable to Old Testament ethics
is then demonstrated in the two chapters that follow: "The Rhetoric
of Hurt and Hope: Ethics Odd and Crucial" and "Bodied Faith and

the Body Politic." The former was an invited lecture presented to the Society of Christian Ethics. In both chapters, Brueggemann carries forward not only the dialectical approach that is central to his theological method but his persistent attention to social and literary dimensions of the text. That attention is not, in these essays, primarily a methodological concern. It is an effort to uncover the role of *social power* (and powerlessness) and *the practice of rhetoric* in Israel's social discourse. Every Old Testament theologian has to come to terms with the place of history and its relation to the theological task. For Brueggemann, the history behind the text or out of which the text comes is very much the stuff of theology; but its primary manifestation is in the social setting, the shaping and character of the text, and the situation of the text. This will be demonstrated at length in the second volume of essays to appear in this series, but it is everywhere apparent in these pages as well. At the same time, no other theologian has succeeded so well as Brueggemann in melding the social and the rhetorical/literary in the service of theology. Social history and literary criticism, as methods, often do not even converse in biblical studies, much less lie down together in a firm embrace. They do so in Brueggemann's theological endeavors.

The centrality and primacy of text and subject matter (as distinct from method) is reflected in the various essays that make up the second half of this collection. They include major treatments of three of the fundamental theological themes of the Old Testament: the aniconic tradition ("Old Testament Theology as a Particular Conversation"), the presence of God ("The Crisis and Promise of Presence in Israel"), and the experience of exile ("A Shattered Transcendence? Exile and Restoration"). In the first of these, the dialectic and tension centers in the aniconic and the iconic, which "reflect very different sociologies" and whose conflict is not a productive one. In the second, "the theological dialectic of *accessibility* and *freedom* for Yahweh is matched by Israel's experience of *assurance* and *precariousness*." The third essay develops "the power of exile and restoration as an imaginative construct" that has its later reflex "in terms of crucifixion and resurrection."

The reference to crucifixion and resurrection is not surprising. The reader of Brueggemann's work in general and the chapters of this book in particular will encounter a canonical freedom and openness that does not hesitate to place the Old Testament in theological resonance with the New. Such resonance is probably due to several reasons, but the primary one is confessional. To think theologically in the light of the whole of Scripture is characteristic of Christian faith, and to filter out one part of the canon is strange and somewhat distorting. This is certainly the case for a Reformed theologian such as Brueggemann, for whom the Testaments do not exist in a dialectic but are parts of a whole, a continuum that allows one at any point either to *presume* the rest of the continuum without reference to it or to *draw upon* it explicitly to undergird and develop what is said. It is unclear at this stage of Brueggemann's work whether or not the New Testament will play a significant part in a formal Old Testament theology should he seek to set one forth, but it is very clear that for him the Old Testament theologian in the Christian community is vigorously engaged with the New Testament. Furthermore, the canonical presumption means *methodologically* that the intratextuality that is so much a part of the way in which Brueggemann works simply extends through the whole of the canon and is not confined to the Old Testament. The unity of the canon is a methodological and theological assumption.

The essays in the last half of this volume develop a theological understanding of a text, again in the kind of dialectic approach that characterizes the other essays and that reflects a dynamic in the material often leveled through in other theological efforts. They are also samples of Brueggemann's theological reading of texts in biblical books to which he has devoted much of his study and for which he has written commentaries: Genesis, Samuel, and Jeremiah. The pieces on the beginning and end of the Samuel books and on the unity of Isaiah demonstrate Brueggemann's particular way of taking up Brevard Childs's canonical focus and the impact on him of the emphasis on canonical shape that is a part of contemporary Old Testament interpretation.

One final note to the reader: Listen for the sounds of other voices. More than any other contemporary Old Testament interpreter, Brueggemann draws in the work of persons from all disciplines and incorporates them in a seminal way in his theology. He is a voracious reader; but what he reads he absorbs, so that the work of persons in theology, psychology, the social sciences, politics, and the like, often provides heuristic possibilities and even basic models for talking about the Old Testament. The broad audience he reaches is due in no little measure to the fact that he sees the Old Testament as having intelligible and significant connections to all sorts of things in this world.

1

A Shape for Old Testament Theology, I: Structure Legitimation

THE ORGANIZATION OF an Old Testament theology is clearly now a quite open and unresolved question. The comprehensive designs of Walther Eichrodt and Gerhard von Rad are now found wanting and we must find a new shape.[1] It is clear that everything follows from a principle of organization so that the elements of an Old Testament theology will fall into place given such a principle. This discussion in two parts proposes a shaping that is, I suggest, reflective of the current scholarly discussion.

I

Several elements of the current discussion may provide a clue for our question:

1. A number of scholars, using various vocabulary, have suggested that Old Testament faith must be understood in a bipolar fashion.[2] All of these suggestions are an attempt to move beyond the

---

1. See the helpful survey of new developments by Henning Graf Reventlow, *Problems of Old Testament Theology in the Twentieth Century* (Philadelphia: Fortress Press, 1985). See also the discussion of hermeneutical dimensions concerning the shape of biblical theology in *HBT* 4, no. 1 (1982) and 6, no. 1 (1984).

2. See chap. 5 for a summary.

dominance of a single center, recognizing that no single motif can contain all of the elements.[3] Such proposals include:

- Claus Westermann on blessing and deliverance;

- Samuel Terrien on the aesthetic and ethical;

- Paul D. Hanson on the cosmic and teleological;

- James A. Sanders on the constructive and critical; and

- Rainer Albertz on *Grosskult* and *Kleinkult*.[4]

Although not directly concerned with Old Testament categories, David Tracy, following Paul Ricoeur, has organized his argument around "manifestation" and "proclamation."[5] In various ways, each of these scholarly proposals intends to be a corrective. In each case, therefore, the first element may be understood as a corrective of a view dominated (as in both Eichrodt and von Rad) by the traditions of cult, credo, election, and mighty deeds of God, to the neglect of the universal, providential way of Yahweh for all of creation. Each of these proposals would insist that the two motifs, variously articulated, must be kept in an ongoing tension and not resolved in either direction. That very tension may be the central dynamic of Old Testament faith.

2. The programmatic books of Brevard S. Childs and Norman K. Gottwald must be taken into account in any assessment of what is possible in Old Testament theology. Even though the two books go in nearly opposite directions, it is important that they have appeared

---

3. On the problem of a "center," see Reventlow, *Problems of Old Testament Theology*, chap. 4.

4. See Westermann, *What Does the Old Testament Say about God?* (Atlanta: John Knox Press, 1979), and his fuller explication in *Elements of Old Testament Theology* (Atlanta: John Knox Press, 1982); Terrien, *The Elusive Presence*, Religious Perspectives, no. 26 (New York: Harper & Row, 1978); and Hanson, *Dynamic of Transcendence* (Philadelphia: Fortress Press, 1978), and his fuller explication in *The Diversity of Scripture* (Philadelphia: Fortress Press, 1982). In *God Has a Story Too* (Philadelphia: Fortress Press, 1979), Sanders presents in a more popular, homiletical fashion the dual hermeneutic of criticism and construction that he has more fully explicated in "Hermeneutics," *IDBSup*, ed. Keith Crim (New York: Abingdon Press, 1976), 402–7. See also Albertz, *Persönliche Frömmigkeit und offizielle Religion*, Calwer Theologische Monographien, no. 9 (Stuttgart: Calwer Verlag, 1978).

5. Tracy, *The Analogical Imagination* (New York: Crossroad, 1981), chap. 5; Ricoeur, "Manifestation and Proclamation," *Journal of the Blaisdell Institute* 12 (1978): 13–35.

at the same time. Surely they are best understood in relation to each other.[6]

Childs seeks to elaborate a notion of the Old Testament as a normative canon that moves beyond critical dissection and historical development. The completed form of the text offers a baseline for normative theology. The implication of Childs's work, it seems to me, is to put the faith claims of Scripture beyond the interplay of historical and literary analysis.

Conversely, Gottwald rigorously moves in the other direction. He sees the text not only as a result of societal conflict but as a literary legitimation of a social movement. In his view, the canonical literature is primarily a settled ideology of a certain partisan experience of reality. In its finished form it claims to be normative, but the really important fact is that it has reached that form through partisan societal interaction. Thus, the canon as canon is the outcome of social conflict, insisting on a certain settlement of the conflict.[7]

Both Childs and Gottwald must be taken seriously. The point is not to choose one to the disregard of the other, although holding them together is not easy. With Gottwald, it is important to see that the text has reached its present form and shape by being *in the fray*. These theological claims did not come out of the sky, nor did they have any prior claim to authority; but with Childs, it can be argued that the text as we have it is *above the fray*, the fray of historical interaction and historical-critical analysis. Whereas Gottwald is sociologically relentless, Childs is theologically reassuring. That tension is part of the richness of this faith claim and is also a part of its problematic that we must study. We know the Bible is fully engaged in the struggle for faithfulness, and yet at the same time we also claim that it is out of reach of that struggle. I suspect anyone who chooses either Gottwald or Childs alone too easily escapes the issues that must be faced.

3. Now on the basis of those two sets of scholarly matters, this and the following chapter seek to advance one particular proposal for an Old Testament theology:[8]

---

6. Childs, *Introduction to the Old Testament as Scripture* (Philadelphia: Fortress Press, 1979); Gottwald, *The Tribes of Yahweh* (Maryknoll, N.Y.: Orbis Books, 1979). Gottwald has discussed ways in which his work and that of Childs relate to each other, in "Sociological Matrix and Canonical Shape in Old Testament Studies," *TToday* 42 (1985): 307–21.

7. Gottwald, *Tribes*, esp. chap. 13.

8. In this and the following chapter I shall be considering Old Testament theology

a. Any theology must be bipolar to reflect the central tension of the literature. The bipolar construct I suggest is that Old Testament faith serves both to legitimate structure and to embrace pain. It will be clear that this argument is informed by the work of Westermann, Terrien, and Hanson, but I wish to suggest very different nuances.

b. This articulation of Old Testament faith seeks to present the faith both as in the fray (Gottwald) and above the fray (Childs). This is a tricky matter that is difficult to articulate, but the point I make is this: Childs and Gottwald have been primarily concerned with how we got the text and what the text is. A theological statement is not concerned with the process and character of the text but with the process and character of God met in the text. Thus, I propose that as Gottwald sees the text emerging in the social process, so the God of this text emerges in the social process. As Childs sees the text as normatively beyond the social process, that is, not changed by historical pressures, so the God met in the text is also beyond reach of historical contingencies. The point is arguable, but I mean to make a connection between the way we view the text and the God whom we may expect to find in the text.

4. The thesis I propose is this: Old Testament theology fully partakes in the *common theology* of its world and yet struggles to be free of that same theology:

a. Insofar as it partakes of that common theology, it is *structure-legitimating*. It offers a normative view of God who is above the fray and not impinged upon by social processes.

b. Insofar as it struggles to be free of that common theology, it is open to *the embrace of pain* that is experienced from "underneath" in the processes of social interaction and conflict.[9]

c. Insofar as this faith enters the fray of Israel's experience, it reflects the *ambiguity of our experiences* about structure and pain caused by structure. I understand this to be at the heart of Gottwald's argument that Israel's sense about God has arisen precisely in connection with the ambiguity and pain of historical experience.

---

as such; but *mutatis mutandis*, the same issues are at play in biblical theology, as Terrien has made clear, in *Elusive Presence*.

9. Karl R. Popper, in a discerning and quite unexpected judgment, has observed that whereas the "winners," those "above," regularly write history (and I should argue create theology), the story of Jesus is one in which Jesus and Jesus' people remember history from below. I should make the same argument regarding remembrance from below about decisive elements of the Old Testament. I cannot now find the exact reference in Popper, but see *The Open Society and Its Enemies II* (Princeton, N.J.: Princeton University Press, 1966), chap. 25.

d. Insofar as this faith makes claims beyond the fray of experience, it offers to the faithful community *a normative standing place* that may not be derived from the common theology but that articulates a normative truth about God not subject to the processes of the articulation. I understand this point to be implied in the canonical position of Childs.

e. A careful understanding of the literature shows that we are *not free to resolve* the tension. The Old Testament both partakes of the common theology and struggles to be free from it. The Old Testament both enters the fray of ambiguity and seeks distance from the fray to find something certain and sure. The God of Israel is thus presented variously as the God above the fray who appears like other ancient Near Eastern gods and as a God who is exposed in the fray, who appears unlike the gods of common theology, a God peculiarly available in Israel's historical experiences.[10]

II

We begin with a characterization of the *common theology:*

1. In 1952, Morton Smith used the phrase in a brief article.[11] The article in retrospect appears to be quite polemical and not very carefully written. Smith offers a critique of those who work too intently at the distinctiveness of the Old Testament. Smith argues that the structure of belief found all over the Near East and in the Old Testament has a common pattern and varies only in detail from culture to culture. That common pattern included the following points:

a. The god believed in is addressed in exaggerated and flattering prayer and praise and is claimed to be the only God, even if it is a minor god in the pantheon. This god is praised by the claim of being incomparable.

b. This god is claimed to be effective in all realms of history, nature, and morality.

c. This god is regularly characterized as both just and merciful, as the object of both fear and love.

d. This god, in any culture, is one who punishes those who offend him or her and rewards those who please him or her: that

---

10. Patrick D. Miller, in "God and the Gods," *Affirmation* 1, no. 3 (1973): 37–62, has most helpfully explored this issue.

11. Smith, "The Common Theology of the Ancient Near East," *JBL* 7 (1952): 35–47.

is, it is a theology of strict retribution. Smith calls this "essentially contractual."

e. Prophets are important in such a system and are everywhere honored, because they know of the god's will and so can speak about the prospects for rewards and punishments. Indeed the prophets are human agents who know what actions can lead to life or death.

Smith's argument is that in one way or another these elements are common in these religions, and Israel is not greatly different. So one can find counterparts to the moral expectations of Nathan, the universalism of Amos, or the monotheism of Second Isaiah. The same factors are everywhere operative.

Now some criticism of Smith's presentation can properly be made. Since he wrote in 1952, we have learned more about the dangers of patternism and the temptation to see the same phenomena everywhere without attending to the peculiar way things are offered in any particular cultural context.[12] Clearly, Smith has no great sensitivity to the political context or circumstance or the impingement of culture in shaping belief in any particular situation. Smith displays no great theological sensitivity about the texture and nuance of statements in relation to religious experience or religious confession. Such a generalization reveals a leveling tendency that runs the risk of reductionism.

Thus, Smith's proposal is offered in a quite heavy-handed way; but nonetheless his proposal is an important one, because it requires us to decide about and recognize the considerable impingement of ancient Near Eastern factors upon the perception and articulation of faith in ancient Israel. It is especially important to assess Smith's article in its scholarly context of the high days of the so-called biblical theology movement, which claimed a great deal for the distinctiveness of Israel's faith (with special reference to von Rad and G. Ernst Wright).

2. In the ongoing debate about that particular form of biblical theology, several other criticisms are now widely recognized as influential. James Barr and Bertil Albrektson have argued in independent statements that the notion of "God acting in history" is not unique and that that claim must be given up. On a broader scale, the same set of criticisms has permitted Childs to declare a crisis and

---

12. See the warning and caution of Shemaryahu Talmon, "The Comparative Method in Biblical Interpretation: Principles and Problems," in *Congress Volume: Göttingen, 1977*, VTSup 29 (Leiden: Brill, 1978), 320–56.

perhaps a death of the movement. More recently, H. W. Saggs has explored the issue with caution and sensitivity.[13]

3. The question appears to me to be worth taking up again because Gottwald has returned to the analysis of Smith, but he has turned the points to a very different argument.[14] In his revisionist version, Gottwald makes these points:

a. the sole high God usurps the entire sacred domain;

b. the sole high God is conceived by egalitarian sociopolitical analogies;

c. the sole high God is coherently manifest in power, justice, and mercy; and

d. the sole high God is interpreted by egalitarian functionaries.

Gottwald has taken the elements of Smith's analysis and expressed them now in terms of his sociological analysis, an element admittedly absent in Smith's presentation. What has happened in that translation is that some of Smith's partisan passion has been removed, and the theological claims are now presented as modes of social analysis and social organization; that is, the motifs assigned to God are understood as functions of social process. Theological categories are understood to have social and political counterparts so that these statements about God now are also understood as statements about the *misuses of human power* and the *proper use of human power;* that is, the high claims for God are now understood also as high claims for political authority in Israel.[15] It may then be that the high claim of Yahweh as the sole high God becomes a way in Israel to order life free from the high claims of the Egyptian pharaoh or the Canaanite city-kings, who also oversee and legitimate politi-

---

13. Much of Barr's critical analysis is now available in his collected papers, *The Scope and Authority of the Bible*, Explorations in Theology, no. 7 (London: SCM Press, 1980; Louisville: Westminster/John Knox Press, 1981). See Albrektson, *History and the Gods: An Essay on the Idea of Historical Events as Divine Manifestations in the Ancient Near East and Israel*, ConBOT, no. 1 (Lund: CWK Gleerup, 1967); Childs, *Biblical Theology in Crisis* (Philadelphia: Westminster Press, 1970); and Saggs, *The Encounter with the Divine in Mesopotamia and Israel* (London: Athlone, 1978). Modest rejoinders more sympathetic to the emphases of the so-called biblical theology movement have been offered by Hanson, *Dynamic of Transcendence*; and by Werner F. Lemke, "Revelation through History in Recent Biblical Theology," *Int* 36 (1982): 34–46.

14. Gottwald, *Tribes*, chaps. 53–54.

15. Ibid., 677–78. The translation of theological motifs into categories of social organization has the effect of removing some of the apparently capricious and disconnected element of the motifs. George E. Mendenhall, in *The Tenth Generation* (Baltimore: Johns Hopkins University Press, 1973), chap. 3, has done the same thing with the notion of the "vengeance of Yahweh" to show that it is an ingredient in a political theory in Israel.

cal expressions of sovereignty. So I suggest, following Gottwald, that biblical theology needs to reconsider its understandings of God in relation to the sociological spin-offs that are implicit in those understandings. In a way Gottwald does not press, however, we must know that these matters are genuinely theological issues.

4. Gottwald's judgment about Israel and common theology is this: "We immediately detect points where Israelite religion stands out as a highly idiosyncratic version of the common theological pattern."[16] The subheading under which he writes is *The Early Israelite Mutations*.

Gottwald's argument is that the common theology is all around Israel, but early Israel in a most peculiar way has appropriated that common theology with decisive mutations in an egalitarian direction. I find Gottwald's argument compelling, given the parameters he has set for his analysis. For the doing of Old Testament theology, however, one must not settle things too quickly. I can think of two factors that make it more delicate than Gottwald's statement suggests:

a. To do Old Testament theology requires more than analysis of the "early Israelite mutations." This is not to fault Gottwald, for that is not what he set out to study; but if one tries to look at the larger picture of the Old Testament, it is clear that the mutations are not as decisive and singular as might be thought. There are no doubt such mutations in Israel. But there are also important parts of the literature that have not gone through the mutation or have in fact resisted it, so that the issue cannot be put sharply in terms of the *common system outside Israel* and the *mutations inside Israel*, for that would be to return to Wright's arguments too easily. Rather, one must say that the Old Testament itself is a mighty struggle between the common theology that has great strength in Israel and the mutations that seek to transform that common theology. It is thus an in-house struggle that concerns Old Testament theology.[17]

---

16. Gottwald, *Tribes*, 679. See his more recent comments, "The Theological Task after *The Tribes of Yahweh*," in *The Bible and Liberation*, ed. Norman K. Gottwald (Maryknoll, N.Y.: Orbis Books, 1983), 190–200.

17. Gottwald is, of course, aware of this. The problem is that the articulations of common theology in the Old Testament (as Smith rightly has seen) are equally reckoned as the faith of Israel. As I worked this through, I had a wonderment. The older view (Wright) has been that Israel fought for its identity against external theological options. It may be helpful to understand this theological struggle as an "in-house" struggle, a view comparable to Mendenhall's and Gottwald's understanding that the conquest was an "inside job." The analogy may be more than a coincidence.

b. Gottwald's argument is largely sociological; that is, he does not address frontally questions of the character of God. Faithful to his method, he treats God in ancient Israel as a *function of the social processes*. To do Old Testament theology, however, one must ask not only about Yahweh as a function of social processes but about the character of Yahweh as a *free agent* who has a life and interiority all God's own.[18] Thus, we need to consider not only mutations in the social processes, or mutations in the articulations of God that serve the social processes, but mutations that are said to be going on in the very person of God. If it may be put realistically, God is seen to be struggling with and deciding how much to be defined by the common theology and how much to break free of that common theology in order to be a God appropriate to the life and character of Israel. One must insist, however, that this is a genuinely theological issue that concerns the character of God and not simply a reflection of social change. As there is a struggle sociologically between the common theology and the mutations (much discussed and debated), so there is a struggle in the person and character of God to be both the God expected and approved in the Near East and the God discerned in and appropriate to the narrative egalitarianism of Israel. The tension is not just in social processes. If theology is to have an integrity of its own, then Old Testament faith is God's ongoing decision about the matter.

5. At the outset, therefore, we affirm and assume:

a. The Old Testament is profoundly linked to the ancient Near East not in marginal ways but in its fundamental shaping. It participates in the common theology in decisive ways.

b. This reality gives some ground for those who regard the Old Testament as indeed a book of justice, law, and retribution. Whatever congeniality with the New Testament that can be made cannot be made by jettisoning that shaping reality.

c. As George E. Mendenhall has seen most clearly, such a grounding of faith and an understanding of reality are politically realistic. One may explore further the extent to which the common theology is taken over as such and the extent to which it has been transmuted. That distinction must be done carefully and in detail without grand theory, but the point here is another one—that in one form or an-

---

18. Gottwald (*Tribes*, 697) is aware of this issue and tries to speak of *agentry* as well as *function*. It is probably the case that he does not go far enough to satisfy the requirements of doing biblical theology. His part 11 clearly indicates he is not unaware of the problem.

other, in a transmuted form or not, the common theology has given the decisive shape to Old Testament faith. If I understand Gottwald correctly, he agrees that Israel has not departed from that shape of reality.

Said another way, the common theology has assured that Old Testament faith is articulated in political images and metaphors, because it serves either in oppressive or egalitarian ways *to give order*, both with reference to the rule of God and with reference to the legitimacy of social institutions. I take it that Gottwald's articulation of this is an important advance beyond that of Smith, not only because of the argument about mutation but because he has shown how the common theology carries with it a ground for social structure and moral coherence.

III

In rough outline, it is clear that this common theology of a contractual kind is structurally crucial for much of the faith of the Old Testament:

1. *The Sinai covenant* (and the traditions derived from it) is surely a tight system of sanctions, of punishments and rewards articulated as blessings and curses. That, it seems to me, is what most needs to be noticed about the recent discussion of treaty and covenant. It is an argument that structurally the Mosaic tradition is a religion expressed in a political metaphor with sanctions and a rule of law that means to supersede and displace every other law.

That this is the main point is not adequately noticed in all the discussions of Mendenhall's hypothesis. Too much energy has been spent on whether the Hittite parallels are accurate; but Mendenhall's point, as seems clear in his later writings, is about the authorization of legal policy and technique, which is firm and beyond challenge.[19] That gain is secure even if, as it now appears, his thesis of Hittite parallels will not be well sustained. At the very least, D. J. McCarthy's judicious conclusion seems appropriate:

---

19. The gains for social theory and social organization in the metaphor of covenant are evident in Mendenhall, "The Conflict between Value Systems and Social Control," in *Unity and Diversity: Essays in the History, Literature, and Religion of the Ancient Near East*, ed. Hans Goedicke and J. J. M. Roberts (Baltimore: John Hopkins University Press, 1975), 169–80. See also his *Tenth Generation*, chap. 8. It is clear that this is an important matter, even if the "Hittite Connection" is in doubt.

> Is it not more reasonable to see theological reflection working toward a full verbal expression of the meaning symbolized in the old covenantal ritual, but that it was still imperfect, in sum developing?...[Urdt] gives a full expression of the covenant idea in the form of a treaty. It reaches what they had been groping for. The treaty analogy for the relation of Yahweh and Israel is thus a flowering of a development, not a root from which covenant ideas grow.[20]

Even if the early community did not use the treaty form, what it did use operated with similar presuppositions and lent itself readily, in due time, to that formulation. Mendenhall's notion of a new foundation for an authorized, ordered society serves Gottwald's argument well. This Mosaic form permits the creation of a counter-community that must fashion its own laws, which are in contrast to that of the oppressive regimes. Thus, the Mosaic tradition bears witness to a theology of justice and love, of reward and punishment, in which futures of life and death are held in the claims of that relationship. At the outset, Israel's religious language intends to legitimate social structures. The theological agent for such legitimacy is also a God who punishes and rewards according to God's articulated will. There is no negotiation or bargaining or softening of that reality. The structure must be taken seriously.

2. It is not different in the *Deuteronomic theology*. As Lothar Perlitt has shown, here we face a much more frontal and full-blown covenant theology. The relation of the Mosaic tradition to Deuteronomic theology is obscure and cannot be traced with any precision, but it is clear that Deuteronomic theology pursues the notion of sanctions, blessing and curse, reward and punishment, with intensity and consistency.[21]

No doubt there are important differences between Deuteronomy and the Deuteronomistic History, and there are more when one moves to the Chronicler, as another articulation of the same issues; but the basic theological structure is not changed, although it is implemented and presented in several ways. The Deuteronomistic History is a sustained portrayal of Israel's royal history from the perspective of Torah obedience and disobedience. Von Rad has seen

---

20. McCarthy, *Treaty and Covenant*, AnBib, no. 21A (Rome: Biblical Institute Press, 1978), 292–93.

21. Perlitt, *Bundestheologie im Alten Testament*, WMANT, no. 36 (Neukirchen-Vluyn: Neukirchener Verlag, 1969). Robert Polzin, in *Moses and the Deuteronomist* (New York: Seabury Press, 1980), has shrewdly noted some continuing restlessness with this view of reality, but I do not think that changes the main structure of the presentation.

that this uncompromising Torah perception is somewhat mitigated by Davidic theology, which defers the consequences of disobedience and allows for God to govern according to free promise; but in large sweep, the Davidic motif leads only to deferral of consequence, not nullification. If the large question of the Deuteronomist is the tense relationship between the Torah summons to obedience and the promise of the monarchy, clearly Torah wins out. The concluding episode of 2 Kings 25:27-30 concerning Jehoiachin does not finally alter that calculus. That settlement is foreshadowed in the promise for monarchy in Deut. 17:14-20, in which the king is utterly subordinated to the Torah and made subject to the Torah teachers. Thus, the Deuteronomic corpus in its main urging stays with the rigor of Mosaic sanctions, and that in turn reflects the tight system of payoffs already noted by Smith and given sociological substance by Gottwald.[22]

3. It can be argued that it is not fundamentally different with *the prophets*. As we shall see with our second consideration (in the chapter to follow), there are important variations on the theme in the prophets, but the variations are all set in a clear basis in contractual theology. As is well known, Westermann has argued that the judgment speech is the basic genre of prophetic speech. For the prophets, the entire historical process is read through the prism of the law court metaphor. Westermann's claim for this genre has become a largely unchallenged truism in the field. If we are to understand the structure of belief in the prophets, we must begin with the judgment speech.[23]

As is now commonly recognized, the judgment speech consists of two elements. The indictment asserts Israel's disobedience, often with an allusion to the old Torah commandments. This is followed by the sentence that, as often as not, is the implementation of the old Mosaic curses. Thus, the judgment speech is structurally seen to derive from the Mosaic structure:

---

22. Von Rad, *Old Testament Theology I* (London: Oliver & Boyd; New York: Harper Brothers, 1962), 334–47. McCarthy, in "II Samuel 7 and the Structure of the Deuteronomic History," *JBL* 84 (1965): 131–38, has allowed a greater place to 2 Samuel 7, which adds some weight to the monarchical element, but the Torah dimension surely is predominant. See Lemke, "The Way of Obedience: 1 Kings 13 and the Structure of the Deuteronomistic History," in *The Mighty Acts of God*, ed. Frank M. Cross, Lemke, and Patrick D. Miller (Garden City, N.Y.: Doubleday & Co., 1976), 301–26.

23. Westermann, *Basic Forms of Prophetic Speech* (Philadelphia: Westminster Press, 1967).

- commandment as the basis for indictment;
- curse as the basis for sentence.[24]

It is worth noting how the scholarly language about these forms has changed. The terms *Scheltrede* and *Drohrede* have dominated the field for a long time. One can hear in them language resonant with that of Smith, for they sound like personal statements of reprimand and anger. The more recent language of *indictment* and *sentence* introduces juridical metaphors to suggest that we are not dealing with personal tyranny or pique but with a rule of law.

What is crucial in the prophetic judgment speech (as in the old covenant structure) is the nonnegotiable linkage between commandment and curse, between indictment and sentence. The one follows the other predictably; that is, the world as governed by God has a structure to it. That structure is known and firm, legitimate and reliable, and it can be transgressed only at cost. Examples of this include Mic. 3:9-12 and Amos 4:1-4. The most startling and clear example is Hos. 4:1-3, in which the violation of commandments is announced as the cause for the withering of creation. Thus, obedience is not simply a social requirement, but it corresponds to the requirements of the very structure of created reality. The Torah is not human rules, but it is the way in which creation has been ordered.

Although the main uses of this statement of structure are negative, this need not be so. The structure of prophetic faith, at least in some of the prophets, assumes that the statement of nonnegotiable structure need not concern guilt and sentence but may concern innocence and blessing; that is, there is at least the theoretical possibility that there could be obedience, and this is tightly linked to well-being. That positive expression, however, does not change the structured, ordered way of reality. So Isa. 1:18-20 and Deut. 30:11-14 allow for the positive working out of the scheme. In the tradition of Hosea, Jeremiah, and Ezekiel, the positive alternative possibility is increasingly muted if not impossible. But the tight structure holds, thus moving toward more complete hopelessness. The prophets are not moral teachers or reformers. Under

---

24. Patrick D. Miller, in *Sin and Judgment in the Prophets* (Chico, Calif.: Scholars Press, 1982), has drawn the linkage of indictment and sentence even closer. He has shown how the punishment announced is often correlated with great precision to the indictment. That, again, has the marks of contractual theology, which countenances no slippage. On the changed terminology, see Gene M. Tucker, *Form Criticism of the Old Testament* (Philadelphia: Fortress Press, 1971), 59–65.

this rubric of common theology they discern what God is about to do. What God is about to do is responsive to Israel's action in relation to God's will. There is no slippage in this reading of reality.

4. Finally, it is clear that the *wisdom materials* hold to a quite similar understanding of reality. Indeed, we should expect to find common theology especially in wisdom, for that literature most readily shares in the worldview of the ancient Near East and most fully reflects that understanding.

Von Rad has most thoroughly explored the perception of reality held from the earliest time in Israel's wisdom.[25] It is not clear whether these simplest sayings are to be set in a context of court or clan, but it is clear that they articulate a sense of orderliness and coherence in life, the interconnectedness of acts and their results.[26] Von Rad has seen that these simple statements should not be taken as simplistic. They are a summary of and a search for moral rationality in life, which may not always be visible or self-evident but which is never in doubt. The wisdom teachers know about a connectedness that, on the one hand, is never fickle and can always be trusted; on the other hand, as that connectedness can always be trusted, so it can never be escaped. No amount of wealth or power or cleverness can circumvent the undoubted linkage of certain kinds of sowing and reaping (cf. Psalm 49). To be sure, the linkage is less explicit than in the Mosaic tradition, less urgent than in the Deuteronomic corpus, and less abrasive than in the prophets; but for all that, it is no less secure.

Klaus Koch has explored the different forms of expression in these varying modes. He has concluded that in some sayings, Yahweh is not an active, present, involved agent in the movement from cause to effect. In such cases, we do not need to speak of *punishments and rewards*, but we can speak of the connection of *deed and consequence*. Consequences are wrought by an automatic, self-fulfilling "sphere of destiny." Such a view departs from that of Smith, who presents a personal God who appears to be capricious. But the shift

---

25. Von Rad, *Wisdom in Israel* (Nashville: Abingdon Press, 1972).

26. This matter has been nicely articulated by Phillip J. Nel, *The Structure and Ethos of the Wisdom Admonitions in Proverbs*, BZAW, no. 158 (Berlin: de Gruyter, 1982), with proper caution about life-setting for the sayings. See the statement of Ludwig Schmidt, *De Deo*, BZAW, no. 143 (Berlin: de Gruyter, 1976), 146; and the early discussion of Hartmut Gese, *Lehre und Wirklichkeit in der alten Weisheit* (Tübingen: Mohr [Siebeck], 1958), 34.

from one idiom to another has caused nothing to change in the basic claim of structure.[27]

It is not different in the basic perspective of the poem of Job.[28] The character Job is in agreement with the friends; both adhere to the same world of moral coherence and reliability. Even in protest, Job does not seek to escape that world. He gladly lives within the world of moral coherence. He insists only that its workings become visible to him. Thus, such a vigorous protest does not at all change the game (although the response of the whirlwind clearly lies outside this view).

Now this is much too general a statement. One could refine and sort things out more precisely, but the central point, I think, cannot be doubted. There is a basic commitment to *contractual theology*, and if that is foundational to the Mosaic traditions, Deuteronomic theology, the prophets, and the wisdom materials, then we may say that it is the foundational construct for Israel's faith.[29] It is not terribly important whether this foundational construct is borrowed, or borrowed and transformed, or whether Israel simply articulated it because it experienced its own life that way. On any of those grounds, it affirms that there is a moral rationality and coherence to life. There are orders, limits, and boundaries within which humanness is possible and beyond which there can only be trouble. Such a conclusion affirms that the Old Testament belongs to its cultural world in basic theological ways, and it warns against any inclination to see Israel's faith too readily as a religion of grace. I suspect that, if one were to investigate it, the same issue is present in the New Testament, which might require a rereading there as well.

---

27. Koch, "Gibt es ein Vergeltungsdogma im Alten Testament?," *ZTK* 52 (1955): 1–42; the English translation, "Is There a Doctrine of Retribution in the Old Testament?," is in *Theodicy in the Old Testament*, ed. James L. Crenshaw, IRT, no. 4 (Philadelphia: Fortress Press, 1983), 57–87. Koch introduces a different conception. For our purposes, however, I regard this difference only as a change within the rubric of contractual theology. Robert G. Hubbard, Jr., in "Dynamistic and Legal Language in the Complaint Psalms" (Ph.D. Diss., Claremont Graduate School, 1980), follows Rolf P. Knierim in exploring the relationship of the two versions of contractual theology.

28. See Horst Dietrich Preuss, "Jahwes Antwort an Hiob und die sogenannte Hiobliteratur des alten Vorderen Orients," in *Beiträge zur alttestamentlichen Theologie*, ed. Herbert Donner et al. (Göttingen: Vandenhoeck and Ruprecht, 1977), 323–43.

29. See Hubbard, "Dynamistic," 3.

IV

Now we need to consider in a more reflective way what this theological foundation may suggest for our critical work:

1. This theology of coherence and rationality must first be *appreciated*. In a variety of ways, this is an assertion of creation theology, the sense that the world is ordered and governed. The world is not chaos; it is not endlessly pliable; it is not yet to be decided. There is an ordered quality to life that will not be mocked. No one is able to fashion a private order according to one's own selfish yearning. There is a transcendent mystery before which everyone must answer, sooner or later. This is a general assertion of God's sovereignty, and one may even say that it is an affirmation of providence. As von Rad has observed, even the wisdom teachers, who want to order all of life in terms of proper conduct, are not blind to the inscrutable coherence that operates in spite of human conduct (cf. Prov. 16:2, 9; 19:21; 20:24; 21:2, 30–31).[30] It is precisely this fundamental conviction that lets social life exist, that permits a measure of humanness, that lets us set limits on our common beastliness, that lets us nurture our children in decency, and that lets there be some public planning and continuity of policy.

2. This theology of moral coherence, which needs to be appreciated, is also *open to exploitation*. Biblical interpreters are still novices at the practice of "suspicion" about theology. We tend very much, with or without the historical-critical methods, to discuss what texts *mean* without attention to their *function*, either deliberately or accidentally; but this general statement about exploitation is, I think, beyond doubt. Every theological claim about moral rationality is readily linked to a political claim of sovereignty and a political practice of totalitarianism. Such linkage need not be so. There is no necessity to it, but it regularly is so. Creation theology readily becomes imperial propaganda and ideology. Then, when the order of life is celebrated, it is the political order with which we agree. Indeed, it becomes the legitimated order from which we benefit and that we maintain in our own interest, if at all possible. The political order may be derived from, reflect, and seek to serve the cosmic order, but derivation is so easily, readily, and frequently inverted that the cosmic order becomes a legitimation for the political order, and so there is a convenient match (often regarded as an ontological match) be-

---

30. Von Rad, *Old Testament Theology I*, 438–41.

tween God's order and our order. What starts as a statement about *transcendence* becomes simply *self-justification*, self-justification made characteristically by those who preside over the current order and who benefit from keeping it so.[31]

In terms of the large public arena, little imagination is needed to see that high contractual theology supports the status quo, the celebration of order. The legitimated power surely stands as a guard against chaos and anarchy. Very often there is a link between creation theology and royal theology. This linkage is conveniently sanctioned in the building of the temple. The temple is a characteristic way of legitimation, not only of God's governance and providential care but also of the particular form of power distribution with the present regime. On the one hand, it is not hard to see the political agenda of David and Solomon concerning temple building. On the other hand, it is possible to see that even with Moses, the leadership of God and the leadership of Moses are easily merged, and protest against Moses' authority results in curse (Numbers 12). Persons in authority, in the ancient and in the modern world, do what can be done to present particular policies in cosmic terms and so are immune to criticism. The present order is traded on as though it were the cosmic order. Even though this is evident publicly in creation theology, no doubt it happens in domestic life with the authoritative claims of wisdom teaching.

3. This contractual theology that serves to legitimate order needs to be submitted to *sharp critique*. I should argue that the main dynamic of the Old Testament is the tension between the celebration of that legitimation and a sustained critique of it. The reason the contractual theology must be sharply criticized is that it lacks a human face when it is articulated consistently. It is a system of reality that allows no slippage, no graciousness, no room for failure.

In the common theology that Smith has outlined, no chance of

---

31. On "suspicion" as an essential interpretive posture, as Ricoeur presents it, see the helpful introduction with a good bibliography by Lewis S. Mudge, in *Essays in Biblical Interpretation* (Philadelphia: Fortress Press, 1980), 1–40. We are only at the beginning of an investigation of the political function of theological order. Hints of the value of such an investigation are offered in the following: Thorkild Jacobsen, "Religious Drama in Ancient Mesopotamia," in *Unity and Diversity* (see n. 19), 65–97; Harry A. Hoffner, Jr., "Propaganda and Political Justification in Hittite Historiography," in *Unity and Diversity*, 49–62; and Conrad E. L'Heureux, *Rank among the Canaanite Gods* (Missoula, Mont.: Scholars Press, 1979), 82–108. Religious claims have their uses, and no doubt these various presentations of created order in the Old Testament have their mundane uses.

forgiveness and no possible move toward newness exists. The most that can happen is a repentance that requires a reentry into the old order with "full purpose of new obedience"; that is, repentance is a return to and a submission to the legitimated order without any questioning of that old order, a doubting of its priority, or a rearticulation in new form that takes into account the situation of those less party to power. Now I am not interested in the speculative question of whether people can live fully obedient lives. That we do not fully obey is, in any case, beyond dispute and poses an enormous question for theology of a contractual kind. I should argue that it is the question posed peculiarly by Israel to the common theology of the ancient Near East: What shall we do with that part of created reality that does not properly submit and become subordinated to the regime that is legitimated?

a. The key element in the critique is *the issue of pain.*[32] The contractual theology of coherence and rationality offers a world in which pain need not occur; and where it does occur, pain is a failure to be corrected. It is a world of perfect symmetry in which God's will is known and can be obeyed. Such a theological system (which we may term "legalism") is expressed in the flattest form of Deuteronomic theology and in the poem of Job, by both Job and his friends. It is also as modern as religions of "possibility thinking," as *consumerism*, in which the right product makes whole, and as *competence* linked to technical reason, in which incompetence is unnecessary and unacceptable.

b. I suggest that this question of pain, a pain experienced as personal hurt and expressed in the lament psalms and in the public outcry that leads to liberation (cf. Exod. 2:23-25), is the main question of Old Testament faith. The traditions of Israel's faith are an interaction between the *full assertion of* common theology, which is relentlessly contractual, and the *protest against* it. Both are present in the text, and the freighted moments of faith are the moments of tension between the two.

c. This question concerns not only the people of Israel or its poets. As the text now stands, the issue of pain is crucial in Israel's portrayal of God. As the text presents it, this is God's question as

---

32. Reference should be made to the important study of Arthur C. McGill, *Suffering: A Test of Theological Method* (Philadelphia: Westminster Press, 1982). Although he makes the argument on very different grounds, I suggest that he understands Israel's main hunch about God from the beginning: the true God must be one who credits pain in decisive ways.

much as it is the question of believing Israel. It is a question of God seeking to present and represent God as taking all of these data into account. Old Testament theology, as distinct from sociological, literary, or historical analysis, must assume some *realism* in the text—that the poets and narrators in Israel do, in fact, speak the mind of God. God's mind is not closed on this question, because God in Israel must decide about the practice of contractual theology and the embrace of pain that permits and requires life outside the contract.

In claiming this realism, I mean to reject the notion that these texts are simply human probings or imagination as Israel discovers more of God and finds, in fact, that the stern God is gracious. Rather, serious theology must insist that God's self-articulation comes as disclosure, so that the biblical artists enter into the struggle in which God is involved.

I mean also to reject an evolutionary notion that Yahweh begins as a common God who ends up gracious. Rather, for this God, such tension is unresolved and works even into the New Testament and into postbiblical Judaism. The tension may surface in different ways in different texts, under the leading of different voices; but the text permits entry into the disclosure of God's own life, which is troubled, problematic, and unresolved.

The issue that Israel and Israel's God (and those who continue this line of reflection) must always face concerns pain—whether pain is simply a shameful aberration that can be handled by correction or whether it is the stuff of humanness, the vehicle for a break with triumphalism, both sociological and theological. What we make of pain is perhaps the most telling factor for the question of life and the nature of our faith. It has to do with the personal embrace of suffering as possibly meaningful in our lives. It also has to do with social valuing of the pained and the pain-bearers—the poor, the useless, the sick, and the other marginal ones. A theology of contractual coherence must excommunicate all the pained and pain-bearers as having violated the common theology. Indeed, the presence of pain-bearers is a silent refutation of the legitimated structures. Visible pain-bearers, therefore, must be denied legitimacy as well as visibility because they assert that the legitimated structures are not properly functioning.

d. Gottwald has applied a sociological critique to this common theology. He shows how it has been radically transformed by the historical experience of Israel. He builds on his hypothesis of early Israel as a liberated community of egalitarianism, a hypothesis I accept. He sees that Israel is founded precisely by those who reject and are rejected by the nonslippage of the world of Egyptian (and Canaanite) totalitarianism. Israel, in contrast to those political forms, is a social movement of the failures and rejects who delegitimate both the rationality of the empire and the coherence of the gods who legitimate those structures.

Doing Old Testament theology, however, requires that the issue should be stated not only with reference to social processes. We must be concerned primarily that the God of Israel is disclosed in this experience as a God different from the structure-legitimating gods of the empire. So it is to be noted and stressed that the new social movement begins with a cry of pain (Exod. 2:23-25) that is heard, perhaps surprisingly, by this nonimperial God upon whom the cry of pain can impinge. The narrative makes clear that this *pain voiced and processed* is the stuff of this new relationship and this new social experiment. The new social reality depends upon Israel's articulated pain as Israel moves away from the Egyptian hegemony of spirit as well as body. The new social possibility depends also upon the remarkable response of this God who takes this hurt as the new stuff of faithfulness. In response, this God makes an intervention in the historical process against the legitimated structures of the day and delegitimates them. What could be a more dramatic expression of a move away from common theology, a move requiring a people that embraces its pain publicly and a God who receives this pain as the stuff of a new faithfulness? In that moment, the beginning point of Israel's faith, the issue has been joined between the old legitimated structures that deny pain and the new structures that receive, embrace, and act out of pain. As there is conflict among social systems, so there is also conflict between the gods, between those who legitimate the structures of repression and denial and the One who forms new history around the reality of pain. (On the conflict of the gods, see the plague narratives and especially Exod. 8:16-19.)

4. This critical assessment of the shape of Old Testament theology is not unrelated to the current cultural situation that is informed by *contractual theology* of the most uncompromising kind:[33]

    a. Contractual theology allows no slippage. It is sure and com-

---

33. I take the risk of moving this discussion out beyond our normal scholarly parameters because of the tasks I understand Old Testament theology to have. See Childs, "Some Reflections on the Search for a Biblical Theology," *HBT* 4 (1982): 1–12. I agree with his judgment that biblical theology must also relate to its second referential group, the community of faith. I take this to mean not only the historic community

prehensive. I submit that this is reflected in such dominant policies of our present situation as arms advances, which can too easily identify the good and the evil, or insensitivity to the marginal, who are dismissed as irrelevant failures.

b. Contractual theology is easily supportive of the status quo and readily becomes available for ideology.

c. Contractual theology is the working of the nonreflective, and it is the useful theology of dominant interests. Stated thus, I submit that there is a strange affinity between this structure-legitimating theology, which is essential to a viable community and which articulates the governance of God, and the easy uses made of it by those who have a vested interest in its articulation and practice.

d. The issue in our time (and I suspect in every culture) concerns the management and resolution of pain, both personal and public. Where pain is not dealt with effectively, both in terms of policies and symbols (liturgy), it will be driven underground, sure to surface in unexpected and harmful ways. For those who can afford it, unprocessed pain is likely to appear as emotional pathology. For those who cannot afford emotional disorder, it is likely to surface as violence and terror.

So far as Christian extrapolations are concerned, the challenge of *pain-embrace* to *structure legitimacy* is presented in the symbol of the cross; but symbols can be misused. The cross is claimed to disclose God's true character as the source out of which new life comes, and yet the language and claims of a theology of the cross are now used to justify a theology of imperial exploitation that ruthlessly condemns pain and sees competence as the stuff of humanness. Such theology, when not criticized and corrected, lacks compassion toward those who are not capable of effective function. In our contemporary values, therefore, just as in the faith of ancient Israel, there is a moving back and forth between the assertion of common theology and the anguish about it, an anguish that protests against it.

---

but the contemporary one. The issue of pain, as I have exploited it, appears to me to be the crucial social issue for the contemporary community of faith.

2

A Shape for Old Testament Theology, II: Embrace of Pain

MY FIRST ARGUMENT, put forth in chapter 1, is that Old Testament faith fully partakes in the common theology of the ancient Near East, as outlined by Morton Smith.[1] In its basic articulation and view of reality, the Old Testament agrees with the common theology of sanctions:

1. This theology provides an ordered sense of life that is lodged in the sovereignty of God, beyond the reach of historical circumstance. It is a way of speaking about God's nonnegotiable governance.

2. This theology appeals to God as creator in relation to creation. It satisfies a religious yearning by an affirmation of providence. Not only does God govern, but there is an order that works through the processes of history, even if that purpose is not always visible.

3. Such a theology tends to serve the ruling class, which regularly identifies the order of creation with the current social arrangement so that the system is the solution. What purports to be an ontological statement always comes out of a process of social interaction.[2] The

---

1. See chap. 1.
2. See the suggestive statement of Carl A. Keller, "Zum sogenannten Vergeltungsglauben in Proverbienbuch," in *Beiträge* (see chap. 1, no. 28), 223–38. Keller's thesis is: The "deed-consequence" construct is not primarily linked to a cosmic principle as "world-order" or self-actualizing "sphere of destiny," but it is a formulation derived from specific social processes (p. 225). In the language of our first argument, these views are evoked in the fray. Keller is clear (perhaps against my view) that these are not theological constructions, but they are observations out of actual experience.

end result serves to legitimate the precarious earthy settlement held at a particular time in a particular circumstance.

4. Although this theology always speaks of God's rule as settled and "above the fray," this theology is always worked out and concerned with being "in the fray"; that is, this contractual theology is never disinterested, detached, objectively clear, or perfectly obvious. It is wrought by power agents who have a sociopolitical point to score and who mean to defeat alternative views and legitimate their own. Methodologically, it is important to recognize that the theological functioning of structure legitimation in heaven always carries with it a hint of the legitimation of certain structures on earth.

I

Clearly, the Old Testament is not simply one more statement of common theology. There is something else going on here to which we must pay careful attention. As the Old Testament is a statement of common theology, it also states the crisis in common theology. The crisis comes about because that theology does not square with Israel's experience of life or Israel's experience of faith, that is, Israel's discernment of God.[3]

Biblical faith, of course, is not static. It is not a set of statements that are always and everywhere true; therefore, contemporary biblical theology must not be reductionist in order to make all of the Old Testament fit together. Rather, the Old Testament is a collage of documents that bring to speech what seems to be going on in Israel's strange linkage with Yahweh. These two, Yahweh and Israel, are lodged in a common theology on their way together. But it is important that they are on the way together and not in a resting place together.[4]

In Israel's practice of common theology, one may suggest that two moves are underway at the same time and in opposite directions.

The point is that the claims that seem to be beyond historical experience are in fact fashioned within the experience.

3. On the crisis of common theology, see Herbert N. Schneidau, *Sacred Discontent: The Bible and Western Tradition* (Baton Rouge, La.: Louisiana State University Press, 1977). He understands that the Old Testament is foundationally committed against common myths; therefore, the community shaped by this book is destined for cultural alienation.

4. For the metaphor of "conversation on the way" as a means of thinking about the theological process, see Paul M. van Buren, *Discerning the Way: A Theology of the Jewish-Christian Reality* (New York: Seabury Press, 1980; part 2, 1983).

On the one hand, there is an *intensification of Yahweh's anger and impatience*. Israel grows more wayward and less inclined to obedience, and, as common theology anticipates, Yahweh grows more taut and harsh. The building of intense anger is evident in the prophets of the eighth and seventh centuries, in the theological constructs of the Deuteronomists, in the events of 587 B.C.E., and in the telling response of Lamentations. The prophets move through all kinds of warnings and indictments to the extreme conclusion of Jeremiah that Yahweh wills the end of the city, of the people, and even of the temple. In the South, about which Jeremiah prophesies, there is a second actualization of Amos's announcement of the end of the North (Amos 8:2). Jeremiah is driven to say that the South has no safe conduct (Jer. 7:1-15). Jerusalem will be a dead crater like Shiloh in the North. This intensification of anger is not chagrin that the end has brutally come. It is, rather, amazement that the end is so long in coming. In retrospect it is clear that the destruction is inevitable and inexorable. The common theology has its say. The outcome of judgment for Jerusalem is tightly tied to disobedience.

II

In the telling of its faith, however, Israel discerned a second move. In the heart of God there is an enormous patience, a holding to promises even in the face of disobedience, a resistance to the theological categories that conventionally give God self-definition. Clearly, this God has reluctance about the singular role of structure legitimation. The God of Israel wills to be other than "the enforcer," and so there emerges an unbearable incongruity. The incongruity concerns a God committed to a structure of sanctions and yet with a yearning for a relationship with this disobedient partner.

It is this incongruity in the person of God that forces the issue that scholars are pleased to call the issue of theodicy.[5] But such a labeling, as usually handled, is much too speculative and cerebral. Rather, the

---

5. The theological problem of theodicy is regularly handled in Old Testament scholarship. See James L. Crenshaw, "Theodicy," in *IDBSup* (see chap. 1, n. 4), 895–96, for a brief presentation of the issues and they several settlements offered in the text. See also the collection of papers edited by Crenshaw, *Theodicy* (see chap. 1, n. 27). The issue of theodicy, however, cannot be contained in a purely literary, reflective treatment. Peter L. Berger, in *The Sacred Canopy* (Garden City, N.Y.: Doubleday & Co., Anchor Books, 1969), chap. 3, has seen that theodicy becomes a problem when the world of plausibility is overwhelmed by facts and social reality that it cannot explain or contain. John Gunnemann, in *The Moral Meaning of Revolution* (New Haven: Yale

problem is that the God of Israel must decide again how much to be committed to the common theology, how many of its claims must be implemented, and how many of those claims can be resisted. That problem is brought to eloquence in the poem of Job, which belongs in the dramatic presentation of this issue. Job makes the argument that the response of God in judgment is disproportionate to any identifiable guilt. The anger of this God seems to go beyond any recognizable warrant, as Job understands it. Perhaps the question raised by this seeming mismatch of disobedience and punishment is not, Does Job serve God for nought? but Does Yahweh judge Israel for nought? The intensification of anger drives Israel's poets to unthinkable thoughts, so the Old Testament undertakes dangerous intellectual and theological probes against the common theology.

There is more here than the intensification of anger. If that were all there was, Israel would not break from the common theology. Israel's theology would be unambiguously structure-legitimating, and it would not be very interesting. Old Testament theology must be bipolar. It is not only about structure legitimacy but also about *the embrace of pain* that changes the calculus. My argument, therefore, in this second of two chapters is that Old Testament theology must attend to the embrace of pain as a posture of both Yahweh and Israel. By *embrace of pain* is meant the full acknowledgment of and experience of pain and the capacity and willingness to make that pain a substantive part of Israel's faith-conversation with its God. Such an act of embrace means to articulate the pain fully, to insist on God's reception of the speech and the pain, and to wait hopefully for God's resolution. The term "pain" here refers to any dysfunction in the relationship with God and to any derivative dysfunction in the disorder of creation or society. The pain may be experienced in quite public or quite private ways. But it is all of a piece, because such acknowledgment and articulation are an assertion that the modes of common theology are not adequate or functional to this experience, which is no longer denied. This is the move made against common theology:

University Press, 1979), chap. 2, has gone further with a sociological understanding of theodicy. It is an argument not that the rules have been wrongly administered, but that the rules are wrong. Thus, revolution means to nullify the settlements made about conduct and payoffs, about who has access and who is denied access. One can make the argument that the exodus event itself was a rejection of the theodicy that was sponsored and legitimated by the Egyptian empire (no doubt with the support of Egyptian religion). The crisis of theodicy is the rejection of the contract and of contractual theology.

1. The practice of pain-embrace *must always be in tension* with the legitimation of structure, never in place of it. It is this tension that is the stuff of biblical faith and it is the stuff of human experience; however, simply to choose the embrace of pain instead of legitimation of structure as a rubric for theology is romanticism. Israel will have none of that. The tension must be kept alive and visible.

2. The embrace of pain is *a crucial minority voice* in the Old Testament that peculiarly characterizes both the God of Israel and the people of Israel. It is surely a minority voice, always fragile against the dominance of structure legitimation, which I have already traced. It can only be and must always be a minority voice. But it is a crucial voice. It is this embrace of pain that opens the Old Testament to the future. It is this radical probe of a new way of relationship that runs toward the theology of the cross in the New Testament and that runs in our time toward and beyond the Holocaust, as Elie Wiesel and Emil L. Fackenheim have seen so well.[6] It is precisely this fragile minority voice that gives a future. Without this voice, the unchallenged tendency of structure legitimation will absolutize the present so that there can be no future that stands apart from and over against the present.[7]

3. The *disregard (or censoring) of pain-embrace* in our time and in every time permits persons and institutions to be unconditionally committed to structure legitimation. Where pain is not embraced, critical uneasiness about every crushing orthodoxy is banished. It is certain that where there is the legitimation of structure without the voice of pain embraced, there will be oppression without compassion. There will be competence without mercy. There will be no need for or possibility of good news. Where there is only the legitimacy of structure without pain-embrace, there is only the good news that the system is the solution, whether the solution is in heaven or on earth. Good biblical theology, indeed good pastoral theology, keeps alive the tension that dares not to be resolved.

---

6. See Emil Fackenheim, *To Mend the World: Foundations of Future Jewish Thought* (New York: Schocken Press, 1982), esp. 278–94.

7. On the critical relation of past, present, and future, see Gary A. Herion, "The Role of Historical Narrative in Biblical Thought," *JSOT* 21 (1981): 25–57.

III

I will consider the embrace of pain as a theological datum in Israel in two parts. Gottwald has considered the issue in *sociological* categories, but it remains for us to consider the *theological* aspects of pain-embrace in Israel. When it is handled only as sociology and not as theological activity, it likely has no serious future.

There is a restlessness in Israel that seeks to move through and beyond or against the common theology, and that restlessness is articulated in *Israel's practice of lament*.[8] Israel's lament is a way of protesting against the common theology. The lament in Israel is a way of asserting that the structure cannot always be legitimated and that the pain needs also to be embraced. This pain, when brought to public speech, impinges upon every structure and serves to question the legitimacy of the structure. The laments of Israel, as Claus Westermann has seen, are not marginal but decisive for the faith of Israel.

The moment when Israel found the nerve and the faith to risk an assault on the throne of God with complaint was a decisive moment against legitimation. The lament is a dramatic, rhetorical, liturgical act of speech that is irreversible. When spoken, it is done and cannot be recalled. It makes clear that Israel will no longer be a submissive, subservient recipient of decrees from the throne. There is a bold movement from Israel's side—a voice that does not silently and docilely accept but means to have its dangerous say, even in the face of God. In risking this form of speech, the conventional distribution of power is called into question. It is no longer placidly assumed that God has all the power and the covenant partner must simply submit. Pain speaks against legitimacy, which now for the first time is questioned as perhaps illegitimate.

Legitimated structure can never again be utterly indifferent to the embrace of pain. It is like Rosa Park's refusing to move to the

---

8. The practice of lament in the faith of Israel has been most carefully studied by Claus Westermann, *Praise and Lament in the Psalms* (Atlanta: John Knox Press, 1981). See also Brueggemann, "From Hurt to Joy, from Death to Life," *Int* 28 (1974): 3–19; and Patrick D. Miller, "Trouble and Woe," *Int* 37 (1983): 32–45. Following the lead of Westermann, a number of scholars have now seen that the structure of the lament psalm characteristically moves to resolution of the trouble, to praise, and to a restored, though changed, relationship. This, however, does not argue against embrace of pain, nor does it mute the power of such speech. Rather, it is to notice that embrace of pain is the only way in which pain can be submitted to God and thus resolved. See my extended discussion of this matter, Brueggemann, *The Message of Psalms* (Minneapolis: Augsburg Pub. House, 1984), 81–88.

back of the bus in Montgomery. Such a refusal means there can be no more business as usual. Such an act of the public embrace of pain makes the questioned structure less above the fray than it has ever appeared to be before. That irreversible risk was so the first time it was uttered. It is so every time this action is undertaken again:

1. Consider the enormous risk of speaking such a lament. Lament-speech takes courage because it pushes the relationship to the boundaries of unacceptability. It takes risk because one does not know how the great God will receive it. It might have been an act of disobedience that would be crushed according to the normal rules of authority and propriety. It requires not only deep faith but new faith. It takes not only nerve but a fresh hunch about this God. The hunch is that this God does not want to be an unchallenged structure but one who can be frontally addressed. Such is the hope or yearning of lamenting Israel. The outcome of such challenge is not known in advance, not known until the risk is run to test the hunch. Such dangerous, restless speech could have been received and reckoned as irreverent, disrespectful disobedience. Because the restlessness, however, is not only Israel's but also Yahweh's, this bold speech of assault is in fact received at the throne not as disobedience but as a new kind of obedience. The gain of Israel's faith is the discernment that this ultimately legitimated structure is indeed open to the embrace of pain, open both for Israel and for God. That can never be known theoretically. It can only be known concretely. The wonder of Israel's faith is that it is concretely risked.

In the risk there emerges a new mode of faith between Yahweh and Israel. In the public utterance of such pain, both parties emerge with freshness. Obedience turns out to be not blind, docile *submissiveness* required by common theology. It is rather a bold *protest* against a legitimacy that has grown illegitimate because it does not seriously take into account the suffering reality of the partner. Where the reality of suffering is not dealt with, legitimate structure is made illegitimate when the voice of pain assumes enough authority to be heard.

2. Before moving on, we may ponder the ways in which conventional theological tendency and conventional church practice have nullified the laments. The laments are not widely used among us, not printed in most hymnals, not legitimated in our theology. Many Christians think the laments are superseded by some christological claim. We have in practice reneged on the bold break made in Israel's protest against the common theology. Unwittingly, by silencing

the break of embraced pain, we have embraced the uncritical faith of structure legitimation. Much biblical faith, as commonly held, has in fact become a support for the status quo by using a theological mode that understands God primarily in the categories of structure legitimation. Such a move is reflected both in liturgical use, where the laments have largely fallen out of the repertoire, and in popular theology as reflected in the catechisms, to say nothing of popular proclamation.

3. The laments are Israel's primary and distinctive departure from the common theology. Erhard Gerstenberger has argued that these speech-forms are not in fact "laments" but "complaints"; that is, they are not acts of resignation but acts of protest.[9] They are not self-pitying meditations on trouble; rather, they are addressed to God. They are speeches that force a new connection between the Lord of Life and the troublesome reality of life, where Israel must live. In this dramatic exchange, Yahweh is recharacterized as the one who must take account of the trouble. God is no longer a trouble-free God, and the trouble is recharacterized as something that now is the proper agenda of Yahweh. Indeed, in these speeches trouble is presented in such a way that it impinges upon Yahweh. Yahweh is no longer free to be a trouble-free God who presides over untroubled legitimated structures; that is, Israel's enormous chutzpah forces a newness upon Yahweh and in Yahweh. Israel's laments force God to recharacterization. This act of forcing God to recharacterization is not an unproblematic venture, theologically. It is in deep tension with the reality of God's sovereign freedom to be whom God chooses to be. Nonetheless, in this liturgical, rhetorical, passionate moment of extremity, such an action is taken. And the remarkable experience of Israel is that God is impinged upon in decisive ways by such an act. Although this rhetorical pattern is a matter of literary interest, it is also a matter of theological marvel and lives in tension with more static theological categories.

4. As Gerstenberger has shown, the laments are refusals to settle for the way things are. They are acts of a relentless hope that believes no situation falls outside Yahweh's capacity for transformation. No situation falls outside Yahweh's responsibility. Israel is the community that refuses to settle for the way things are, refuses to accept the legitimated structures, refuses to accept a God who is positioned above the fray, refuses to accept guilt and blame for every

---

9. Gerstenberger, "Jeremiah's Complaints," *JBL* 82 (1963): 393–408, esp. n. 50.

dysfunction. Indeed, such a theological hunch does not believe that the doctor knows best, does not believe all authority is ordained by God, does not believe city hall (in heaven or on earth) cannot be fought.

This is a rhetorical form of civil (sometimes uncivil) disobedience that turns out to be a way of obedience.[10]

IV

The restlessness as lament is pervasive in Israel, and in each case it forces a break in Israel's version of common theology:

1. Surprisingly, *Moses first models such protest*. That is surprising because it is also Moses who articulates the heaviest theological sanctions in Israel. But Moses is a bold man of faith who believes that as the covenantal sanctions legitimate structures, so also the faithful must press God to embrace and deal with the pain. The prayers of Moses are radical and dangerous protests that throw down the gauntlet to God:

> Alas, this people have sinned a great sin; they have made for themselves gods of gold. But now, if thou wilt forgive their sin—and if not, blot me, I pray thee, out of thy book which thou hast written. (Exod. 32:31-32)

> If thy presence will not go with me, do not carry us up from here. (Exod. 33:15)

> Moses was displeased. Moses said to the Lord, "Why hast thou dealt ill with thy servant? And why have I not found favor in thy sight, that thou dost lay the burden of all this people upon me? Did I conceive all this people? Did I bring them forth, that thou shouldst say to me, 'Carry them in your bosom, as a nurse carries the sucking child, to the land which thou didst swear to give their fathers?' Where am I to get meat to give to all this people? For they weep before me and say, 'Give us meat, that we may eat.' I am not able to carry all this people alone, the burden is too heavy for me. If thou wilt deal thus with me, kill me at once, if I find favor in thy sight, that I may not see my wretchedness." (Num. 11:10-15)

---

10. It is clear that much of "proper faith" is in fact an act of civility to keep the issues of injustice from having visibility. See the insightful analyses of John M. Cuddihy, *The Ordeal of Civility* (New York: Basic Books, 1974); and Norbert Elias, *Power and Civility* (New York: Pantheon Books, 1982).

The most extraordinary thing about these prayers is that in each case, Moses prevails.[11] The prayers are uttered in conflict with God. Moses assaults the throne. Each time God is impinged upon and must do a new thing because of the pressure of the prayer of Moses. It turns out that God is not so fully closed off and settled that there will be no relenting.

2. The *lament psalms of the Psalter* follow in the way of Moses. I mention especially Psalm 88 as the most dangerous, unresolved, and perhaps hopeless of all the laments.[12] It is an unmitigated accusation against God. The hurt is not that the speaker is "shunned" (*rāḥaq*, vv. 7, 18) but that Yahweh causes the hurt. The verb is in the hiph'il. The linkage is drawn here most closely between the trouble and the throne. With incredible boldness, the pain of the speaker is left unresolved at the throne for God to ponder. The speaker does not blink or waver, is not intimidated, accepts no responsibility for the problems, and proposes no way out. The trouble, unbearable as it is, is left there. And if there is to be a next move, it will have to be on the part of God. God may wish to be above the fray, but this speaker relentlessly draws God into the fray. This is embraced pain playing brinkmanship with legitimated structure.

Things have now been quite inverted. What gall! Such prayer must be a galling experience for God, but note unmistakably that it is an act of hope. It is still addressed to God, and there is a waiting for God's new answer—"until hell freezes over." All parties know that God will have to make a new response. No old, conventional response will do. Israel will give God as long as God likes. God must re-decide, for pain makes a new requirement of legitimacy. Can we even imagine what it is like to pray that way when circumstances have jeopardized all conventions, when the restlessness can no longer remain silent under the incongruity? The corpus of lament psalms provides a primary datum for this pole of biblical theology. The power of Israel's prayers to evoke from God a new posture of relationship is stunning; however, it is not everywhere the case in the Old Testament. Many times, Israel does not offer such a challenge.

---

11. See George W. Coats, "Humility and Honor: A Moses Legend in Numbers 12," in *Act and Meaning: Rhetoric in Biblical Literature*, ed. David J. A. Clines, David M. Gunn, and Alan J. Hauser, JSOTSup, no. 19 (Sheffield: University of Sheffield Press, 1982), 97–107. Coats shows that the "meekness" of Moses entails the bold capacity to intervene with God on behalf of Israel.

12. It is worth noting that this is the psalm utilized by William Styron, in *Sophie's Choice* (New York: Random House, 1979), 505–6, to articulate the depth of despair by his central character, Stingo: "Dat is some fine Psalm."

On other occasions, as in Job, the challenge is rejected. But in the lament psalms themselves, this remarkable theological transaction does seem to make changes in both parties. Such theological adventurism is a high-risk action, but Israel found it to be substantive and not simply speculative, wishful thinking.

3. *Jeremiah brings the lament tradition to intense, personal speech.* The speech of Jeremiah occurs when the intensity of God's anger and God's restlessness against Judah has become full. Jeremiah is his own man. His passionate poetry, however, brings to speech the full trouble of his people, so he speaks as Israel at the eleventh hour.[13]

His word is a harsh accusation (Jer. 20:7-12). Jeremiah knows that God has seduced him (v. 7), yet he says that God is his "dread warrior" (v. 11). It cannot be both ways, yet Jeremiah is unsure and wavers. I suggest Jeremiah puts the poem that way not only because he cannot decide but also because he wants to force God to decide. For God seems not yet to have decided about how to be present to Jeremiah—as a reliable stream or as a deceitful brook, as a balm in Gilead or as an incurable wound. The voice of pain takes the trouble to the throne; and in that act of the poem, God's presumptive categories of self-characterization are shattered.[14]

4. The lament tradition comes to its fruition in the *harshness of Job*, who is surely informed by Jeremiah. As has been noted often, the protesting posture of Job still stays with the normal presuppositions of the common theology of deed and consequence; however, the poem as such (as distinct from the character of Job in the poem) is intended to move out of those presuppositions:

a. The extraordinarily harsh protest of 9:19-24 decisively nullifies the dominant theology. Job defiantly concludes that the theology of legitimated structure does not work:

> Though I am blameless, he would prove me perverse. . . . It is all one; therefore I say, he destroys both the blameless and the wicked. . . . He mocks at the calamity of the innocent.

---

13. William L. Holladay, in *Jeremiah: Spokesman out of Time* (Philadelphia: United Church Press, 1974), chap. 7, has provided a helpful summary of the current discussion. See my own assessment of the matter, Brueggemann, "The Book of Jeremiah: Portrait of the Prophet," *Int* 37 (1983): 130–45. It is not necessary, I think, to decide if these complaints are personal or articulations for the community. It seems plausible that both factors are present.

14. On the transformative hurt of God as it relates to Jeremiah, see Abraham J. Heschel, *The Prophets* (New York: Harper & Row, 1962), chap. 6. My own inclination, as distinct from Heschel, is to say Jeremiah not only expresses God's pain but also evokes it in his own speech.

Job now has enough pain that he has the courage to challenge the dominant theology and the readiness to dismiss pain.

b. The great refusal of Job is reinforced with the speeches from the whirlwind, which also refuse to respond any longer to questions of the old rationality. That tight system of deeds and consequences is not explicitly denied any more than it is affirmed. Rather, it is disregarded as if to say that, in future conversations, Job as well as God should not appeal to it, but should ignore it. As the poem is shaped, Job lingers longer in loyalty to the old theology (old truth) than does God, who moves beyond it. This shift in agenda in the whirlwind supports James L. Crenshaw's judgment that creation theology is a response to the question of theodicy now grown too large for history and morality.[15] What is offered is perhaps not a new ground for theodicy but a dissolving of the question.

c. Finally, we should note that in 42:8 it is Job and not the friends who spoke what is "right." The verdict in Job's favor indicates that the obedience received and valued by God is not simply submissiveness and docility, but it is the courage to stand in the face of the Holy One and force the issues in new directions. What is right about Job is not just the final settlement of 42:6, however that is understood, but the whole tradition of speech that refuses to accept the conventions of the accepted order.

My proposal is that the *countertradition* articulated by Moses-Psalms-Jeremiah-Job is pervasive and important enough to be regarded as a major point of tension with the common theology that we have found in many parts of the text:

First, it is clear that this is a rigorous protest against the common theology, which assumes that the firm order of God is equitable. Common theology assumes that if something is amiss, it must be the fault of the protester. This countertradition of texts refuses to accept that assignment of fault and returns the compliment to God. The most remarkable thing is that God is characteristically presented as the one who receives and takes seriously that bold counterspeech.

Second, this theological stance insists and affirms that the legitimated order (that is, God's order) can be addressed, assaulted, impinged upon, and transformed. There is, through this speech, a changed dynamic between the parties. That changed dynamic gives authority to the hurting one over against the transcendent one. It affirms and respects the voice of pain as a proper partner in the

---

15. Crenshaw, "The Problem of Theodicy in Sirach," *JBL* 94 (1975): 47–64.

work of theology. It acknowledges that the cry in the fray reaches the one above the fray. God is inevitably drawn back into the fray, from which "canon" seemed to immunize.[16]

Third, the risk in this tradition of protest is a dangerous one whenever it is undertaken. The fact that such an assault is accepted one time gives no assurance that it will be the next time. It is only in the concrete, nervy act of such speaking that one can know when such conduct is acceptable. One never knows, until the bold act is done, whether one has gone too far. Any new speech of this kind that is boldly probing may be the probe that goes too far and evokes the rage of the legitimated one under attack. The regular experience of Israel, however, is that in the moment of honest risk, Israel characteristically discovers that the speech is not only not resisted, but it is taken seriously in a way that permits a newness.

This theological tendency has no place in the pattern discerned by Smith. The reason for that is important. Smith has rightly seen that in the common theology there is a claim of the unqualified authority of God, conventionally asserted with the words "omnipotent, omnipresent, omniscient." The lament tradition begins to question that claim and to reshape the agenda of power in subversively covenantal ways. The lament critiques common theology. It invites this God to participate in the critique that will permit a newness.

V

It is clear that this restlessness against the intensity of anger impinges upon Israel. But note that the same restlessness with common theology is at work with God. There are hints (only hints) that God begins to feel increasingly uneasy about conventional forms, about standard characterizations of what makes a god a god.

Now in saying this, I am making some delicate assumptions about

---

16. The matter of canonization points not simply to a literary authority but also to a theological normativeness. Canonization too easily suggests that the God articulated in the canon is above the fray. So Gottwald, in "Sociological Matrix" (see chap. 1, n. 6), writes: "Literature, especially canonical literature, is not disinterested. Every text has its sociological matrix and interest, whether we can easily identify it or not. And the final act or series of acts that fix a canonical shape have a sociological matrix and interest as well." My point here is that the embrace of pain requires and permits the God who has been thus canonized in the literature to enter back into the historical process where pain is the vehicle for new characterization. On the problem of canon in relation to static categories, see the helpful discussion of Sallie McFague, *Metaphorical Theology* (Philadelphia: Fortress Press, 1982).

the nature of the biblical text. I am not arguing that this is simply a clever literary fiction in which the biblical writers present whatever god they need to keep the play going. Nor am I arguing that this is flat, descriptive reporting on the mind of God. Rather, I am assuming that the biblical text is an imaginative literary enterprise in which the writers are like dramatists who create new scenes about God but who are readily surprised by the moves made by the lead character, almost against the intent and beyond the imagination of the author.[17] The hints we shall consider portray the surprising efforts of Yahweh to break beyond convention and articulate a new identity.

Yahweh is indeed getting free of the pigeonhole of common theology. Throughout the Old Testament, it is likely correct that Yahweh never fully breaks through. But there is a restlessness, a probing, a daring alternative that is proposed and lingered with, only then to be withdrawn.[18] And these restless probes may be the primary material for Old Testament theology:

1. The first such narrative text is the flood of Gen. 6:5—8:22.[19] It is not about destructiveness or a lot of water but about the troubled heart of God. Or said another way, the narrative is not about the anger of God but about the grief of God.

At the beginning of the narrative, two motifs are in tension. The text is carefully wrought to hold the tension in place. On the one hand, we have conventional lawsuit theology:

The indictment: There is wickedness of imagination, evil continually.

The sentence: I will blot out. (Gen. 6:5, 7)

This is contractual theology. Such wicked acts warrant such responses of punishment. If that were all we had, it would be a

---

17. See in this connection Dale Patrick, *The Rendering of God in the Old Testament* (Philadelphia: Fortress Press, 1981). Note particularly his references to Hans Frei and David Kelsey.

18. Such bold probing of God has been eloquently characterized by Samuel Terrien, *Job: Poet of Existence* (Indianapolis: Bobbs-Merrill, 1957), 113–17. Terrien quotes T. S. Eliot to good effect: "There are only hints and guesses, / Hints followed by guesses; and the rest / Is prayer, observance, discipline, thought and action. / The hint half-guessed, the gift half-understood, is / Incarnation." That is how it is with the problems we mention here.

19. See my exploration of this text, Brueggemann, *Genesis* (Atlanta: John Knox Press, 1982), 73–88.

simple, uninteresting story. On the other hand, intertwined with that
structure is a disclosure of the heart of God:

> The Lord was sorry,
> It grieved him to the heart,
> I am sorry I have made them. (Vv. 6-7)

These lines take us into the interiority of God, where things are troubled and far from clear.[20] The former system gives the public facts
of the case. The disobedient deserve to die. The other inclination
reveals the internal sense of God that does not easily move into a
public form. This combination of public system and internal inclination is a radical theological disclosure. God has an internal life that
does not conform to contractual norms. Things are at play and are
yet to be decided. There is anguish, uncertainty, ambiguity, mixed
feelings, and presumably some option. This is not how the high gods
work who punish evil and reward good, so we are put on notice of
a theological risk here on the part of Yahweh.

The narrative proceeds just as it should have, if there were only
common theology. There is water, destruction, and death. The story
could and should have ended in Gen. 7:24. There is more to the
story only because there is more to God. "God remembers."[21] God
is self-reflective and has a past to which appeal is made. God makes
commitments and subsequently honors them. God is not an automatic principle. At the center of the story is a person who cares.
Caring is what legitimated structure cannot do.[22]

---

20. This aspect of God's character is affirmed from an unexpected source. Bertil
Albrektson is best known for his insistence that the biblical God is not unique for action
in history. In *History and the Gods* (see chap. 1, n. 13), however, he writes: "We learn
about Yahweh's purposes and intentions, his true nature and the innermost thoughts
of his heart, his gifts and his claims, which make him different from all the other gods
of the ancient Near East" (p. 122). It is that distinctiveness that is narrated in this text.
See Gottwald, *Tribes* (see chap. 1, n. 6), 674–75, for his comment on Albrektson.

21. On "God Remembers," see Ralph W. Klein, "The Message of P," in *Die Botschaft
und die Boten*, ed. Jörg Jeremias and Lothar Perlitt (Neukirchen-Vluyn: Neukirchener
Verlag, 1981), 57–66. Klein argues that, in the P tradition, "signs" such as the rainbow
and circumcision are established to help God remember. In the flood narrative, such
special reminders are not necessary. The importance of Klein's argument for our
discussion is that it also points to the interiority and life of freedom that Yahweh has.

22. I do not want to push the theme of "caring" too far, but reference might
be made to Carol Gilligan, *In a Different Voice* (Cambridge: Harvard University
Press, 1982). The theme has theological, as well as psychological, developmental
dimensions.

The conclusion of this narrative in Gen. 8:20-22 is well-known. In the end, the waters are driven away. There is a promise that it will not happen again. Yahweh makes a new resolve and a new promise. In the end only one thing remains the same: "... the inclination of the human heart is evil" (v. 21). That has not changed. Humankind is seen to be resiliently and relentlessly evil.

A new relation, however, is possible. The human heart in 8:21 is as it was in 6:5. The change that makes a new future possible is wrought not in the human heart but in Yahweh's heart, which is filled with sorrow, grief, regret. The flood is about the inundation of God's person. The narrative tells about a new resolve on God's part, which takes God outside the framework of "evil imagination" and "blotting out," that is, outside the lawsuit of contractual theology. There is here a disclosure that Yahweh has heart trouble, knows something of pain, and does not act finally to legitimate order. To be sure, in 8:22 there is again a guaranteed order, but it is on the other side of God's turned heart. Pain for Yahweh has caused a turn in the flood and a turn in the narrative and—we dare to think—a turn in the theological enterprise.

2. Genesis 18:16—19:22 presents the same tensions we have been considering elsewhere.[23] In 19:1-29, there is the old, patterned story. Except for the mitigation concerning Lot's family in vv. 12-23, the story is flat and predictable, according to contractual theology:

vv. 1-11:   the presentation of wickedness and outcry—indictment

vv. 24-28:   fire and brimstone—sentence

The structure is a simple judgment story befitting conventional, traditional theology.

What interests us more, however, is the counternarrative in 18:16-33, which lives in tension with the older narrative of 19:1-29. In 18:16-19, there is an extravagant credentialing of Abraham, perhaps the most extravagant of all of Scripture. The simple story of guilt in chapter 19 could be operative without Abraham, but the introduction of Abraham in this alternative version allows for slippage and surprise. In 18:30 there is the verdict, but there is no flat, automatic

---

23. See my exploration of this text, *Genesis*, 162–76. Joseph Blenkinsopp, in "Abraham and the Righteous of Sodom (Gen. 18:23-32)," *JJS* 35 (1982): 119–32, has provided a most discerning history of interpretation of this passage.

rush to judgment. Abraham is present, and his presence means there are promises to be kept and impossibilities to ponder (see v. 14).

Verses 22-23 contain some of the most remarkable material in the Old Testament:

a. An important textual issue appears in v. 22. The corrected text, as we have it, has Abraham standing before the Lord in a posture of proper deference. But we are told that the uncorrected form of the text reversed postures and placed Yahweh deferentially before Abraham for questioning and instruction. Indeed, that is the tone of the narrative.

b. In vv. 13-24, Abraham poses the question to Yahweh about the judge judging equitably. Admittedly, the issue is not very much developed. It is not argued here that the presence of the innocent should save the guilty; it is only proposed that the innocent should not be destroyed with the guilty. But the question introduces for Yahweh a new theological sensitivity. It is as though Abraham has posed for Yahweh a new question about what kind of god to be, whether to notice people in their concreteness or to operate like the usual gods in rather summary fashion.

c. The double question is answered by Abraham in v. 25: "Far be that from thee!" The term is *ḥll*, which may mean unworthy, profane, unacceptable—that is, incongruous with the holiness of God's character, upon which God had not yet reflected. Abraham identifies such harsh judgment as inappropriate to and incompatible with the character of God even though God has not yet arrived at this insight about self-characterization.

The acknowledgment by Yahweh of the rightness of Abraham's argument is given in v. 26. There then follows in vv. 27-33 the wonderful and amusing negotiation between God and Abraham about the minimum number that might save the city. In its outcome, the narrative is thoroughly Jewish because the bottom line is the minimum of ten, a minyan. The story ends rather abruptly with the mutual departure. Abraham and Yahweh had gone as far as they could with this bold and dangerous exploration of a new characterization of God and a new practice of righteousness.

Clearly, the narratives of Gen. 18:16-33 and 19:1-29 reflect very different theological efforts, the second being written out of exactly the purview presented by Smith. The present form of the text links them, but they do not flow easily. Chapter 19 is an automatic playing out of the story of guilt and punishment. But chapter 18 lingers over the decisions that Yahweh has yet to make. In this narrative God is open to and instructed by Abraham about the reality of hurt and need in the human arena.

In the present form of the text, one can conclude that after such a radical probing, the narrative pushes along with business as usual to its terrible, predictable ending. Abraham's dangerous proposal to God is in vain. The *probe* of chapter 18 did not change the *convention* of chapter 19. The standard act of structure legitimacy is not penetrated by the embrace of this more nuanced human reality, but perhaps that is to miss the point of literary finesse. The unthinkable has now been thought. The unutterable has now been uttered. The question has now been asked of the judge of all the earth: Shall not the judge of all the earth do right? Will not the *šōpēṭ* do *mišpāṭ*? The question cannot be unasked. It lingers in the mind of God and God must decide afresh what that means. The effect of such a probe is to give God some distance so that there are options, so that God is not taken for granted. The voice of real human hurt is embraced there in the context of the question of righteousness and justice. And although the old theology is implemented in chapter 19, it has been questioned and placed in jeopardy by the probe of chapter 18. The old, presumed systems of settlement are now placed in question. As we shall see, the question persists.

3. Our third text, Hos. 11:1-9, is well-known and perhaps the most important for the point being made. This poem is a rather conventional judgment speech. Much of the tradition of Hosea adheres to judgment speech conventions and is even more rigorous and harsh than is much of Amos. Indeed, stereotypes that treat Hosea as a "prophet of love" without further reflection miss the main point. In this text, vv. 2-3 are a recital of God's graciousness, intertwined with an indictment:

> They went from me;
> they kept sacrificing to the Baals,
>   and burning incense to idols....
> They did not know that I healed them.

They forgot who was God (cf. 8:14), and the sentence in vv. 4-7 is flat and predictable: exile, even death. That much is common theology, and that should be the end of that. There the poem might have ended. That is where we conventionally stop with contractual theology. The wonder is that the poet stays with the poem beyond this point. The greater wonder is that the God rendered in this poem focuses attention on the continuing question of Gen. 18:25 when one might have thought vv. 4-7 to be God's last thought on the question.

It is, however, precisely where the end is expected and justified that the poem takes on a new vitality. In v. 8a God poses four rhetorical questions.[24] They are introspective questions, to which the answer is not known ahead of time, even to God; that is, this is not mere rhetoric, but a genuine probe. Yahweh probes for a new way of relating that moves beyond the end to which v. 7 had brought things. It is important that the poem, in moving to this newness wrought in pain, makes explicit reference to the dilemma of Genesis 18–19. The reference to Admah and Zeboiim is to be taken as a reference to Sodom and Gomorrah. It is as though God now recalls that narrative. God now remembers what was done there against the urging of Abraham, how painful it was, and considers whether it should be done again, this time against the proper, beloved covenant partner. The question is a dangerous one for God to ask. All the old notions about what it means to be God come into play. The question is asked four times. Then there is a reflection on what this question does to God.

The reference back to Genesis 18–19 may be intensified by the use of the verb *hāpak* (v. 8), which the Revised Standard Version renders "recoil." It is the verb used in Gen. 19:25, 29 to characterize the earthquake. In that narrative God is not touched by the destruction that is externally executed against the wicked cities. Now, in this remarkable turn by the poem, God does not cause the earthquake against Israel, which is as deserving of it as Sodom and Gomorrah.

Now God takes to God's own heart the pain and the upheaval that one expects to be actualized. God's heart is impinged upon (not unlike in the flood story). God is unable to do the warranted act precisely because God is no longer able to be a one-dimensional legitimator of structure. Now God is transformed by the embrace of pain in God's own person, which changes the calculus with reference to Israel. What had been done to Sodom and Gomorrah is now done to God's own person.[25] The next phrase in v. 8 is difficult. If the term *nhm* is retained, it holds for us the same term used to characterize

---

24. J. Gerald Janzen, "Metaphor and Reality in Hosea 11," *Semeia* 24 (1982): 7–44.

25. I would not want to press the poetry into excessively rigid categories, but I take warrant from Eliot's "hint-guess of Incarnation." This formulation of the matter, when read in light of Genesis 18–19, affirms that God takes into God's person what rightly belongs to Israel. It is a step in the direction of saying, "He died that we might live."

God's regret in the flood narrative (Gen. 6:6). If the conventional emendation is taken and the term is rendered as *rhm*, "compassion," then the impact upon God's own body is intensified.

So the probing questions of v. 8 are answered in v. 9. There will be no destruction. The "Holy One" is the one who makes the new decisions. This Holy One knows that there are promises to keep. What happens in this moment of the poem is that God's holiness is recharacterized as compassion. The move made here is not unlike the one proposed in Gen. 18:23-25 by Abraham, although the words are different. Finally in v. 9, God resolves not to act like *'îš*, a human being. God will not act in destructive, retaliatory ways, because God has broken with the usual human notions of retribution.[26] It is as though the whole enterprise of contractual theology is here treated as an unworthy human construct. God has until now been laboring under this reading of reality. But in this moment of acute pain, when the hurt of Israel is taken into God's own heart, that conventional reading of earth and heaven is nullified and God assumes a new posture toward the covenant partner.

This is bold poetry on the part of Hosea, for the poet hazards the mind of God. What is discerned is that God has broken all the conventions. Common theology is rejected as a human construct and a human expectation, a mode to which God need not conform.

God's break with the common theology is not an easy step. It is a break wrought only in moving grief, only in solidarity with the grief of Israel. It is when God can grieve that there is a possibility of breaking out of such conventional categories.

4. The poem of Jer. 30:12-17 presents yet another articulation of the same issue in Israel's discernment of God. The key literary problem in this poem is how to relate vv. 12-15 to vv. 16-17. The first element announces that the pain is incurable and the last two verses promise healing. The theological issue is how God makes the move from harsh rejection to positive intervention. Conventional critical treatment assumes that vv. 16-17 are a later redactional addition to soften the previous verses. The problem with such an approach is that it violates the poem and dissolves all of the possible poetic playfulness.

---

26. Psalm 82 is also a discussion over what constitutes the godness of God. It is argued that care for the marginal is what makes God God. The other gods are condemned to die as mortal, no doubt because they lack the compassion of God and only serve themselves according to human standards. The term *mortals* (NRSV) there is *'ādām* (not the same term as in Hos. 11:9), but the point seems parallel.

If we are to take the poem as it stands, then we must seek within the poem ground for the move to v. 15.[27] In v. 14 Yahweh asserts that "no one cares." The odd turn is justified, if the final *kî* in v. 17 is read as causative. That is, I will be healing *because* "they have called you an outcast." In v. 17, the nations are said to repeat the very formula that was in the mouth of Yahweh in v. 14.

That is intolerable. As long as the issue is between the two covenant partners, Yahweh can be harsh and final. But when the nations (as outsiders to the relationship) make the same judgment, Yahweh is evoked (or provoked) to new action, which turns out to be saving. I submit that the break with contractual, structure-legitimating theology articulated in vv. 16-17 is made because Yahweh is brought much closer to the hurt that Israel experiences. Contact with that hurt causes Yahweh to assume a new posture and to recharacterize the future of Israel.

VI

I have touched only a few texts, and even these could be probed in greater depth. Other texts could be cited; but even with the other texts, the Old Testament offers no more than a probe, a hint, or an urging. This is not the main presentation of faith, which is still dominated by the power of structure legitimation. But the presence of such texts is important for discerning the dynamic of Old Testament theology.

The following conclusions may be suggested on the basis of these considerations:

1. The dominant mode of the Old Testament is contractual, a quid pro quo—a mode that serves to legitimate structure in heaven and on earth.

2. Where the countertheme of pain-embracing is present, it does not supersede or nullify structure legitimation but only lives in tension with it. That tension must be kept alive in all faithful biblical theology. I do not believe one can say there is a development from one to the other, but there is an ongoing tension, unresolved and unresolvable.

3. In the Old Testament, the voice of pain is a minority wonderment, never a central proposal, but this gives vitality and openness to

---

27. See my discussion of this passage in chap. 15.

the entire enterprise. Thus, these texts of probing perform a function in Old Testament theology disproportionate to their number and strength.

4. Insofar as Old Testament theology is related to the life of the church, this way of organizing our understanding of the text may be peculiarly poignant in our cultural context. There is a great tendency now, both religiously and politically, to want the text to serve purposes of structure legitimation. This is no doubt powered by the enormous fear and sense of chaos that are close at hand. But such a way of treating the text, for whatever reason, requires pushing the text unambiguously back into a pattern of contractual theology that ignores the hints and probes that are offered. The probes of pain-embrace affirm that the text asserts more than mere contract. The text understands that God's good news consists in more than structure legitimation. Human personhood in the image of this God always entails pain-embrace, which causes transformation and breaks beyond contractual relationships.

Israel, from its earliest time, had understood this. In the early and programmatic formulation of Exod. 34:6-7, the tension is already spelled out.[28] On the one hand, God takes violators seriously, well into the future. On the other hand, this same God is merciful and gracious. No doubt the text contains a deep incongruity, but the God of the Bible does not flinch from this incongruity. It is this incongruity that makes human life possible and makes biblical theology endlessly problematic and promising. This double focus can be carried through in a biblical theology that probes what structure legitimation and pain-embrace mean for our understanding of God, of Israel, of human personhood, of church, of creation.

The God portrayed here is an ambiguous one, always in the process of deciding.[29] For Israel, the issue is whether to be "like

---

28. On this crucial passage, see Gottwald, *Tribes*, 686–91. The continuing power of this tension and the continuing vitality of the articulation of Exod. 34:6-7 are evident in Walter Harrelson, "Ezra among the Wicked in 2 Esdras 3–10," in *The Divine Helmsman*, ed. Crenshaw and Samuel Sandmel (New York: Ktav Pub. House, 1980), 21–39. On pp. 35–39, Harrelson comments on the remarkable exegesis of Exod. 34:6-7 offered in 2 Esdras.

29. In the terms offered here, there is no doubt that God is "in process." It may be that such an articulation opens to an interface with so-called process theology. Perhaps so. But I am unconvinced about the enormous metaphysical superstructure of process philosophy as being useful for interpreting the Bible. It appears to me much simpler and more effective to deal with social/covenantal/personal metaphors on the Bible's own terms. In another context I have suggested that process theology is inherently more conservative than is recognized in some quarters.

the nations" or to be a "holy people." Israel dared to say that its
God, Yahweh, lived in the same ambiguity: whether to be "like the
other gods" or to be a holy God, "the Holy One in our midst,"
who had learned from Abraham fresh subversive notions of *ṣĕdāqâ*
and *mišpāṭ*.[30] The God-question is intimately linked to the character of Israel in the Old Testament. And the sociological tracings
of Norman K. Gottwald are intimately linked to theological questions proper. Israel as a social experiment could have little positive
prospect unless it sojourned with a God who noted, responded to,
and embodied the pain that Israel was also to embody. Yahweh's
probe of godness away from the gods of the Egyptian empire is at
least as important as Israel's probe of a sociology alternative to that
of the empire.

---

30. Robert Polzin, in *Moses* (see chap. 1, n. 21), 36–43, has seen that, at least
in Deuteronomy, the issues of Yahweh's uniqueness and Israel's distinctiveness are
intimately linked.

3

The Rhetoric of Hurt
and Hope: Ethics Odd
and Crucial

WHAT IS IT ABOUT the Old Testament that is so odd and disruptive and restless, that refuses to behave itself and act with civility? What is it about the Old Testament that is peculiarly crucial to ethics, especially to Christian ethics, and that is voiced nowhere else? These two questions converge: what is disruptive is also what is distinctive, and this uncommon, uncivil element is crucial to our ethical conversations in part because it is so odd.

Israel was shaped as a distinctive community by the character of its discourse. The Old Testament as an embodiment of that rhetorical world is odd and crucial because it mediates ethical reflection through *disclosures of hurt and articulations of hope*. The human experiences of hurt and hope not only provide the materials for Israel's conversation about ethics but also supply the categories for ethical discussion, ethical criticism, and ethical possibility. I suggest that hurt and hope are the most characteristic aspects of Jewish experience and discourse, aspects that can be embraced in Christian discourse but protest against a Christian discourse that is excessively rationalistic, positivistic, or romantic. Thus, though we may legitimately say that the voice of the Old Testament is essential for Christian ethical reflection, we cannot claim to have properly heard these texts unless we have heard in them a challenge to and a judgment against our own typical practices.

Hurt as a Category of
Ethical Reflection

Israel's faith arises in an experience of disorder that works against full human existence. That disorder may be understood *cosmically*, as in Israel's protest against chaos and its affirmation of creation (cf. Gen. 1:2; Isa. 45:18-19). That disorder may be understood *naturally*, as in the cases of barren mothers whose wombs are unopened except by the power of promise (cf. Gen. 11:30; 21:1-7). Most characteristically, however, the experience of disorder that preoccupied Israel is historical disorder arising out of unjust, exploitative, oppressive arrangements of social power and social goods. That experience is definitional for all of Israel's ethical reflection.

The exodus event, narrative, and memory clearly give classic expression to this paradigmatic disorder. The exploitative situation of the Egyptian empire is not thought to be cosmic or natural. It is a contrived disorder that the powerful (albeit legitimate) have perpetrated against the weak and marginal. That proto-event shapes Israel's ethical discourse. It is conventional in theological interpretation of the exodus to focus on God's powerful deliverance. In fact, the hurt of Israel is the driving reality of the exodus tradition.

Notice what it requires and what it costs to identify the bondaged situation of the empire as a situation of hurt. It is extraordinary that a conventional and routine condition of the empire becomes identified in Israel as a hurtful disorder. Such an identification requires that the imperial situation of "normalcy" be reperceived and redescribed as abnormal and unacceptable. To acknowledge normalcy as hurt is a fundamental act of courage and of subversion, which in the moment of expression delegitimates the claims of the empire and initiates the process of dismantling the empire.

The cruciality of hurt as a category of ethical reflection in ancient Israel requires the following steps, which provide a map of Israel's ethical formation:

1. The reality of hurt is *experienced and noticed*. This in itself is no small matter. To experience and notice hurt already indicates some critical distance from the totalism of the empire so that the ones in bondage can differentiate between imperial, ideological claims and the reality of their own bodies![1] Hurt supplies no impetus for ethical discourse until it is experienced and noticed, until it is embraced as

---

1. The term "totalism" is helpfully explicated by Robert J. Lifton, *The Broken Connection: On Death and the Continuity of Life* (New York: Basic Books, 1983), 293–301.

real and legitimate. The bodily embrace of hurt provides the material base of Israel's ethical tradition and articulates the otherness of Israel in every situation of social inequity.

2. The experienced, noticed reality of hurt is *voiced*. The act of giving voice to hurt in "cry and groan" is a bold act of self-assertion. Moreover, the bold act of self-assertion is at the same time an act of dangerous political subversion because, with the most elemental and incontrovertible authority, the voicing of hurt announces that the system is not working. The primal ethical act in Israel is gaining voice against the pseudoreality of the empire. The empire, after all, can tolerate experienced hurt as long as it is not voiced. Moreover, the empire will go to great lengths to keep the hurt from coming to voice. The empire, concentration of dehumanizing power that it is, cannot for long survive voiced hurt.

3. The hurt, so the Old Testament asserts, is not only voiced, but *heard*. The grief and anger experienced, noticed, and voiced on earth (in the empire) are received, heard, credited, and taken seriously in heaven (Exod. 2:23-25). When it first cried out in pain, Israel addressed no one and did not know its cry would be heard. Israel cried because it had to, but it knew of no one to address. The hurt of Israel, however, does not float in an unreceptive space. It is heard by none other than Yahweh, who becomes in the moment of hearing the God of Israel. This God, alone in the world of the gods, is like a magnet that attracts and draws hurt to God's own self.

In this moment of communication about hurt, we are close to the central oddity of the Old Testament. That oddity occurs in two parts. On the one hand, this community has *a bold voice for hurt*. It is prepared to take the risk and subvert the settled world because of its hurt. Israel will speak. On the other hand, this God has *an attentive ear for hurt*. Yahweh is now implicated irreversibly in Israel's hurt. God is bonded to Israel around the quintessential human reality of hurt. The God of Israel will never again be unhurt or unaware of Israel's hurt. God takes the hurt of earth into God's own life and heaven is thereby transformed.[2] The hurt, noticed and voiced, becomes the peculiar mode of linking earth to heaven, Israel to Yahweh.

The God of Israel hears. "Hearing" in Israel entails not only lis-

---

2. The conviction that God receives and transforms human hurt is expressed in the hymn "There's a Wideness in God's Mercy": "There is no place where earth's sorrows / Are more felt than up in heaven; / There is no place where earth's failings / Have such kindly judgment given."

tening but also acting; to hear means to obey. The God who compels
Israel to *šěma'* (Deut. 6:4) has first of all "shemaed" Israel. In obedience to Israel's cry of hurt, God acts, intervening not only to cherish
the hurting ones, not only to stand in solidarity, but also to act in
power against those who initiate, sponsor, and perpetuate the hurt.
The voiced hurt of Israel is the material base from which the holy
power of God is activated to transform, destabilize, and reorder the
world.

4. This odd drama of hurt noticed and voiced on earth, heard
and obeyed in heaven, becomes *incorporated into Israel's liturgy*. It
becomes the parlance through which Israel engages in symbolic mediation of its own identity and presence in human life. The initial
event of voiced hurt—against chaos, against barrenness, against slav-
ery—so grasps and shapes Israel that it becomes central to Israel's
liturgical enterprise of remembrance, self-identity, and vocation. Israel ceaselessly recites, "We cried out—God heard our cry." That
formula stands at the center of the old credo recitals. That formula
governs Israel's songs of thanksgiving, which reiterate earlier songs
of complaint that have now been answered and resolved. Israel's
rhetoric is saturated with reminiscences and reenactments of this
transaction of voicing pain and being heard.

In shaping its liturgy in this way, Israel does more than remember. Israel also socializes its young and initiates them into this mode
of experience, speech, social perception, and public practice. The
liturgy is a model for social relations. In this act, Israel asserts, "This
is who our God is. This is who we are. This is what we do. This is
how the world is." Without the liturgy, the next generation might
let the hurt go unnoticed and unvoiced, might let the world become settled, might reckon social hurt to be a normal, acceptable
cost for social tranquility. The liturgy invites the next generation
of Israel into the subversion, subverting ideologies of social power
that foster docility. The liturgy in Israel subverts imperial ideas of
a god who neither hears nor obeys pain. At the center of Israelite
ethics, birthed in the exodus, persistently modeled in the liturgy, is
a foundational, critical restlessness and a refusal to endure disorder
passively.

5. This formative moment of communication, of noticing and being heard, of Israel's voicing and God's responding obedience to
hurt, cannot be kept and contained in the liturgy. It spills over into
public life and public policy. The odd alternative Israel practices against
the empire is not simply an act of worship. Israel must deal with

socioeconomic, political matters. All those matters, however, must be submitted to and shaped by the decisive event of hurt.

That definitional reality, kept alive through the symbolization of worship, required the attentiveness of the public leadership in Israel. They must think again about social power and social goods in light of this odd foundation. Israel now knows, with the memory available and the liturgy ringing in its ear, that public power cannot be arranged for stratification, exploitation, and oppression. Such social order is a disorder that will generate more cries to Yahweh against the status quo, and such cries will provoke Yahweh into decisive transformative activity. A cry of oppression will mobilize this hearing God against any agents of hurt (cf. Exod. 22:21-27). Israel's public power and its institutional forms must be ordered to eliminate the cause of such voiced hurt. Thus, the hurt drives Israel to radical egalitarian models of social relationships. Specifically, Israel's lawgivers limit bondage and curb indebtedness (Exod. 21:1-2). Out of such an imperative of hurt voiced and answered comes provision for the Sabbath (Exod. 20:8-11), the year of release (Deut. 15:1-11), and the year of the Jubilee (Lev. 25:1-12). The hurt organizes public life away from the threat of hurt. The laws are made by the people who still remember the hurt, if not directly, then through the liturgy. Those laws are sanctioned and guaranteed by the God who is enmeshed in Israel's hurt.

6. Israel is largely preoccupied with its own life and the ordering of its own house. It understands itself as the community of voiced hurt and is preoccupied with the God who has attended to its own hurt. Hurt, however, will not be contained in such a narrow range of social experience. Israel dared to imagine that such *hurt is a common human experience* generated wherever there are skewed power relations. Moreover, Israel understood that its voiced hurt was definitional for the character of Yahweh. From those two convictions, closely rooted in direct and available experience, Israel concluded that social hurt, wherever it is generated, outside of Israel as well as inside Israel, is the concern of Yahweh. This God attends to hurt wherever it is present. To be sure, such an awareness lies at the margin of Israel's text, but it is there in ways beyond denial.

The more inclusive affirmation of hurt voiced on earth and obeyed in heaven is nowhere more clearly expressed than in the book of Amos. Amos speaks oracles assaulting other peoples who have practiced cruelty. In most of the cases cited, the affront for which various peoples are castigated has nothing to do with Israel but concerns the configuration of power and policies that generates social hurt. The oracles of the prophet articulate Yahweh's attentiveness to such social reality without respect to Israel (Amos 2:11, 13). At the end of the book of Amos (9:7), it is asserted that Yahweh, the God of Israel's exodus, has also caused exoduses for Syria and the Philistines, two of Israel's perennial enemies. We are not told what lies behind those deliverances. We may, however, imagine that those people also cried out in their hurt and that Yahweh heard and obeyed their hurt. Clearly, the cruciality of hurt shapes Israel's field of knowledge, language, and practice concerning ethics.

Hope as a Category of Ethical Reflection

Israel's faith anticipates the decisive resolution of every human disorder so that full, joyous, peaceable human existence will be possible. Israel's anticipation is that chaos will be overcome by creation. Israel's confidence is that barrenness will be overridden by birth. Most characteristically, Israel's conviction is that bondage will be transformed into the glorious liberty of the children of God. Israel's hope is that there will be a decisive and radical reordering of social power and social goods so that all may have enough, none will have too much, and all will live together in harmony (cf. Exod. 16:18; Mic. 4:4).

Thus, I suggest that hope constitutes the second governing category for Israel's ethical discourse, the foundational conviction that more and other than the present can not only be expected but can rightly and legitimately be insisted upon. That enormous act of expectation is obviously a theological act, a conviction that the world (and our social experience) is held in a larger governance. That act of expectation is also a profound, elemental material yearning rooted in the very bodies of the hurting ones, a yearning that moves with authority from hurting bodies to hoping lips.

Such hope originates, then, in bodily hurt rather than in the word of God. I am aware of the difficulty of arguing the unorthodox claim that the origin of hope is hurt; however, such a reading of the Old Testament is possible both because Israel's faith is characterized by uncompromising materiality and because in such yearning and such speech Israel is acting out its true identity as creature of God. Israel is saying and acting back to God the very intent of the creator, summoning the creator to do what had been intended in the very act of creation. Israel's hope is an insistence that this body of hurt is not our final condition and is not God's final intention. Israel's faith and Israel's experience assert that the present, absolute though it may appear, is open to destabilization, available for new gifts from God. The defining features of Israel's hope constitute a precise parallel to the distinctive features of Israel's response to the reality of hurt.

1. In defending the claim that Israel's hope originates in hurt and precedes the word of God, I want to emphasize that Israel's notice of its pain is the beginning of *Israel's felt hope*. Those who are incapable of noticing their hurt, the ones numbed to despair and resigned to conforming docility, do not hope. When human pain is noticed, however, it is noticed as unnatural and abnormal, and finally as unacceptable. Thus Israel, at the outset of its subversive way in the world, already imagines that its life could and must be different. Israel, in being Israel, refuses to accept conditions of social hurt as permanent or legitimate. Thus, noticed pain prepares the way for voiced hope.[3]

2. The voiced pain of Israel is *a reach beyond silenced suffering* to whomever has authority beyond the present crushing, pain-producing system. Israel does not yet know the name of the one to whom and for whom it reaches, but it reaches nonetheless.[4] Thus, Israel's pain, voiced as "cry and groan," is a first inchoate voice of hope, daring to assert that somehow there is another arrangement of life; somewhere there is a listener who will be more attentive and more powerful and more faithful than the perpetrators of hurt are in their enormous power and in their massive infidelity.

In many of Israel's cries of hurt, the speech of Israel moves finally to imperatives: "hear, save, help" (cf., e.g., Ps. 22:19-21). The sound of an imperative is not present in the initial voicing of the exodus. It is, however, the pattern in many of the Psalms. The imperative that governs the petition of hurting Israel becomes more than noticed pain. The imperative coming from the pain is Israel's first effort at voiced hope. Those who genuinely hurt dare to speak a command, even to the throne of God. Hurt impels such a command to the one

---

3. On the dialectic of pain and speech, see the poignant analysis of Elaine Scarry, *The Body in Pain: The Making and Unmaking of the World* (New York: Oxford University Press, 1985).

4. Erhard Gerstenberger, in "Der klagende Mensch," in *Probleme biblischer Theologie*, ed. Hans Walter Wolff (Munich: Chr. Kaiser Verlag, 1971), 64–72, has shown how complaint in Israel is indeed an act of hope.

who can assuage the hurt. Such speech is a daring, unsettling act, for earth does not characteristically address heaven with such shrillness. In this act, nonetheless, Israel dares to address the ear of the awesome, unapproachable one who now must be approached. It is the approach of urgent petition that is Israel's refusal to end in suffering despair.[5]

3. The hurt of Israel is thus an act of insistence, protest, petition, complaint, and finally hope. It is, against all resignation, an assertion of an alternative, albeit wholly inchoate. When that inchoate, abrasively disguised act of hope reaches the ear of God, it is not only received by God; it evokes in God a resolve to move Israel to a better alternative. The startling affirmation of biblical faith is that *this God accepts the groan, takes it into God's own person, and speaks it back to hurting Israel as promise from on high.*[6] In the primal text of Exodus 3, God answers Moses:

> I have seen the affliction of my people who are in Egypt, and have heard their cry because of their taskmasters; I know their sufferings, and I have come down to deliver them out of the hand of the Egyptians. (Vv. 7-8a)

As quickly as the rhetoric has God receiving the hurt, the very next words are a promise from God: "to bring them up out of that land to a good and broad land, a land flowing with milk and honey, to the place of the Canaanites" (v. 8b). This is the normative sequence in the conversation of Israel. Israel cries out to God; God enters the hurt; God makes a promise. That promise is elementarily and characteristically a promise of land, a zone of well-being, justice, freedom, peace, safety, and dignity.

In this passage from Exodus, we are at the ethical pivot in Israel, between hurt expressed and hope returned. As the cry of Israel dismantles the regime of the empire, so the hope of Yahweh, in the form of promise, relentlessly criticizes the present and displaces

---

5. Frederick Jameson, in *The Political Unconscious: Narrative as a Socially Symbolic Act* (Ithaca, N.Y.: Cornell University Press, 1981), concludes that "all class consciousness—or in other words, all ideology in the strongest sense—... is in its very nature utopian" (p. 289).

6. The classic form of this exchange in the Old Testament is the exchange of Israel's complaint and Yahweh's "salvation oracle." That connection was classically articulated by Joachim Begrich. See Walter Brueggemann, "From Hurt to Joy" (see chap. 2, n. 8), 3–19; and Patrick D. Miller, *Interpreting the Psalms* (Philadelphia: Fortress Press, 1986), 48–63.

present power arrangements with an alternative future that is concrete, public, and political, but utterly transformed. This answering, transforming promise of God becomes definitional for Israel's life. Faith asks what is promised. Ethics follows by asking about embrace of and action toward that assured alternative.

4. The definitional act of oracle, which moves directly and immediately from critique of the present to an alternative future, takes place in Israel in a known, nameable moment with Moses. In that moment, Israel's ethics takes on its odd and crucial character. That known and nameable moment when Israel is given its life and Yahweh becomes a wholly new God is not an isolated, remote moment, however. That moment becomes endlessly replicated in liturgy. *Israel's liturgy is regularly a voicing of God's alternative future* that stands over against every present.

The form in which that replicated hope of God is voiced is the prophetic promises.[7] As we have them, these promises are on the lips of individual persons. The traditioning process of Israelite rhetoric, however, makes it most probable that prophetic oracle is reflective of covenantal proclamation in the worship of the community.[8] Israel meets with Yahweh regularly to hear a voiced future that lives in deep tension with every settled pattern. The purpose of such liturgy is to shake loose Israel's excessive attachment to the present, to assert that the present, even the one we like, is in deep jeopardy because this God envisions reality out beyond present arrangements.

Examples of this hope received, transformed, and spoken back to Israel are well known:

---

7. In the faith of Israel, behind the prophetic promises, there are the much older narratives that initially disclosed Yahweh's promissory character. The basic study of these texts is that of Albrecht Alt, "The God of the Fathers," in *Essays on Old Testament History and Religion* (Oxford: Blackwell, 1966), 1–77. Through the mediation of Gerhard von Rad, Alt's great insight has been influential in theology. See especially the use made of it by Jürgen Moltmann, *Theology of Hope* (New York: Harper & Row, 1967).

8. This connection has been emphasized especially by Sigmund Mowinckel. See also works by Aubrey R. Johnson and Alfred O. Haldar. Critical reviews of this scholarship are provided by Otto Eissfeldt, "The Prophetic Literature," in *The Old Testament and Modern Study*, ed. Harold H. Rowley (Oxford: Clarendon Press, 1951), 119–34; and by Ronald E. Clements, *One Hundred Years of Old Testament Interpretation* (Philadelphia: Westminster Press, 1976), 60–70. Attention should also be paid to the work of Henning Graf Reventlow, *Das Amt des Propheten bei Amos*, FRLANT, no. 80 (Göttingen: Vandenhoeck and Ruprecht, 1962), and *Liturgie und prophetisches Ich bei Jeremia* (Gütersloh: Gerd Mohn, 1963).

It shall come to pass in the latter days
    that the mountain of the house of the Lord
shall be established as the highest of the mountains,
    and shall be raised up above the hills;
and people shall flow to it,
    and many nations shall come, and say:
"Come, let us go up to the mountain of the Lord,
    to the house of the God of Jacob;
that he may teach us his ways
    and we may walk in his paths."
For out of Zion shall go forth the law,
    and the word of the Lord from Jerusalem.
He shall judge between many peoples,
    and shall decide for strong nations afar off;
and they shall beat their swords into plowshares,
    and their spears into pruning hooks;
nation shall not lift up sword against nation,
    neither shall they learn war any more;
but they shall sit every man under his vine and under
        his fig tree,
    and none shall make them afraid;
for the mouth of the Lord of hosts has spoken.
            (Mic. 4:1-4; cf. Amos 9:11-14; Jer. 31:31-34)

The course of scholarship concerning these promissory oracles is particularly interesting. An older, still lingering view is that the oracles are in principle late, that is, exilic.[9] According to this view, they are designed only to counteract despair and to tone down the harshness of the earlier judgment speech forms. Now, however, as the promise passages are studied more closely, and as we think more carefully about the political function of promissory language, it is possible to locate some of the oracles of promise in an earlier period, that is, the pre-exilic period. They are offers of an alternative spoken in the context of the dominant culture and summoning Israel to an

---

9. My impression is that the exilic origin of prophetic promise came to be an assumption of scholarship that was seldom argued, but was taken for granted. See the judicious review of the problem with reference to Jeremiah and Ezekiel by Siegfried Herrmann, *Die prophetischen Heilserwartungen im Alten Testament*, BWANT, no. 85 (Stuttgart: Kohlhammer, 1965); and notice Gerhard von Rad's terse comment, *Old Testament Theology II* (New York: Harper & Row, 1965), 138. For a general review, see Gene M. Tucker, "Prophecy and the Prophetic Literature," in *The Hebrew Bible and Its Modern Interpreters*, ed. Douglas A. Knight and Tucker (Philadelphia: Fortress Press, 1985), 325–68.

alternative that lies beyond the administration of the present but that has active power now for those who take it up.

Among the promises is the promise to transform the situation of curse, caused by rapacious economic policy.[10] The cursed situation of greedy politics is stated by Amos:

> Therefore because you trample upon the poor
>   and take from him exactions of wheat,
> you have built houses of hewn stone,
>   but you shall not dwell in them;
> you have planted pleasant vineyards,
>   but you shall not drink their wine.
> For I know how many are your transgressions,
>   and how great are your sins.
>   (Amos 5:11)

The promise that counters this curse imagines a social situation in which destruction is ended and settled life made possible:

> They shall build houses and inhabit them;
>   they shall plant vineyards and eat their fruit.
> They shall not build and another inhabit;
>   they shall not plant and another eat.
>   (Isa. 65:21-22; cf. Amos 9:14)

Israel's boldest ethical imagination is rooted exactly in the resolve of God to transform the public life of the human community. The promise points beyond present circumstance and asserts that the present is not permanent and that Israel may act toward another assured possibility.

5. What is assured by God is at the same time commanded as human action. The vision of an alternative *spills over into public policy*. Thus it is expected, hoped, presumed, and, therefore, commanded that Israel will live its life differently. The clearest statement of promissory public policy is found in the book of Deuteronomy. The book of Deuteronomy is the clearest statement of covenantal ethics in the Old Testament and of anticipation that public power can be

---

10. On this particular form of curse, see Delbert R. Hillers, *Threat-Curses and the Old Testament Prophets*, BibOr, no. 16 (Rome: Biblical Institute Press, 1964), 28–29.

organized differently.[11] The commands of Deuteronomy reflect the belief that the "land of Canaan" (now become the "land of promise") can be organized in radically new ways. The land need not be organized in the greedy, brutalizing, exploitative ways that are called "Canaanite." This enormous anticipation, however, is not just a grand vision, but it turns on quite concrete and practical public acts. The vision of God is to be enacted, one element at a time, in daily practice.

Perhaps the most daring and demanding of these commands is the "year of release" in Deut. 15:1-18. The law is in three parts: The first concerns the cancellation of debts to a member of the covenant community after seven years (vv. 1-6). Bad credit, that is, poverty, was the primary cause of imprisonment in the ancient economy. This law proposes to undermine the entire debt and credit system. The second part is an expository reflection on the law of release, reflecting on the presence of the poor in the community (vv. 7-11). It expresses an awareness that the poor are open to special exploitation and in need of special care from the community. In this section, there is a warning that the poor may cry in need. It may be a cry of hurt or a cry of hope; when that cry is sounded, it will be "sin in you." The third section makes provision for release and urges that the released bond-prisoner not be sent away empty-handed (vv. 12-17). The released slave must be given sufficient means to reenter the economy with dignity.

What interests me the most in this passage is the fact that the infinitive absolute is used six times:

- surely bless (v. 4),

- surely hear (v. 5),

- surely open (v. 8),

- surely lend sufficiently (v. 8),

- surely give (v. 10), and

- surely furnish (v. 14).

---

11. Lothar Perlitt, in *Bundestheologie* (see chap. 1, n. 21), has argued that covenant theology appears for the first time in Deuteronomy. I regard Perlitt's judgment as most doubtful. In any case, my own statement is a theological and not a historical judgment. On the theological significance of covenant theology, see Ernest W. Nicholson, *God and His People* (Oxford: Clarendon Press, 1986), 191–217.

The infinitive absolute is a rhetorical device that restates the root verb in a second, absolute form in order to give heavy stress to the verb. It is striking that this proclamation of law, which warns against a cry and which alludes to the exodus, is permeated with the infinitive absolute. I suggest that the urgency reflected in the grammatical form is based on the promissory character of a counterethic. The urging of the law is this: If Israel does not act in the way urged here, it will never break from the dominant Canaanite pattern. Israel will regress to the dominant, conventional ethic that is never liberating, never giving, never generous, never heeding, and therefore never blessed.

The rhetoric of Deuteronomy falls somewhere between law and sermon.[12] This peculiar rhetoric reflects the radical counterethics of the tradition of Deuteronomy. At the same time, the teaching must provide a substantive statement of an alternative social possibility and must motivate Israel to take the risks entailed in that social possibility. The mandate of Deuteronomy is to transform social situations that produce cries of despair and oppression. Thus, the tradition of Deuteronomy makes a theological-moral appeal concerning bold transformations of socioeconomic, political practice. The rhetoric reflects the determined conviction that another way of social organization is indeed possible.

6. The primary concern of commands in the Old Testament is the community of Israel. The primary horizon of liturgy is the community of Israel. Both the liturgy and the commandments, however, spill over the boundaries of Israel. Israel's enormous act of hope, addressed to God and answered back by God, takes into account *the well-being of the nations* as well as the well-being of Israel.

The liturgy of world-scope is voiced in the great psalms of enthronement. It may be that these psalms are a self-announcement by the Jerusalem establishment and so are carriers of Jerusalem ideology. Taken on their best reading, however, they also offer a gospel: "Say among the nations, 'Yahweh reigns [has just become king]'" (Ps. 96:10). The rule of Yahweh is thus extended to the nations; this rule does not refer to the dynastic rule of the Jerusalem establishment. The rule of Yahweh for the nations means that the nations may also participate in the hope of Israel, may also be addressed by

---

12. Von Rad, in *Studies in Deuteronomy*, SBT, no. 9 (Chicago: Henry Regnery, 1953), uses the apt phrase "law preached" (p. 16).

the promises of Yahweh, and so are invited to the same counterview of reality.

One of the ostensible reasons for the witness of the texts about "God's mighty deeds"—that is, God's acts that fulfill hope—is "that all the earth may know there is a God in Israel" (1 Sam. 17:46). In the narrative of 1 Samuel 17, Yahweh's victory occurs so that "the Philistines may know"; the rhetoric, however, clearly refers not only to the Philistines but to all the non-Yahwistic peoples around Israel. That the "nations may know" is in part threat, judgment, and warning. Beyond that, however, the nations are invited to share in the hoped-for new world that belongs to the promises of Yahweh.

The hope of Yahwism for "the healing of the nations" is included in the oracle already cited from Micah 4:

> Many nations shall come and say:
> Come, let us go up to the mountain of the Lord. . . .
> For out of Zion shall go forth the Torah. (v. 2)

On the one hand, all nations submit to the Torah, to a share in the mandates for the world God has promised. On the other hand, "nation shall not lift up sword against nation." The hope of Israel is not narrowly a hope for Israel, but it is a hope to which the nations are invited. We may imagine that as the nations are invited to the hope, so the hurt of the nations also has credence at the throne of Yahweh. Thus hurt and hope are definitional for Israel; hurt and hope are also taken seriously in the transactions between the nations and God. The ethical categories in Israel are readily usable in and available for the nations.

The Textuality of Hurt and Hope

Two sets of ethical questions emerge from Israel's discourse: (1) *Who hurts* and who causes hurt? (2) *Who hopes?* What makes hope possible? And what does hope make possible? The Old Testament shows us that hurt and hope are irreducible issues in ethics, and my thesis is that *voiced, obeyed hurt* and *voiced, trusted hope* constitute the oddity and the cruciality of Old Testament ethics. In this section I want to emphasize and explore the fact that Old Testament ethics always considers *voiced* hurt and *voiced* hope, that is, hurt and hope mediated through time in speech. Such mediating speech is constitutive

for Old Testament ethics and represents another aspect of its odd-
ness and cruciality. When we insist on the voiced quality of ethics, we
are driven to textuality—to the precise, concrete modes and practices whereby Israel becomes a community of ethical discourse. This
means that we cannot extract principles from Israel's text, but the
how of the text is integral to the what of ethics.[13] The several acts
of hurt expressed as complaint and lawsuit, the several acts of hope
expressed as oracle and promise, and the narratives that track the
dynamic of hurt and hope are neither accidental nor incidental to
Israel's ethical discourse. They are the way ethical discourse is con-
ducted in Israel, the only way it can be done in Israel. To understand
and appropriate Israel's ethic, we must enter into the voicing that
shapes Israel and characterizes the god of Israel. The purpose of
such voiced hurt and hope is to deabsolutize and to destabilize the
present (which is held under critical scrutiny in Israel), to loosen
the grip the present has on Israel's imagination, and to invoke an
alternative that God assures and that Israel may embrace and obey.

The voiced character of Israelite ethics is important in three ways.
It becomes a vehicle for three elements of Israel's faith that are
indispensable to Israel's identity.

1. The textuality of this ethics provides a steady, unembarrassed
way *to keep the holy power and purpose of Yahweh decisively present in ethics*.
Israel's practice of conventional speech leaps over many epistemological problems in its innocent assumption that Yahweh is a key
character in speech and a key actor in public ethics. When Israel
fails to speak of hurt and hope, Yahweh as a vital force is soon silenced and eliminated.[14] Ethics is transformed away from covenantal
transactions.

2. The textuality of this ethics assures that *hurt and hope are mediated in active, transformative ways that give energy, courage, and stamina*.
Israel's textual tradition of ethics is not escapist religious talk; it is
praxis that moves the women and men of Israel into the drama of
hurt on its way to hope. The transformations wrought in the rhetoric
of Israel are transformations of imaginations; the world is perceived,
engaged, and dealt with differently. Without this rhetoric, there is

---

13. On the interrelatedness of "what" and "how," see Gail R. O'Day, *The Word
Disclosed* (St. Louis: CBP Press, 1987), 11–15.

14. Hans W. Frei's *The Eclipse of Biblical Narrative* (New Haven: Yale University
Press, 1974) constitutes the definitive study of the loss of a particular mode of rhetoric and its costs for the community. Frei has not explicitly explored the ethical
implications of his argument, but they are clearly suggested in his analysis.

yes

not enough of voiced pain to destabilize, not enough of voiced hope to energize. Members of this speech-practice are situated in a peculiar way midst the intransigent forms of brutalizing power, neither withdrawing nor capitulating.

3. This textual tradition of ethics provides a linguistic community that is sustained *through the generations*. Ethical reflection in Israel is profoundly and decisively intergenerational. On the one hand, the text provides models for ethical discernment in each new generation and authorizes new voices to sound hurt and hope. On the other hand, because of the canonizing process, the textual voice of the older, original generation is not received and heard simply as the voice of an older generation. It is heard and received as the inexplicable voice of holy power and holy purpose, which intrudes awkwardly into ethical discussion and insists on having its subversive say. Thus, for example, the command of the year of release may be an old Levitical teaching. It is now, however, the enduring command of God with which every generation must come to terms. In this rhetoric, Israel must say not only "This is how we talk" but, in the end, "This is how God talks."[15]

This rhetorical mediation of hurt and hope, I suggest, is not marginal for ethics but matters enormously for the categories in which we do ethics. Alasdair C. MacIntyre has observed that each tradition of ethics has linguistic particularity.[16] I cannot imagine a community of discourse for which linguistic particularity is more odd or more crucial than it is for the Old Testament community of ethical discourse. This linguistic particularity ensures these elemental human categories in the conversation that both settled power and settled knowledge want to eliminate.

Social Intention and Establishment Silence

My argument that the *textuality of hurt and hope* is definitional for Israel's modes of ethical discourse reflects the powerful influence of

---

15. George A. Lindbeck, in *The Nature of Doctrine* (Philadelphia: Westminster Press, 1984), has paid the most careful attention to modes of speech as crucial to the sustenance of a community of faith. Lindbeck has focused on human speech; my second phrase, "This is how God talks," is an extrapolation from Lindbeck's analysis.

16. MacIntyre, in *Whose Justice? Which Rationality?* (Notre Dame, Ind.: University of Notre Dame Press, 1988), 9.

NB

the emerging methods of sociological criticism and literary analysis in Old Testament study.

The developments of sociological criticism suggest that every text and every interpretation of text are socially embodied acts, reflective of a specific social interest.[17] Indeed, there is no ethical reflection in ancient Israel that is not advocacy and polemic. The distinctive focus on hurt and hope indicates that this community particularly values the social interest and social rhetoric of the marginal. Voiced hurt is the speech of the oppressed and marginalized, for their hurt is most available. Voiced hope is the speech of those who can hold the present loosely enough to receive alternatives yet to be given. Sociological analysis has made clear that such voiced hurt and voiced hope are always enormously daring, dangerous, and risky, because there are established interests that also generate texts of another kind and resist both these voicings.

Literary analysis is teaching us that texts are never simply reportorial; all texts are acts of social construction. They are always imaginative proposals, acts of world-construction from a particular position of advocacy.[18] The texts of hurt and hope are peculiarly rich instances of such creative efforts because they seek to draw the imagination of the community outside the hegemony of the dominant regime. The dominant regime—social, economic, political, religious—has constructed a world in which hurt is denied and hope is domesticated or precluded. The texts of the dominant regime seem true, established, correct, and authorized.

Texts of hurt and hope, to the contrary, demand another world. It is a world artfully voiced but touched by the reality long denied, domesticated, and precluded. This rhetoric of hurt and hope is an affront to established social power. The passionate voices of complaint and lament, the powerful oracles of hope, the narratives of hidden, inscrutable transformation—these are not escapist comments of transcendentalism, but they are acts of power perpetrated by the powerless through the only power available to them. Thus

---

17. The basic study of the relation of text and social interest is Norman K. Gottwald, *Tribes* (see chap. 1, n. 6). On prophetic speech and social interest, see Robert R. Wilson, *Prophecy and Society in Ancient Israel* (Philadelphia: Fortress Press, 1980). Robert Gordis, in "The Social Background of Wisdom Literature," in *Poets, Prophets, and Sages* (Bloomington: University of Indiana Press, 1971), 160–97, has explored the same connections in relation to sapiential texts.

18. On the social advocacy inherent in texts, see Richard Harvey Brown, *Society as Text: Essays on Rhetoric, Reason, and Reality* (Chicago: University of Chicago Press, 1987).

the convergence in recent time of sociological and literary analysis is important in seeing that Israel's ethical discourse is inherently subversive. It witnesses against the silenced, silencing power of an absolute present in which there is no serious speech, no palpable holiness, and no groaning opening toward humanness.

Employing these sociological and literary insights, I have made an argument about a specific family of texts that have a certain rhetorical, social intention. It is important to acknowledge that alongside this tradition of speech and text, there were also *powerful voices in ancient Israel* (and therefore powerful texts in the Old Testament) *that had no sympathy with or interest in the realities of hurt and hope.*[19] There were powerful voices reflecting socioeconomic and political interests that wanted both hurt denied or stifled and hope domesticated or eliminated. As texts become political acts in order to voice hurt and hope, so texts may also be political acts to silence hurt and hope. I will mention three broad classes of texts that favor establishment silence:

1. In my book *Israel's Praise*, I have argued that *hymns* are a genre of speech in Israel that can escape from and cover over pain, hurt, rage, and loss in order to support an uncriticized status quo.[20] When hymns are sung that lack "reasons," they offer a symmetrical world in which no transformation is possible. Such hymns propose and sponsor a God who does not act and a social structure that cannot be subverted.

2. *Wisdom sayings*, as reflected in the book of Proverbs, seek to endorse and legitimate a powerfully symmetrical world. With a few important exceptions, this wisdom teaching claims that social reality is a set of reliable relations of deeds and consequences that can be known and "worked."[21] There are pitfalls and dangers, but these come about because there has been a departure from the proper choice and a disregard of what is wise. When one stays prudently inside the program, the dangers can be avoided. In such a comprehensive system, hurt is transformed into guilt and hope is reduced

19. On the interests that resisted the egalitarian vision of early Israel, see Robert B. Coote and Keith W. Whitlam, *The Emergence of Early Israel*, SWBA, no. 5 (Sheffield: Almond Press, 1987); and the several articles in *Semeia* 37 (1987).

20. Brueggemann, *Israel's Praise: Doxology against Idolatry and Ideology* (Philadelphia: Fortress Press, 1988).

21. The crucial exceptions are noted by von Rad, *Old Testament Theology I* (see chap. 1, n. 22), 439, and *Wisdom* (see chap. 1, n. 25), 98–101. Cf. Koch, "Doctrine of Retribution" (see chap. 1, n. 27).

to the payoffs of the system. Everything is contained and the system is the solution.

In the completed corpus of wisdom materials, this reduced claim of the book of Proverbs does not everywhere prevail. In the arguments of Job and Ecclesiastes, the problem of evil does raise its insistent head, permitting the acknowledgment and voicing of genuine hurt.[22] Thus, as Claus Westermann has shown, the poems of Job introduce laments into the sapiential conversation and shatter the claimed totalism of the proverbs.[23] The first inclination of wisdom, however, is to domesticate the question of theodicy, to make hurt a necessary personal burden, and to make hope either unnecessary or impossible.

3. The *temple apparatus* of the Jerusalem establishment seeks to argue that everything needful for full life is adequately offered in the guaranteed presence of the temple, either through the routinization of sacrifice, through the reassuring purity of the cultic system, or through the assured willingness of God to take up unconditional residence in the midst of the royal complex. Such temple worship tends characteristically to reduce and domesticate hurt and hope, to rob them of their power, to eliminate their vitality, and to minimize their abrasion.

Thus I submit that the tension in the Old Testament over ethics is a dispute over who shall speak and who shall have voice. We may believe that in the history of Israel the power to silence was largely successful, both in economic-political and in cultic-liturgical terms. What strikes me, however, is that the canonical literature is not an exact correlate to or replica of sociopolitical reality; that is, there are voices in the canon that likely were muted in the mainstream public process of ancient Israel. I submit that the canon has become a place where hurt and hope are honored and taken seriously. Historical criticism has often sought to reduce the canonical voice to the sober realities of the historical process. Canon, however, is another voice reflecting another courage and another freedom, always voicing a challenge to historical reality. Canon, then, is not only holy voice with its attendant claims of inspiration and revelation. It is also a zone of freedom and courage where human voices of hurt and hope may sound that are permitted nowhere else.

---

22. Peter L. Berger, in *Sacred Canopy* (see chap. 2, n. 5), 58–60, has explored the issue of theodicy in relation to the realities of social suffering and social well-being.

23. Westermann, *The Structure of the Book of Job* (Philadelphia: Fortress Press, 1977), 31–66.

The Threat of Voicelessness

This determination to silence the voices that speak of hurt and hope
is a powerful temptation in any age, not least so in our own. In our
own contemporary task of ethical reflection and in our own context
of ethical responsibility, this Israelite tradition of the rhetoric of hurt
and hope is crucial because, if voices of hurt and hope can be fully
and finally silenced, then the dominant voices can have their unchallenged, uninterrupted say. In the face of this odd, crucial tradition of
ethical discourse, ours is a situation in which the ideological power of
silence is formidable indeed. Given the categories of my argument,
I suggest there are three strange comrades at work together, comrades committed to silencing the voices of hurt and hope in order
that the dominant present may become absolute—without protest
from hurt and without alternative from hope:

   1. A first factor is *technological ideology* that believes that manipulation in the interest of management is the way real power works. In
such an ideology, words do not count at all.[24] What counts is access
to technology. The gathering of power through the manipulation
of vacuous symbols is reserved for the cunning and the fortunate.
The others are eliminated from the payoffs given the competent
and are thereby excluded from the economic and political process.
Technological ideology and its handmaiden, consumer advertising,
have no place for the cries of the wretched or the hope of the
quarrelsome. Everything is reduced to systems of continuity with a
no-surprise, no-intrusion future. The only way to preclude surprise
and intrusion is to prevent decisive speech. That condition is nearly
accomplished among us, so that even ethical discourse, when robbed
of serious human speech, can become a comrade in voicelessness.

   2. In my field of Scripture study, *historical criticism* has become a
mode of silencing the text by eliminating its artistic, dramatic, subversive power. I do not wish to overstate my critique of historical
criticism.[25] It is, nonetheless, increasingly clear that historical criti-

---

24. On the crisis of speech when language is subsumed under technique, see the
programmatic essay by Eugen Rosenstock-Huessy, *Speech and Reality* (Norwich, Vt.:
Argo Books, 1970). See also Wendell Berry, *Standing by Words* (San Francisco: North
Point Press, 1983), 24–63; and Jacques Ellul, *The Humiliation of the Word* (Grand
Rapids: Eerdmans Pub. Co., 1985).

25. The most frontal attack on historical criticism is that of Walter Wink, *The Bible
in Human Transformation* (Philadelphia: Fortress Press, 1973). Since his publication, a
great deal has happened to sustain his argument. Perhaps his extreme language was
essential to advancing the conversation.

cism is no objective, disinterested tool of interpretation, but it has become a way to trim texts down to the ideology of Enlightenment reason and autonomy and to explain away from the text all the hurts and hopes that do not conform to the ideology of objectivity.[26] In the end, the text is thereby rendered voiceless. It becomes only an echo of the passionless containment of knowledge by the teaching, interpreting monopoly. The voiced text is the natural partner and practice of the marginal who depend on such texts. If the texts can be silenced by their disuse or reinterpretation, then the marginal lose their chance of speech and of power. In an odd interpretive maneuver long established among us, we tend not to notice that the voiceless text has been made into a silent support for the status quo, holding all memory in a contained present, numbed to protest, resistant to alternative, and all in the interest of objectivity.

3. A third factor that seeks to silence the voice of hurt and hope is *moralistic, scholastic religion* that is incapable of self-criticism. This religious enterprise embodies modes of certitude that resist the human struggle of hurt and hope. This enterprise claims to take the text seriously, but it does so only to the degree that the text can be made to conform to settled ideological positions. As the dramatic play of human hurt and human hope is denied, so also the interplay of God's sovereignty and graciousness is denied.[27] Everything is flattened theologically, so that God's freedom is overcome. Everything is flattened in the text, so that texts can serve only a coded certitude. Everything is flattened about human protest and human possibility. When everything is flattened for God, for text, and for neighbor, there is nothing left about which to speak and, therefore, no speech. This religious enterprise, so rich in certitude, is thus impoverished in terms of the speech in which the Bible specializes. If the texts are to be read in this enterprise, they must be read with their power silenced. They become only convenient vehicles for ideology of a settled, brutalizing kind.

The great threat in our ethical situation is voicelessness. The convergence of technological ideology, historical criticism, and moralistic, scholastic religion constitutes a powerful lobby advocating silence. In our society as much as in any, that lobby exercises enormous power. The bet of the biblical text, against this lobby, as well

---

26. The clearest exposé of the ideology of "objectivity" in Scripture study is the work of Elisabeth Schüssler Fiorenza, *Bread Not Stone* (Boston: Beacon Press, 1984).

27. On that interplay, see chaps. 1 and 2.

as the bet of the community that heeds this text, is that the voices of
hurt and hope will not and cannot be silenced. It is the resilience of
the protesting word of revelation that George Steiner celebrates in
his reflections on Jeremiah 36–39: "The truth will out. Somewhere
there is a pencil-stub, a mimeograph machine, a hand-press which
the king's men have overlooked. . . . The Temple may be destroyed;
the texts which it housed sing in the winds that scatter them."[28]
These voices cannot be silenced because hurt is irreducible in its
anguish, and hope is irreducible in its buoyancy. That anguish and
buoyancy on the lips of human persons are also anguish and hope in
the very person of God, whose text this is. Thus, our context for ethical reflection is not simply the matrix of silence so powerful among
us. It is also the odd welling-up of voices of hurt and hope in our
contemporary world, almost always authored and powered by this
text.

It is a cause for marvel, gratitude, astonishment, and repentance
that the current powerful lobby for silence has not yet prevailed. Ethical discourse in this textual community is rooted in the conviction
that the voicing is our modest, urgent task, a voicing that troubles
the interests of people like us. It is odd that this voicing is regarded
as God's word. It is crucial that God's word be voiced on the human
lips of those who refuse the current idolatries, in the very name of
unsilenced holiness.

---

28. Steiner, "Our Homeland, the Text," *Salmagundi* 66 (1985): 21. For this reference, I am grateful to Robert P. Carroll, *Jeremiah: A Commentary*, OTL (Philadelphia:
Westminster Press, 1986), 668.

4

Bodied Faith and the
Body Politic

IN OLDER, SEEMINGLY better days, the Bible spoke with a single voice concerning faith and morals. Only lately have we noticed that the single voice of the Bible was possible and credible only because there was a hegemony of interpretation, a small, homogeneous community of interpreters who spoke from the same perspective and for the same vested interests.

I

Interpretive history has witnessed two moves that have subverted that singled voiced hegemony of interpretation:

First, for over a century, the emergence and dominance of historical-critical work has situated texts in different contexts and so has relativized the absolute voice of the Bible.[1] Historical criticism was not especially interested in theological interpretation. Indeed, the great critics were indifferent to theological dimensions of interpretation. Nonetheless, the single voice has been relativized by such criticism.

---

1. In some measure, the critique made of historical criticism by religious conservatives is, in my judgment, correct. Historical criticism is in principle committed to the relativization of the text. The alternative offered by religious conservatives, however, is of very little help. More recent methods of criticism that attend to literary evocation and social interest seem to me to be significant gains for the interpretive enterprise.

Second, more recently and more importantly, sociological criticism has required us to see that not only many contexts but also many vested interests are reflected in the text of the Bible, interests that tend to correspond with the vested interests of various contemporary communities of interpretation.[2] This second development in recent interpretation has shown not only that there is not a single voice in Scripture but that there is no disinterested voice in the text. Every voice in the text is in some measure a voice of advocacy.[3] Sociological criticism forces us not only to recognize pluralism but also to acknowledge that any obvious and easy theological, transcendental claim is denied to the text. We are left with a series of local theologies whose advocacies are in deep tension with each other.[4] Moreover, these various local advocacies cannot be harmonized and are not easily or readily adjudicated.[5]

These two developments in interpretation, historical criticism that has relativized the single voice of Scripture and sociological criticism that has acknowledged the power of advocacy, pose difficult questions for theological interpretation. How could such a text—relativized, interested—be heard as the word of God? How could such a text function as critical norm for any serious and disputed ethical issue? To these questions I will propose a provisional answer.

I suggest there are two available strategies in response to such pluralistic advocacy:

First, one can concede the pluralism to be decisive for the text and pick one voice among the many as normative;[6] then other, competing voices are disregarded, denied, or reinterpreted in our treatment of the text. Although this is clearly a partisan approach, it is an approach commonly used. In more formal garb, such a strategy appeals to a "canon within the canon"; that is, a text is found that judges all other texts, and to which all other texts must submit.

---

2. It is beyond dispute that interest is at work in the interpretation of many feminists and other liberationists. What is not so readily acknowledged is that interest is also at work in the "objective" interpretation of scholars who would eskew a liberationist hermeneutic. It is important to recognize that there is no standing ground outside interest in current hermeneutical disputes.

3. In Old Testament studies, the work of Robert Polzin, *Moses* (see chap. 1, n. 21), has made the clearest case for "voices" of advocacy in the text.

4. See Robert J. Schreiter, *Constructing Local Theologies* (Maryknoll, N.Y.: Orbis Books, 1985).

5. See chap. 7.

6. On the problems and possibilities in theological pluralism, see David Tracy, *Plurality and Ambiguity: Hermeneutics, Religion, and Hope* (San Francisco: Harper & Row, 1987).

This approach is evident in classic Lutheran theology with its focus on the book of Romans; it has been used in Roman Catholicism with its characteristic appeal to the Petrine confession; and it is currently used by feminist and other liberation hermeneutics.[7] Indeed, I suspect that in practice, this is an almost inevitable interpretive move, for if one does not select a place in the text from which to interpret, one may be immobilized by the unresolvable diversity of the text; or one may settle for the least common denominator that ends in an embarrassing blandness.

The second strategy is to see whether one can move underneath the differences and advocacies in the text and locate a foundational claim that is everywhere present in the text. Recent attempts to establish such a shared norm include Rolf P. Knierim's focus on righteousness and Paul D. Hanson's accent on community.[8] If one is to proceed in this fashion, one must ask of the proposed norm allegedly found everywhere in the text:

- What are the decisive categories in the claim?
- Is the proposed norm everywhere in the text?
- Where in the life and testimony of the biblical community is the norm rooted?
- What does the norm criticize and how is that critique voiced?

There are enormous difficulties in pursuing this strategy in legitimating the Bible as a norm for ethical criticism. On the one hand, there is a danger that the norm is made so inclusive and comprehensive that it becomes innocuous and in fact no norm at all. On the other hand, one may in fact be focusing on a canon within the canon and, simply by assertion, extending it to the places where in fact it does not operate.

Recognizing these hazards, I will seek to utilize this second strategy and articulate a norm for theological, moral criticism to which the biblical text in all its parts bears witness and that I therefore judge to be a canonical norm. I may, however, be falling into the trap of a quite partisan textual tradition. If that is so, I will live with that

---

7. In my own church tradition, the United Church of Christ, at a national level, Luke 4:18-19 has come to operate as a "canon within the canon."

8. Knierim, "The Task of Old Testament Theology," *HBT* 6, no. 2 (1984): 25–27, 91–128; Hanson, "War and Peace in the Hebrew Bible," *Int* 38 (1984): 341–62, and *The People Called* (San Francisco: Harper & Row, 1986).

failure, and I submit in any case that this norm is crucial and decisive for biblical faith, even if it is a partial tradition of advocacy. Thus
I shall argue (1) that the claims of a particular tradition of the text
make a particular testimony most poignantly and most passionately,
and (2) that the same claim is present pervasively in the text and
beyond the particular tradition where it is most clearly rooted—that
is, my proposed norm for ethical criticism is rooted particularly but
operates pervasively in the biblical text.

II

My thesis is this: In the face of the rich pluralism and passionate
interestedness of the biblical text in its various local voices, the text
everywhere is concerned with *the costly reality of human hurt* and *the
promised alternative of evangelical hope;* that is, the Bible is peculiarly
preoccupied with hurt and hope. Those public realities, mediated
through various textual traditions in the Bible, constitute a biblical
basis for asserting theological, moral norms. Four dimensions of the
central claim of hurt and hope are decisive for the norming authority
of the Bible:

1. Hurt and hope are *powerful and pervasive social realities* in the
biblical community, realities expressed and realities remembered.
The Bible is not a theological literature cast in a transcendental voice
as though it is a message from the sky. Against my perspective there
are, to be sure, interpretive practices that tend to be variously pietis-
tic, mystical, romantic, and gnostic. These practices tend to construe
the Bible from above; such a religious propensity, however, has little
to do with the main claims of the Bible.

Religious claims in the Bible are mediated through and wrought
in the midst of the anguish and the hurt of actual human reality. The
Bible is exceedingly honest about the reality of evil and its costs.[9]
Moreover, the Bible believes that evil is not natural but is largely initiated by human arrangements of power and ideology, contrived by
some, costly to others, and given various religious legitimations. The
theological word for such systemic distortions of arrangements of social power for some and against others is *idolatry*.[10] Thus idolatry is
not a narrowly religious issue. It concerns perversions in the order-

---

9. See the splendid discussion of Jon D. Levenson, *Creation and the Persistence of
Evil* (San Francisco: Harper & Row, 1988).
10. On the theological issues related to idolatry, see Matitiahu Tsevat, "The Prohibi-

ing of communal life. The Bible knows about the profound risks that are connected to various practices of social oppression. The Old Testament emerges in the midst of imperial (Egyptian) oppression; it is concluded in the shadow of imperial (Babylonian) oppression. The ministry of Jesus takes peculiar notice of marginated people who suffer in the midst of social power unfairly managed and ideologically legitimated.

The powerful social reality of the biblical communities, however, is not simply evidenced in the exercise of hurt. The social reality of hurt is matched by the social experience of hope, by the relentless insistence that social hurt is not permanent, that oppression is not for perpetuity, that marginality is not absolutely ordained. Hope for an alternative possibility lives in the very bodies and on the lips of suffering people who refuse to accept present social reality as permanent reality.[11] Notice that I have made this assertion about hope without direct reference to God. At a practical, social level, the human agents who fund these texts are people who believed that a radical newness is possible in the historical process, a radical newness variously experienced in the exodus liberation, in the exilic homecoming, and in the resurrection.[12] The lived reality of the communities reflected in the Bible constitutes the candid, daring practice of hurt and hope.

2. Hurt and hope are *pervasive theological claims in the* text. That is, the text discloses that the humanly experienced realities of hurt and hope not only matter to the experiencing human community, but matter decisively to the God of the Bible. This discernment and articulation of God mark an extraordinary theological break in religious history. We do not know how to assess the reality of this theological articulation; for our purposes, it does not matter greatly if this is a claim assigned to God by human persons (as Feuerbach), or a claim owed directly to God. Either way, the Bible bears witness to a God with a most peculiar way of being God. The God of the Bible is unlike the other gods of that ancient context; this is a God who binds God's own self to the needs, hopes, and destiny of this people.[13] It is

tion of Divine Images according to the Old Testament," in *Wünschet Jerusalem Frieden,* ed. Matthias Augustin and Klaus-Dietrich Schunck (Bern: Peter Lang, 1988), 211–20.

11. Elaine Scarry, *Body in Pain* (see chap. 3, n. 3), 161–326.

12. See my comment in Brueggemann, *Revelation and Violence: A Study in Contextualization* (Milwaukee: Marquette University Press, 1986), esp. 33–36.

13. This binding and bonding are articulated most directly in the phrase, "I will be your God and you shall be my people." See Rudolf Smend, *Das Bundesformel,* ThStud, no. 68 (Zurich: EVZ Verlag, 1963).

this acknowledgment of God's peculiar way in the world that lets us claim that the Bible is a decisive disclosure, that is, revelation.[14]

One peculiar and primal text in this regard is the initial self-disclosure of God to Moses (Exod. 3:7-8). This statement in God's own mouth is God's initial entry into the exodus story after the theophany of Exod. 3:1-6. In that episode of the burning bush, Yahweh speaks only to summons Moses and to identify God's self with the ancestors in the book of Genesis. It is, however, vv. 7-8 that bear most directly on our theme.

These verses voice God's decisive attention to Israel's hurt:

> I have seen the affliction of my people who are in Egypt, and have heard their cry because of their taskmasters; I know their sufferings, and I have come down to deliver them out of the hand of the Egyptians.

God sees, hears, and knows. In response, God acts.[15] The act of God is extraordinary, for in "coming down," this God is unlike any other god in readiness to be at risk with this hurting community. God enters the hurt produced by imperial oppression, because such imperial oppression is intolerable to Yahweh. Yahweh will intervene because the hurt is unbearable and must be overcome. The story of Yahweh in the Bible is the narrative account of God's powerful intervention whereby social hurt is ended.[16]

Verse 8b shows that God not only moves against hurt. God also acts in hope by announcing to Moses a radical, alternative future:

> ...to bring them up out of that land to a good and broad land, a land flowing with milk and honey, to the place of the Canaanites, the Hittites, the Amorites, the Perizzites, the Hivites, and the Jebusites.

The alternative asserted by Yahweh is in no way derived from present circumstance, but is indeed a fresh resolve on God's part to

---

14. Paul Ricoeur, *Essays on Biblical Interpretation* (Philadelphia: Fortress Press, 1980), 119–54, has explored the ways in which human testimony about God comes to be accepted as revelatory and finally as revelation.

15. On the problematic of this phrase, see Werner E. Lemke, "Revelation" (see chap. 1, n. 13).

16. Emphasis should be placed on compassion in a consideration of Yahweh's entry into human hurt. Compassion is Yahweh's bodily response to hurt. On the term, see Phyllis Trible, *God and the Rhetoric of Sexuality*, OBT (Philadelphia: Fortress Press, 1978), 39–53; see the New Testament counterpart, *splangnizomai*, which also bespeaks a bodily response. More programmatically, cf. Abraham Heschel, *Prophets* (see chap. 2, n. 14), esp. chaps. 15 and 18.

impinge decisively in the public process of land management, population deployment, and power arrangement. These two verses together, in the very mouth of God, portray the God of the Bible as *vigorous against social hurt* (vv. 7-8a) and *powerfully resolved to work a public hope* of land and well-being for the marginalized of the empire (v. 8b). Both aspects of the text, overcoming hurt and introducing hope, are crucial for God's identity and role in the text. God will not tolerate the pain of oppression. God will create an alternative of liberated community outside imperial domination.

3. Hurt and hope as experienced social reality and as proclaimed theological reality are *given voice in a distinctive rhetoric*, peculiarly congruent with the substance of hurt and hope. Only recently have we paid attention to how Israel speaks its faith in the text. We are now aware that the rhetoric in which faith is cast is crucial for the passion, power, authority, and credibility of faith.[17] In the end, the Bible is an exercise in rhetoric, and we must pay attention to its particular, specific casting.

The biblical text utilizes rhetoric peculiarly appropriate to the practice of hurt.[18] That rhetoric is the speech of lament or complaint in which the speaker insistently complains about present circumstance, assaults those who are responsible for it, and insists on a transformation of that circumstance. Clearly, such speech is not casual; it is surely not neutral; and it is not descriptive or speculative. It is urgent, imperative, and passionately, clearly linked to actual experience. It is speech that is indeed a life-and-death matter. The life of the speaker is at stake in speaking, and the life of the speaker is at stake in being seriously heard by God.

The classic examples of this speech are found in the lament psalms. Claus Westermann, following Hermann Gunkel, has explored the stylized, patterned way of such speech.[19] The key elements of the rhetorical practice are complaint that describes the situation of trouble and petition that, by way of imperative, expects the addressed one (God) to intervene and transform; that is, the lament form lives and is uttered at the expectant edge of what does

---

17. Gail R. O'Day, *Word Disclosed* (see chap. 3, n. 13), esp. 11–15. George A. Lindbeck, in *Nature of Doctrine* (see chap 3, n. 15), has observed how the forms of language are decisive for faith.

18. MacIntyre, in *Whose Justice?* (see chap. 3, n. 16), has explicated the way in which every ethical tradition has its own distinctive linguistic practice and its own peculiar narrative matrix.

19. Westermann, *Praise and Lament* (see chap. 2, n. 8).

not yet exist. The speech of lament seeks to evoke or even force a newness from God that would not happen without this bold insistent speech. The explication of hurt in the speech of Israel is not analytical, diagnostic, or descriptive. It is rather militant, urgent protest whereby the underling—the humiliated and marginated—speaks, seizes authority, and addresses hurt to power. Israel's rhetoric of hurt provides a moment of repositioning between speaker and addressee. The powerless one utters power, the marginal one occupies the center of authority and insists on action. As Sigmund Freud later understood in a highly specialized context, there is no substitute for voiced protest that constitutes an act of shrill delegitimation and an act of abrasive expectation.

The lament speech apparently evoked an assurance of intervention from God, who is attentive to Israel's hurt.[20] Because of such an assurance of intervention, the pleading speech of Israel is abruptly transformed into praise, celebration, and well-being. We do not understand dramatically, liturgically, or theologically what transpired in this exchange to effect such a decisive change in rhetoric. We can only observe that the texts characteristically move from hurt to joy, from hurt to hurt resolved.[21] Israel's rhetoric maps a way for transformation that operated in the public imagination of Israel and, we dare imagine, in the public policy of Israel.

Conversely, Israel also devised rhetoric appropriate to its passion for hope. Hope, as a social, theological practice in Israel is not a vague confidence that things will improve. It is, rather, a conviction of an inversion of circumstance through an abrupt giving of new gifts, a decisive intrusion by God that will make "all things new." Hope is trust in an alternative future that will not be derived or extrapolated from the present, but will be given in the very face of the present.

Israel fashioned speech to carry this radical expectation of a new future. Although hope is carried and voiced in old narratives,[22] the most noteworthy and obvious speech form for hope is the prophetic oracle of hope.[23] The oracles characteristically begin with "In that

---

20. The classic hypothesis of this shift in rhetoric is that of Joachim Begrich, "Das priesterliche Heilsorakel," in *Gesammelte Studien zum Alten Testament*, TBü, no. 21 (Munich: Chr. Kaiser Verlag, 1964), 217–31.

21. Brueggemann, "From Hurt to Joy" (see chap. 2, n. 8).

22. See Westermann, *The Promises of the Father* (Philadelphia: Fortress Press, 1980), and David J. A. Clines, *The Theme of the Pentateuch*, JSOTSup, no. 10 (Sheffield: University of Sheffield Press, 1978).

23. Westermann, "The Way of the Promise through the Old Testament," in *The Old*

day," or "Behold, the days are coming." In both formulae, the oracle asserts and assures a coming, unspecified, but guaranteed time, a time when new gifts will be given by God and old circumstances will be overcome. Then war will yield to peace, hostility to reconciliation, sadness to joy, oppression to justice, and, ultimately, death to life. The language of hope is no doubt hyperbolic, as is the preceding language of complaint. What counts in this overstated speech is the daring voicing of an alternative world, an alternative that claims to be the resolve and intent of God.

The critical intention of this form of hopeful speech should not be missed. Every status quo seeks to devise ways not only of legitimating but also absolutizing the present. The present may not be perfect, but it is the best practical possibility that is conceivable. To critique that present is both unwise and treasonable. These oracles of promise function precisely as protest against such ideology; they delegitimate and deabsolutize the present by asserting that a better future is imaginable and is part of God's sovereign intention.[24] The effect of such speech as an act of hope is to loosen the grip of the present upon the imagination of the community and to expose the present as one among many chooseable options.

Thus both *complaint about hurt* and *promise of hope* are acts of rigorous criticism of every present. The present is protested because it generates hurt. The present is asserted to be less desirable and faithful than what is promised in the theological tradition. Israel's speech enacts both Israel's critical social discernment and its theological passion. Both social discernment and theological passion depend upon this distinctive characteristic rhetoric of Israel.

4. This practice of speech concerning hurt and hope is characteristically Jewish.[25] Admittedly, such a claim is extremely problematic, both because any characterization of Jewishness is endlessly difficult and because our argument is largely circular. Acknowledging these

---

Testament and Christian Faith, ed. Bernhard W. Anderson (New York: Harper & Row, 1963), 200–24, has provided a useful typology for the various genres of promises in the Old Testament.

24. On the power of promise in the face of ideology, see Paul Ricoeur, *Lectures on Ideology and Utopia* (New York: Columbia University Press, 1986).

25. Ricoeur, in *The Symbolism of Evil* (Boston: Beacon Press, 1967), comments on the speech of the prophet: "The prophet . . . does not 'think' in the Hellenic sense of the word; he cries out, he threatens, he orders, he groans, he exults. His 'oracle,' which gives rise to chronicles, codes, hymns, and sayings, possesses the breadth and the depth of the primordial word that constitutes the dialogical situation at the heart of which sin breaks forth" (p. 53). What Ricoeur says of the prophet in a less direct sense characterizes more broadly speech that is Jewish.

formal problems of definition, this speech (and therefore the claims of God carried in the speech and the social sensitivities and expectations fostered by the speech) draws us close to what is central and definitional about biblical faith as a voice of social criticism.

Jewish forms of speech, insofar as we may call the speech patterns of the biblical faith by such a term, are spectacular alternatives to other modes of speech. Given the ancient options, it is clear that this historicizing, politicizing, protesting, imagining language of the Old Testament is contrasted with the rational speech of the Greeks or even with the dramatic speech of Greek playwrights.[26] This language of memory and hope, of complaint and praise, gives identity in Israel and is very different from therapeutic speech, from managerial speech, from all speech that reduces language to technique.[27]

Although the term is freighted with difficulty, we may call Israel's odd speech "covenantal." It is speech that dares to bind the destiny of speaker and listener together in a common burden and common possibility. Insofar as this speech is address to God and address by God, we may say this speech is a bonding of heaven and earth, a linking of the power of holiness and the possibilities of human history, a bonding and a binding that reshape holy power in terms of human history and that recharacterize human history with reference to holy power. When holy power and human possibilities are bound together, a different practice of social relationship is both permitted and required. It is no longer possible to skew social relations toward either a flat, one-dimensional rationalism that ends in oppression or a flat, one-dimensional transcendentalism that escapes public reality. Now the public process is radically recharacterized, reshaped, redescribed, and resignified in terms of bonding and binding.

Israel's tradition of testimony, so far as I know, is distinctive in speaking principally about hurt and hope and in positing such a binding.[28] On the one hand, this conversation, which bespeaks new

---

26. James A. Sanders, in "Adaptable for Life: The Nature and Function of Canon," in *Magnalia Dei: The Mighty Acts of God*, ed. Frank M. Cross et al. (Garden City, N.Y.: Doubleday & Co., 1976), 531–60, speaks of Israel's traditions involving a process of "depolytheizing, monotheizing, Yahwizing, and Israelitizing" (p. 541). My reference to historicizing and politicizing is consistent with his intention.

27. The reduction of language to technique is reflected in the research of Robert Bellah et al., *Habits of the Heart* (Berkeley: University of California Press, 1985). More generally on the reduction of language, cf. Eugen Rosenstock-Huessy, *Speech and Reality* (see chap. 3, n. 24). On the language of memory and hope, see Dietrich Ritschl, *The Logic of Theology* (Philadelphia: Fortress Press, 1987), esp. 14–27.

28. On "testimony" as a life-and-death mode of speech, see Ricoeur, *Essays*, 123–30.

social relations, traces the movement of hurt from human experience to the reality of God; that is, hurt begins in "we groaned and cried out" (Exod. 2:23) and ends at God's throne with "I have seen the affliction of my people . . . and have heard their cry" (Exod. 3:7). It is the cry from earth to heaven that creates new social possibility. On the other hand, this conversation traces the movement of hope from the throne of God to human experience; that is, hope begins in the assertion "I will bring you to a good land" (Exod. 3:8) and ends at the human level: "[The Lord] gave their [the kings'] land as a heritage, . . . a heritage to Israel his servant" (Ps. 136:21-22). It is the intrusion from heaven that makes new possibilities on earth available. The conversation between God and Israel, between heaven and earth, between holy power and human experience, is about pain taken seriously and hope given buoyantly.

Hurt received and *hope given* are the central affirmations of this tradition. It is a great oddity that this Jewish characterization of social reality has not finally been silenced. Moreover, this characterization of social reality cannot be silenced because it lives so close to the bodily realties of human experience, for our bodies do hurt and they do hope. Because this tradition relentlessly honors the voice of the body, it is altogether Jewish to understand the body politic as the body in which hurt and hope are irreducible elements in fashioning a good life and a viable community.[29] This tradition knows that well-being depends on the faithful, bodily hosting of hurt and hope and the faithful, daring voicing of the same hurt and hope.

III

I have made a sweeping claim that the categories of hurt and hope are characteristic of the spectrum of the canonical literature of the Old Testament. My claim is that hurt and hope constitute the common thematic of the Old Testament, even in the midst of the enormous plurality of the canonical text. Even though there are many voices in the text, the various texts are endlessly preoccupied with this agenda of hurt and hope. I shall seek to show that the text in its pluralism is indeed constant on this focus:

1. It is not difficult to see that the practice of voiced hurt and

---

29. On the irresistible voice of the body, see Ernest Becker, *The Denial of Death* (New York: Free Press, 1973); and Aarne Siirala, *The Voice of Illness: A Study in Therapy and Prophecy* (Philadelphia: Fortress Press, 1964).

voiced hope is central to the *pentateuchal traditions* of narrative and law. I have taken as my "clue text" Exod. 2:23-25 and 3:7-14. In the first of these texts, Israel speaks hurt and Yahweh responds. In the second, Yahweh acknowledges hearing the hurt and then makes a promise in response to that hearing. These exchanges stand at the originating point in the Mosaic tradition that constitutes the main narrative of the Pentateuch. The stylized narrative of exodus-wilderness-sojourn-Sinai is a counternarrative. It legitimates, envisions, and enacts a community that is counter both to the exploitation of the empire and to the rapacious practices of the city-states.[30] In the stylized credos, the central affirmation of the rhetoric is that "we cried" and "God heard." The completed narrative thus sponsors and voices a critical alternative to oppressive social arrangements that generate hurt and preclude hope.

The most important aspect of the pentateuchal tradition for our subject is the law. Law in the Pentateuch is not positive law. It is deeply rooted in and informed by the narrative memory and commitments of Israel; that is, the law in Israel is an attempt to give sustained, institutionalized form to the countervision of the Moses narrative. We completely misunderstand if we imagine that the laws of the Pentateuch are simply rules for order. They are, rather, acts of passionate protest and vision whereby Israel explores in detail how the gifts and vision of the exodus rescue can be practiced in Israel on an ongoing basis as the foundation for society.

As God acted in response to a cry of hurt, the law is an attempt to devise institutional power arrangements in which those in authority, those who have legitimate power, those who "know good and evil," are responsive to hurt and attentive to the dangers of exploitation. Clear and obvious examples of law in response to hurt are the laws about oppression of strangers and loans to poor neighbors:

> You shall not wrong a stranger or oppress him, for you were strangers in the land of Egypt. You shall not afflict any widow or orphan. If you do afflict them, and they cry out to me, I will surely hear their cry; and my wrath will burn, and I will kill you with the sword, and your wives shall become widows and your children fatherless. If you lend money to any of my people with you who is poor, you shall not be to

---

30. The basic study of this core tradition is by Gerhard von Rad, *"The Problem of the Hexateuch" and Other Essays* (New York: McGraw-Hill, 1966). Norman K. Gottwald, in *Tribes* (see chap. 1, n. 6), 489–598 passim, has made clear the countercultural social function of the traditions.

him as a creditor, and you shall not exact interest from him. If ever you take your neighbor's garment in pledge, you shall restore it to him before the sun goes down.... If he cries to me, I will hear, for I am compassionate.

(Exod. 22:21-27)[31]

At the center of the two laws is the recognized capacity for "crying out." Two aspects of this act of "cry" are important. First, it is expected and recognized that the abused will have a serious voice. They are not in principle silenced and they cannot be silenced. Hurt counts in the power-processes of Israel. Second, such a cry is a serious political threat to established interests, because such a cry has public consequences. There is nothing romantic about political power in Israel.

There is also nothing excessively transcendental about this threat. The threat is related to the power and intent of God, but the implementation of the threat is through historical means. Thus the two legal statements nicely balance a theological affirmation ("I am compassionate," v. 27) and a political sanction ("I will kill you with the sword," v. 24). The sanctions for the sake of the abused are legitimated by the God of the exodus, but they are enacted through political means. Israel well understood that violence against a neighbor will evoke severe political cost and hurt, because the political process takes place in an assured moral structure. The political process, that is, the legal tradition in Israel, is never autonomous but always includes reference to the will of God.

Israel's torah instruction is an act of hope. This is an odd sort of claim but one that is crucial to the lawmaking process in ancient Israel. It is striking that much law in Israel is anticipatory, envisioning an alternative ordering of public power.

The clearest case of such anticipation of a public alternative is in Deuteronomy. The law in Deuteronomy is cast in anticipatory ways under the rubric "when you come into the land." The rhetorical situation created and assumed by Deuteronomy is that Israel is not yet in the land but fully expects to receive the land as a gift from God.[32] In the presumed world of Deuteronomy, the land is still organized in

---

31. On the social ethos and intention of these laws, see Eckard Otto, "Rechtssystematik im altbabylonischen 'Codex Esnunna' und im altisraelitischen 'Bundesbuch,'" *UF* 19 (1987): 175–97.

32. The same metaphor of "not yet in the land" is taken up in Hebrews 11 as a way of speaking about "faith."

noncovenantal, exploitative—that is, disobedient—ways. The land need not be ordered in that way, however, and it will in the end not be ordered that way. Israel's anticipated political-economic ordering of the land will be a concrete practice of the liberating purpose and sovereignty of Yahweh. Quite specifically and concretely, Deuteronomy works out in daily practice how the promises of Yahweh will be embodied with reference to day laborers (24:14-15), runaway slaves (23:15-16), poor debtors (24:10-13), brutalized defendants (25:1-3), and even birds in a nest (22:6-7). The law is not simply codification of common practice, but it reflects a didactic urgency and a keen resolve that covenantal obedience will lead to transformed public practice.

Perhaps the most vigorous act of hope in the law of Israel is articulated in the various provisions for the release of slaves and the cancellation of debts. The extreme case among these provisions is the year of the Jubilee proposed in Leviticus 25. With reference to this provision, it is our inclination to ask if the provision of the Jubilee was ever in fact enacted. We assume that if it was not enacted, then it need not be taken seriously. Such a question and such an assumption, however, fail to understand the visionary, anticipatory function of law in Israel. It is crucial that Israel imagined, hoped for, believed in, and awaited such a social practice.[33]

In the less spectacular provision for release in Deut. 15:1-11, arrangements are made to cancel debts at the end of seven years and to release the bond servants. In v. 4, it is asserted, "There will be no poor among you." The statement is clearly an act of hope; it imagines an alternative social situation when the year of release is properly implemented. The hope is made conditional: "...if you will really obey my voice." There is indeed "a more excellent way," but its appearance depends on Israel's action. We may assume that this concrete *act of hope* is related precisely to the *voice of hurt* that finds indebtedness, bondage, and the accompanying degradation to be unbearable. The memory of the exodus and Israel's own oppression and cry give poignancy to Israel's long-term legal practice. It is the memory (and the hope) that impinge

---

33. On cancellation of debts as the root idea of forgiveness, see Patrick D. Miller, "Luke 4:16-21," *Int* 29 (1975): 417–21. On the radical nature of forgiveness, see Hannah Arendt, *The Human Condition* (Chicago: University of Chicago Press, 1958), 236–43, esp. 239 n. 76. On the social potential of the Jubilee teaching, see Sharon H. Ringe, *Jesus, Liberation, and the Biblical Jubilee*, OBT (Philadelphia: Fortress Press, 1985).

upon Israel's present socioeconomic, political practice in daring and transformative ways.

I do not argue that all of the Torah narrative and law is ordered according to the issues of hurt and hope. I suggest only that these motifs are present in powerful and shaping ways. It is evident that in the legal provisions (with particular reference to the cultic material) there is an inclination to change the subject away from hurt and hope. This is done both by substituting cultic presence for intruding hope and by resolving social hurt in liturgical affirmation. I am uncertain whether and to what extent such cultic practice (as in the book of Leviticus) tends to tone down the raw authority of hurt and hope or tends to legitimate transformative social practice. I suspect there is a tension in the function of the material in Leviticus.[34]

Israel knows in all its bones that hurt and hope are crucial for its life and faith. It finds such concerns inconvenient and costly, however, and so it contains hurt in cultic transactions (sacrifices) and hope in the celebration of reliable holy presence. Although resistance to processing hurt and hope is anticipated in both narrative and law, such a counterpressure cannot quiet the centrality of hurt and hope in Israel.

2. *The prophetic corpus* is perhaps the clearest expression of hurt and hope as the categories of criticism in the Old Testament.[35] The standard form of prophetic criticism is the judgment speech composed of an indictment and sentence. That form is cast in juridical language, which explicates accepted legal antecedents. The judgment speech is well-suited to present God as the tribunal before whom aggrieved parties may bring their complaints and file their charges.[36]

The framing of the prophetic judgment speech, however, develops two other rhetorical strategies. On the one hand, Yahweh is presented not only as the judge who gives the verdict and pronounced sentence but also as the prosecuting attorney who files the complaint and gives the evidence. A variant on this usage is that the prophetic speaker on behalf of God brings the charge and estab-

---

34. On this tension, see Fernando Belo, *A Materialist Reading of the Gospel of Mark* (Maryknoll, N.Y.: Orbis Books, 1981).

35. On prophetic criticism, see Michael Walzer, *Interpretation and Social Criticism* (Cambridge: Harvard University Press, 1987).

36. See Westermann, *Basic Forms* (see chap. 1, n. 23); and Gene M. Tucker, "The Law in the Eighth-Century Prophets," in *Canon Theology and Old Testament Interpretation*, ed. Tucker et al. (Philadelphia: Fortress Press, 1988), 201–16.

lishes the indictment. The dramatic character of the rhetoric is not always clear and simple. What is clear and simple, however, is that the prophets bring to speech the abuse, exploitation, injustice, and violence that distort the community and that cause destruction. In the prophets, the hurt is presented in order to explicate the consequence. The covenant curses of famine, war, pestilence, exile, and death intrude because of the social production of hurt. The perpetration of hurt evokes a response of hurt from God that injures the perpetrators. The prophets thus bespeak a morally coherent world in which injurious social transactions result in damage to the perpetrators. Social hurt is taken seriously, and those who practice it will eventually be caught in the hurt they perpetrate and suffer from it.

On the other hand, the juridical metaphor is in tension with more intimate images, through which God is presented as wounded lover or dismayed parent. In this poetic maneuver, social reality is articulated as wound to the person of God, even as the body politic is wounded by wrong social relation.[37] In the metaphor of wound and healing, the central issue is sickness and suffering and not the legal categories of violation, guilt, and punishment. Especially in the poetry of Hosea and Jeremiah, the metaphor of illness is powerfully used to voice social criticism against a social arrangement that is systemically destructive.

Characteristically, the prophets do not speak directly about the social system. They prefer personal and interpersonal images by which allusion is made to systems of social reality. The outcome of such prophetic proclamation is indeed death and destruction. The judgment Yahweh has originally worked against the Egyptian empire is now worked against Israel itself.[38] This rhetorical development of turning God's anger against Israel makes clear that Yahweh's commitment to human well-being and Yahweh's resistance to human exploitation and brutality override even Yahweh's massive commitment to the community of Israel. The perpetration of hurt is more fundamental for Yahweh than other commitments, even a commitment to the Israelite community of faith. Thus, as the social norm of hurt and hope operates on behalf of God's people, it may also be turned against that people.

---

37. See chap. 2.

38. Jer. 21:5 shows the prophet using the same language earlier used against the Egyptian oppressors. The stylized language of the credo is now turned against Judah. On the "anti-exodus," see William L. Moran, "The End of the Unholy War and the Anti-Exodus," *Bibl* 44 (1963): 333–42, and his reference to Lohfink.

The practice of hope by the prophets is well known and hardly needs explication. I have the impression, however, that the promises of the prophets have been misunderstood and discounted for two reasons. First, religionists have been excessively preoccupied with "fulfillment" so that Christians like to make lists of the fulfillments of the Old Testament promises, as though they were in fact predictions.[39] Second, historical criticism has been preoccupied with locating the date and setting for each promise. The effect of such a preoccupation is to explain away the power of hope, for such scholarship seeks a time and place of utterance that are palatable and minimize the abrasion of the promise. Such a critical approach fails to notice that such rhetoric is never palatable to established power. The preoccupation among scholars to determine what is "genuine" or "not genuine" among the promises amounts to a refusal to take the promise on its own terms.[40]

All such reasoning, religious and critical, misreads and misunderstands the intent of the promise. The promises are acts of powerful social criticism. They intend to evoke and nurture alternative imagination and to counter the absolutist claims of the status quo; that is, the promises are bold, subversive political utterances designed to delegitimate the commonsense world of plausibility sponsored by the dominant ideology. The effect of promise is to make alternative, imaginative commitments thinkable so that the poems effectively dismantle old commitments and invite the community to civil disobedience, that is, to violate the ideological claims of the status quo.

In broad stroke, the promises may be situated in two different contexts. On the one hand, the promises may be uttered in contexts of prosperity and well-being, that is, before 587 B.C.E.[41] In such con-

---

39. A case in point is that in the program notes for the Atlanta Symphony, an ad provides a list of the fulfilled promises of the Bible. Such a crude way of handling the Bible turns up incongruously amidst the sophistication of the community of the symphony.

40. To focus on or disregard the distinction of "genuine" and "late" is a most important methodological issue. That issue is now most clearly dramatized in a canonical approach to the text that means to bracket out the historical-critical distinctions of "early" and "late." Such a canonical approach loosens the text from a particular historical placement and pays attention to the continuing authorizing power of the text as original speech. See James L. Crenshaw, "Wisdom," in *Old Testament Form Criticism*, ed. John H. Hayes (San Antonio: Trinity University Press, 1974), 253–56, on this peculiar usage.

41. In the case of the Northern Kingdom, the comparable date is 722 B.C.E. *Mutatis mutandis*, the "before" and "after" are synonymous for the North and South.

texts of well-being, the promises articulate the terrible gap between present reality and God's intended reality. The dominant culture always wants to offer present reality as a close replica of God's intention. On the other hand, the promises may be uttered in a situation of despair and defeat, that is, after 587 B.C.E., as in the clear cases of Jeremiah, Ezekiel, and Second Isaiah.[42] In this latter context, the promise moves against the resignation and despair of the exilic community. It proposes an alternative to the absolutist claims of the host empire. In both cases, in situations of prosperity and well-being and in situations of exile and despair, the promise is an authorization for faith, perception, and action beyond the accepted practices of the dominant rationality. The social function of promise is not simply solace and reassurance; it is abrasive critique and counterauthorization. Such a function makes fulfillment less important and the concrete historical locus of the utterances of minimal importance.

The prophetic lawsuit and the prophetic promise voice hurt and hope in powerful fashion. These two modes of speech confirm that hurt and hope matter decisively to the God of Israel. What has been less noticed and understood is that these speech forms for hurt and hope are powerful critical interventions in Israel's public life. This critical function of lawsuit and promise is evidenced in the reaction of establishment authorities to prophetic utterance, as for example concerning Amos (Amos 7:10-17) and Jeremiah (Jer. 36:22-26). Although it has not been so much noticed, it is plausible to conclude that the sound of hope evokes as much resistance from the status quo as does the voicing of hurt. Both sounds undermine present patterns of power, perception, and reality.

3. The voices of hurt and hope predominate in *the Psalms*. The most crucial (and neglected) part of the Psalter is the large collection of psalms of complaint and lament. In a highly stylized way, these psalms are precisely voices of hurt that protest against present reality. Sometimes the protest is an appeal (petition) to God against the enemy who has injured. On other occasions, the speech of complaint is direct address to God that accuses God of causing injury and injustice. Thus, the lament poems function as zealous criticism of the present; they announce that present arrangements are dysfunc-

---

42. On the peculiar significance of these three prophets, see von Rad, *Old Testament Theology II* (see chap. 3, n. 9), 263–77; and Brueggemann, *Hopeful Imagination* (Philadelphia: Fortress Press, 1986).

tional, unbearable, and unacceptable. Moreover, Israel believes that if Yahweh can be mobilized, the present circumstance is unnecessary and need not persist.

The voice of hope in the Psalter is less easy to identify, but it is everywhere sounded. We may identify three aspects of the power of hope in the Psalter.

First, the lament psalms themselves are protests expectant of change. Erhard Gerstenberger has seen that complaint with an imperative petition is an act of hope, fully anticipating that God can and will hear the petition and act to transform the circumstance.[43] While the utterance of hope is most often a distinct element in the Psalms, the complaint itself is an act of hope. Thus Psalm 88, for example, has no positive resolution. It is unrelieved complaint. Yet its very utterance is a refusal to accept present circumstance as God's most faithful act. The complaint psalms are offensive to us because in them, not even God is protected from criticism. In these prayers, the last residue of transcendentalism is overcome and even God is expected to change. Unlike Psalm 88, most of the lament psalms culminate in an actual statement of confidence, assurance, and praise. These psalms characteristically announce that the protest has "worked." God will create a better circumstance for the speaker in time to come.

Second, more speculatively, Sigmund Mowinckel has argued that the cultic use of the Psalms is the root of eschatological hope; that is, Israel worshiped regularly in order to enact and receive the gifts that were mediated in the liturgy. Over time, so Mowinckel has concluded, the liturgy failed to keep its promises and mediate its gifts. Eventually the driving hopes of Israel were pushed away from the present moment of worship, and made to be hope for the future. Mowinckel's central theme is the expectation of the "true king."[44] The true king, according to the hypothesis, is to appear in an act of worship. When he does not appear, however, the hope for a true king is eventually pushed into the future and becomes "messianic hope." The royal psalms thus become bearers of a hope that lives outside and beyond any present possibilities that worship can fulfill.

---

43. Gerstenberger, "Der klagende Mensch" (see chap. 3, n. 4). See also Anneli Aejmelaeus, *The Tradition Prayer in the Psalms*, BZAW, no. 167 (Berlin: de Gruyter, 1986), 1–117.

44. Mowinckel, *Das Thronbesteigungsfest Jahwäs und der Ursprung der Eschatologie, Psalmenstudien II* (Amsterdam: Schippers, 1961), and *He That Cometh* (New York: Abingdon Press, 1954).

The Psalter becomes the literary deposit for keeping that long-term hope alive and available in Israel.

Third, Brevard S. Childs has observed that the Psalms in their final, canonical form constitute a corpus of eschatological literature.[45] Childs underscores the confidence in God that is the core and substance of Israel's hope. The Psalms give voice to a thoroughly theonomous conviction. The God addressed, accosted, and summoned in the lament is the one who is counted on to make the world new.

The analysis of Mowinckel and the observations of Childs are certainly helpful. In my judgment, however, they do not see or state clearly the critical function of hope in its present moment of utterance. Hope is not simply deferral of expectation into some future time; hope is also a dismantling of the present. In the singing of the Psalms, the participants begin to yield their uncritical citizenship in the present in order to await and live toward a "better city" here enunciated and envisioned.

4. *The wisdom tradition* is the most difficult dimension of the Old Testament for my thesis on hurt and hope. As is often the case, wisdom proves a challenge to any large, comprehensive scheme of interpretation for the Old Testament. Nonetheless, because the wisdom teachers lived close to experienced reality, it is possible to see that, even here, the elemental human realities of hurt and hope are powerfully present.

Even though it is customary in wisdom studies to proceed from the stability of Proverbs to the disorientation of Job, it will be useful for our argument to reverse the procedure and to begin with Job. The book of Job is indeed wisdom literature that is saturated with the voice of hurt. Indeed, the central issue of the book of Job is hurt that is beyond any rational or conventional explanation.

We may identify two aspects of hurt in the poem of Job that need concern us:

First, the poem of Job, as Westermann has shown, is constructed around speeches of lament and complaint.[46] The use of lament and complaint in a sapiential context is a daring rhetorical move. The lament form is obviously not a "sapiential form," but the poet has been forced to use speech forms that lie outside the scope of wisdom in order to voice his extraordinary argument.[47]

---

45. Childs, *Introduction* (see chap. 1, n. 6), 511–23.
46. Westermann, *Structure* (see chap. 3, n. 23), 31–66 passim.
47. The conventional instruction of wisdom intends to articulate the limits of safe

The speech forms that voice hurt, that is, laments, are indispensable for the dramatic argument of the total poem of Job. As has long been recognized, it is the rhetorical and theological dissonance between Job's complaints and the speeches of the friends that gives dramatic power to the total enterprise of the poem. If the speeches of lament are removed, the poem collapses. The intent of the complaint speeches of Job is to mount a massive critique of the sapiential conventions of the friends, who imagine the world to be equitable, symmetrical, and well-ordered. The poem of Job exposes the friends' claim as false ideology, incongruent with the stubborn reality of facts.[48] Any claim that the world is well-ordered must deal with the stubborn realities of moral disorder articulated by Job.

The second, minor motif of hurt in the poem of Job is the awareness that the well-off must be responsive to the voice of hurt in the community. In his nostalgic remembrance of better days, Job says that he was blessed

> ...because I delivered the poor who cried,
>   and the fatherless who had none to help him.
> The blessing of him who was about to perish came upon me,
>   and I caused the widow's heart to sing for joy.
> I put on righteousness, and it clothed me;
>   my justice was like a robe and a turban.
> I was eyes to the blind,
>   and feet to the lame.
> I was a father to the poor,
>   and I searched out the cause of him whom I did not know.
> I broke the fangs of the unrighteous,
>   and made him drop his prey from his teeth.
>   (Job 29:12-17)

---

conduct. It can be argued that lament speech becomes necessary and appropriate when experience drives Israel to the limit or beyond it. In the categories of Ricoeur, the laments in Job are "limit expression" that correlates with Job's "limit-experience." Cf. Ricoeur, "Biblical Hermeneutics," *Semeia* 4 (1975): 107–35.

48. On the polemical, critical function of Job, see Ernst Bloch, *Atheism in Christianity: The Religion of the Exodus and the Kingdom* (New York: Herder & Herder, 1972), 110. Gustavo Gutiérrez, in *On Job: God-Talk and the Suffering of the Innocent* (Maryknoll, N.Y.: Orbis Books, 1987), has taken up the point but with much greater theological sensitivity. For a subtle analysis of this problem in Job, see Herbert Fingarette, "The Meaning of Law in the Book of Job," in *Revisions: Changing Perspectives in Moral Philosophy*, ed. Stanley Hauerwas and Alasdair MacIntyre (Notre Dame, Ind.: University of Notre Dame Press, 1983), 249–86.

Job does in his community what God does for Israel in bondage. Job is an imitator of God in attending to human hurt.

In his great oath of innocence, Job claims for himself:

> If I have rejected the cause of my manservant or
>   my maidservant,
> when they brought a complaint against me...
>   (Job 31:13)

Job is the voice of hurt that assaults false power arrangements on earth and in heaven. Moreover, Job is the model listener to the voice of hurt who hears and responds in decisive and transformative ways.

The book of Job deals with the unacknowledged residue of human reality after the book of Proverbs has made its best claim. The book of Proverbs seeks to instruct about success, well-being, security, and prosperity in a well-ordered society. That teaching tradition seems to know nothing of hurt, wants nothing to do with hurt, and has no need for hope. The book of Proverbs, more than any other literature in the Old Testament, is a literature against my thesis because it celebrates a good present-tense circumstance that can fend off the unsettling of both hurt and hope.

I suggest, however, that a more careful, critical reading of Proverbs permits us to notice the presence of hurt and hope at least at the edge of awareness in the book of Proverbs:

a. The teachers in Proverbs know about social hurt. Their teaching is a defensive maneuver to distance their treasured social reality from the threat of hurt; that is, the proverbs teach how to avoid getting hurt. That defensive maneuver is in part a sociological act that identifies strategies for avoiding poverty. It is also in part a constructive, rhetorical power play designed to override the reality of hurt and to read hurt out of existence. J. David Pleins has shown that poverty (to take one representative issue) is acknowledged in Proverbs as a real social fact.[49] Given that acknowledgment, however, the strategy of Proverbs is not to deal with the problem of poverty, or to eradicate it, or to address its causes, but simply to avoid it. Positively, the teacher believed that "right living" can avoid social hurt. Thus, the teachers know all about "sorrow" (1:1), "hunger" (10:3), "poverty" (19:4), "shame" (10:5), "violence" (10:6, 11), and "ruin" (10:8, 14, 15); but all those dangers can be avoided. The purpose of

---

49. Pleins, "Poverty in the Social World of the Wise," *JSOT* 37 (1987): 61–78.

wisdom instruction is to teach how to avoid and stay untouched by such a threat.

Negatively, hurt is defined out of existence by labeling it "sin" or "foolishness." These teachers, advocates of certain social privilege and advantage, work to distance their social privilege and advantage from the unwelcome social reality of hurt. This redefinition is done by translating *trouble*, which may be fortuitous but which most often is a product of skewed social relations, into *fault*. When redefined in this way, it is no longer trouble that needs attention but only the avoidance of "foolishness." Such a translation and redefinition of trouble constitute self-serving ideology. The teachers do not want to hear or to notice the power and pervasiveness of trouble with which Job struggled. They want the hurt to be unacknowledged, because when it is unacknowledged, it need not be faced as a social fact.

This strenuous strategy of denial, however, serves only to call attention to the reality of hurt. The argument of the book of Proverbs, then, is not about whether there is hurt in the world or whether there needs to be hurt in the world. It is, rather, an argument that little oases of well-being can be constructed that provide protection from the immediacy and power of hurt. The strategy of Proverbs, thus, is to handle hurt so that it does not function as an audible criticism but only as a failure that is to be condemned, disregarded, and dismissed. The capacity to translate hurt into some more manageable social product is an effective ideological act. In the face of that act in the book of Proverbs, however, the poem of Job is a poignant reminder that such a defensive, ideological strategy can work for a short time, but not finally.

b. In a similar way, we might conclude that hope is not on the horizon of the book of Proverbs. Pleins can say "that the writers of Proverbs do not look beyond the hard realities of this life in anticipation of a new order," and he is correct. Here the voice of hope is quieter and very different than that in the prophets.[50]

We may, however, identify four proverbs that suggest that even the wisdom teachers had on their horizon a future that God would give:

> The hope (*yḥl*) of the righteous ends in gladness,
>> but the expectation (*qwh*) of the wicked comes to nought. (10:28)

---

50. Ibid., 67, 70.

The righteous do have a hope and expectation; it is very different from the future sought by the wicked.

> The desire (*'wh*) of the righteous ends only in good;
>   the expectation (*qwh*) of the wicked in wrath. (11:23)

In this proverb, the parallelism is not between hope and hope (*yḥl*, *qwh*), but between desire and hope. It is telling that the righteous are identified with a desire. Perhaps the word for desire is simply a synonym for hope; it has, however, a different nuance, bespeaking self-satisfaction, even self-indulgence. The future expected by the righteous is only characterized as good. This is enough, however, to indicate that even the proverb hopes in a way that pushes into the future. Even the prosperous righteous anticipate a more blessed, joyous state of well-being yet to be given. Indeed, that hope and expectation are the impetus for the teaching of the sages.

The last two proverbs I will cite are especially important:

> Surely there is a future (*'aḥărît*),
>   and your hope (*qwh*) will not be cut off. (23:18)

> Know that wisdom is such to your soul;
>   If you find it, there will be a future (*'aḥărît*),
>   and your hope (*qwh*) will not be cut off. (24:14)

In these two instances, the wisdom teachers affirm that there is an "afterward," a time of well-being for the wise, righteous, responsible, and obedient, a time to be distinguished from this present time, a time that will be better than the present. That better time, however, depends on finding wisdom.

This hope is subdued and truncated. Moreover, we may imagine that the future wished by the teachers is very much like the best of the present. Their hope is domesticated, predictable, and in large part under the control of one's present choices. Nonetheless, it is important that even in this most disciplined, self-celebrative literature that seeks to guarantee the present, there is an explicit hope. Frederick Jameson's study of utopia and ideology has helped me in understanding this strange juxtaposition of conservatism and hope. "Ideology" is set against utopia and is a refusal to hope beyond the best of the present; that is, ideology is rhetoric that legitimates the status quo. Jameson, however, dares to conclude that even such ideology is an act of utopia, an act of "futuring" for a better place, that is, a utopia.[51] The teachers of proverbs have in mind a future state of society in which the choices, hopes, and values of the righteous will everywhere pertain. Even in the book of Proverbs, such a state manifestly does not now exist. Their teaching about the future has force because the wisdom teachers believe that such a society can be formed. It depends on human wisdom, but it is in the end the gift of a faithful God who honors human effort.

For two reasons I cite this odd twist that Jameson gives to hope. First, I wish to establish that even the wisdom teachers are voices of hurt and hope, albeit in quite peculiar ways. Second, I wish to assert that hope can be managed as a reactionary strategy in the interest of the status quo; that is, hope can have its energy and danger siphoned off, routinized, and domesticated so that it is no longer a threat or critique. I judge that such a domestication of hope is evident in the book of Proverbs.

In sum, then, I conclude that the Old Testament in all its major elements is indeed a voice of hurt and of hope:

> *The Pentateuch* is an account of protest and promised deliverance, a collection of laws of warning and possibility;
>
> *The prophets* speak in judgment speeches of complaint and oracles of promise;
>
> *The Psalms* are constituted by songs of lament and complaint, and by petition and doxologies of alternative possibility;
>
> *Wisdom instruction* concerns an anticipated possibility, and cries of protest and restlessness.

The Old Testament is a literature of richly diverse voices. It cannot be reduced to any single theme or set of themes. Its pluralism is vigorous and unavoidable. I submit, however, that its pluralism is a sustained reflection on the most central and foundational of human experiences. These various literatures in different ways concern the irreducible human realities of hurt and hope.

IV

These voices of hurt and hope function in the Bible as a sustained act of criticism. It remains for us to ask: Toward what object is

---

51. Jameson, *Political Unconscious* (see chap. 3, n. 5). Jameson's definitional categories are from Karl Mannheim. See also Ricoeur, *Lectures*, esp. 289.

this criticism addressed? I should answer: The fundamental criticism of biblical faith is against *voicelessness*, against a society in which
speech about power and powerlessness is banished and in which social power is so concentrated that it need no longer listen and is
no longer capable of hearing. The voice of pathos and possibility
sounded in these texts is the Bible's great gift against all the strategies of voicelessness, strategies that were so powerful in the ancient
world and in our own situation. While the text comes out of a series
of social situations quite remote from our own, the text nonetheless
continues to exercise originating authority among us.[52]

I shall identify two aspect of voicelessness that I take to be crucial
among us:

1. *When the voice of hurt is absent*, we end in *psychic numbing*. We become incapable of speech, of sensitivity, of noticing, of compassion, of
caring, of intervening, of transformation. Robert J. Lifton has studied a series of extreme cases of psychic numbing among Viet Nam
veterans, in the face of nuclear totalism, and among the doctors who
operated the German death camps.[53] These are the most extreme
cases of human brutality we can imagine from our own time. Less extreme cases of psychic numbing wrought through human brutality
have to do with all the enforced silences among powerless, marginal
peoples, among the abused, the aged, the children, the disapproved,
and the excluded. The institutions of elitist culture, of technological
media, and of the powerful corporate economy have little patience
with such voices. Moreover, in their impatience, these established
forces have the capacity and often the will to silence the marginated
voices of hurt and hope. Where such silencing happens, our vision
of humanity shrivels and brutality becomes conventional.

The primary critical function of the Bible is to keep the voice of
hurt present in the public process. That voice, so cherished and honored in the Bible, is the voice of the marginal, whose testimony is
oddly transmitted to us, in the canonical process, as the voice of God.

2. *When the voice of hope is silenced*, we end in *deep despair*. We come
to believe that nothing is possible, no gifts remain to be given, no
newness will be received, no transformations can be undertaken.

---

52. It is the intention of Childs, in *Introduction*, that the canonical status of the text
looses the text from its original historical locus and permits the text to continue to
speak with powerful theological authority in always new circumstances.

53. Lifton, *The Future of Immortality and Other Essays for a Nuclear Age* (New York:
Basic Books, 1987), esp. 50–59, *Broken Connection* (see chap. 3, n. 1), and *The Nazi
Doctors: Medical Killing and the Psychology of Genocide* (New York: Basic Books, 1986).

Where there is such despair, we not only end in personal depression and loss of energy; at the same time, we generate public docility. If there is no newness, then life cannot get any better than it is now. We become members of a public body easily administered. We become accommodators to the power of the present. Because all the pieces of reality are now on the table, we acquire whatever we cay by cunning, by greed, and by violence. It is no large step from despair to violence and to the arms race, which is an act of utter hopelessness.

The primary critical function of the Bible is to keep the voice of hope present in the public process. That voice, for which the Bible is a principle custodian, continues to shatter our perimeters of reality. It does so on behalf of the marginal who refuse to believe the present is ultimate. It does so in the name of God, for whom all things are possible, even the impossible.

Thus the Bible is an odd, subversive voice that refuses to be silenced. That voice is *an act of material reality*, reminding us that our irreducible bodies will speak relentlessly against the imposed silence. Our bodies will not be silenced and, therefore, the body politic must finally face the material reality of hurt and hope. The voice, so material in its embodiment, is at the same time a daring *enactment of a transcendent claim*. We imagine that this voice is in some way the governing will of God, for voicelessness is indeed atheism in pursuit of autonomy. We foster silence because we imagine there is no one to address and no one to whom we must listen. Against such silence, the voice that bespeaks hurt and hope is sounded as the very voice of God. Social reality and the will of God converge in speech of a particular kind. It is called revelation; what it reveals is a holy restlessness and an indefatigable yearning. Such revelatory speech, however, is not excessively transcendental. It is a cry of the abused, an assault by a prophet, a maxim by a teacher, a hymn by the chancel choir. These voices—cry, assault, maxim, hymn—are all restless, all disclosing.

My claim, therefore, is that hurt and hope constitute a common theme that permeates the pluralism of the Bible. When we stay inside the Bible, we notice the stark differences in the text from one part to another. We are aware of how different is wisdom from the Pentateuch, the Psalms from the Prophets. When, however, we think about this text vis-à-vis technological modernity, romantic therapy, bureaucratic management, authoritarian moralism, and consumer propaganda, this text has a relentless, agreed-upon claim. The pluralism so evident in the Bible pales before the central conviction of the text: Our bodies, gifts of God, sponsor truthful voices that must be taken seriously. Public ethics is the serious passion of bodily voices that can be killed, but not silenced.

The Bible is framed at beginning and end by magisterial voices of hurt and hope. At the very beginning of the text, a cry of hurt is set at the boundary of the historical process. Cain has killed his brother. Of course. Family violence permeates the historical process. The revelatory news of the narrative is this: The dead one will not be silenced. The cry of the violated one will not be disregarded. So we are told, "The voice of your brother's blood is crying to me from the ground" (Gen. 4:10). The cry will persist. The cry is the very stuff of the process of creation. The creation is marked by the abrasive protest of hurt.

At the far limit of the Bible, bracketing all the material since the murder of Cain, is the ultimate voice of hope and promise:

> Behold, the dwelling of God is with humankind. God will dwell with them, and they shall be God's people, and God will be with them; God will wipe away every tear from their eyes, and death shall be no more, neither shall there be mourning nor crying nor pain any more, for the former things have passed away. (Rev. 21:3-4)

No more mourning; no more crying; no more pain on the earth—for the former things have passed away!

We live, in the meantime, between the cry of Cain and the promise of John. Until the promise is kept, the public, ethical process consists in attending to the pain still present, the cry still voiced until former things do indeed pass away and the promised newness comes.

5

A Convergence in Recent
Old Testament Theologies

THIS CHAPTER CONSIDERS the shifted ground that is evident in several publications in Old Testament theology. Although not more than a provisional judgment can be made, it is possible that a striking convergence of categories indicates a break in the long-standing stalemate in Old Testament theology. That stalemate, as assessed by Henning Graf Reventlow, has posed the *history of traditions* approach of Gerhard von Rad over against the more *systematic* categories of Walther Eichrodt.[1] The major criticisms of these positions have been widely accepted even though scholars have only slowly made progress beyond these two alternatives.

Concerning von Rad, the following points merit attention:

1. It may be argued that his approach is not genuinely a theology, but it is on the brink of being a history of the religion of Israel.

2. The category of "history" with its ambiguous and diverse meanings is problematic, and von Rad has not been able to resolve satisfactorily the matter of the gap between confessed and critical history.

3. In his last major publication, *Wisdom in Israel*, von Rad himself seemed to be moving away from his own synthesis.[2] That book seems to suggest that the wisdom (and creation?) materials are not derived

---

1. Reventlow, "Basic Problems in Old Testament Theology," *JSOT* 11 (1979): 2–22.

2. Von Rad, *Wisdom* (see chap. 1, n. 25).

from or responses to the historical traditions but rather offer a distinct, alternative, and perhaps competing theological posture. Thus von Rad's own work permits one to infer a critique of his work.

For all these reasons, the synthesis of von Rad is very sharply in question. (Such a frontal critique is on hermeneutical grounds, even without reference to the more specific critical question of the status of the "credo," a matter so crucial for von Rad's entire program.)

Concerning Eichrodt, criticism, as one expects, runs in the opposite direction:

1. The governing category that becomes the master key is in part imposed upon the material rather than read out of it.

2. In any case, the governing category, indeed any single governing category, cannot accommodate all the material. Thus, it becomes necessary either to force material into the category or to ignore part of the material.

3. Other attempts after Eichrodt to locate a "center" or to identify a governing category are not much more successful and represent little methodological advance beyond Eichrodt.[3]

For all the criticism, however, subsequent attempts have been unable to move past these alternatives. It is our purpose here to call attention to three books that are very different in perspective from each other but that converge in their proposals of a fresh perspective.

I

Claus Westermann has for some time given attention to the distinctive role of blessing in the Old Testament. He has suggested that "blessing" embodies a perspective in the Old Testament quite different from that of "deliverance." In *Elements of Old Testament Theology*, he has pursued the theme to show the way in which it can aid in understanding the Old Testament more generally.[4]

Westermann's book is not singularly concerned with the development of the dialectic of blessing and deliverance. It presents a

---

3. Cf. Gerhard Hasel, *Old Testament Theology: Basic Issues in the Current Debate* (Grand Rapids: Eerdmans Pub. Co., 1975), chap. 3. Hasel shows how Eichrodt is the first in an ongoing sequence of those who seek a "center."

4. See esp. Westermann, *Blessing in the Bible and the Life of the Church* (Philadelphia: Fortress Press, 1978), but also his important adumbration in "Creation and History in the Old Testament," in *The Gospel and Human Destiny*, ed. Vilmos Vajta (Minneapolis: Augsburg Pub. House, 1971), 11–38; see *Elements* and the earlier and shorter presentation, *What Does the Old Testament Say* (for both see chap. 1, n. 4).

sketch of how an Old Testament theology might be shaped, and so it includes many other materials as well. The book is characterized in the following ways: (1) as reflective of Westermann's intense work on the Psalms and particularly on the movement of petition and praise;[5] (2) by the strong influence of von Rad in the structure of the book, especially in terms of the dialogue of God's initiative and human response; and (3) by the way in which the more particularistic motif of the elect community comes to dominate, especially as Westermann looks toward the New Testament. Thus, even though he is intensely interested in blessing, on balance the tilt seems to be in the direction of the historical, that is, the deliverance motif.

Our interest here, however, is to focus on the pair of deliverance/ blessing without reference to the New Testament. Of the former of these, deliverance, Westermann stays close to the now familiar categories of historical credo, the exodus-Sinai tradition, and the covenant themes of Deuteronomy. He pays special attention to the role of the mediator in the formation and maintenance of the community of deliverance.

In the development of the countertheme, he is attentive to the creation narratives, the Psalms, and the wisdom materials. In contrast to the historical concreteness of deliverance with its once-for-all particularity, the blessing theme is concerned with the reliable processes of life and death, birth and well-being.[6] It is this tradition that takes in a universal scope (p. 99) and is articulated in the priestly and royal institutions. Following earlier work,[7] Westermann gives attention to the ways in which the Old Testament draws the two together, especially in Genesis 12–13 and in the Balaam songs of Numbers 22–24. The major gain of this statement is that Westermann summarizes his various studies on these matters and brings them together to offer a new structure for understanding Old Testament faith. The new element is that the blessing theme is now a full counterpart to that of deliverance. His shrewdest example of this, with reference

---

5. See Westermann, *The Praise of God in the Psalms* (Richmond: John Knox Press, 1965), reprinted in *Praise and Lament in the Psalms* (Atlanta: John Knox Press, 1981).

6. Special attention should be drawn to the two works of Rainer Albertz, *Weltschöpfung und Menschenschöpfung*, Calwer Theologische Monographien, no. 3 (Stuttgart: Calwer Verlag, 1974), and *Persönliche* (see chap. 1, n. 4). As Westermann's student, Albertz is heavily indebted to Westermann's constructs. But he has also forged ahead in making some major proposals of his own. In both books he has proposed a dialectic that shapes the material somewhat differently but that, nonetheless, greatly illuminates the general issues of this discussion.

7. See Westermann, "Way of Promise" (see chap. 4, n. 23).

to 2 Kings 6–7 and Josh. 5:11, is a contrast between the "bread of deliverance" and the "bread of blessing" (cf. also Deut. 11:10-12).[8]

II

The second study is that of Samuel Terrien, *The Elusive Presence*.[9] As might be expected, Terrien's main effort is to show that the sapiential and hymnic materials must be centrally included in an Old Testament theology. Negatively he argues that the historical-covenantal materials have been unduly and disproportionately stressed. Thus, he seeks to establish a balance in which the covenantal/historical materials are seen as one side of a dialectic, but not the whole matter.

Terrien's way of proceeding is to consider the main theme of the "presence of God," which he rightly discerns as "elusive." His statement is magisterial in its ability not only to comprehend an enormous variety of Old Testament materials concerned with theophany, epiphany, and call, but also to link this to the Gospel reports concerning the birth, transfiguration, and resurrection of Jesus.[10] Thus, he proposes a new way of seeing the interrelatedness of Old and New Testaments; however, for our purposes, the theme of God's elusive presence is not the main point. Conceivably, he might have made his same argument in relation to another theme.

What concerns us more is the dialectic that Terrien finds everywhere in various forms. The largest pair would be that of the *ethical and the aesthetic*. By the aesthetic he refers especially to the sapiential and psalmic materials. These are concerned not so much with duty as with beauty. They understand that the world cannot be encapsulated in a propositional, unambiguous statement to which a mandatory response is made. Rather, reality is complex and must be honored in its elusive, ambiguous, and playful dimensions. For that reason, the mystery and wonder of reality cannot be subsumed under or confined to the concrete particularity of Israel's salvation-Torah tradition.

Terrien focuses especially on the contrast or tension between the covenant traditions and the emergence of the temple appa-

---

8. Westermann, *Elements*.

9. Terrien, *Elusive Presence* (see chap. 1, n. 4).

10. Ibid., chap. 9.

ratus.[11] For that reason, his identification of the antithesis is not neat and clean. It cannot be reduced to a single formulation, and he considers it from many different angles. Pursuing a line already suggested by Murray Newman[12] and now taken up by many persons, Terrien develops the tension between the glory-oriented South and the name-oriented North, also congenial to von Rad's proposal concerning ark and name.[13] Thus, the temple establishment must be understood neither as simply derivative from nor as a perversion of the Mosaic tradition. It is a countertheme that is a correction providing genuinely alternative resources. It is possible, even likely, that Terrien has placed too positive a reading on the Davidic achievement. But he sees that David is ambiguous, holding together erotic passion and a keen sense of social justice.[14]

Terrien skillfully articulates a number of other dialectics that follow the governing one of ethical/aesthetic. These include:

"ear/eye"
"north/south"
"time/space"
"name/glory"
"ethical passion/emotional contemplation"
"ethical ear/mystical eye"
"ethical demands/spiritual delight"

Presumably, a number of other pairs might have been suggested, but such multiplication is not necessary. The point of Terrien's proposal is that there are other dimensions of Israel's faith that must be given attention but that have been screened out of scholarly consideration by the domination of ethical/covenantal/historical categories. Terrien neither denies these nor denies that they have been rightly interpreted in the recent enthusiasm over covenant. But alongside or over against this stress, other traditions embody elements of faith that are important. Thus, it is this dialectic of elusive presence that hints at the "insidiousness of intellectual idolatry" and exposes "the corruptibility of the covenant theology."[15]

---

11. Ibid., 186–213.
12. Newman, *The People of the Covenant* (New York: Abingdon Press, 1962).
13. Von Rad, *Studies* (see chap. 3, n. 12), chap. 3.
14. Terrien, *Elusive Presence*, 281.
15. Ibid., 369.

III

The third book is a much more modest proposal to the theological community and does not intend to be a substantive presentation of an Old Testament theology. Paul D. Hanson, in *Dynamic of Transcendence*,[16] addresses a very different problem, namely what now is to be done with a theology of the mighty acts of God. On the one hand, Hanson values the tradition of G. Ernest Wright (and less directly the influence of von Rad), although he is not insensitive to the criticism leveled at such a theological perspective. On the other hand, he appeals to the philosophical proposal of Gordon Kaufman, who suggests that it is the whole course of history that constitutes the one sovereign act of God, so that focus cannot and need not be made to the specific acts.[17] Thus the problem Hanson seeks to address is the concrete particularity of specific acts and the cosmic claim of God that is universal in scope.

Hanson's earlier book, *The Dawn of Apocalyptic*, with its paradigm of visionary/pragmatic, leads us to expect him to be dialectical in his presentation.[18] And we are not disappointed. In language strikingly similar to that of Westermann, he speaks of the "twin confession of deliverance and preservation."[19] Hanson is aware that every statement about Israel's faith, both as presented by Israel and as presumed in our study, must be dialectical. His statements on this include:

- synchronic/diachronic

- experience/tradition

- web of conditions/confessional heritage

- theological consolidation/prophetic creativity

- new event/heritage

The most comprehensive dialectic he proposes, however, is that of "cosmic vector and teleological vector," which he links to the visionary/pragmatic dialectic. By the cosmic vector, Hanson refers to a concern in the text that appeals to those who think in large terms

---

16. Hanson, *Dynamic Transcendence* (see chap. 1, n. 4), esp. 101 n. 8.

17. Cf. Kaufman, *God the Problem* (Cambridge: Harvard University Press, 1972), 119–47.

18. Hanson, *The Dawn of Apocalyptic* (Philadelphia: Fortress Press, 1975).

19. Ibid., 29.

about *structure and system* in reality, and he sees this as pertinent for those more philosophically inclined who discern reality systemically. By the teleological vector, he refers to those who think in more linear and concrete fashion of a series of new events on their way to a particular fulfillment. Such persons tend to focus on identifiable events discernable in the historical process. It is the particular merit of Hanson that he is attentive to the sociological element in tilting toward one or the other of these vectors:

> Historical sociological analysis can reconstruct the situation of each segment and plausibly explain why each responded as it did, given its particular social status, ideology, etc. That is to say, the hierocratic leaders tended to appeal to the need for ordered structures and the disenfranchised tended to envision divine intervention and reversal.[20]

Hanson argues that the entire theological community is needed to embrace this material adequately. No ideological bias in one direction or the other, for example, historical/philosophical, can dominate or deny the other its rightful place.

IV

These three books obviously come from very different directions with very different intents. Clearly, none is dependent on any other, although Westermann's previous work has been the most visible; but for these independent statements, the convergence of argument is important. Thus, we may correlate:

Westermann: deliverance/blessing,
Terrien: ethical/aesthetic,
Hanson: teleological/cosmic.[21]

---

20. Ibid., 68. For a more general discussion of sociological method and perspective, see Robert W. Friedrichs, *A Sociology of Sociology* (New York: Free Press, 1970).

21. I have not included in this discussion Ronald E. Clements, *Old Testament Theology: A Fresh Approach* (Atlanta: John Knox Press, 1979). I regard it as an important book that is related to the issues discussed here; however, Clements presents matters differently. He presumes a major move of the faith of Israel is from *cultic-* to *Torah*-centered religion. He does not present this as an ongoing dialectic but as a developmental move. Such a dialectic suggested by Clements could be seen as parallel to the three suggested here.

We must, of course, allow for differences of nuance and terminology, and I have no desire to flatten out the differences that are real. But with those allowances, the governing dialectic in each case bears strong resemblance to the other two. Thus, if we can consider the first member of each pair together, we have deliverance/ ethical/teleological. All these clearly make reference to the historical/ covenantal tradition upon which both Eichrodt and von Rad focused and to which Wright gave such singular attention. In the analysis of all three of our authors, this is legitimately understood as a confessing tradition that remembered and recited old particular memories and anticipated new divine disruptions not unlike those already known.

It is the second half of each pair, however, that interests us— blessing/aesthetic/cosmic—for it is the special intent of Westermann and especially Terrien to assert the legitimacy of this second element and to insist that without it, biblical faith is not well discerned. Hanson's agendum is somewhat different, but it comes to the same thing. Hanson argues that unless "act of God" be understood in terms of cosmic intentionality, "act of God" is only a slogan without hermeneutical effectiveness.

In proposing this dialectic in a variety of forms, Westermann, Terrien, and Hanson have offered a fresh paradigm for Old Testament theology that escapes the totalitarianism of Eichrodt's "center," and the historicism of von Rad's approach via the history of traditions. All three scholars admit the legitimacy of the historical/covenantal stress, but all three insist it must live in the presence of the alternative tradition that corrects, informs, and modifies.

V

The fact of this convergence from three very different perspectives is in itself important. I suspect that their appearance together has changed in irreversible ways the approaches that can be taken to Old Testament theology. One of the major intentions of all three scholars is surely to be celebrated: They intend to be genuinely ecumenical. Their ecumenism means that, as Christian scholars, they intend to be attentive to Jewish interpretation, tradition, and experience, and that they intend to point toward the New Testament in a much less mechanical and simplistic way. These two claims may seem to run in opposite directions, but both are surely important. Both will remove Old Testament theology from the isolation in which it has been widely practiced. Hanson especially has seen that the reality of the believing community is a constitutive factor in Old Testament interpretation and, therefore, that the ongoing claims of both synagogue and church must be taken into account.

A number of issues may be raised about this convergence of presentations. The following seem to be important at a first reading:

1. In what way is the central dialectic a genuine and well-balanced dialectic? And to what extent is the blessing/aesthetic/cosmic emphasis only a minority report that must not be given equal status? That, it would seem, is a crucial methodological issue. Perhaps it is the nature of a dialectic that this question can never be fully answered. But it makes a great deal of difference whether we begin with the assumption that the deliverance/ethical/teleological—that is, Mosaic—tradition is normative and that the other themes are critiques and challenges, or whether we view the two trajectories as equal partners to be taken with equal weight and seriousness.[22] I suspect that is an unfinished piece of business with von Rad.

The question is most apparent in Terrien. He is not unaware that the influence of the "religion of the eye" entered Israel in a decisive way with the temple and the accompanying Solomonic apparatus. Terrien is not unaware that this innovation was something of a syncretistic development in Israel. If Westermann's way of presentation is preferred, however, then it may be argued that the natural processes of life and death, birth and growth, are not late emergents or syncretistic developments but are simply a part of life experience and are there from the very beginning.

Terrien's way of presenting the issue leaves the matter open. On the one hand, he, along with Westermann, finds the dialectic well put already in the Torah. The traditions of creation and salvation history are together in Israel's most authoritative literature, the Torah of Moses. Yet Terrien's book is structured to suggest that the dialectic is to some extent between the old Mosaic material (Torah) and the psalmic-sapiential materials (*Kethubim*). Perhaps we are not required or permitted to choose between these; yet it would make a good deal of difference. If we take the dialectic in the Torah itself, then the aesthetic/cosmic dimension is essential and constitutive. If, on the other hand, we refer the aesthetic matter primarily to the

---

22. See Walter Brueggemann, "Trajectories in Old Testament Literature and the Sociology of Ancient Israel," *JBL* 98 (1979): 161–85.

Writings, then the aesthetic/cosmic materials are primarily critical and not constitutive, as James L. Crenshaw has seen so well.[23] Even though the dialectic has now been articulated, it is not clear to what extent it is a genuine dialectic and to what extent it is a *normative statement* together with a *sustained criticism* of it.

2. Closely related to the question of the status of the dialectic is the sociology of the dialectic. It should be apparent that the two trajectories—of deliverance/ethical/teleological and the counter of blessing/aesthetic/cosmic—are not socially disinterested. Hanson is most acutely aware of it, and Terrien only alludes to the matter. But the point is that the two trajectories embody alternative worldviews and different epistemologies, surely reflective of social circumstance, social vision, and social commitment.

If these dialectics are to become a paradigm for Old Testament theology, then decisions of a sociological kind will need to be made. The intrusion of sociology in our study (certainly recognized by all three of our authors) is not modernizing or appealing excessively to the social sciences, but it is an attempt both to hear the text faithfully and to be self-critical about the implications of scholarly methodology. By reference to the work of George E. Mendenhall and Norman K. Gottwald, even if details of their analyses are in dispute, it seems clear that the deliverance/ethical/teleological trajectory reflects a community not greatly benefited by present social arrangements and therefore hopeful for and prepared to receive an upheaval that would position them differently in terms of social power.[24] Conversely the hymnic tradition of those who affirmed the wonder, beauty, symmetry, and order of reality is not likely to be that of those who are denied the beauty or crushed by the order. Thus, the articulation of the dialectics now invites us to be attentive to the *social function* of the literature in forming, maintaining, and legitimating communities, in sanctioning and evoking change, in constructing and criticizing social reality.

3. The dialectic is closely related to the question of canon. It is the special merit of James A. Sanders to have shown that canon in Israel is characterized both by its stability and its flexibility.[25] On the one hand, there are some constants that are commonly affirmed, but

---

23. Crenshaw, "Popular Questioning of the Justice of God in Ancient Israel," in *Studies in Ancient Israelite Wisdom* (New York: Ktav Pub. House, 1976), 289–304.

24. See also the discussion of the work of Mendenhall and Gottwald in *JSOT* 7 (1978), for both summary and critical review.

25. Sanders, "Adaptable for Life" (see chap. 4, n. 26).

those constants lie behind the dialectic. Or is the dialectic itself the shape of the constant? The former would seem to be the argument of the older efforts at Old Testament theology. The latter may be the argument of our present writers. So we have the question: What is the stable factor? On the other hand, Sanders has shown that the canon endures and continues to be authoritative because it is flexible. But is its flexibility more or less at random, free to go this way and that? Or is there a kind of predictable ordering to the flexibility as it gets pushed toward one social group or another, one social perspective or another? Does the flexibility mean that each group can find what it wants? Or might it mean that each social group is met by what it does not want to encounter? Is the flexibility primarily *confrontational or accommodating*? Likely, Sanders would say it is flexible in being any or all of these.

4. The richness of the dialectic in these three discussions poses the question of *canon within the canon*. That now is the suspect phrase. So far as I am aware, of our three authors, only Hanson refers to it, and then somewhat critically.[26] But I wonder if both the dynamic of the dialectic and the flexibility/stability issue require us to pursue the question. Surely the dialectic did not develop as a whole piece but precisely by conflict in the community, a very partisan conflict over what was normative. Thus the term *canon* may be used in more than one way, both as the final form of the total literature (so Brevard Childs) or as the principle of criticism within the final form:[27]

a. The tri-part canon of the Old Testament itself suggests that perhaps the dialectic in its several forms is not balanced and symmetrical. Evidently the Torah is in some sense normative over the *Kethubim*. Both parts of the dialectic are certainly in the Torah itself, but not in a balanced way. Undoubtedly the deliverance/ethical/teleological motif dominated the Torah. So in some sense the ques-

---

26. Hanson, *Dynamic Transcendence*, 65.

27. Childs, in *Introduction* (see chap. 1, n. 6), concentrates on the completed product so that he is not interested in the conflictual processes by which it was formed. Indeed, his program is precisely to overcome inordinate attention to that process that tends to relativize the finished literature. The difference of perspective is noted by Sanders, in "Adaptable for Life," 552 n. 1. Childs's perspective precludes any consideration of "canon within the canon," for the literature is seen of a piece in its present form. But note Sanders's comments on "canon within the canon" in the same note. It is an important distinction to make, because discussions about canon can thus go in very different directions. There is currently a tendency to lump all such discussions together.

tion of canon discerns the dialectic as an interaction of Torah and
Writings, surely not an equal interaction.

   b. With the criticism, if not rejection, of von Rad's credo hypothesis, one may wonder if within the Torah some parts hold priority
or are more decisive.[28] It is perhaps a new question in light of these
three discussions. It is my impression, however, that the criticism
of von Rad's hypothesis concerns the *critical ground* on which it is
founded but not the *substantive claim* he made for the theological
intentionality of the literature.

   c. At least Westermann and Terrien (and perhaps in a different
way Hanson) have written to urge a corrective balance. On the short
term, the urging of that balance is a protest against the overem-
phasis given to the historical/covenantal tradition that by itself is
particularistic and narrow. That may be a fair, objective urging, or
it may be simply a reflection of our own circumstance as scholars
and believers. Either way, we should recognize that the great vitality of the covenant emphasis did not arise from the "Hittite Treaty
Hypothesis" but from the situation of the Confessing Church in Germany, vis-à-vis the rise of National Socialism. Thus, in Basel there
was not only the more or less objective work of Eichrodt but the
passion of Karl Barth, who has greatly influenced a whole generation of exegetes. Historical reality, therefore, requires more of us
than the yearning to be free from a partisan, uncritical "kerygmatic"
emphasis.[29] It requires that we take account of the interrelatedness
of historical circumstance and interpretive emphasis. It is clear that
however it might have been verbalized, the "German Christians" had
preempted the trajectory of blessing/aesthetic/cosmic in a new fertil-
ity religion. Appeal was made to the more radical trajectory to find
standing ground for social criticism. This is not to say it was "correct"
but to observe that the practice of canon within canon and the tilt of

---

   28. On the various critiques of von Rad's credo hypothesis, see Gottwald, *Tribes* (see
chap. 1, n. 6), 723 nn. 72–73, for a bibliography.

   29. On the cruciality of covenant for Barth, see *Church Dogmatics*, vol. 3, no. 1 (Edinburgh: T. & T. Clark, 1958), and vol. 4, no. 1 (1956), chap. 13. On the influence
of Barth on exegetical presuppositions and the movement beyond Barth, see Erhard
Gerstenberger, "Psalms," in *Old Testament Form Criticism* (see chap. 4, n. 40), 184–88.
Gerstenberger notes (p. 193) the possible connection of Eichrodt to Barth concerning
the covenant as a governing metaphor. The movement away from the perspectives of
Barth cannot be doubted, but perhaps it indicates a lack of self-knowledge and self-
criticism to view this as a liberation and an unqualified advance. On the character
and significance of Barth's exegesis, see Childs, *Biblical Theology* (see chap. 1, n. 13),
110–12.

the dialectic are not unrelated to the matters of interest, worldview, and social setting.

d. Obviously the believer and the scholar are now in a very different time and place from that generation that tilted interpretation toward covenant. Perhaps it is important to recognize that our time and place are not superior to or better than. It is simply our time and place. It may be a time and place when such confessional vitality is not appropriate or at least not felt. But that should be assessed knowingly.

In our time and place, as these three discussions make clear, it is important to preserve the dialectic, to try to see it whole, and to honor the balance that is there. But that should be done with self-knowledge and not with any pretense that we do so with more objectivity, neutrality, or detachment than the generation of the 1930s and 1940s. We do so because our scholarly paradigms are also heavily shaped by our circumstance. Our circumstance just now is one of some ease between the confession community and the academy, reflected nowhere more clearly than in the desire for a "general hermeneutic" that applies general literary criticism to the Bible "like every other document." That may be a correct way just now, but we should not miss the hermeneutical commitments that are implicit in such a decision. It would seem ludicrous in retrospect to have expected that generation of the 1930s and 1940s to have utilized such a perspective.

Two matters seem clear about such a movement of ease: First, the intention to hold the dialectic in balance and to see the matter whole is itself an important *sociological decision*. It is to accept *a holistic epistemology that moves away from passion and commitment* to a scholarly stance removed from the intense claims of some of the material; that is, the maintainers of such a neat dialectic are not likely to be the ones who defy pharaoh for the sake of freedom. Such a decision appears to be an appropriate posture, but we should be aware that we are doing it. Second, it is clear that such a balanced view that refuses to take a side in the dialectic, appropriate as it may be, is not one from which any critical faith could be mounted. I do not suggest that such a critical faith should be mounted but that such a practice of a balanced dialectic is indeed a decision about it, even if unwittingly made.

e. Although we are attracted so much to a dialectic mode of thought, the question of canon within the canon is not silenced. It is kept alive especially in the liberation movements that refuse such a balanced dialectic. They see it as silencing particularity, as deadening the critical principle, and as incompatible with the Bible and the God of the Bible, both of which are viewed as having a bias toward the "have-nots."[30]

How are we to face that issue? Do we finally arrive at a break between the academy and the confessing community? That, I suggest, is an area we must pursue. We must take care that dialectical thinking as embodied in these three studies is not used to cover over either the pain or the passionate hearing of the text that takes place in other quarters. I do not suggest that is the intent of any of our three authors, each of whom is acutely sensitive to these matters. Nor do I suggest that our paradigms for disciplined study should be dictated by self-serving interpretations. But this consideration does remind us that there are no paradigms of study, even properly dialectic ones, that do not move back toward economic reality and its accompanying epistemology. Willy-nilly, our perspectives and paradigms are also not free of self-serving.

5. Finally, one other comment on the dialectic is suggested here. Hanson pays attention to the current issue of diachronic and synchronic interpretations, and the matter is implicit in the pairs presented by Terrien and Westermann. I am especially helped by Hanson's analysis. He suggests that this methodological issue is not an isolated question we are free to resolve on "objective" grounds. It has intense substantive implications. Hanson does not go so far as to correlate diachronic/synchronic with his larger dialectic of teleological/cosmic, but he does offer hints that are worth pursuing.

How one regards the matter of diachronic and synchronic ways depends on how one perceives the issue. There is no doubt that synchronic, that is, systemic, interpretation is welcome, if by diachronic is meant the kind of flat analytical approach that never yields meanings. By these three studies, I am moved to ask two questions about diachronic and synchronic, both of a sociological kind:

  a. If we assume that the general form of dialectic presented in these studies is correct, could it be that we must correlate diachronic/synchronic to the two kinds of texts so that texts of the deliverance/

---

30. See Lee Cormie, "The Hermeneutical Privilege of the Oppressed," *Catholic Theological Society of America Proceedings* 33 (1978): 155–81. On the matter of "canon within the canon," see the perceptive comments of Jon D. Levenson, "The Davidic Covenant and Its Modern Interpreters," *CBQ* 41 (1979): 214–15. He rightly distinguishes between history of religion and theology concerning the legitimacy of canon within the canon. But after all, our concern here is not history of religion, but theology.

ethical/theological must be diachronically discerned and, conversely, that texts reflecting matters of blessing/aesthetic/cosmic should be synchronically understood? This is not to suggest, for example, that the historical character of the Song of Moses (Exodus 15) should be protected as a thirteenth-century event; rather, it may be seen as a statement concerning a once-for-all (deliverance) commitment-demanding (ethical) break of newness (teleological). And perhaps to treat it synchronically, whatever one's intent, serves to dull the particularity and silence the scandal of newness, so that it can be contained in a systemic and closed epistemology.[31] Conversely, such a correlation of synchronic/diachronic with the other matters discussed here may suggest that any attempt to understand texts in the blessing/aesthetic/cosmic vector in any way but synchronically denies to them the character and claim they mean to make.

b. In this series of quite provisional wonderments, I come finally to the most provisional of my wonderments, namely the sociology of scholars who practice these dialectics in various ways. Where we work and with whom, where we publish and for whom, surely reflect both economic and epistemological commitments. That in turn may help locate interpreters in relation to these two vectors in various ways (and see texts characteristically in one way or another). My unscientific impression is that the closer a researcher is to a confessing community, the more likely interpretation will reflect a commitment that is of the deliverance/ethical/teleological variety and therefore be drawn to a method that reflects particularity. Conversely, the more one is placed in the academic context of commitment only to objectivity, the more texts are likely to be handled systemically, that is, in terms of a closed set of signs that manage to contain newness and reduce particularities to typologies. Such a placement would appear to be crucial for one's canon within the canon (that is, the material one prefers to study) and one's method of interpretation. It would seem to me, both in terms of the *substance* of the dialectic and our use of *methods*, that the point is not that we should be committed enough or objective enough to tilt in one direction or another, but rather that we practice enough self-knowledge and self-criticism to be aware of what we are doing. The choice of substance as well as

---

31. See the comment of John Collins, "The 'Historical Character' of the Old Testament in Recent Biblical Theology," *CBQ* 41 (1979): 199–204, which seeks to go behind the convention of "history and myth" to speak about historicizing paradigms. His attention to different kinds of claims for different kinds of literatures is salutary, moving beyond simplistic alternatives.

the practice of method are likely to be in the service of "preservation or liberation," either in appreciation of a system or in challenge
to that system. Such a criticism of our criticism might serve to affirm
in telling ways that matters of substance and method are elusive and
subject to corruption.

6

Futures in Old Testament Theology

THE ONLY TWO THINGS sure about Old Testament theology now are:

1. The ways of Walther Eichrodt and Gerhard von Rad are no longer adequate.

2. There is no consensus among us about what comes next.

So it is not only a time of uncertainty. It is also a time of experimentation in which many things may be tried. On the one hand, one is sure to be criticized regardless of what one does; but on the other hand, one is unlikely to be criticized too deeply, because no one is sure.

These four points occur to me:

1. The distinction of "what is meant" and "what it means," between descriptive and normative articulations (most clearly stated by Krister Stendahl),[1] is increasingly disregarded, overlooked, or denied. That may be good or bad, but it is happening. No doubt there are many reasons for that. Most directly, the reason is our hermeneutical awareness that between the text and any theological rendering of it, there is, in David Kelsey's words, "imaginative construal."[2] And that imaginative construal is never obvious in or dictated by the text itself, but it is always in some way the constructive, creative work of

---

1. Stendahl, "Biblical Theology, Contemporary," in *IDB* (New York: Abingdon Press, 1962), 1:419–20.

2. Kelsey, *The Uses of Scripture in Recent Theology* (Philadelphia: Fortress Press, 1975), esp. 159, 163, 215.

the renderer, no matter how tightly the descriptive task is intended. Thus, as we may have more interest in what it "means," we may be less sanguine and more suspicious about any statement of "what is meant."

One can hardly take in the extent to which that hermeneutical self-awareness has changed things. Such self-awareness about our constructive role was undoubtedly known to be operative when Stendahl wrote, but it was not at all practiced or even acknowledged among us. And now one cannot utter an interpretative word without hermeneutical self-awareness. That makes the task much more delicate, as well as much more risky and free. Indeed, it may immobilize or cause failure of nerve. The emergence of hermeneutical questions was in the first instant simply an intellectual development, but that intellectual development surely reflects what Langdon Gilkey calls "an ending of the Enlightenment."[3] Gilkey has written on the problematic of distinguishing what it meant and what it means.[4] Our context is not the positivism either of objective critical scholarship (which purports to be descriptive) or of a theological kind (which claims to give objective norms). Our context puts the creative, constructive role of the interpreter under scrutiny.

2. In some ways, the practice of Old Testament theology is continuous with and builds upon all other methods and disciplines in the field. In some other ways, however, it is distinctive, distinctive because the word "theology" makes a claim. Old Testament theology is not simply a synonym for "value" or "meaning," but it has implicit within it a substantive acknowledgment. Or to say it another way, Old Testament theology is not free to handle the text only in relation to its "sense" but also must attend to its "reference." The very notion of biblical theology indicates a very different judgment about the character of the text.

That issue, I think, is clearest when Old Testament theology is assessed alongside the important practices of rhetorical criticism and the newer modes of literary criticism. Those approaches are peculiarly fitted to speak about the meaning and sense of the text. Brevard S. Childs has observed how his approach to canon has im-

---

3. Gilkey, *Society and the Sacred: Toward a Theology of Culture in Decline* (New York: Crossroad, 1981), esp. 4. See his summary statement, "The New Watershed in Theology," *Soundings* 64 (1981): 118–31.

4. Gilkey, "The Roles of the 'Descriptive' or 'Historical' and of the 'Normative' in Our Work," *Criterion* 20 (1981): 10–17.

portant commonalities with those approaches.[5] But quite explicitly, in those disciplines, the meaning and sense are said to be contained only within the text, indeed evoked by this particular text. Such an approach rightly urges a peculiar match between the mode of expression (irony, lyric) and the subject expressed (holy mystery). But it is all there in the text. Old Testament theology is not permitted to get by so nicely. It presumes that there is a reference not fully held in the text to which the text is referred. It is a tricky responsibility to ask about that reference as disclosed in other texts or in any part of the life of the community that lives before and after the moment of the sense in this text.

I suggest that means, willy-nilly, that one who practices Old Testament theology, as distinct from rhetorical or literary criticism or history of religion, is likely to understand one's self as nurtured by and accountable to a concrete community of reference that has already decided some things. That means that there is likely to be something of a partisan quality that rubs at two points. It rubs, first of all, against the academy whose claim it is to withhold every partisan commitment, even though this is not true in fact. Second, it rubs against the hermeneutical notion that wants to keep every statement of commitment in some kind of state of tentativeness. I think that we must recognize that doing Old Testament theology requires that such decisions of reference cannot be held in abeyance and must be acknowledged as proper to the work, and they are proper to the work even if subject to close scrutiny. The scrutiny, however, must not be *that* such a decision of reference has been made but *what* it is in particular. Thus a community of faith must make a decision about reference. The academy may criticize and assess the decision, but it may not fault the community or the proposal of a theology for having made such a decision.

3. The problem of doing Old Testament theology, I suspect, is that we desire to replicate the architectural comprehensiveness of Eichrodt and von Rad. We would like at the beginning to have a comprehensive paradigm that relates all the parts to each other, and it is immobilizing not to have one. But because our discipline (and indeed our culture) is in a time of scattering—intellectual and otherwise—such comprehensive models are not likely to emerge quickly. In the meantime, we seem to be reduced to problems that may or may not eventually lead to comprehensive models. So it is my im-

---

5. Childs, *Introduction* (see chap. 1, n. 6), 74–75.

pression that methodologically, Old Testament theology must and may proceed by the offer of theses for conversation and critique without exposition that includes and accounts for everything. The theses may not add up to a grand design, but they may permit the building of a consensus about the shape and character of the task. My urging here is that we not judge ourselves or others by the mode of grand design but that we accept a mode probably more appropriate to our cultural moment of scattering and our intellectual moment of the hermeneutical self-knowledge.

Having said that, by trial and error (in contrast to the abrupt designs of Eichrodt and von Rad), it does seem to me that a shape for Old Testament theology is indeed emerging. That fresh shape, to which I have pointed elsewhere,[6] is also represented in the work of both James A. Sanders and Paul D. Hanson. That shape is hardly a grand design, but it does suggest a way to proceed that is reflective of our situation. I refer to the "two trajectories," which Hanson variously calls "visionary/pragmatic," "teleological/cosmic," or "form/reform,"[7] and which Sanders refers to as "prophetic/constitutive." In other contexts that may be characterized as "covenantal/sapiential," or "ethical/aesthetic." The terms are not precise, and precision is not important for our purposes.[8]

The point to be made is that we might cease to ask about a *center* for Old Testament theology[9] and ask about boundaries, edges, limits, parameters, within which faith proceeds and beyond which it may not legitimately go. It appears to me that on every great theme or conviction, one may find in the Old Testament a debate that at some points is heated and at many other points goes along unresolved and that at some point may come to resolution or consensus. One may characterize the boundaries around the matter of cultural *embrace* and cultural *criticism*; that is, in every issue, one may ask the extent to which Israel borrows, appropriates, coheres with the general practices of the ancient Near Eastern culture and the extent to which it makes its own distinctive statement out of its own concrete

---

6. See chap. 5 and Brueggemann, "Trajectories" (see chap. 5, n. 22).

7. Hanson uses the terms variously in *Dawn* (see chap. 5, n. 18), and in *Dynamic Transcendence* (see chap. 1, n. 4). In his *Diversity* (see chap. 1, n. 4), 16, he uses the poles of "form" and "reform."

8. Sanders, *God Has a Story Too*, 17, 132–33, and his more programmatic statement on the same issues, "Hermeneutics" (for both, see chap. 1, n. 4).

9. On the quest for a center, see esp. Rudolf Smend, *Die Mitte des Alten Testaments*, ThStud, no. 101 (Zurich: EVZ Verlag, 1970). See the review of the issue of a center by Henning Graf Reventlow, *Problems* (see chap. 1, n. 1).

experience, which has the effect of transforming cultural forms and values.[10] One may characterize the boundaries around the economic categories of *haves* and *have-nots*, with the derivative political yearning for equilibrium or transformation.[11] One may sense it around the debate that Israel is "like the nations" or is *'am qādôš* about God, who is sovereign in conventional ways and faithful in the ways of pathos. When the search for a center is given up, we do not need to find a right or normative answer given on any one of these questions. It is clear, however, that in both directions, at both parameters, there are limits beyond which Israel does not go in its texts. And these limits beyond which Israel does not go set the parameters for Old Testament theology. Then one may explore the tension and dynamic between the edge-points. I suggest that the work of Hanson and Sanders is well suited for such an exploration, not yet undertaken in a programmatic way.

Two comments: First, I suggest that where an Old Testament theologian locates herself or himself in study is reflective of her or his reference group, academic or ecclesiastical;[12] and, therefore, we may attend much more to the reference group in discerning the decisions which shape the study, for every study is shaped by some reference group. Second, in such a way, I am interested in the tendency of scholars who operate at a parameter of cultural embrace, wherein there is a tendency to discern Israel more, rather than less, like the nations. Regularly in such discussions, it is averred that in this "one respect," Israel is distinctive. It is odd but worth noting that that "one respect" is not the same among various scholars but regularly is found somewhere. All are agreed that there is at least one aspect of distinctiveness midst the much commonality, and that seems to me to be the shape of much of the current discussion. How we tilt depends not so much on the text, but on our communities of reference. I think, for example, that von Rad's community of reference in the Confessing Church of the 1930s has not been sufficiently taken into account in assessing his credo hypothesis or, indeed, in seeing the shift he made in the 1960s toward an emphasis on wisdom. Such

---

10. See chaps. 1 and 2 as well as the carefully nuanced statement of Patrick D. Miller, "God and the Gods" (see chap. 1, n. 10).

11. Norman K. Gottwald has posed the question of boundaries in exceedingly sharp terms in *Tribes* (see chap. 1, n. 6). Gottwald has made the point well that Old Testament theology cannot ignore the critical issues of sociology and social theory.

12. Note that Childs, in "Some Reflections" (see chap. 1, n. 33), has urged that both academic and ecclesiastical references are legitimate and essential to the intellectual task of biblical theology.

a way might permit us to understand our own efforts better without imagining them to be "the new truth."

4. Finally, a comment in three parts on the future task of Old Testament Theology:

a. It may be a scandalous and idle hope, but I would wish for a cessation of the endless formal reflections on method, which stay with form and do not touch substance. It seems to me that the field has now been sufficiently surveyed. We are now as free as we are likely to be of the old paradigms. There is now need for substantive proposals. It is my judgment that what is now needed are probes of a substantive kind about the theological claims and affirmations of this text. Those substantive probes surely must reflect hermeneutical decisions and move beyond such decisions to substantive articulations and, no doubt, commitments reflective of communities of reference that will be criticized. Such substantive probes are likely to serve us best, but those can be made only in the context of a community of reference. Grand design is possible when one is above such communities, but I think such aloofness is now unlikely or impossible.

b. I do not understand Jürgen Habermas very much, but I want to comment on his move from hermeneutical to anticipatory modes of knowledge.[13] The hermeneutical enterprise by itself may lead to a relativizing, so that we end up being unable to say anything because we are so aware of our own relative vantage points. Habermas, however, has urged that we practice anticipatory knowledge, which hopes for a social vision yet to be given.

That is, I submit, pertinent to us. Jews and Christians will agree that these texts are in their main reference anticipatory, either in the Old Testament or in the New Testament, as the coming Kingdom or the coming Messiah.[14] That means that the texts are inevitably critical of the way things now are and unreservedly in hope of an alternative to be given. This may be the point at which Old Testament

---

13. Habermas, *Knowledge and Human Interests* (Boston: Beacon Press, 1971). See the helpful commentary by Thomas McCarthy, *The Critical Theory of Jürgen Habermas* (Cambridge: MIT Press, 1979).

14. I take it to be agreed and not in need of argument that biblical theology of the future will have in some way to be a conversation between Jewish and Christian discernments. A splendid prolegomenon for such an undertaking is provided by Paul van Buren, in *Discerning the Way* (see chap. 2, n. 4). Note especially David Tracy's shrewd judgment on the difference such an agenda can make, in "Religious Values after the Holocaust: A Catholic View," in *Jews and Christians after the Holocaust*, ed. Abraham J. Peck (Philadelphia: Fortress Press, 1982), 87–107.

theology is distinguished from all other parts of Old Testament study that are rightly analytical and not anticipatory. So the debate at the two parameters that I have suggested is not just a controversy about how it is, but it is a freighted, interest-filled conversation about what will be.

c. This leads to the third element of this point. If we need to move from formal to substantive matters, and if the texts are elementally anticipatory, then I suggest that Old Testament theology cannot be left at the margin of our interest. Nor can we wait until we become so seasoned that we can no longer write monographs. These texts make claims that are of great urgency in our common life. Otherwise, we would not spend our life on them. It is important that we are not so fascinated with method, so content with writing for each other, so preoccupied with subjective niceties that we do not have our say to the human culture around us out of these texts. That is, is it not, the purpose of humanistic study?

I do not want to be a reductionist. But I submit that there is general agreement among us—Jews and Christians, liberals and conservatives, philologists and rhetorical critics—about the main claims of this tradition that matter to any culture caught in technique, consumed in fear, and capable of such inhumaneness and exploitation as we now witness. I do not suggest that our discipline be used for propaganda, ideology, or partisanship. That is why the theological enterprise is always kept under a discipline of critical methods. But I suggest that Old Testament theology is an enterprise that must participate in the life of the mind and body (politic), for these texts do disclose an alternative world. My wonderment is whether, in the interest of precision and niceties and our fascination with methodology, we have not forgotten what it means to take the text theologically. Such a theological reception of the text may yield nothing immediate, but it may mediate truth and therefore life in the face of the ideologies around us. The purpose of each study is to try to articulate the main claims of the text. Those main claims, few of us would doubt, could matter to our culture, but some in our culture have a great stake in keeping our study marginalized in scholarly niceties in order to keep the main claims from visibility. The way to do that is to stay with formal issues in the avoidance of substantive claims, to be endlessly critical, to avoid any act of anticipation. Doing biblical theology is obviously difficult. It could also disturb critical slumber.

7

Old Testament Theology as a Particular Conversation: Adjudication of Israel's Sociotheological Alternatives

IT IS CLEAR THAT WE must probe new ways of organization in Old Testament theology. Neither the thematic organization around a single motif, as proposed by Walther Eichrodt, nor the alternative of a recital of traditions, as modeled by Gerhard von Rad, claims scholarly assent any longer. In a variety of ways, many scholars now propose a bipolar scheme that juxtaposes two emphases that live in vital and apparently irresolvable tension.[1]

My own proposal is that one pole, the conserving, constructive tradition, be understood as "the legitimation of structure," whether that be moral, theological, social, political, or economic structure, and that the other pole, the transformative, critical tradition, be understood as "the embrace of pain."[2] This second pole reflects the anguished recognition that no legitimation of structure fully takes into account the specificity, immediacy, and harshness of pain as it is experienced by those not fully valued by the legitimated structure. I have argued that this tension lies at the core of the dynamic of Old Testament faith and that it is definitional for Israel's understanding of God, for Israel's characterization of human persons, and for Israel's strategy for organizing public life.

---

1. On the status of Old Testament theology, see George Hasel, "Biblical Theology: Then, Now, and Tomorrow," *HBT* 4 (1982): 61–93; and Henning Graf Reventlow, "Basic Problems" (see chap. 5, n. 1). See also chap. 5.

2. See chaps. 1 and 2.

My beginning point is to explore in more detail this bipolar way of organizing the Old Testament material and to consider the processes by which this dialectic was maintained and kept alive in Israel's faith and life.

Aniconic God

Old Testament faith is actively and vigorously *aniconic;* that is, the God of Israel cannot and will not be represented in any visible, manageable form.[3] The Commandments of the Torah center around Yahweh's aniconic character. Von Rad, Walther Zimmerli, and Werner H. Schmidt have shown that the first two Commandments of the Decalogue (Exod. 20:3-6) are at the very center of God's self-presentation.[4] From the outset, this God will be unaccompanied by any other divine agent in Israel's life, will claim full allegiance, and will share that loyalty with none other. For our purposes, the Second Commandment is even more decisive. This God must not be articulated in any fixed, stable, predictable form. It is in the very character of this God to be free, unaccompanied, and unencumbered.

This, of course, does not suggest that God has no form. Such anthropomorphic language as God's eye, hand, and heart, show that Israel had no capacity or inclination to deny or speak without reference to God's embodied person. Indeed, even in God's startling self-disclosure to Moses, God's face may not be seen, but God's back is seen (Exod. 33:23). It is not that God has no form, but that that form is not available to Israel. This insistence is at the center of the profound theological reflection of Deut. 4:1-31. The primal meeting at Sinai is remembered and presented as a meeting with a voice, but with no form (vv. 12, 15). The voice sounds commandments that will be obeyed. The denial of form precludes images. The voice of commandment sets the primal mode of meeting as one between sovereign and obedient subject. The preclusion of images assures

---

3. Patrick D. Miller, in "Israelite Religion," in *Hebrew Bible* (see chap. 3, n. 9), recognizes an aniconic inclination as a distinctive mark of Israel's religion: "While various proposals have been put forward to identify central elements of discontinuity or uniqueness in Israel's religion, the most likely candidates are the initial demands of the Decalogue, the claim of exclusive worship by Yahweh, and the aniconic requirement" (pp. 211–12).

4. Von Rad, *Old Testament Theology I* (see chap. 1, n. 22), 203–19; Zimmerli, *Old Testament Theology in Outline* (Atlanta: John Knox Press, 1978), 109–24; and Schmidt, *The Faith of the Old Testament* (Philadelphia: Westminster Press, 1983), 69–84.

God's priority and precludes Israel's management of God. God will command and not be managed. Israel will obey and not administer God.

The aniconic character of Israel's God implies more, however, than an absence of images. To stay with issues of religious phenomenology is to miss the point of Israel's theological affirmation concerning Yahweh's incomparable character. The aniconic God of Israel is contrasted with all the other gods who are well-known in Israel's tradition.[5] Yahweh's incomparability is expressed in various ways:

1. Yahweh is an inscrutable *novum* in Israel's memory. God's way with Israel had an identifiable break point, a beginning point. Israel does not raise metaphysical questions but deals with historical memories. In the various traditions that we have conventionally designated as J, E, D, and P, it is clear that Israel probed a number of hypotheses about Yahweh's first being present to and known in Israel. Whether one follows either J's innocent proposal that Yahweh was always known[6] or the more self-conscious suggestions of E (Exod. 3:14)[7] and P (Exod. 6:2)[8] that Yahweh was known only in the events around Moses, it is clear that Israel was dazzled by this God that was unlike other gods. This God has created fresh historical possibilities for Israel, certainly in the slave community of Moses but also in the barrenness of Abraham and Sarah. Yahweh's readiness to act unlike gods characteristically act is narrated by Israel, but the intrusion that creates historical possibility is covered in hiddenness, for the name of the God who hears Israel's cry (Exod. 2:23-25) is and

---

5. Yehezkel Kaufmann, in *The Religion of Israel* (Chicago: University of Chicago Press, 1960), has most militantly insisted upon this characteristic. See the critical commentary on Kaufmann by Jon D. Levenson, "Yehezkel Kaufmann and Mythology," *Conservative Judaism* 36, no. 2 (1982): 36–43. Kaufmann understands the issue from inside the tradition whereas Levenson attempts to present the material as a critical observer. These different postures clearly lead to different perspectives. My effort here is to understand how Israel's own insider perspective construed the issues.

6. The classic statement concerning the relation of Yahweh in the Moses traditions and the antecedents in the Genesis materials is that of Albrecht Alt, "God of the Fathers" (see chap. 3, n. 7). Norman K. Gottwald, in *Tribes* (see chap. 1, n. 6), esp. chap. 43, makes use of Alt's paradigm to propose a pre-Yahwistic Elohism that has both continuity and discontinuity with the radicalness of Yahwism.

7. On the matter of continuity and discontinuity reflected in Exod. 3:14, see Frank M. Cross, *Canaanite Myth and Hebrew Epic* (Cambridge: Harvard University Press, 1973), 44–75.

8. Zimmerli, in *I Am Yahweh* (Atlanta: John Knox Press, 1982), 7–13, has focused on Exod. 6:2 as crucial for Yahweh's self-disclosure.

remains enigmatic.[9] Not only will this God show no form, but even God's name is given so that it is not accessible to Moses and Israel. Thus, not only is the eye prohibited access to God, but even the ear is given only partial entry to the inscrutability.[10]

2. Nor is Yahweh's aniconic character articulated in a vacuum without reference to the other gods. On the contrary, Yahweh's character is articulated with direct reference to, and in tension with, the other gods. Because Yahweh's character concerns relation to the other gods and is conflictual, the language of Yahweh's character and self-presentation is political in its tone and implications. Thus the First Commandment, "There will be no other gods before me," means that the throne room of Yahweh's sovereignty will brook no rival, entertain no alliance, share no splendor.[11]

Yahweh's unencumberedness precludes alliances with the other gods. This is not formally stated until the exilic period, but it is definitional for Yahweh. In the P materials of Exodus 14, in which Yahweh joins issue with the gods of Egypt, Yahweh asserts, "I will get glory over pharaoh" (Exod. 14:4, 17). The getting of glory, acquiring of sovereign splendor, clearly means the routing of other claimants who happened to be allied with the royal power of pharaoh.[12] In Second Isaiah, where Yahweh is in conflict with Babylonian gods and Babylonian imperial power, the claim is parallel, "My glory I will share with no other" (Isa. 42:8, 48:11). Yahweh will not share glory with Babylonian gods or political authority with Babylonian authorities. Thus, at the two pivot points, vis-à-vis Egyptian power in the early period and vis-à-vis Babylonian power in the late period, Yahweh will not be confused with, traffic with, or even deal with the

---

9. Dennis McCarthy, in "Exodus 3:14: History, Philology and Theology," *CBQ* 40 (1978): 311–22, has advanced the discussion by proposing that we desist from etymological judgments and pay attention to the function of the passage in its context. McCarthy's urging is an important critique of a great deal of scholarship that has not been noticeably productive.

10. Samuel Terrien, in *Elusive Presence* (see chap. 1, n. 4), has especially contrasted the religion of ear and eye. See also Jon D. Levenson, *Sinai and Zion* (New York: Crossroad, 1985), 150.

11. Henning Graf Reventlow, in *Gebot und Predigt in Dekalog* (Gütersloh: Gerd Mohn, 1962), 26–28, has proposed that the so-called First Commandment is not a commandment but a decree from the throne concerning the actual state of affairs in the throne room of Yahweh.

12. On the triumph and power of Yahweh's presence in this tradition, see Thomas W. Mann, *Divine Presence and Guidance in Israelite Traditions: The Typology of Exaltation* (Baltimore: Johns Hopkins University Press, 1977), chap. 5. On the same theme in another context, see P. D. Miller and J. J. M. Roberts, *The Hand of the Lord* (Baltimore: Johns Hopkins University Press, 1977).

other gods who are allied with the empires. Yahweh's aniconic character has political implications because Yahweh is unlike the other
gods whom the empire has forced into iconic roles for the sake of
legitimation of royal power.

3. Yahweh's aniconic character, as it articulates Yahweh as a historical *novum* with Israel and as it polemicizes against the gods of the
empire, moves Yahweh's self-identity in a peculiar direction. Yahweh is unencumbered with reference to the other gods, unwilling
to share glory, unallied with the other gods, rejecting the gods of
the empire. Yahweh's aniconic identity distances Israel's God from
the conventional ways in which gods are imaged by the practitioners
of and pretenders to imperial power. Yahweh's imageless character
means that Yahweh is disengaged from the ways of worldly power.

The stunning outcome of Yahweh's aniconic character leads to
a surprising "therefore. . . ." The "therefore" is remarkable, unexpected, inscrutable. We do not know how it follows, but it does
follow in Israel's portrayal of this God. That Yahweh is unencumbered permits/causes Yahweh to be allied with and engaged for the
marginal ones who go by the name of Yahweh.[13] Yahweh's foundational characteristic is that having an imageless identity makes
Yahweh available for and attentive to those who do not participate in the image-making, image-enhancing, image-producing, and
image-consuming ways of imperial life.[14]

This odd move on Yahweh's part is articulated in the theologically
primitive poem of Psalm 82, in which a new argument for the character of godness is presented. Formally, throughout the ancient Near
East and throughout the heavenly realm, the assumption has been
that godness consists in omniscience, omnipresence, and so forth.
Dramatically, these criteria for godness cause Yahweh, the God of
Israel, to join issue with and dispute the other gods and finally to

---

13. The matter of this alliance has been articulated on the most rigorous critical
grounds by Gottwald, *Tribes*, chap. 49. The subtopic of the chapter is "Mutual Rein-
forcement of Yahwism and Social Egalitarianism." Gottwald's argument is intended,
I believe, to permit either a theological or a sociological reading. That alliance of
course is pivotal for much liberation theology and is encapsulated succinctly in the
Conference of Medellín's reference to a "preferential option for the poor."

14. It is exceedingly important and often unnoticed that the stuff of idols is characteristically silver and gold. That is, visible location of God happens characteristically
where there is surplus of precious metals. It does not follow that those without such
surplus wealth do not seek to locate God, but clearly they cannot do it so well, so
convincingly, or so visibly. The juxtaposition is an important critical point and not
an accident of circumstance. A critical understanding of fetishism is pertinent to the
connection.

separate from them. Appropriately, the ultimatum of Psalm 82 is not a hymnic statement of order (as might be done in the equilibrium of the empire) but an imperative addressed to the gods by the voice of the marginal, petitioning Yahweh to make a move appropriate to the new definition of God:

> Give justice to the weak and fatherless;
> maintain the right of the afflicted and the destitute;
> Rescue the weak and the needy;
> deliver them from the hand of the wicked. (Vv. 3-4)[15]

This same presentation of Yahweh's distinctiveness is found in the pivotal Song of Moses (Exod. 15:1-18). The hymn asks doxologically, "Who is as Yahweh?" The implied answer is "None."[16] But the hymn not only asserts Yahweh's incomparability. It specifies the incomparability of this God who is unencumbered, shares no glory, and asserts a new criterion for godness. The specificity is that this Yahweh challenges and opposes pharaoh and all the theological claims of the empire. The power of this God is mobilized for the slave community against the claims of the empire. To be imageless is the other side of Yahweh's propensity to be allied with those who are excluded from the safe, privileged world of religious image. Because gold and silver are the stuff of images, Yahweh will not be associated with all the accumulations of silver and gold, that is, with all such monopolies of religious aggrandizement.

The *monopoly of glory* (not shared with Egyptian and Babylonian imperial gods) and *attentiveness to marginality* (attending to the needy) are twin aspects of Yahweh's aniconic identity. Yahweh is unimpressed with the splendor of images in relation to the practice of the gods. That leaves Yahweh free to pay attention precisely to those who are nullified by the practice of images and the social

---

15. On an interpretive perspective that reflects this affirmation, see the collection of essays edited by Willy Schottroff, *The God of the Lowly* (Maryknoll, N.Y.: Orbis Books, 1984).

16. On Yahweh's incomparability, see C. J. Labuschagne, *The Incomparability of Yahweh in the Old Testament* (Leiden: Brill, 1966). The incomparability is most eloquently and powerfully articulated in Isaiah 40–55, which follows the trajectory of Exodus 15. The primal poem of Exodus 15 ends with a reference to a settled place, to be sure; but in the context of the exodus narrative, that settled place surely attends both to Yahweh's freedom and Israel's liberation. To interpret otherwise fails to take into account the social intentionality of the poem. The sociopolitical implications of Second Isaiah's liturgic assertions are not difficult to discern.

monopoly they legitimate. This remarkable convergence of themes is well articulated in the doxology of Isa. 57:15:

> For thus says the high and lofty One
>   who inhabits eternity, whose name is Holy;
> I dwell in the high and holy place,
>   and also with the one who is of a contrite and humble spirit,
> to revive the spirit of the humble,
>   and to revive the heart of the contrite.

This very different God announces a decision for a new habitat: on high and with the low, but not in the big house with pharaoh.

Aniconic Community

This articulation of Yahweh's aniconic character makes clear that the aniconic dimension of Israel's faith is not and cannot be contained in purely religious categories. The aniconic God lives in polemical tension with the gods of the empire. The counterpart, which is characteristic and definitional for Old Testament faith, is that Israel models, constructs, and advocates an ordering of human community that is also aniconic; that is, it refuses to assign to any visible structure, form, or symbolization the power or significance of holiness, or to seek there the power for life. In a word, Israel knows that *images in religion* accompany inequities of social power in society, which inevitably result in disproportions of social goods and social access.[17] The location of God in a place or object proposes that the power of life can be identified and located and, therefore, controlled and administered. Thus, the imaged gods of Egypt and Babylon are experienced by Israel as the proponents and legitimations of social systems that enslave and oppress. Images in heaven warrant monopolies on earth.[18]

---

17. This linkage has been most clearly articulated by Karl Marx in his early programmatic statement: "The criticism of heaven is thus transformed into the criticism of earth, the criticism of religion into the criticism of law, and the criticism of theology into the criticism of politics" (*The Thought of Karl Marx*, ed. David McLellan [London: Macmillan Press, 1971], 22).

18. On images in relation to economics see Luke T. Johnson, *Sharing Possessions* (Philadelphia: Fortress Press, 1981). Johnson writes of "riches being one of the classic objects of idolatry. When we look at the matter more closely, however, we see that every form of idolatry is a form of possessiveness....An idolater is one who, quite literally, seeks to have God in his pocket. The power worshipped is shown service

Conversely, an *imageless God* accompanies *a social vision* and *social practice of equality and justice*.[19] The aniconic claims of Israel's faith cannot be contained in heaven but, characteristically, spill over and insist upon the practice of justice on the earth. The radical social vision of the Old Testament is not an invention of the prophets but is already contained in Israel's primal discernment of God who wanted the people who were enslaved by the empire "let go."

This inalienable connection between the character of God and the shape of community is evident in the primal theophany to Moses (Exod. 2:23-25; 3:1-6, 7-14).[20] At the center of the text is the theophanic confrontation of the burning bush. In that meeting, Moses has disclosed to him Yahweh's imageless, holy presence, but it will not do to consider that disclosure as a religious experience in a vacuum (as Samuel Terrien is wont to do).

The meeting at the burning bush occurs in a quite particular context. Preceding it, Moses had committed a dangerous act of violence against the empire (Exod. 2:11-15), thereby delegitimating the claims of the empire. We would call it an act of terrorism, but it is really a symbolic dismantling of the authority of the empire and the monopoly for which it stands. In Exod. 2:23-25, it is precisely when one pharaoh dies and another takes power that Israel cries out. The change in imperial masters characteristically creates the hope of a new social possibility. That hope comes in the form of cries and groans when Israel recovers for an instant its voice of pain and hope. That voice evokes Yahweh. Thus, the violent delegitimation by Moses and the hopeful groan of oppressed Israel are the context of theophany.

The burning bush episode is immediately followed by a credolike promise in the mouth of Yahweh who has "come down" (3:8). This recital of Yahweh's self-disclosure is followed, on the one hand, by the enigmatic name of Yahweh that retains God's freedom (3:14)

---

precisely so that it can be controlled. The idolater seeks to *own* god, and since the true God cannot be owned, the idolater fashions one more amenable to manipulation" (p. 55).

19. I am grateful to M. Douglas Meeks for this pivotal insight from which comes the substance of my argument. My conversations with him over an extended period have pressed my exegesis in this direction. Meeks has articulated this matter with precision in various places, but see esp. *God the Economist: The Doctrine of God and Political Economy* (Minneapolis: Fortress Press, 1989).

20. Paul D. Hanson, in "War and Peace" (see chap. 4, n. 8), esp. 345–46, has shown how Yahweh's character is enacted in the faith community. See his book on community in the Bible, *People Called* (see chap. 4, n. 8).

and, on the other hand, by a social vision of departing the empire for a land of freedom and justice (3:16-17). The verb "come down" (3:8) is decisive. The theophany is not an end in itself; it asserts the availability of this God precisely to this violent mediator and this groaning community of pain and hope that awaits a better possibility.

Yahweh is engaged in a radical social practice that creates an alternative social possibility. This is true even in the Priestly version of Exodus 14 where Yahweh will "get glory over pharaoh." Getting glory over pharaoh is to establish Yahweh's liberating sovereignty in place of pharaoh's enslaving sovereignty. Yahweh's central disclosure is "let my people go," a phrase parallel in function to "I will get glory," thus juxtaposing the phrases of Exodus 14 in verses commonly regarded as J and P. The two statements do not stand as cause and effect but, rather, "letting my people go" is Yahweh's very mode for "getting glory."[21] As Yahweh breaks with the other gods in Psalm 82, so Yahweh engages in Israel's break with imperial social practice. The theophany is in the service of promissory history and against the imperial arrangement of life, which is by definition antipromise, antihope, and ends in despair and brutality.

The assertions of the Decalogue articulate the aniconic impetus toward alternative society. The opening self-identification already articulates the juxtaposition: "I am Yahweh who delivered you from bondage." "I am Yahweh" is indeed an enigmatic statement of God's inscrutable character.[22] That enigmatic identity is explicated precisely in an act of social liberation and not in any other way. The refusal to be imprisoned by any name is counterpart to the formation of a community that resists fragmentation, compartmentalization, and, therefore, repression.

We have already suggested that in the list of the Decalogue, the first two Commandments on exclusiveness and absence of images fully assert Yahweh's aniconic character. This beginning is answered by the second tablet, perhaps especially by the Tenth Commandment, "You shall not covet." It is now clear that the Tenth Commandment is not a general statement about envy, jealousy, or greed, even though that in itself would not speak against our argument, but

---

21. The same self-assertion of Yahweh's sovereign pride is made in Ezek. 36:22-32, only here the operational word is "holy" rather than "glory"; but the point is the same. The saving effect for Israel is an incidental by-product of Yahweh's uncompromising self-concern.

22. Zimmerli, in *I am Yahweh*, 1–28, has given the decisive understanding of the formula.

the commandment concerns precisely land-tenure systems and land practice in society. "You shall not covet your neighbor's field or your neighbor's house." Without being reductionist, it is not too much to say that the center of the social experiment that was ancient Israel was an attempt at a revolutionary land-tenure system with important implications for the relation between peasant and urban dweller, between tribe and state, between the power of taxation and the practice of land grants.[23]

We know from the Joseph narrative (Gen. 47:13-26), now presented as a prelude to the exodus story, that Egyptian land policy was based on the premise that finally all land reverted to the throne. Surely that sense of legitimated social monopoly is not unrelated to the imaged gods who legitimated pharaoh and authorized the monopoly that was state policy. In Genesis 47, Israel engages in a hermeneutic of suspicion calling into question every social monopoly and every religious justification for such social monopoly.[24]

The imageless God Yahweh, however, has no interest in or need for monopoly. Yahweh does not covet, does not crave territory or goods (cf. Ps. 50:9-15). Indeed, Yahweh has no need for any land or produce that others may generate. Yahweh's decisive action of letting the people go was a decisive act against the coveting gods and against policies of social monopoly. Thus, the Tenth Commandment is a proposal for an alternative land practice that is congruent with Yahweh's character as a liberating God who permits no images. God's character requires Israel to organize life in ways that are not usurpatious.

The laws of the Torah are then an attempt to develop social prac-

---

23. See Marvin L. Chaney, "You Shall Not Covet Your Neighbor's House," *Pacific Theology Review* 15 (1982): 3–13. That Israel's faith is closely related to a transformation in land-tenure systems is now clear from an important new direction of scholarship represented by Gottwald, Chaney, and Robert B. Coote, among others. Gottwald's programmatic statement concerns the withdrawal of tribal groups from the Canaanite land-tenure system: "Our image of Israel's formation must be that of a profound discontinuity in the hierarchic feudal social fabric of Canaan, a rupture from within centralized society. This rupture was accomplished by an alliance of peoples who withdrew directly from the Canaanite system with other peoples who, beyond the centralized system's immediate reach in the hinterland of Canaan, refused the customary path of being drawn into that system and accommodating themselves to it" (*Tribes*, 326). See also Coote, *Amos among the Prophets* (Philadelphia: Fortress Press, 1981), 24–45.

24. On the religious underpinnings of such imperial social monopoly that was regarded as legitimate, see Donald Gowan, *When Man Becomes God* (Pittsburgh: Pickwick Press, 1975). The arrogant social practice of Genesis 47 is of a piece with the poetic claims in the mouth of the empire in Isaiah 47.

tice and organize social institutions that are resonant with Yahweh's aniconic character. As Paul D. Hanson and Fernando Belo[25] have shown, the laws of the Torah are not all inclined to this singular transformative vision, but those that seem most faithful to Yahweh's radical and initial self-disclosure in the exodus are indeed expressive of such a transformative vision. Thus, *law implements as social policy and social practice this articulation of God.* God is not simply a religious concept but a mode of social power and social organization.[26] We mention first Exod. 22:21-27, which warns against exploitation of sojourners, the poor, widows, and orphans, that is, the socially marginal, powerless, and vulnerable. Two things are of interest for us: First, the motivation offered in v. 21 is to remember "that you were slaves in Egypt." The warrant for social policy is the memory of the action of the imageless God who intervenes against the empire. Second, twice in this unit, it is said that the abused may "cry to Yahweh," who will act against the oppressor. This cry, which is now situated in the legal material, is the same cry of the vulnerable that we have seen in Exod. 2:23-25. There it was the cry of needy Israel against the empire that evoked the solidarity of Yahweh. Here it is the cry of the needy against the strong within Israel, which also evokes Yahweh to act for the exploited weak against the abusive strong. The reality of God's passion is mobilized in social policy. What had been a memory against the empire now is an act against oppressive tendencies within the very community shaped by the memory.

The Tenth Commandment on coveting receives its full exposition in the law of Jubilee (Leviticus 25), which I understand as egalitarian social practice as a mode of Yahweh's aniconic rule.[27] Two central affirmations are made: First, "The land is mine" (Lev. 25:23); therefore, none of it may be administered according to the modes of the empire. Second, "They are my servants whom I brought forth out of the land of Egypt; they shall not be sold as slaves" (25:42). This God aims at two social practices: keeping land out of the hands of

---

25. Hanson, "The Theological Significance of Contradiction within the Book of the Covenant," in *Canon and Authority*, ed. George W. Coats and Burke O. Long (Philadelphia: Fortress Press, 1977), 110–31; Belo, *Materialist* (see chap. 4, n. 34), esp. his theses on 38–59.

26. The most remarkable statement of this equation is found in Jer. 22:16, in which equity for the poor is synonymous with knowledge of Yahweh. See the discerning interpretive comments of José Miranda, *Marx and the Bible* (Maryknoll, N.Y.: Orbis Books, 1974), 47–50, 62–69.

27. On the theological future of the Jubilee tradition, see Sharon H. Ringe, *Jesus* (see chap. 4, n. 33).

the rapacious and keeping people out of the service of the abusive. Because Yahweh does not covet and has no designs for self concerning either land or people, these assertions about land and people are liberating. It is Yahweh's claim of sovereignty that nullifies the pretensions of the other gods, that vetoes other social practice, and that gives Israel space for humanness and warrant for justice. Yahweh's refusal to covet permits Israel to order its life according to land policies that are free of coveting.

Iconic Realities

The Old Testament is not able to be untouched completely by the iconic realities all around it. Ancient Israel is never literally iconic, for the God of the Old Testament never received an imaged expression. But one can detect in the Old Testament a temptation toward the iconic. It is a truism of scholarship that Israel borrowed fully from the religious offers in the culture around it, which had a propensity for iconicity. There is surely an inclination toward iconic religion in the Old Testament even though it never comes to full expression.[28]

That iconic inclination, however, should not be interpreted primarily in terms of syncretism or the seductions of other religions.[29] Rather, I should say that Israel found the aniconic claims of its own faith theologically too rigorous and pragmatically too demanding. That is not to say that Israel had a need to *see* God in any literal sense. Rather, Israel had a need to *locate* God, to be able to identify Yahweh's place and the locus of Yahweh's power; that is, Yahweh's freedom put Yahweh's faithfulness to Israel profoundly at risk, and the development of iconic tendencies is an effort to secure Yahweh's fidelity and presence, even if Yahweh's freedom is thereby placed in jeopardy. In general, we may say that this iconic

---

28. It is important to acknowledge two points. First, I am using the term "iconic" not only in a literal sense concerning actual physical embodiments but in a more general sense concerning the inclination to fetishism and the social practice of location of the deity. Second, I speak of the Old Testament and not Israelite religion in its popular forms. Thus, for example, there may be evidence of the emergence of figurines in the early period and there surely were such distortions later as in Elephantine, but those lie outside the argument of the text.

29. Levenson (*Sinai*, 38) suggests that the Israelite polemic against idols indicates not distance between the two cultures, but proximity, not the radical nature of Israelite distinctiveness, but its precariousness. Levenson may be correct but I am not persuaded. Levenson's argument seems to me to be lacking in the sociopolitical-economic factors related to the issue of religious conflict.

temptation is the move from theophany to cult. Theophany is the disclosure of Yahweh's presence with surprising immediacy. Cult is the attempt to routinize, manage, make predictable, and perhaps control that presence. Here I will mention three texts that evidence Israel's propensity to the iconic:

1. The most obvious reference is the narrative of the golden calf in Exodus 32. The narrative unfolds in these scenes:

vv. 1-6   Aaron makes the calf in the absence of Moses.

vv. 7-14   Yahweh and Moses discuss the threat of the calf.

vv. 15-24   Moses and Aaron discuss the calf.

vv. 25-29   Moses summons the Levites to act in judgment to purge the evil.

Clearly, in this Mosaic-Levitic casting of the narrative, orthodox Mosaic faith is adamantly against the iconic.[30] But it is equally clear that the well-pedigreed Aaron, leader of an elitist priesthood, is responsible for the reality of the calf. As the issue is joined between Moses and Aaron, it is clearly the priesthood of the Sinai tradition that resists translating Yahwism into icons, whereas it is the priesthood linked to Jerusalem that succumbs to icons and is under indictment.[31]

Equally important is the actual commentary about the calf:

> Aaron said to them, "Take off the rings of gold which are in the ears of your wives, your sons, and your daughters, and bring them to me." So all the people took off the rings of gold which were in their ears, and brought them to Aaron. (Vv. 2-3)[32]

---

30. Gottwald (*Tribes*, 381–89) proposes that it was the Levites, the group to which Moses was attached, who were the bearers "of the experience of the god Yahweh as a deliverer from political oppression." There is no doubt that they emerged in the canonical account as the bearers of orthodoxy. See Robert Polzin, *Moses* (see chap. 1, n. 21), 29–42, on the struggle of the text to maintain and modify orthodoxy as it became unbearably rigid.

31. On the history and conflict between the priesthood, see Cross, *Canaanite Myth*, chap. 8.

32. Herbert C. Brichto, in "The Worship of the Golden Calf: A Literary Analysis of a Fable on Idolatry," *HUCA* 54 (1983): 5, makes the interesting observation that the gold rings that are offered are precisely those of the ear, not the nose or any other part of the body. Because Israel is a community summoned to listen, it may be especially telling that it is the adornment of the ear that is offered and given. The transaction may hint especially at a distortion of listening.

Aaron explains his action to Moses in the same language:

> I said to them, "Let any who have gold take it off"; so they gave it to me, and I threw it into the fire, and there came out this calf. (V. 24)

The temptation to iconic religion is linked to the reality of gold. This community is no longer the one that desperately confiscates gold from Egyptian masters (see Exod. 11:2).[33] Now it is a community of established gold. We may believe that the confiscated gold is evidence of an economic surplus. Clearly, the implementation of the iconic tendency by Aaron is now correlated to an economic situation that makes such gold available.

2. It is too much to claim that the temple is iconic. If, however, we understand iconic as the concern to locate God's faithfulness and God's presence, then the temple intends and does indeed serve such a function.[34] The temple is clearly both an articulation of God's presence and an articulation of social power in a monopoly. It is the monopoly of social power that makes possible the surplus of gold that not only permits but requires the iconic interest in security.

In 2 Sam. 7:1-7, the tension that is foundational to Israel is well presented. It is significant that David's interest in the temple occurs when he is secure from his enemies (v. 1), and he himself is situated in affluence in a house of cedar (v. 2; cf. Jer. 22:13-16). Iconic tendencies occur in Israel when there is a social context in which *surplus value* can function with reference to the *location of God as patron*. It is clear that the debate that follows in 2 Sam. 7:1-7 (like the more extended debate over kingship in 1 Sam. 7-15) reflects the actual struggle for the heart of Israel. There is approval for the temple (v. 3), but then there is the retraction of that approval (vv. 4-7) for the sake of Yahweh's freedom to come and go. This debate reflects a tension over God's character. I suggest that the tension exists not only in Israel's reflection upon God but in the very character of God as that character is rendered in Israel's literature.[35] It also reflects a

---

33. On the motif of slaves confiscating gold and silver at the time of deliverance, see David Daube, *The Exodus Pattern in the Bible* (London: Faber & Faber, 1963), 55–61. That situation of desperate seizure, however, is now transformed into a situation of surplus.

34. See John M. Lundquist, "What is a Temple? A Preliminary Typology," in *The Quest for the Kingdom of God: Studies in Honor of George E. Mendenhall*, ed. Herbert B. Huffmon, Frank A. Spina, and Alberto Ravinell Whitney Green (Winona Lake, Ind.: Eisenbrauns, 1983), 205–10.

35. See chaps. 1 and 2 and Gottwald (*Tribes*, 686) on this unresolved and unresolv-

social situation in which there is sufficient means now concretely to represent and guarantee Yahweh's presence. The iconic temptation is not purely religious; it reflects a social situation of being secure enough and affluent enough no longer to be open to the risk of the free God of Moses. The socioeconomic factor of rest and riches is congruent with the function of surplus gold in Exodus 32.

3. The tension between freedom and faithfulness is also expressed in 1 Kings 8, a text the Deuteronomists have linked to 2 Samuel 7. There can be no doubt that the royal temple initiated by Solomon embodies royal affluence and extravagance (vv. 63-64). Such a social situation requires the steadiness and reliability of an ever-present God. The hymnic fragment of vv. 12-13, judged to be very early temple theology, offers and affirms the temple as a place where God would predictably dwell. There are no qualifiers to assert Yahweh's freedom or elusiveness but only a flat, innocent claim of God's full presence.

That some in Israel noticed the danger (or perversion) of such a claim is evident in vv. 26-30, which are more alert to the problem and which seek a formulation that will affirm Yahweh's locatable presence without denying Yahweh's real freedom.[36] But the very presence of this voice of qualification in vv. 27-30 confirms the heavy-handed flatness of the original claim of vv. 12-13. It is clear that the temple is tempted toward an uncritical theology of presence sponsored by the royal apparatus, which has acquired an economic monopoly that needs to be legitimated and protected.

In all three texts—Exodus 32, 2 Samuel 7, 1 Kings 8—there is a push toward God's locatable presence. In each case, the claim is reflective of an economic situation of affluence, and in each case the claim is subjected to harsh criticism and is rejected. The economic factor is evident:

a. in the gold of Aaron (Exod. 32:23-24),

b. in the rest and cedar of David (2 Sam. 7:1-2), and

c. in the extravagance of Solomon (1 Kings 8:63-64).

The criticism and rejection is evident:

---

able tension. On the rendering of God in ways that allow for the freedom of Yahweh's character, see Dale Patrick, *Rendering of God* (see chap. 2, n. 17).

36. On the problem of the locatable presence of Yahweh and various solutions to the problem, see Tryggve N. D. Mettinger, *The Dethronement of Sabaoth: Studies in the Shem and Kabod Theologies* (Lund: CWK Gleerup, 1982).

 a. in Moses' rebuke of Aaron and the calf project (Exod. 32:19-21),

 b. in the warning against a Davidic temple (2 Sam. 7:4-6), and

 c. in the challenge of presence (1 Kings 8:27-30).

There surely is an important dynamic in Israel's faith that juxtaposes the reality of the economic factor of affluence and the theological criticism of that surplus. There were voices in Israel who were prepared to present faith in Yahweh as a faith on its way to iconic practice.

The Iconic and Social Inequity

We have seen that Moses' aniconic faith had linked to it a radical policy of social justice. Conversely, the iconic tendency we have seen is also reflective of and in the service of a social policy. If the iconic tendency is, in each case, reflective of and tied to economic affluence (as I hope I have shown), it will not surprise that the iconic tendency is reflective of social policies in the service of social monopoly that benefits the affluent. I propose a connection between iconic inclinations in religion and social policies of stratification that support inequity and that advance social monopoly and social marginality.

Israel's primal commitment out of the exodus-Sinai texts is to a militantly aniconic faith and a vigorously egalitarian society, but the reality of that militant faith and that vigorous social vision was difficult to maintain. It was difficult to maintain not primarily because of external pressures but because of the shape of Israel's own life. As Israel became a community securely established, as slaves became masters, as peasants became managers of surplus property, the yearning for a locatable God was accompanied by a modified social policy and practice that legitimated and authorized social distinctions, political stratification, and differential economic advantage.[37] We may cite two texts that evidence the shift to iconic religion and to stratified social policy:

1. In Judg. 8:22-28, Israel makes its first request for monarchy, a social organization that evidently was in tension with Israel's initial social vision. The men of Israel ask Gideon to initiate a monarchy,

---

37. This political reversal is evident already as early as Joshua 9 and the subservience of the Gibeonites. It is remarkable that this community so fresh from subservience itself should immediately take the other side of the same relationship. On the text, see Gottwald, *Tribes*, 521–25.

which he refuses to do. According to the narrative, Israel is not yet
ready for such a radical shift and is fully aware of the problem of
such a shift. Kingship is perceived to be inimical to Yahweh's rule:

> I will not rule over you, and my son will not rule over you; the Lord
> will rule over you. (Judg. 8:23)

But what is telling in the narrative is that Gideon asks for and
receives gold from the community:

> And Gideon said to them, "Let me make a request of you; give me
> every man of you the earrings of his spoil."... And they answered,
> "We will willingly give them." And they spread a garment, and every
> man cast in it the earrings of his spoil. And the weight of the golden
> earrings that he requested was one thousand seven hundred shekels
> of gold; besides the crescents and the pendants and the purple gar-
> ments worn by the kings of Midian, and besides the collars that were
> about the necks of their camels. (Vv. 24-26)

We may be astonished that this community, usually reckoned in
the book of Judges to be primitive and unsophisticated ("rustic"
is a favorite word of scholars), has such a deposit of gold. We
may be further astonished that Gideon had the *hutzpah* to con-
fiscate it for himself. We may be finally astonished that Israel
"willingly" complied (v. 25).[38] The narrative reflects Israel's rapid
transition to a money economy. Such an active utilization of gold
suggests that shifts are being made in Israel's self-understanding.
It is telling that there is a juxtaposition between Gideon's readiness for gold and his refusal of kingship. Presumably, the problems
are easier to spot with political temptation than with economic
temptation.

Finally, v. 27 reports that Gideon made an ephod and "Israel
played the harlot." We do not know what an ephod is,[39] but it is
clearly a sacral object. The ephod is enough linked to religious activity and sacramentalism to evoke harlotry on Israel's part, that is,
a betrayal of and distortion of Yahwism. The Gideon narrative is
a clear case in which the move to a static cultic practice is closely
linked to a changed social practice evidenced in the availability of

---

38. The Hebrew is an infinitive absolute.
39. On ephod, see G. Henton Davies, "Ephod," *IDB* (New York: Abingdon Press,
1962), 2:118–19. Whatever it was, it is socially symbolic of elitist power.

God.[40] We may note in passing that in Judges 17, the readiness to construct a graven image and a molten image for Yahweh is related to an offer of eleven hundred pieces of silver (v. 3), and in v. 10, the priest is offered ten pieces of silver for his services. Although this narrative does not criticize the act of image-making (as in the Gideon narrative), the connection of money and icon is again evident.

2. The major evidence for this disruptive social practice in Israel's faith is in the Solomonic arrangement of faith and social policy. Solomon is best known as the temple builder. The Deuteronomic presentation of 1 Kings 3–11 clearly is organized so that the temple dedication in 1 Kings 8 is the centerpiece of the Solomonic sketch. In that report on the dedication of the temple, we have seen that the high liturgic claim is made in the anthem of vv. 12-13. This extreme statement of the location of God as an institutional patron is criticized in vv. 27-30 and dismissed in the sarcastic, debunking observation of v. 9:

> There was nothing in the ark except the two tablets of stone which Moses put there at Horeb, where the Lord made a covenant with the people of Israel.

There is no doubt that Solomonic prosperity and affluence were built on the emergence of new social inequities that violated the Mosaic vision and celebrated a monopoly of wealth and power in the hands of some at the expense of others, a monopoly that was unprecedented in Israel. The capacity to keep God's location predictable seems to come with economic-political monopoly.

Three evidences of this monopoly in the Solomonic narrative may be cited:

a. There is the difficult question of forced labor.[41] In 1 Kings 5:13-18, a levy of forced labor in Israel is reported (cf. 4:6). In 9:27, it is denied that the forced labor policy was applied to Israel. Even though it is disputed whether Israelites were included in the forced

---

40. The impact of Gideon's request on the community may not be without parallel to Mark Twain's "The Man That Corrupted Hadleyburg," in *The Complete Short Stories of Mark Twain*, ed. Charles Neider (Garden City, N.Y.: Doubleday & Co., 1957), 349–90.

41. Isaac Mendelsohn, in "On Corvée Labor in Ancient Canaan and Israel," *BASOR* 167 (1962): 31–35, has provided a careful analysis of the problem.

labor program, the main point is that the narrative can, without embarrassment or apology, assume that such a policy is well in place for
Solomon, and it is reported without qualification or criticism. It does
not matter greatly for our purposes if it included Israel or not. The
policy itself is evidence that a very different theology, along with a
very different social practice, has emerged in Israel.

b. In 1 Kings 4:20-28, immediately after the identification of the
royal bureaucracy in 4:1-6 and the tax system in 4:7-19, we are given
a picture of the economic extravagance of the Solomonic enterprise,
which is based on arms and taxes and which claims well-being, happiness, and security for every person. But the narrative must be read
discerningly. Such extravagance for some does not emerge from an
egalitarian social practice. The development of a royal elite both
stems from and legitimates social inequalities in this community—a
community that was an innovation in the Near East aimed precisely
against such inequality.[42]

c. That such a social practice is to be assigned to Solomon is evident in the report of social unrest in the latter part of the narrative
and perhaps in the latter part of his reign (chaps. 11–12). The understated conclusion of his reign reports (1) that Solomon followed
the foreign gods of his foreign wives (thus the emergence of iconic
religion, 11:1-8); (2) the warning of judgment directly from the Lord
(11:9-13); (3) two rebellions by Hadad and Rezon that he suppressed
(11:14-26); (4) the subversive activity of the prophet Ahijah that
includes the identification of Jeroboam as a principal threat (11:29-
40); and (5) the negotiations with Rehoboam that seek redress from
the oppressiveness of his father (12:1-20). The picture given in these
two chapters is of a man and a regime that, from the perspective of
the primal vision of Israel, have lost their way. The troubles named
in 1 Kings 11 and 12—foreign gods, political rebellion, prophetic
denunciation—are of a piece. They present a social order that is
alienated from the reality of Yahweh and that practices exploitative
rule in politics and economics. It takes no special insight to suggest
that the capacity to locate God in the temple belongs together with
the capacity to exploit with a "heavy yoke" and with "whips" (1 Kings
12:11).

---

42. On the development of a royal elite, see George E. Mendenhall, "The Shady
Side of Wisdom: The Date and Purpose of Genesis 3," in *A Light unto My Path*, ed.
Howard N. Bream, Ralph D. Heim, and Carey A. Moore (Philadelphia: Temple University Press, 1974), 321–34; and Eric W. Heaton, *Solomon's New Men: The Emergence
of Israel as a National State* (London: Thames & Hudson, 1974).

Polarities in Tension

On the basis of this analysis I propose an arrangement for presenting the main tendencies of Old Testament faith:

- aniconic religion/egalitarian social practice (the combination of which I have called "pain-embracing").

- iconic religion/monopolistic social practice (the combination of which I have called "structure legitimation").

The first pair—aniconic religion/egalitarian social practice—is established in the structure of the Decalogue that begins in Yahweh's exclusive aniconic claim and ends in a prohibition of coveting. The second pair—iconic religion/monopolistic social practice—does not find such paradigmatic expression. Iconic religion is evidenced in royal-temple practices that deny Yahweh freedom and reduce the deity to a status of reliable, predictable patron. The derivative social system for which Yahweh is patron and legitimator is embodied in the monarchy that characteristically gathers silver and gold (cf. Deut. 17:14), that is, engages in economic monopoly. It is precisely the accumulation of silver and gold that is expressed in the iconography of images. The social system in turn enhances the static claims of Yahweh as patron.

This tension in Old Testament faith between aniconic and iconic religion and between egalitarian and monopolistic social practice is a paradigm for Old Testament theology, now utilized and articulated in a variety of ways among scholars:

- Samuel Terrien: ethical ear and contemplative eye;

- James A. Sanders: critical and constitutive;

- Claus Westermann: deliverance and blessing;

- Paul D. Hanson: visionary and pragmatic, reformative and formative, teleological and cosmic;

- Jon D. Levenson: Sinai and David;

- Fernando Belo: debt cancellation and purity.

Indeed, we may conclude that this polarity is the primary paradigm that is emerging among scholars, even though it may be nuanced in a variety of directions and named by a variety of labels.[43]

It appears to me that the sociotheological significance of this polarity either has largely gone unrecognized by scholars or, if recognized, has not been pursued in a way that helps discern the claims of the two tendencies. The scholars cited tend to present these poles in a restrained, descriptive way. Indeed, there is an eagerness in some quarters to try to be more evenhanded because it is judged that the accent has been too heavy on what I have termed the aniconic/egalitarian tendency. For doing a serious biblical theology, however, the claims and tensions of these poles must be recognized as very important, critical, substantive issues. It is not sufficient simply to put the two poles next to each other:

First, the two poles of aniconic/egalitarian and iconic/monopolistic belong to and reflect very different sociologies, of the marginal and the well-established, of the have-nots and the haves. The reading of every theological text requires sociotheological alertness, if not suspicion. The matter of God's freedom or locatability, of God's aniconic sovereignty or iconic availability, is a matter freighted with social significance. One cannot simply cite the polarity without an awareness that the two are in profound tension. How one articulates that tension matters enormously for the role of biblical faith in contemporary society. Second, the polarity is not to be understood with a simple reference to economics, to having or not having. It relates more broadly to a whole view of social reality. The first set of terms alludes to a theological tradition in which Yahweh is primarily a transformative agent and in which the social community is under way in transformation from monopolistic to egalitarian practice. Conversely, in the other tradition, Yahweh is essentially a conserver of present cultural arrangements and values. Consequently society is celebrated as a viable arrangement in which problems are to be contained within the limits of the system. Thus, every articulation of God makes an important substantive decision about the character of human life, but in its personal and public dimensions.

---

43. See the following: Samuel Terrien, *Elusive Presence;* Sanders, "Adaptable for Life" (see chap. 4, n. 26), and *God Has a Story Too* (see chap. 1, n. 4), 127; Westermann, *What Does the Old Testament Say* and *Elements* (for both, see chap. 1, n. 4); Hanson, *Dynamic* and *Diversity* (for both, see chap. 1, n. 4); Levenson, *Sinai;* and Belo, *Materialist.*

Third, it can be argued that the first pole of that set of tensions articulates what is distinctly Israelite, whereas the other pole tends to emphasize what Israel has in common with other Near Eastern religions. The issue of distinctiveness and commonality in Israelite faith is complex and problematic, and I do not ignore that fact. Thus, for example, I am aware that even the telling of the exodus tale, which is decisive and distinctive for Israel, is cast in the mythic language of the Near East.[44] Nonetheless, the distinctive elements that belong to the transformative tradition tend to be concerned with historical liberation practice, critique of land-tenure systems, and prophetic critique of social-economic power monopolies. Conversely, the other tendency, as Levenson has argued so well, tends to move in mythical, spatial imagery in which the language, religious parallels, and cultural references are of a less distinctive character. Levenson has wisely warned against drawing this distinction too sharply, because the conserving theological tradition also partakes of some elements of transformative vision.[45] Nonetheless, I suggest that the tension between the traditions is a real one. It is a discussion of the ways in which Israel, in its social theology, is a distinctive people (Deut. 7:6-11) and the ways in which Israel is willing and eager to be "like the other nations" (1 Sam. 8:5, 20).

Fourth, it must at least be noted that the canonical presentation provides some clues about the relative claims of the two traditions. The primary canon of Torah is, to a very large extent, committed to the tradition of transformation, whereas it is after the canon of Torah, in a less authoritative canonical position, that the conserving claims of royal-temple theology have their say.[46] This canonical preference is somewhat mitigated by the presence of creation theology and priestly legislation in the Torah, but the central dynamic of the Torah concerns transformation, both theological and sociological. Israel's faith characteristically returns to exodus, not to creation.

It must be recognized that both theological tendencies are important and both belong properly and necessarily to Israel's articulation of faith. Both, moreover, operate in Israel's socioeconomic self-understanding. Surely both tendencies respond to and satisfy

---

44. See Cross, *Canaanite Myth*, 121–44; and P. D. Miller, *The Divine Warrior in Early Israel* (Cambridge: Harvard University Press, 1973), 113–17.

45. See also Levenson, *Sinai*, 89–184, 214–17.

46. On the cruciality of the tradition of transformation, see Walter Harrelson, "Life, Faith and the Emergence of Tradition," in *Tradition and Theology in the Old Testament*, ed. Douglas A. Knight (Philadelphia: Fortress Press, 1977), 11–30.

important religious needs and yearnings, and both must be taken seriously. Nonetheless, the discernment of their relative importance and power is crucial for an understanding of Old Testament theology because they legitimate very different forms of social life. It is clear that the two tendencies cannot honestly be harmonized. If, indeed, one engages in such reductionism, the settlement will predictably be made on the grounds of the conserving tradition.

Traditions in Tension

Much Old Testament theology, as indicated above, is organized around the issue of aniconic versus iconic tendencies in the heart of Old Testament traditions. I submit that the matter of two trajectories in tension is likely to be an emerging scholarly paradigm that will dominate theological exposition for the coming decades.[47] While I am fully supportive of that paradigm, I here make no special appeal for it, but I simply observe the power and rapidity with which that paradigm has emerged. It is my judgment that its power and its attractiveness among us are reflective of our worldview and our social experience at the end of the twentieth century. It is not necessary to be a Marxist to see how broadly the categories of social analysis in class terms and the reality of class conflict are operative among us. The rise of the Third World, the emergence of liberation movements around the world, the awareness of how the established church functions as the legitimator of the status quo, the restlessness and uneasiness of voices of transformation within the legitimating church—all bear witness to the fact that the issues are now set for us in a quite different way than heretofore. I am interested in how this self-consciousness on our part not only impinges on our economic, political perceptions, but how it plays an influential role in our theological articulations and indeed in our hermeneutical categories.

The recognition of this tension as a main theological issue in the Old Testament is the point of our study. This recognition corresponds to the growing awareness that this same tension is the overriding social concern in the contemporary world. The governing metaphors of Old Testament faith are essentially conflictual, both

47. The scheme of two trajectories in tension is particularly influential in Gottwald's analysis of the early period; for the late period of the Old Testament, see esp. Hanson, *Dawn* (see chap. 5, n. 18).

because Yahweh lives in dispute with the other gods and because Israel's social practice is in tension with the available cultural alternatives. Indeed, Israel as a historically identifiable community was wrought precisely out of this dispute among the gods. The community that still looks to this text as authoritative will continue to be wrought precisely in this same dispute among the gods, a dispute that is enacted in the arena of social-economic politics and that will continue until the full coming of God's kingdom and the establishment of the sovereignty of this transformative One.

This recently emergent paradigm, which I judge to be peculiarly appropriate to and congruent with our cultural context, is to be contrasted with at least three other models that have served us well but were respondent to other cultural situations:

1. It has long been clear that a hypothesis of religious developmentalism or evolution is no longer a viable model for biblical interpretation, even though that notion continues to exercise enormous popular power.[48] That view, shaped and influenced by intellectual models of the nineteenth century, must now be rejected on two grounds. First, it is clear that Yahweh does not emerge or evolve but intrudes abruptly as a genuine *novum* in Israel's experience, in conflict with all previously known gods.[49] Second, as Gottwald has indicated, there is also not social evolution from tribe to state, but the social vision of the tribe appears as an abrupt alternative to the claims of the state system. The conflictual, rather than developmental, reality of Yahweh's self-identity as rendered by Israel's storytellers and poets is thus wrought in and through conflictual social reality. If we do not understand that social reality through which Yahweh's character is wrought, we shall misunderstand the character of Yahweh.[50]

---

48. William F. Albright, in *From the Stone Age to Christianity* (Baltimore: Johns Hopkins University Press, 1957), delivered the telling blow against such evolutionism. In retrospect, it appears that Albright's "organismic" articulation was not as remote from developmentalism as appeared at the time. In Brueggemann, "*The Tribes of Yahweh:* An Essay Review," *JAAR* 48, no. 3 (1980): 441–51, I have suggested that Gottwald's shift of paradigms is as decisive for this generation of scholarship as was that of Albright for his generation.

49. On the conflict, see the citation to Gottwald in n. 6.

50. I do not imagine that this hermeneutic of conflict, which finds conflict decisive both in the social process and in the character of Yahweh, is "contextless" or that it is the absolute model. I have no doubt that it is shaped and evoked by the intellectual-political climate of our generation of scholarship as much as the developmental hypothesis was evoked by the climate of Hegel, Darwin, and Spencer. The conflictual character of the contemporary world is reflected in the emerging libera-

2. The credo hypothesis of von Rad, although widely criticized, continues to have enormous attractiveness.[51] It is clear that that hypothesis from 1938, which eventuated in the so-called Biblical Theology Movement, is best understood in relation to the courageous action of the Confessing Church in Germany in the 1930s. Indeed, that model of Scripture study echoes the claims of the Barmen Declaration and the courage of that faith community to assert its distinctive identity in the face of an alien oppressor. The power of the hypothesis is found in the congruence between that theological crisis in Germany and the actual practice of Old Testament faith and tradition in the face of Egyptian, Canaanite, Assyrian, Babylonian, and Roman oppression. Von Rad and his cohorts grasped that fundamental analogy for their own theological work.

Gottwald has presented von Rad's hypothesis in a revised form so that Gottwald's work may be understood as mediation between the credo paradigm and the *traditions-in-conflict* model proposed here.[52] Gottwald has shown, as the tradition of von Rad did not in any intentional way (though it may be inferred), that the credo recital is a social practice that both joins issue with countertruth and carries within it the seeds of revolutionary social practice. Thus, Gottwald's handling of the materials is in continuity with that of von Rad, but he has introduced into the discussion the dimension of social realism and critical analysis of social function, and that has changed the terms of the conversation. The credo cannot be presented simply as a recital of faith, which it is, but it must also inevitably be understood as an act of revolutionary social practice that becomes embodied in the social construction through the Torah of Sinai.[53]

---

tion movements as they impinge on world order, on social structure and institutions, and on the life and mind of the church. It is inevitable that such forces would shape our hermeneutical inclinations.

51. The hypothesis is given its normative expression in von Rad, "The Form-Critical Problem of the Hexateuch," in *The Problem* (see chap. 4, n. 30), 1–78. The criticisms are now many and well-established.

52. Gottwald (*Tribes*, chap. 13) makes a helpful distinction between "cultic modalities and narrative themes." He has seen that the credo is not merely a recital but an ideological articulation that means to challenge and refute alternative readings of reality; that is, he has presented the credo much more in conflict, although von Rad had of course understood the point. Gottwald's presentation makes more intentional use of the tools of social analysis.

53. The Torah is Israel's practice of what Peter Berger calls "the social construction of reality." Norbert Lohfink, in *Great Themes from the Old Testament* (Chicago: Franciscan Herald Press, 1982), 55–75, has suggested that the Torah recital of Deuteronomy not only shapes the mind-set and perceptual field of Israel but is a "constitution" for the development of public institutions with a division of power.

3. My proposed traditions-in-conflict model also moves against every attempt to find a single theme or center for Old Testament theology. The classic attempt to find such a center is that of Eichrodt around the theme of covenant. By definition, the identification of a single theme as an organizing principle serves to exclude the tension or conflict among the traditions. Against such excessive reductionism, however, the model proposed here does not embrace von Rad's conclusion that there is no organizing principle, but it asserts that the organizing principle must be found at the interface between theological affirmation and social vision.

We may comment on two attempts at an organizing principle. Terrien has organized biblical faith around the theme of God's presence, which he discerningly characterizes as "elusive."[54] Terrien's masterful treatment is something of a breakthrough because he has found a single theme, but at the same time, he is attentive to the inherent tension between the ear and the eye, the ethical and the contemplative in the theme of presence. Thus, his proposal is not to be criticized in the same way as Eichrodt's. Perhaps Terrien's major weakness is that the various articulations of Yahweh's presence through ear or eye are left largely unrelated to the social-political realities to which they are joined. The result is a kind of transcendentalism that seems to miss much of Israel's powerful discernment that Yahweh's presence is always intensely related to social experience and social reality. Terrien seems to be largely unaware that every affirmation of God's presence is inevitably a comment on social reality and social practice.

Recently, Rolf P. Knierim has proposed that "righteousness of God" be taken as the organizing principle, and he is able to show that this theme is present in all parts of Israel's theological reflection.[55] There is much that is fresh and convincing in his presentation. The reservation I have is that Knierim does not apply social criticism to the notion of righteousness and therefore understands it in a rather undifferentiated way. For example, it makes a great deal of difference whether righteousness is handled in a conserving or transformative way. No doubt both ways are present in various tex-

---

54. Terrien, *Elusive Presence*. See my review of his book, "Canon and Dialectic," in *God and His Temple*, ed. Lawrence E. Frizzel (South Orange, N.J.: Seton Hall University Press, 1981), 20–34. In retrospect I wish Terrien had paid more attention to the social contexts in which the "events of presence" are embedded. Only in that way does their literary-social function become clear.

55. Knierim, "The Task" (see chap. 4, n. 8).

tual traditions, but unless they are critically assessed in terms of their social function, they tend to be handled in a reductionist way.

It may be that the effort to find a single unifying theme is also reflective of a certain intellectual context that values system and coherence. Thus, even to pose the question as we have posed it is already to say something decisive about transformation and the subversion that belongs to transformation. A single theme does not allow for the reality that there are always minority voices that will not and must not be subsumed and co-opted. Attention to the text means to listen to and for those minority voices that characteristically have an alternative way.

Thus, I suggest that the models of developmentalism, confessional recital, and single-focused theme are all efforts at Old Testament theology that can be understood in certain cultural contexts. In our specific context, however, the movement of scholarship suggests that "traditions in tension" is congruent with our particular theological responsibility.

Adjudication

If we are to organize Old Testament theology in this way around the poles of transformation and conservation, around legitimation of structure and embrace of pain, around what is distinctive and what is held in common with other religious traditions, around aniconic and iconic discernments of God, we are left with the question: How are we to adjudicate the relative authority of the two trajectories in any particular expository situation? I suggest we are regularly presented with hard choices about this adjudication and that a choice inevitably must be made. To the question of such adjudication, I propose an answer in two dimensions, neither of which escapes the problematic of the hermeneutical circle:

First, how these two tendencies are adjudicated with their relative claims of authority largely depends on one's dialogue partners.[56] The text is heard differently, depending on the conversations in which one is engaged and in whose presence the text is interpreted. We are learning in powerful ways about the contextualization of all theological interpretation. The voices of liberation theology do not object to being charged with contextualization (for example, they

---

56. See Douglas Hall, "Who Tells the World's Story? Theology's Quest for a Partner in Dialogue," *Int* 36 (1981): 47–53.

speak as advocates of the poor) if the same reality of contextualization is conceded for established Euro-American interpretations that
characteristically speak as legitimators of established social interest.
Clearly, all interpretations are in some measure shaped and determined by the voices present in the conversation.[57] Thus, how one
credits traditions of theology and social practice depends on one's
conversation partners. It will not do to imagine that Scripture interpretation is objective. We need, first, to notice and acknowledge the
operation and importance of conversation partners and, second, to
assess critically if those particular conversation partners are agents
of distortion or if they help us discern rightly and faithfully. A range
of possible dialogue partners is available and we need to be aware of
that full range of options, none of which embodies objectivity.[58]

The second issue in such adjudication of dialogue partners is to
try to clarify the norms by which the proper partners are identified.
The choice of dialogue partners through which the two traditions
are adjudicated is not one of arbitrary choice or personal preference.
Rather, the choice must be one that is appropriate to the material
itself. This is to acknowledge that the question of a proper conversation partner is a dialectical matter. On the one hand, the identity of
the partner determines the character of the text. On the other hand,
the character of the text is decisive for choosing the partner. Karl
Barth argued this point when he insisted that "the *object* of theology
is determinative of the method and not vice versa, as he believed had
become the case since the Enlightenment and Schleiermacher."[59]
Barth's general argument is that *scientific* method requires that the
method fit the subject, that theology must find methods appropriate
to the God it will present.[60] I argue in similar fashion that a respon-

---

57. Jürgen Habermas, in *Legitimation Crisis* (Boston: Bacon Press, 1975), 105–43,
proposes that the final establishment of truth and legitimacy depends on communication. Who is in the conversation shapes social reality. He suggests that the "ideal
speech situation" occurs when all affected parties have a voice. Such an ideal situation
of communication is closely parallel to the intent of the kingdom of God as a model
of human community.

58. On the problem and deceptiveness of objectivity, see Donal Dorr, *Spirituality and
Justice* (Maryknoll, N.Y.: Orbis Books, 1984), 40–51; and programmatically, Alvin W.
Gouldner, *The Coming Crisis of Western Sociology* (New York: Basic Books, 1970). A stun-
ning negative example of a destructive partisan interpretation in the guise of scholarly
objectivity is presented by Robert P. Ericksen, *Theologians under Hitler: Gerhard Kittel,
Paul Althaus, and Emmanuel Hirsch* (New Haven: Yale University Press, 1985).

59. S. W. Sykes, "Barth on the Centre of Theology," in *Karl Barth: Studies of His
Theological Method*, ed. Sykes (Oxford: Clarendon Press, 1979), 29.

60. That the character of the subject should determine the method of study is

sible critical method requires dialogue partners that are appropriate
to the subject itself. The *community of interpretation* must be congruent with the God of the text and the perspective on reality offered
by the text.

From that methodological commitment we make the following
judgments. These judgments are not simply formal, but must be
substantive:

1. The interpretive community must be primarily concerned
for justice because the God of the text is primarily concerned for
justice.[61]

2. The interpretive community must be in alert and suspicious
dialogue with the great political empires because the text itself
stands largely in contradiction to the great empires—Egyptian, Assyrian, Babylonian, Persian, and Hellenistic. It presents those empires as systems of legitimation, technology, methodology, ideology,
and epistemology that serve order and not justice. The Old Testament presents Israel and Israel's God as always having a vision of
justice that challenges the great forces of order that are present in
every part of the literature.

3. The interpretive community must be in tension with the great,
comprehensive religious systems because the text itself, derivative
from the character of this God, is characteristically in tension with
the Canaanite, Babylonian, and Hellenistic religious systems. Those
great religious systems that are characteristically iconic create the
kinds of images that offer the false and seductive promise that
humankind can secure its own existence. Israel and its text are persistently in tension with, if not in conflict with, the notion of any
religion that imagines it can secure its own existence.

4. The interpretive community must be committed to a scandal in
the face of the imperial alternative of order and the religious alternative of security, because this text and its God practice such a scandal
against just such systemic order and comprehensive security. The
scandal is that the text is image-rejecting because of the holy, jealous
God who will fit into no preconceived scheme of divinity.

I have already conceded that this way of adjudicating the iconic

---

not only true in theology but in science. See Liebe F. Cavalieri, *The Double-Edged
Helix* (New York: Columbia University Press, 1981), esp. the foreword, "Convergence," by Ruth Nanda Anshen, III. The argument is that old methods belong to
old understandings of the subject.

61. Knierim, in "The Task," has argued the point in terms of God's righteousness
that is evidenced as justice on the earth.

and aniconic is not unambiguous and that it finally depends on a hermeneutical decision. That hermeneutical decision is not subjective and arbitrary, however, but is informed by the text at hand. Thus, on theological grounds, I make this decision: The God of the Old Testament is fundamentally aniconic and the social practice that is derived from, referred to, and authorized by this God is a social practice of the aniconic, that is, a refusal of oppressive relationships and a refusal of economic, political monopoly, and, therefore, a social practice of egalitarianism. The appropriate conversation partners, therefore, are those who can honor that aniconic character, who are capable of suspicion about the gods in heaven and the powers on earth, and who are prepared to engage in criticism, both of the gods and of the socioeconomic derivations from that God.[62]

This conclusion is drawn in response to one simple question: With whom does the God of the Bible make a regular abode? To whom does this God regularly attend? The answer is that the God of the Old Testament has taken as primary partner in the conversation of history the poor and needy, the "mixed multitude" (Num. 11:4), the disestablished swarm whom Gottwald has identified as peasants, whom the credo tradition names as slaves. That is, the aniconic God regularly finds partners among the socially marginal; therefore, the interpretive task must be carried on with and in the presence of the socially marginal and politically vulnerable, the ones of broken spirit and contrite heart, because they are the ones congenial to this subject matter of the interpretive conversation. A New Testament extrapolation from this conclusion is that God's aniconic character is embodied in the suffering, crucified Jesus whose best friends were publicans and sinners and the crowd who hung on his words (Luke 19:47-48). The interpretive task, then, must be carried out under the practice of suspicion that is not only theological but sociopolitical and psychological as well. In our recent intellectual history, this suggests that the aniconic contributions of Karl Marx and Sigmund Freud loom large for our work.

It should be clear that a very different interpretive conversation would be held if we conclude that the God of the Bible is fundamentally iconic. Then the proper partners for conversation would be the voices of social conversation and construction, but I judge such partners to be in important ways incongruent with the God of Israel.

---

62. On doing theology as conversation, see Paul van Buren, *Discerning the Way* (see chap. 2, n. 4).

Thus, I propose that the adjudication of these traditions in tension grows out of a conversation. It matters enormously who is included in that conversation, and the appropriate participants in that conversation are, in large measure, determined by the very character of God. Such a conversation emerges among barren women, unhealed persons, hungry crowds, oppressed slaves, homeless sojourners, ritually disqualified lepers—a conversation that leads to a theology of the cross. An alternative conversation would lead, with iconic premises, to a theology of glory, but that is a conversation incongruent with the God who hears the cries of the poor, assaults the structures of the empire, and frees slaves.

Finally, I want to point to two pieces of the conversation that I believe embody the practice of theological interpretation urged here:

1. I regard the two letters of the American Roman Catholic bishops on nuclear arms and economics as among the most important religious events of recent time in America. I submit that their importance is that the bishops have publicly asserted the profound tension that exists between the claims of the gospel and the dominant values and policies of the American system. To assert that profound tension is an act of enormous courage because Americans are accustomed to imagine a comfortable congruity between the gospel and dominant American values. That tension may yet be handled in a variety of ways that remain to be determined, but the public articulation of the tension seems to me to be integrally related to the aniconic tradition of biblical faith. Indeed, the response of officialdom to the two letters indicates that the letters are perceived as theologically and socially aniconic, that is, acts that delegitimate the sustaining symbols of the system. The letters are a critical and crucial declaration that God is not located in theological claims and pretensions that legitimate monopoly in politics and economics. The bishops have shown in powerful ways how theological claims and social reality go together, and it is clear that the bishops do their theology in the presence of God's peculiar friends, the marginal.

2. I tread on dangerous ground to comment on the conversation that Leonardo Boff is having with church authorities. Boff has asserted God's aniconic character in ways that matter for sociotheology. His daring use of the categories of "production and consumption" in relation to the Eucharist and the monopoly of administrative power over the sacraments as means of production and

consumption has been inevitably misunderstood.[63] But it is a point he had to make, given his discernment of God's aniconic character. Clearly, Boff's primary theological partners in conversation are those who have no access to the "production of Eucharist" and who are voiceless in its "consumption." The mistaken response to Boff is predictably iconic. The categories of production and consumption, it was asserted, are not applicable because the sacrament is a gift from heaven. The practitioners of iconic religion, who are invariably practitioners of social monopoly, shrink from aniconic criticism because such criticism, even in a theological mode, always quickly assaults the monopoly of power and goods.

I suggest then that the questions of Old Testament theology for us are the same as they have been since Aaron in Exodus 32.[64] To what extent is the community able to bear God's aniconic character and the social implications of that aniconic character, and to what extent is that dangerous reality compromised in terms of heavenly icon and earthy monopoly? Participants in this conversation are left to ponder this:

> For thus says the high and lofty One
>> who inhabits eternity, whose name is Holy;
> I dwell in the high and holy place,
>> and also with the one who is of a contrite and humble spirit,
> to revive the spirit of the humble,
>> and to revive the heart of the contrite. (Isa. 57:15)

If God's name were not so holy and if God's habitat were not with the humble, our interpretive task would be very different, surely more palatable to the ways things are in the world.

---

63. See Boff, *Church: Charism and Power* (New York: Crossroad, 1985), 110–15.

64. On Exodus 32 and the problem of iconic religion in general, see Christoph Dohmen, *Das Bilderverbot*, BBB, no. 62 (Bonn: Peter Hanstein Verlag, 1985), 66–153. Dohmen's analysis of a clash of social systems is congruous with my analysis in this chapter.

8

The Crisis and Promise
of Presence in Israel

THE PRESENCE OF GOD in the life of God's people is an important and difficult problem in the Old Testament.[1] That Yahweh should be present to God's people is obviously important, but equally important is how Yahweh should be present and how Israel should speak about God's presence.[2] The various traditions present the issues on a broad spectrum,[3] on the one hand drawing upon and embodying the common presuppositions of Near Eastern mythology and cult practice, and on the other hand reflecting upon the distinctive liberationist experience and traditions of Israel's Mosaic memory. In broad scope, the common traditions of the Near East are concerned with the assurance of God's presence and with accessibility guaranteed. But the Mosaic tradition, which we will discuss, is concerned with articulating Yahweh's freedom from Israel and capacity to stand apart from and over against Israel, thereby asserting that Israel's access to Yahweh is characteristically precarious.

---

1. I want to acknowledge Samuel Terrien's masterful treatment of the theme of this chapter in *Elusive Presence* (see chap. 1, n. 4). Although my major argument is independent of that of Terrien, I am glad to note a general agreement with him and appreciation for several points of suggestion taken from him.

2. On the interplay of presence and language, see Peter C. Hodgson, *Jesus—Word and Presence* (Philadelphia: Fortress Press, 1971).

3. On the traditions of the spectrum seen in schematic fashion as continuing trajectories, see Walter Brueggemann, "Trajectories" (see chap. 5, n. 22); and Odil H. Steck, "Theological Streams of Tradition," in *Tradition and Theology* (see chap. 7, n. 46), 183–214.

Thus the theological dialectic of *accessibility* and *freedom* for Yahweh is matched by Israel's experience of *assurance* and *precariousness*. It is no small matter to speak of the issue so that these two agendas are kept in responsible tension with each other.[4]

The topic is a large one in which different literary efforts present different nuances to the dialectic. Here we will confine ourselves to the focal text of Exod. 33:12-23. We will consider the ways in which that articulation of the problem may illuminate the issue of divine presence as it is also apparent in some New Testament traditions. This study is offered in pursuit of the motif of *face* as a metaphor for *presence* in an attempt to consider the linkage and interplay between an Old Testament theme and some possible New Testament counterparts.[5] This is no attempt to trace a historical development from the Mosaic to the New Testament traditions, and no doubt there are various important steps in that development that might be considered. Rather, I intend to be attentive to the *canonical claims* made in the Old Testament and the New Testament for a common theologou-

---

4. On the dialectic of accessibility and freedom, see Walter Brueggemann, "Presence of God, Cultic," in *IDBSup* (see chap. 1, n. 4), 680–83. It is no longer possible to assume a simplistic contrast between Israelite faith and its religious context; see, for example, J. J. M. Roberts, "Divine Freedom and Cultic Manipulation in Israel and Mesopotamia," in *Unity and Diversity* (see chap. 1, n. 19), 181–90. Rather, the argument here concerns the tension between an accommodating culture-religion and a critical faith over against present cultural arrangements. That tension is within Israel, and both postures are genuinely Israelite. That issue is nowhere more evident than on the matter of divine revelation. Following Claus Westermann and Jürgen Moltmann, it may be possible to use the words "epiphany" and "theophany" to characterize the two types, but that depends upon definition of the words. So used, they refer respectively to the disclosure of what has always been and to the emergence of a genuine newness with the coming of God. For a full summary of the discussion, see Rolf Knierim, "Offenbarung im Alten Testament," in *Probleme* (see chap. 3, n. 4), 206–35. I do not presume that there is a proper Israelite and a Near Eastern way of divine presence but that there is a strong tension in Israel among its various ways of understanding the issue. Thus while his point is well taken, I do not assume that Menahem Haran, in "The Divine Presence in the Israelite Cult and the Cultic Institutions," *Bib* 50 (1969): 253–58, has effectively disposed of the issue, because Haran appears to ignore the political dimensions of the issue that require attention. I hope to indicate that this issue about presence is at the same time a dispute over models of social relationships and distribution of social power.

5. It is appropriate to speak of *face* as "metaphor"; see Terrien, *Elusive Presence*, 311. Face is surely rooted in a quite concrete reference (vehicle) and is handled imaginatively to bear surplus meanings (tenor). On the use of metaphor for Scripture study, see Phyllis Trible, *God and Rhetoric* (see chap. 4, n. 16), chap. 1. On the possibility of surplus meaning see Paul Ricoeur, *Interpretation Theory* (Fort Worth: Texas Christian University Press, 1976). Wather Eichrodt, in *Theology of the Old Testament II* (London: SCM Press, 1967), 36, means something different and less by a "metaphorical sense" of face.

menon. Thus, this chapter seeks to suggest some new connections in an attempt to contribute to methodological matters now before us.

I

There can be little doubt that Exodus 33 is the most sustained and delicate attempt to deal with the problem of Yahweh's presence/absence in Israel.[6] The chapter appears to be a loosely constructed collection of diverse traditions, all of which struggle with the issue of presence,[7] but the various elements seem to have no necessary connection to each other. We may identify at least four elements: (1) vv. 1-6 (itself a complex piece) in which the presence of Yahweh is said to be in jeopardy even though there is a command to leave the mountain; (2) vv. 7-11 on the tent of meeting;[8] (3) vv. 12-17, a conversation between Yahweh and Moses, with the tone of conflict; and (4) vv. 18-23, a theophany in which the presence of Yahweh draws near to Moses. Of these four elements, we are here concerned with the last two, vv. 12-17 and 18-23.

The source analysis of this chapter is notoriously difficult and not likely to be of great help. It is clear that we are dealing with early (JE?) materials not to be confused with the more sustained Priestly attempts at the problem of presence. To be more specific, however, is highly subjective and we must leave the question open.[9]

More important than an identification of sources is the crucial location of this text in the Sinai-sojourn materials. Exodus 32–34 contains a remarkable acknowledgment by Israel's tradition that Israel's history with Yahweh is fractured and that the well-being assured in the covenant of Sinai is in jeopardy. One could have wished for a direct linkage between the fidelity of covenant in Exodus 19–24 and the sojourn in the land, but Israel's memory is more

---

6. Werner H. Schmidt, in *Das Erste Gebot* (Munich: Chr. Kaiser Verlag, 1969), can write: "The individual narratives of Exodus 33 discuss the theological problem of how God's presence on Sinai and his presence with the wandering people of God stand in relation to one another and they attempt in different ways to solve it" (p. 7, n. 1). Cf. Martin Noth, *Exodus* (London: SCM Press, 1962), 253.

7. For representative treatments of the critical problems, see Walter Beyerlin, *Origins and History of the Oldest Sinaitic Traditions* (Oxford: Blackwell, 1965), 18–26, 98–126, 133–143; and Brevard S. Childs, *Exodus* (London: SCM Press, 1974), 582–600.

8. On the tent in relation to ancient Near Eastern religion, see Richard J. Clifford, "The Tent of El and the Israelite Tent of Meeting," *CBQ* 33 (1971): 226–27.

9. Beyerlin attempts a close source division, whereas Noth believes that is impossible. See the comments of Childs, *Exodus*, 584.

candid. There is not fidelity even at the mountain; therefore, there is not unmitigated well-being in the covenant from the first moment. Whatever historical issues may be behind this text, these three chapters insist on realism about the character of the relationship. They insist that a formulation of Yahweh's presence in Israel may not be a cultic, liturgical resolution immune to historical threat, but that Israel's formulation of divine presence must be full in the face of historical slippage. It is perhaps the skewed character of history, skewed by disobedience, that makes the matter of God's presence both so important and so problematic. Insofar as the "hunger for transcendence" and eagerness for "religious experience" are currently cultural realities, one may suggest it is the skewedness of disobedience that makes them currently both so important and so difficult. Even the disobedient community is able to discern that we are made for presence, and when that is in jeopardy, everything is in jeopardy.[10]

Thus, chapter 33 is placed precisely between the disobedience of 32 and the new beginning of 34. By the beginning of 33, everything is in danger.[11] There is no assurance of continuation. What Yahweh is to do with recalcitrant Israel is still an open question (33:5). Thus chapter 33 forms a bridge over the abyss between the forfeiture of 32 and the "second coming" of Yahweh in 34, characterized by law, theophany, and covenant, grounds for a continued history. But the ground that cannot be found in Israel (cf. 32) is now found only in Yahweh (34). This bridging function of 33 may be more closely drawn in the chapter itself. In v. 3, there is a negative looking back to the fracture of 32: "I will not go up in your midst." In vv. 19-22, with the double use of "pass by," there is a positive looking forward to a new beginning wrought in chapter 34. Israel in this text is placed

---

10. On the current "hunger for transcendence" and theological efforts to deal with it, see the discussions of Peter L. Berger, *Rumor of Angels* (Garden City, N.Y.: Doubleday & Co., 1969); and Langdon Gilkey, *Naming the Whirlwind* (Indianapolis: Bobbs-Merrill, 1969). Although these books intend to be descriptive of the situation and not constructive theology (though Gilkey is intentionally more constructive than Berger), neither of them frontally makes the link of *presence* and *obedience*, upon which the Mosaic tradition insists. The dialectic of ethics and aesthetics that Terrien presents is much more useful in making that claim out of the Mosaic tradition. On absence and presence as an issue in contemporary theology, see the suggestive essays, *The Presence and Absence of God*, ed. Christopher F. Mooney, S.J. (New York: Fordham University Press, 1969).

11. Childs (*Exodus*, 582) entitles his discussion of the chapter "God's Presence Endangered." This is surely the main point, though derivatively much more is endangered, even the existence of Israel.

between the sin of 32 and the covenant of 34, between the negation of 33:3 and the affirmation of 33:19, 22. And between them, there is the lament of vv. 4-6, the tent of vv. 7-11, and the hard bargaining of vv. 12-17. Between 33:3 and 33:19, 22, Israel must come to terms with the strange reality of Yahweh's presence that comes in a way quite sufficient, but in a way not expected by conventional religious standards and not wished for by Moses and Israel.

Verses 12-17 are placed at the heart of that moment between negation and affirmation.[12] In this unit, everything hangs in the balance; but as we shall see, at its end, nothing is settled. Indeed, nothing can be settled except that Yahweh retains the initiative and the relationship will have to be on Yahweh's terms. That is, however, precisely the situation at the beginning of 32 that evoked that crisis. Thus the problem of presence is made acute, enduring, and unresolvable only because of the character of Yahweh and Yahweh's sovereign ways in the relationship.

We are not faced simply with the problem of *presence* but with the *presence of Yahweh*. The matter is not a general religious one, but one concerning the unaccommodating character of this God. It is disregard of the distinctiveness, even jealousy, of Yahweh that has permitted the contemporary question of presence to become a general religious question. Israel's royal trajectory has this inclination, which is resisted by Moses.

I call attention to two especially helpful analyses of the unit. James Muilenburg has paid particular attention to the rhetorical movement of the passage, urging that it is easily divided into two exchanges.[13] In both vv. 12-14 and vv. 15-17 there is a request from Moses and a response on the part of Yahweh. Moreover, Muilenburg has been especially attentive to the verb "know" (*yāda'*), which occurs six times in the passage and in which he rightly finds the clue to the unit.

I shall not attempt to advance upon Muilenburg's rhetorical analysis, but I make three additional comments:

1. We may be more closely attentive to the six uses of *yāda'*, for

---

12. Following Childs, the break between vv. 17 and 18 surely seems correct but has not been conventional. I hope my analysis will indicate further reasons for this division.

13. Muilenburg, "The Intercession of the Covenant Mediator (Exodus 33:1a, 12-17)," in *Words and Meanings: Essays Presented to David Winton Thomas*, ed. Peter H. Ackroyd and Barnabas Lindars (Cambridge: Cambridge University Press, 1968), 159–81. Muilenburg includes v. 1a in our passage, which is plausible but not necessary to our analysis.

they indicate a strong dissonance in the dialogue. Of the six uses, five of them (vv. 12, 12, 13, 13, 16) are in the mouth of Moses, of which one (v. 12) is a quote from Yahweh. It is Moses who introduces the theme of knowing. The four uses are an urging on Moses' part to know as he is known. He wants to be the active agent of knowing. His demand is imperative to the point of abrasion, for he addresses Yahweh as though Yahweh were an unresponsive equal. The other two uses, in vv. 12 and 17, although one is quoted by Moses, are in fact the same statement by Yahweh, a lordly, unaccommodating reassurance that yields nothing and only asserts, "I know you by name." Thus, it is not enough to see that both parties use the key verb. The use by both parties is not to express agreement or compatibility but is used rhetorically to show the conflict of the one who insists and the one who grants nothing. At the end of the unit, Moses is given nothing new to know and Yahweh is still the only subject of the verb with any substance.

Moses wants to know, but he is not given to know. Perhaps it is possible to see in this exchange of the verb an analogue to the primordial couple (Genesis 2–3) who want to know and be like God. At most it is a hint.[14] But the drama that might have been used to suggest *communion* in fact only serves to stress the *distance*. The mess of chapter 32 is not overcome. There will not be easy identification, for what follows it is an important provisional conclusion that the very text that is concerned with *presence* in fact asserts *distance and incongruity*.

2. Muilenburg mentions the fivefold use of the formula "find favor in eyes" (vv. 12, 13, 16, 16, 17), but he does not exploit it for interpretation.[15] Again the phrase is four times placed in the mouth of Moses as suppliant (vv. 12, 13, 13, 16), with the first of these being a quote from Yahweh. The other three suggest an intense and anxious desire for assurance that Yahweh will not give. It is like asking for a sign (cf. Judg. 6:36-40) by one who can scarcely believe. The two other uses of the phrase by Yahweh (v. 17, in addition to the quote in v. 12) again concede nothing and press Moses to rely only on the word of assurance, which he already had at the beginning of the pericope and which he found so hard to trust. Thus, the

---

14. On the assertive dimension of Moses as presented in the tradition, see George W. Coats, "The King's Loyal Opposition: Obedience and Authority in Exodus 32–34," in *Canon and Authority* (see chap. 7, n. 25), 91–109. The emergence of the heroic suggests links to the pursuit of knowledge in Genesis 2–3.

15. Muilenburg, "Covenant Mediator," 169.

double statement of Yahweh, "I know you by name, you have found favor in my sight" (vv. 12, 17), provides an envelope for the unit, but there is little development. The last assurance is nothing more than the first assurance repeated and it remains precarious throughout. Moses had hoped for a more certain assurance, but it is not given. The same precarious one is given again.

Most striking is the fact that while this unit purports to be about presence and likely cultic presence, Yahweh insists on keeping the conversation in historical, political language, the language of precariousness. There is here little indication of cultic symbol or liturgical enactment. There is only the word of the king who holds life and death in his hand. This fivefold formula is surely one drawn from the realm of royal politics.[16] It speaks of the *power* one holds over another and the complete *dependence* of the one on the other. Moses is driven to trust this lordly, invisible word and nothing more.

How little change there is in Yahweh's response to Mosaic uncertainty is indicated by the fact that Moses is left precisely where Aaron was in 32:1 when the free, invisible God did not provide enough assurance. Moses, like his community, wants more than will be granted.

3. The analysis of the two formulae, "know" and "find favor in the eyes of," surprisingly shows their absence in the middle of the unit, in vv. 14-15. In these two verses, we have a quite different exchange. Thus, in refinement of Muilenburg's double structure, perhaps we may argue that "know" and "find favor in the eyes of" in vv. 12-13, 16-17 provide an envelope for 14-15, which speaks in a very different idiom. Here, and only here in these verses, are an assurance and a questioning of assurance that contrast with the plea/response structure Muilenburg uncovered. Now the conversation flows the other way. In the middle of the *plea/response* structure there now appears *promise/protest* in which the dynamics are quite different.

By such an analysis, the promise of v. 14 is the center of the text,

---

16. The formula characteristically occurs in contexts of abasement before a king who holds the power of life and death in his decree. Cf. Gen. 47:29; 50:4; 1 Sam. 25:8; 27:5; 2 Sam. 14:22; 16:4; 1 Kings 11:19; Esther 5:8; 7:3; 8:5. It is used in a curiously triangular way in 1 Samuel between Saul, David, and Jonathan as the narrative works its way to the new kingship. Cf. David Jobling, *The Sense of Biblical Narrative*, JSOTSup, no. 7 (Sheffield: University of Sheffield Press, 1978), chap. 1. It is also used of Moses to indicate his leadership (Num. 32:5), and in a derivative theological sense with Moses in Num. 11:11-15 and with David in 2 Sam. 15:25. The primary sense, however, is political, asserting unequal power relations, and indicating postures of superiority and subordination.

for it is both the response to the first plea and the promise that evokes the protest of v. 15. It looks both ways. It contains two parts:

> My face goes (with you)
> I give you rest.

The first of these seems to introduce a more visible cultic assurance (on which see below), but the second element of the promise is again doggedly historical. The motif of "rest" may indicate that what is being promised is leadership on the way to the land.[17] The central promise of Yahweh then is one of historical dynamic again calling to sojourn (cf. v. 1) and not a stable, even static "placement" for which Moses seems to yearn.[18] Ironically, in his challenging response of v. 15, Moses presses only the first element of the promise and is silent on the second.

This analysis suggests that Moses' request and insistent repetition of it seek to avoid the circumstance that produced Aaron's radical act in chapter 32. But Yahweh's response and promise here concede nothing that changes the circumstance. Yahweh insists that Moses (and Israel) must walk utterly by faith. Yahweh is the only knower. Moses is given to know nothing beyond the promise unencumbered by visible assurances.[19] The desire for presence is kept uncompromisingly historical.

That historical definition of presence (as opposed to anything cultic or epiphanic) is enhanced in v. 16 by the use of the term "distinction" (*pālâ*). That term has already been used in three passages in the exodus narrative:

> But on that day I will set *apart* the land of Goshen, where my people dwell, so that no swarms of flies shall be there; that you may know that I am the Lord in the midst of the earth. (Exod. 8:18, Eng. 22)

---

17. To be sure, the term "rest" here is not the usual one for rest as promised land; however, the possible links to the ark and the general theme of guidance make this the most plausible meaning. Cf. Thomas Mann, "Pillar of Cloud," *JBL* 90 (1971): 25. Although it is a problem that the rest is to Moses specifically and not to Israel, the context, I believe, requires such a reading. See Childs (*Exodus*, 594), who is cautious on the point; and Beyerlin, *Sinaitic Traditions*, 100–110.

18. On the temptation to a static placement of God, see the discussion of Walter Krebs, "Der sitzende Gott," *TZ* 30 (1974): 1–10. On the interplay of revelation and promise, see Knierim, "Offenbarung," 218.

19. On "knowing nothing" in relation to the yearning to know, see the discussion of Paul below and esp. 1 Cor. 2:2, in which Paul resists the religious knowing of Corinth: "For I decided to know nothing among you except Jesus Christ and him crucified."

But the Lord will make a *distinction* between the cattle of Israel and
the cattle of Egypt, so that nothing shall die of all that belongs to the
people of Israel. (Exod. 9:4)

But against any of the people of Israel, either man or beast, not a
dog shall growl; that you may know that the Lord makes a *distinction*
between the Egyptians and Israel. (Exod. 11:7)

These three uses[20] indicate that the distinctive action of Yahweh toward Israel (in the three uses progressively presented as land/cattle/
people) concerns *historical deliverance*; that is, it has to do with an
action and not at all a presence or an appearance. Interestingly, in
8:18 the verb "know" (so central in our passage) is used as the conclusion of distinctiveness, "that you may know that I am Yahweh in the
midst of the earth."[21] And in 11:7 the verb "know" is closely linked
to "division."

Thus, it is possible to suggest that out of the plague-exodus
narrative, our unit makes a play on the juxtaposition of know/
distinguish. Our text agrees with the exodus narrative that the
deliverance-separation-leadership theme is the ground of knowing
and certitude, and Yahweh here will not permit Moses to change the
subject in the interest of religious certitude.

In the midst of a demand for "face," the stress clearly falls on
historical, political language that looks back to exodus (*pālâ*) and
stretches forward to land (rest). Moses is granted only the assurance
of guidance.[22] Now perhaps we may see why in the conclusion of
v. 17, Yahweh seems to grant Moses' request and yet has conceded
nothing. The reason is that in a conversation that purports to be
about visible revelation, likely cultic, the resolution is kept tightly
in the idiom of historical trust. All three of our observations—(*a*)
that the demand to "know" is not granted, (*b*) that the formula of
assurance is essentially political, and (*c*) that in vv. 14-15 a different universe of discourse is operative[23]—indicate that the claim for

---

20. See also the possible use in Exod. 8:19 (Eng. 23), though that use is improbable.

21. On the formula, see Walther Zimmerli, "Erkenntnis Gottes nach dem Buche
Ezechiel," reprinted in *Gottes Offenbarung*, TBü, no. 19 (Munich: Chr. Kaiser Verlag,
1963), 41–119. On this text and the linkage of *know* and *distinguish*, see pp. 61–62.

22. On the theme of guidance, see Thomas W. Mann, *Divine Presence* (see chap. 7,
n. 12). For our purposes it is important that Mann shows the cluster of themes of
guidance and leadership to be insistently political. His argument is that this language
used in Israel theologically is reflective of political realities in its origin.

23. By this it is not at all suggested that these verses are an intrusion. Rather the
unit is constructed to show that the envelope of "know-favor" is brought to focus on

more immediate, intense, and sure guarantees of presence is turned aside in yet another summons to radical trust of Yahweh in a dangerous pilgrimage. Thus, it may be, as Muilenburg suggests, that this is a liturgical presentation; but if so, it is a liturgy of a peculiar kind, polemical in its rejection of normal notions of divine presence, reflective of Israel's more radical trajectory.[24] The purpose of such a liturgy is to drive Israel back out of the presumed safety of the shrine into the risks of Yahweh's history.

The other analysis of the text to which reference must be made is that of Samuel Terrien.[25] Largely accepting Muilenburg's rhetorical analysis, Terrien probes the language for its theological claim. I find myself in close agreement with Terrien's analysis, although I would make one point quite differently. Terrien presents vv. 12-23 in one developing, dramatic unit, seeing three requests by Moses and three divine responses:

The First Request (33:12-14)
    The Plea for Knowledge of God (vv. 12-13)
    The Divine Answer to the First Plea (v. 14)

The Second Request (33:15-17)
    The Plea for Continuing Presence (vv. 15-16)
    The Divine Answer (v. 17)

The Third Request (33:18-23)
    The Plea for the Vision of Glory (v. 18)
    The Divine Refusal (vv. 19-20)
    The Divine Concession (vv. 21-23)

That analysis has much to commend it; however, Terrien also suggests that a quite different issue is raised in his "Third Request." For reasons that I hope become apparent, I am inclined to juxtapose vv. 12-17 and 18-23 in a more abrasive way than does Terrien.

---

the radical trust required of the *face* that must be trusted and the *rest* that cannot be grasped.

24. Muilenburg, "Covenant Mediator," 181. This suggestion is rejected by Childs, *Exodus*, 585.

25. Terrien, *Elusive Presence*, 138–52. I am glad to acknowledge that the two scholars who have treated the text most suggestively, Muilenburg and Terrien, are my teachers. My debt to both of them, not only in this study but generally, is very great.

II

Verses 18-23 (which Terrien views as a continuation of the same conversation) appear to change abruptly the character of the discussion. Verses 12-17 were indeed a genuine exchange in which each party dealt seriously with what the other had said. Verses 18-23 are quite in contrast to that. In three ways I suggest this unit is removed from the angers and passions of history that set it apart from vv. 12-17.

1. There is no real exchange, and Moses is not a party to the text. He speaks once, in v. 18; but his request is, in contrast to the contentiousness of what has preceded, bald and passionless. It does not seem to be as much a plea or demand that has grown out of historical experience as it is a device by the narrative to announce a theological theme not to be discussed. In any case, it is here a very different Moses, one who does not press his point at all. I regard v. 18 as not really a plea speech but a thematic heading for what follows. All of vv. 18-23 appear to be a somewhat removed, balanced theological reflection or meditation on the problem of divine revelation. It is offered by someone who is not informed by the dispute that has just ended but by someone who meditates on the mystery of the divine character and the nature of Yahweh's commitment to Israel.[26]

2. That this is a meditation or a reflection rather than an authentic exchange is evidenced by the new motif of "see." That was not at all the agenda in vv. 12-17.[27] It is clear that "see" in v. 18 is a new agenda from a quite different theological perspective, likely from the Zion-Jerusalem tradition.[28] The shift from "know" in vv. 12-17

---

26. I suggest that such a reflective theological statement, removed from the dangers of history as presented in vv. 12-17, may be particularly identified with the Jerusalem royal-temple establishment, for whom much is at stake in the question of accessibility and freedom. It is surely the case that the theologoumenon of glory was a continuing agenda of the Jerusalem theologians, for the obvious reason of connection with the claims of the king. On its subsequent use by the Priestly tradition, also rooted in the Jerusalem apparatus, see Westermann, "Die Herrlichkeit Gottes in der Priesterschrift," in *Forschung am Alten Testament*, TBü, no. 55 (Munich: Chr. Kaiser Verlag, 1974), 115–37.

27. The RSV in v. 13 follows the LXX in rendering the verb "show" or "let me see," but vv. 12-17 stay consistently with the theme of "know" as distinct from "see/show" in vv. 18-23. Thus the rendering of the RSV is misleading and distracts from the singular focus of "know" in the Hebrew text.

28. Terrien characterizes the Mosaic tradition thus: "For the northern theologians of the Elohist tradition, the visual faculty of man, the symbol of his sensorial and rational ability to know, is enlisted only in a preliminary way. Sight is submitted to hearing. Man never sees God, but the word is heard. The eye is closed but the ear is opened. Hebraism is a religion not of the eye but of the ear" (*Elusive Presence*, 112). But when he comes to speak of "glory" and the move to the eye, he writes: "A long-

to "see" in vv. 18-23 is not a development in a single discourse, but it reflects the agenda of an alternative theological tradition. This text, I propose, seeks to resolve the question of *knowing* in terms of an answer of *seeing*.[29] The yearning for *evangelical assurance* (which can only be a word of promise as it is in vv. 12-17) is here transformed into an offer of *cultic certitude*, and that changes issues completely.

3. That this is a reflection upon the character of God is evident in that after v. 18, Moses disappears from the text. This is not genuinely covenantal, for Moses has no role to play. Three times, in vv. 19, 20, 21, Yahweh makes a fresh statement with *wayō'mer*, but it is as though it were only a self-address, as though God were struggling for a way to be revealing yet transcendent, precisely the issue of the Jerusalem establishment that wanted to avoid the threat of historical revelation. The three entries of Yahweh do not allude to the historical issues of exodus-sojourn-land. They fall within the horizons of a community that thinks primarily in terms of the possibilities of cult. The three speeches of Yahweh are not evoked in turn by Moses. They have, rather, the character of a divine soliloquy.[30]

The three statements of Yahweh present three facets of revelation, each of which needs to be set alongside the other two. Thus, I am not convinced that there is development from the first to the third, from "refusal" to "concession." Except for reasons of emphasis, they could as well be presented in another order, for none of the three features is nullified by the other two. The second speech (v. 20) reasserts what must be an old premise of biblical faith.[31] That

---

ingrained theology of glory in Zion had prevailed ever since the foundation of the temple" (p. 203). Subsequently (p. 422), he speaks of the alliance of ear and eye.

29. See the distinctions in verb usage suggested by Frank Schnutenhaus, "Das Kommen und Erscheinen Gottes im Alten Testament," *ZAW* 76 (1964): 1–22; Schnutenhaus refers to the contrast of historical and cultic epiphany. Beyerlin (*Sinaitic Traditions*, 106–7) asserts that in Israel the "face" relates to theophany and not to image. In this he reflects the same distinctions in the notion of presence that Moltmann has pursued more theologically. See Knierim's discussion on knowing and seeing, "Offenbarung," esp. 215–20. Special attention should be called to the exchange of Zimmerli and Rolf Rendtorff and a review of their positions by Robinson. Cf. Moltmann, *The Crucified God* (London: SCM Press, 1974), 166ff.

30. On the matter of divine soliloquy, see Roderick A. F. MacKenzie, S.J., "The Divine Soliloquies in Genesis," *CBQ* 17 (1955): 277–86. J. Gerald Janzen, in studying Hos. 11:8-9, has suggested that the soliloquy of Yahweh presented there is not simply a rhetorical device but is in fact a fresh exploration by Yahweh concerning Yahweh's relation to Israel; see Janzen, "Metaphor" (see chap. 2, n. 24). I suggest that in parallel fashion, this soliloquy by Yahweh, crafted in three statements, is presented as a fresh decision by Yahweh regarding a self-presentation to Moses, who asks too much. Thus it is bold reflection by theologians, at the very dangerous edge of theological thought.

31. It is reflected in Gen. 32:30 and in Judg. 6:23; 13:22. For purposes of our

is the beginning point of the problem of visible revelation. It is *dangerous*. The second facet is the assertion of divine gracious *freedom* in v. 19, which in structure echoes Exod. 3:14. I would not label it, as does Terrien, "refusal." Rather, it establishes the ground and basis of God's initiative. It is not refusal; it simply asserts that anything seen will be Yahweh's doing and not forced by Moses. Third, there is the staggering *disclosure* of vv. 21-23, the only one in which the divine name is given as subject for the verb of speech. But the *disclosure* of vv. 21-23 in no way nullifies the *danger* stated in v. 20 nor the *freedom* claimed in v. 19.

Terrien has rightly seen the marvelous juxtaposition of two word pairs in this narrative. First, Moses asks to see *glory* and is given to see *goodness*. Glory undoubtedly reflects a high cultic view of presence.[32] As is now well-established, goodness pertains to covenantal relatedness and tilts toward *action*, not *appearance*.[33] Thus, even in the unit that ostensibly concerns *seeing God*, that is immediately and decisively denied. The sharp juxtaposition of "glory" in v. 18 and "goodness" in v. 19 is set to assert that the theme of glory announced in v. 18 is the wrong theme and cannot be dealt with until it is reformulated in acceptable terms. Second, there is the play of face/back, in which again Yahweh grants something but not at all what is asked. To these may be added a third, that Moses asks to *see* (*har'ēnî*) and the answer is "I will *proclaim*" (*qārā'*). Thus even the idiom is transferred from the visible to the audible. These three pairs—glory/goodness, face/back, see/proclaim—suggest a keen sense of irony in which the response that appears to concede in each case quite radically redefines the issues to conform to the purpose and character of this God who is ill at ease in discussions about revelation. The Moses of v. 18 (a device to broach the subject) wants more than can be given. Thus the response of vv. 19-23 may be correct teaching in response to a popular misconception of v. 18.[34] The name of Yahweh (v. 19) that is

---

subsequent discussion, it is also important to note uses of the motif in John 1:18 and in 1 John 3:2.

32. On glory as a theologoumenon of the Jerusalem royal establishment, in addition to the work of Westermann and Terrien already cited, see Bernard W. Anderson, *Creation versus Chaos* (New York: Association Press, 1967).

33. Muilenburg ("Covenant Mediator," 180–81) has cited studies showing that "know" may in certain uses be a covenantal word. The same argument has been offered for "good" as well. For the bibliography on *ṭôb* as a treaty term meaning friendship, see Dennis McCarthy, *Old Testament Covenant* (Oxford: Blackwell, 1973), 15 n. 12, for his citation of William L. Moran, Delbert R. Hillers, and Abraham Malamat.

34. On the tension between popular religion and more intentional theology, see

gracious freedom and sovereign graciousness means that final certitude cannot be given. The request reflects an agenda belonging to religion, a yearning for epiphany. But Yahweh stays free of such religious certitude. The three statements of Yahweh in vv. 19-23 reflect in the present form not a redactional process that added on various motifs but a divine soliloquy in which Yahweh (and Yahweh's theologians) work out a new way to give an *assurance* that is not a *certitude.*

III

Thus, we conclude that vv. 12-17 and 18-23 reflect quite distinct contributions to this mediating chapter on presence. Characteristically these two units are dealt with separately in the commentaries, as is every other part of the chapter.[35] No effort generally is made to discern any organic intention in their being together. It is the special merit of Terrien's exegesis that he has held them together. For reasons given above, however, I suggest that they cannot be treated as an original unit as does Terrien, although that approach is preferable to an atomistic approach often followed. More likely than either such treatment—that is, to treat such units as only *fragments* or to see them as an *original unity*—I propose that they were originally independent traditions that faced quite different issues but were wrought together for fresh purposes that we may discern in their present form. The one, vv. 12-17, reflects a tradition of covenantal dispute; and the other, vv. 18-23, presents a more detached rumination on the theme of freedom and disclosure.

We must, however, consider what has been intended and accomplished by bringing these very different elements together. We

---

Judah Benzion Segal, "Popular Religion in Ancient Israel," *JJS* 27 (1976): 1–22; Martin Rose, "Schultheologie und Volksfrömmigkeit," *WD* (1975): 86–104; and *Der Ausschliesslichkeitsanspruch Jahwes*, BWANT, no. 6 (Berlin: Kohlhammer, 1975); James Crenshaw, *Prophetic Conflict*, BZAW, no. 124 (Berlin: de Gruyter, 1971); and Rainer Albertz, *Persönliche* (see chap. 1, n. 4). Again note that the antithesis here suggested is not between an Israelite and a non-Israelite, pagan perspective. Both are genuinely Israelite. The text reflects a battle for the life of Israel, but it is not a matter of an alien, outside, or foreign intrusion. It is, rather, a dispute that reflects interests, both theological and political, well within the confines of Israel.

35. Thus, in addition to Beyerlin and Childs, see Noth, *Exodus*, 253–58; and Philip Hyatt, *Commentary on Exodus* (London: Oliphants, 1971), 313–18. Umberto Cassuto, in *A Commentary on the Book of Exodus* (Jerusalem: Magnes, 1967), 432–37, does treat vv. 12-23 as a unit. This is an exception and anticipates Terrien's analysis.

assume that their joining is more than an artificial editorial act, but that something organic is intended, that is, the creation of a new juxtaposition impacting both units. Clearly the principle of combination is to join together themes on *face*, but that joining is not by an external device of *Stichwort*. Canon criticism asks not only about the links between Old Testament and New Testament but about the ways in which various elements are juxtaposed in the tradition to create intentional new configurations. The juxtaposition of vv. 12-17 and 18-23, I suggest, is an example of such an intentional new configuration, for their linkage permits both of them to mean something more than and different from either taken alone.

The theologoumenon *face*, it is now generally agreed, came to mean *cultic presence*.[36] While it became stylized simply to mean the cultic place, it is probable that it referred, in its origin, specifically to an image or representation of the deity, which was kept in the shrine and which worshipers could see. Thus, it likely grows out of a quite concrete, visible notion of presence. It was, as has been widely argued in the exegesis of Gen. 1:26-28, a common practice to set up representations to assert presence and rule.[37] But the usage of image or representation of the deity should not be trivialized, as though the image was equated with or identified with the actual deity. Certainly any reflective religion is aware of a distinction between agent and representation. Having said that, however, it is likely that the necessary and deliberate ambiguity of image as presence and distance is inevitably tilted toward presence, so that when the representation is fully seen, the deity is fully present. And undoubtedly that tilt toward presence may be understood quite crudely or with

---

36. Terrien (*Elusive Presence*, 159 n. 78) has cited the standard discussions. They include Wolf E. H. von Baudissin, " 'Gott schauen' in der alttestamentlichen Religion," *ARW* 18 (1915): 173ff.; E. Gideon Gulin, "Das Antlitz Jahwes im Alten Testament," *AASF* 17, ser. B (1923); Friedrich Nötscher, *"Das Angesicht Gottes schauen," nach biblischer und babylonischer Auffassung* (Würzburg: C. J. Becker, 1924); Aubrey R. Johnson, "Aspects of the Use of the Term PNYM in the Old Testament," in *Festschrift Otto Eissfeldt*, ed. Johann Fück (Halle: Niemeyer, 1947), 155–59; and Joseph Reindl, *Das Angesicht Gottes im Sprachgebrauch des Alten Testaments* (Leipzig: St. Benno, 1970). Of these, the study of our passage by Reindl (pp. 56–69) is most pertinent to the present discussion. Summary statements may be found in Edmond Jacob, *Theology of the Old Testament* (London: Hodder & Stoughton, 1958), 77–79; and Eichrodt, *Theology of the Old Testament II*, 35–39.

37. That exegesis has been especially prominent under the influence of Gerhard von Rad, *Genesis* (London: SCM Press, 1972), 57–60. See the particular nuance given this by Westermann, *Genesis* (Minneapolis: Augsburg, 1984–86), where "rule" is linked to the caring of the shepherd.

sophistication, but clearly the representation seen inclined a practice more toward accessibility than toward freedom.[38]

The cultic function of face is likely primary in the religious world of the Old Testament; but George E. Mendenhall, following Ernst H. Kantorowicz, suggests that this normal cultic practice concerned with presence may also be understood as a political representative concerned not with *presence* but with *authority*.[39] Thus, the face of the royal one is not undialectically an announcement of *being present to* but also *being lord over*. Deut. 4:37 regards the face as a political metaphor of sovereignty; and Exod. 34:9 also looks in a more covenantal, relational direction. Mendenhall's suggestion is one that is characteristically peculiar to his own work, but insofar as it is a cogent one, this gives yet another dialectic of *cultic presence with* and *political sovereignty over*. There is no doubt that singular attention to cultic presence can serve to nullify the historical-political claims of the ruler said to be present in this way, and that is the ground for Yahweh's resistance to full disclosure. Such full "seeing of the glory" would give full assurance of presence to Moses and Israel, but it would dimin-

---

38. For a review of the scholarship on the matter of visibility as presence, see Karl-Heinz Berhardt, *Gott und Bild* (Berlin: Evangelische Verlagsanstalt, 1956). It is especially noteworthy how the motif of nomadic background has influenced scholarship in light of the study of Norman K. Gottwald. Equally important, conversely, is the extreme reticence with which the problem of images has been linked to political criticism.

39. Mendenhall, "The Mask of Yahweh," in *Tenth Generation* (see chap. 1, n. 15), 32–66, has investigated the Israelite theologoumenon of cloud (with reference to face) in light of the royal ideology of the Near East—with reference to the *melammu/puluḫtu* of the king, the manifestation of splendor that asserts the sovereignty and authority of the king, and its counterpart of the god. On our passage, see pp. 59–60. It is important to Mendenhall's argument that the "glory" can be given and revoked, lost when conquered by a superior agent. Thus it is not indelible but lives in the dangers of historical power. What is of prime importance for our discussion is that Mendenhall's interpretation is consistently political, dealing with the dynamics of historical interaction and not with eternal religious categories. I urge in this chapter that the interplay of Yahweh and Moses in our text concerns their relative power and authority and that Yahweh's reticence about the divine face is that Yahweh wishes to make a commitment to Moses but without placing Yahweh's sovereignty in danger. In the latter part of the chapter, I suggest that when the face of Jesus is understood in such political terms, the conflict in the text is greatly illuminated. Kantorowicz, in *The King's Two Bodies* (Princeton, N.J.: Princeton University Press, 1957), presents the Tudor fiction of the king as two persons, one the historical person with legal rights and limits, the other the invisible person of absolute perfection. The curious interplay between the two in a thoroughly political atmosphere concerns us because the issue is surely acute for the biblical notion of the presence of God. Even though the two bodies may be a "man-made irreality" (p. 5), the notion reflects acknowledgment of a serious political problem concerning the king as human body and "body politic," concerning God as *present to* and *free from*.

ish if not nullify the distance essential to freedom, sovereignty, and leadership.[40]

On the full seeing of the glory as the endangerment of sovereignty, we may also refer to the reception given the Babylonian envoys by Hezekiah in Isaiah 39. Peter H. Ackroyd has called attention to the central importance of *see* in this passage. The passage states:

> He *showed* them his treasure house, the silver, the gold.... There was nothing in his house or in all his realm that Hezekiah did not *show* them.... "What have they *seen* in your house?" Hezekiah answered, "They have *seen* all that is in my house; there is nothing in my storehouses that I did not *show* them." (39:2-4)[41]

The showing of the glory in Exodus 33 is not unlike the action of Hezekiah. When it is seen, it comes into their power. The notion that seeing means to *come into power over*, or *possession of*, may be linked to Mendenhall's insight that the face has to do with political authority. Thus, even though we may be dealing in the first instance with a problem of cultic presence, it is clear that underneath such a question is the issue of authority, freedom, and sovereignty of a quite political kind. All of that is at issue in the seeing and not seeing the face. The critical issue of the face is enhanced in fresh ways by the juxtaposition of these two texts.

Thus, the yearning for religious security is perceived in Israel as an issue of Yahweh's sovereign freedom. Characteristically in Israel,

---

40. It will be evident that our perspective assumes the close interplay of religious language and political reality. Mendenhall in his various writings has indicated what happens when the critical distance between political reality and religious authority is collapsed, or conversely, when politics is cast as religious ideology. On myth and ritual as a way of overcoming the distance between humankind and mythical being, see Thorkild Jacobsen, "Religious Drama" (see chap. 1, n. 31). The result is a political absolutism, for there is no transcendent principle to which appeal can be made in criticism of the present political arrangement. Thus the "freedom, sovereignty, and leadership" of Yahweh are not just polite religious concerns, but they have everything to do with Israel's vision of political freedom and justice. Surely New Testament interpretation will be illuminated as these political issues are taken into account with reference to the face of Jesus as the glory of God. Both Mendenhall and Gottwald, following the general insight of Karl Marx, have pursued the linkage of religious claim and political modeling. (For their literature, see my "Trajectories," 10–11.) The "seeing of the glory" is linked to the diminishment of authority. Yahweh's refusal to be seen is allied to a resolve not to be at the disposal of or disposed by Yahweh's creatures, subjects, and partners.

41. Ackroyd, "An Interpretation of the Babylonian Exile: A Study of 2 Kings 20, Isaiah 38–39," *SJT* 27 (1974): 329–52.

such cultic concerns can never be separate from the matter of historical freedom. The double program of *genuine cultic presence* and *real historical freedom*, I suggest, is the reason for the juxtaposition of our two passages.

Both vv. 12-17 and 18-23 are concerned with the problem of God's face to Israel. The history of translation and interpretation of these units has not addressed in any depth the problem with the symbol of face. On the one hand, the theologoumenon has suggested ready access and direct meeting. On the other hand, it has seemed dangerously materialistic and primitive. The Greek New Testament happily can distinguish between "face" (*prosōpon*) and "presence" (*enōpion*), but the Hebrew has no such device. As a result, translators have tended to use face and presence by choice, using face for times when things are protected theologically or when nothing is at issue and presence when there is a desire to speak intentionally and in freighted ways about God's presence. Although that gives translators and interpreters some freedom and some opportunity for precision, as is always the case, such choices tend to disguise the issues. Thus, in our text the RSV translates *pen* in vv. 14-15 as "presence," but in vv. 20, 23 it is rendered "face."[42] But the tradition itself does not make that distinction, and it must not be made if we are to understand what was intended and accomplished in the juxtaposition of these two texts.

We have seen that at the center of vv. 12-17 stands this exchange:

My *face* will go with you. . . .
If your *face* does not go with us, do not carry us up. . . .

---

42. The MT unflinchingly uses "face" in both units; however, the LXX already dissolved the tension. LXX rendered "face" in vv. 20, 23 (*prosōpon*); but in vv. 14-15, it rendered "I myself" (*autos*). In this, the LXX has been generally followed by translators:

	Living Bible	*New English Bible*	*Jerusalem Bible*
v. 14	"I myself"	"go with you in person"	"I myself"
v. 15	"you"	"go with you in person"	"you"
v. 20	"see glory of my face"	"my face . . . see me"	"see my face . . . see me"
v. 23	"face"	"face"	"face"

Thus "face" is retained only in v. 23 (and to some extent in v. 20) where the rendering "face" is necessary to give the text meaning. Elsewhere the term to express a tension has been resolved and the distance in the theologoumenon has been overcome. See the comment of Muilenburg ("Covenant Mediator," 172 n. 3) on the importance of the concreteness of the term.

We have also seen that in vv. 18-23, along with the glory/name/ goodness, there is the double use of face, presumably with concern to protect the freedom of the face:

> You cannot see my *face*,
> for man cannot see me and live....
> My *face* will not be seen.[43]

The first of these (vv. 14-15) is a *promise* that Moses found adequate, though hard to trust. The second (vv. 19, 23) is a *hedge* that held Moses at a distance. The reservation of the second means that the first requires radical trust, for it is an accompanying companion who will not be seen, even when trusted. The first means that the second, which is an important hedge for freedom, is not a denial or refusal but an inscrutable affirmation. Taken together they deny, on the one hand, that Israel is left to its own resources, for the face accompanies. On the other hand, they reject any presumption upon Yahweh, for the face maintains its incredible freedom.

The juxtaposition of the two establishes a remarkable evangelical dialectic. There is a harsh clash between the two texts, a clash that Terrien's analysis perhaps softens too much. It is a clash of traditions (I judge a northern, prophetic or covenantal tradition and a Jerusalem tradition of presence).[44] Each serves to correct the other, but both serve also to enhance and underscore the other. For it is never claimed that the unseen face should not be trusted. Nor is any hope given that the face, if trusted enough, may be seen. The one who asked to *see* is driven back to a request simply to *know*, but he is not given to know either. He is *known*. And that is enough.[45]

---

43. The identity of face and self is evident here. That is both the power and the problem with the theologoumenon. See Johnson, "Aspects," 158–59; and Reindl, *Angesicht Gottes*, 64. On the analogue in the study of Mendenhall, he observed that "*puluhtu* is a linguistic substitute for the person himself" (p. 53).

44. Although I believe the two units reflect diverse communities of cult and tradition (likely northern and southern, surely Mosaic and royal), I suggest no correlation with conventional assignments to J and E. Such a correlation would be very nice, but there is no basis for it.

45. The dialectic of "know" and "see" is thus reshaped as the dialectic of see-know/ known. The latter, upon which vv. 12-17 insists, means that Moses is addressed and named. Thus the contrast established is not far removed from the more familiar one of see/hear, for to be known is to listen to one's name being called. To be known and to hear are protests against every iconic attempt to control. See Erwin W. Straus, "Aesthesiology and Hallucinations," in *Existence*, ed. Rollo May (New York: Basic Books, 1958), 139–69, esp. 158–59 on the contrast of seeing and hearing. Hearing, says Straus, makes one the receiver, and obedience is "foreshadowed." In seeing, one is

Putting it that way, with Yahweh the subject of the verb, clashes with every royal religion that is enamored of image, vision, appearance, structure.[46] The temptation of all such static religion is to make God an object of adoration, visibility, observation, and veneration, an object of a human subject. The juxtaposition of texts offers a radical criticism of all such religions, asserting that Yahweh is subject, not object, and that historical pilgrimage is undertaken faithfully in Israel precisely when Israel accepts itself as the object of Yahweh's summons and leadership, of Yahweh's mercy and compassion. Thus, hunger for transcendence is displaced by an affirmation of election, for the one known is the one called and sent. The face is not *at rest*. The face is turned toward Canaan to *give rest*. And that shatters every category of Israel's would-be religion.

IV

Now it is our concern in this discussion to make a move to the New Testament. That is always a precarious move methodologically, because given our historicist predilection, we are not disposed to make that move as the early church seems readily to have done. We are not, however, here engaged in tracing the history of a motif. Rather, we are concerned with canon criticism, with the ways in which authoritative texts are taken up subsequently and used afresh, both as critique and as resource, to function with reasserted authority.

I urge that the theme of God's face—*present in Israel* but *hidden from Israel*—is one important way in which the early church articulated its faith around Jesus of Nazareth. The reality of Jesus affirmed to his

---

an active agent. Moreover, the eye is the agent for "identification and stabilization." More directly on seeing and hearing, on control and receiving as expressed in the Old Testament, see von Rad, *Old Testament Theology I* (see chap. 1, n. 22), 212–19, on the prohibition of images. Terrien (*Elusive Presence*, 152) contrasts the two under the rubric of name/glory: "The name demands active participation in the totality of life. The seeing of an image—or the cultic symbol of glory—tends to lull the worshipers into the delights of passive spirituality and the loss of social responsibility." Thus the prohibition of images in the Decalogue is the negative counterpart to the initial assertion of Yahweh's sovereignty in the First Commandment.

46. In the field of image/vision/appearance, it may seem strange to include "structure"; however, I am here building on the linkage of religious claim and political model. There can be no doubt that an iconic religion is likely to be found in a structured society that tends to be uncritical of its own social, political ordering, thus with a tendency to absolutizing. Thus by adding the word "structure" to this cluster, I mean to hint at the political implications of "seeing God." See Knierim, "Offenbarung," 219–20, with particular reference to Exod. 6:3 and Isa. 6:9.

community that in Jesus, the God of Israel was fully and powerfully present. And yet he did not look like the God of Israel. Thus it is precisely the passionate faith of the Jesus community that acutely posed the problem of presence, and the notion of "face" was an important means of speaking about that presence.

I have first selected three texts that speak of the *face of Jesus*. They are not linked in any way by the flow of tradition so that critical study would draw them together. I have selected them because they reflect facets of the reality of Jesus that made promises and caused problems to the early church:

First, it is clear that the early church had to face up to the human reality of Jesus, who was an affront, given the high theological claims made for him. Nowhere is he more of an affront than when he set his face (*prosōpon*) to go to Jerusalem (Luke 9:51,53). That Lucan presentation, which marks a turn in the narrative, includes two sticky features. First, that the face is to go to Jerusalem caused him to be rejected.[47] Second, in vv. 57-62, the one who has just set his face delivers his most radical and most demanding call to discipleship, in which he acknowledges that he has nowhere to lay his head and calls his disciples to the same risk he embraces. There is no explicit typological reference here to Exod. 33:14-15, but the face to Jerusalem is surely parallel to the face going with Israel in pursuit of the promise.

The face of Jesus, that powerful christological theologoumenon (cf. Matt. 11:10; 17:2; Mark 1:2), is at this point the concrete, historical raw face of the crucified. We are not dealing here with an image honored and safe, set apart and serene. Rather the face that *goes with* is *over against* all the powers of the day. Indeed the poverty-stricken humanness of his face in which he is disfigured (Isa. 53:2) and given a form of humiliation (Phil. 2:7-8) is precisely the problem, and it comes to this:

---

47. There is no doubt that the "face toward Jerusalem" is intended by the Gospels (if not by Jesus) as a dominical act. Cf. Ernst Lohmeyer, *Lord of the Temple* (London: Oliver & Boyd, 1961), 34–35. It is telling that Lohmeyer, without any interest in the issues we are considering, uses language pertinent to our question: "There is therefore a dualism involved in the entry as there is in the entrant. As the *Hidden One* he enters like any other honored Rabbi; as Son of Man, however, he enters with *the secret glory of the king*, coming to his people.... Under cover of this triumphal entry, therefore, it becomes evident just how closely the person of the Son of Man and the fact of the temple are bound up with each other" (p. 35, italics mine). Perhaps the lordly way to Jerusalem is indicated in Mark 11:11. When Jesus enters the temple, he "looked around at everything." His seeing may be like the seeing Hezekiah permitted in Isaiah 39, that is, coming into possession and control. Cf. James M. Robinson, *The Problem of History in Mark*, SBT, no. 21 (London: SCM Press, 1957), 52–53.

Then they spat in his face, and struck him; and some slapped him. (Matt. 26:67)

And some began to spit on him, and to cover his face[48] (*prosōpon*), and to strike him. (Mark 14:65; cf. Luke 22:64)

Such statements may be taken as innocent historical narrative, but they correspond remarkably to the face that goes before, that stands in the midst of, and yet is not seen. The face of God, in the crucified face of Jesus, cannot be recognized. It is the face of a dangerous, threatening king, and it must be abused. We have seen that Exod. 33:12-23 took the notion of God's face and set it into the dangers of history. Now in the trial scene of Jesus, that present, assurance-giving, but unrecognized face is taken for the threat that it is. But curiously, the hiddenness of the face here comes from the other side. In Exod. 33:18-23, the face is hidden because of massive glory. Here the face is hidden so to speak from the other side, "from below," unrecognized for its shamefulness and weakness, which are the transfigured form of glory.[49]

In the trial scene, the powers of this age seek to nullify that face, for in all its vulnerability it is a radical criticism and dangerous threat to all the religious posturing of those with safer images. The action of

---

48. It is difficult to know how much should be made of this phrase. It can be taken simply as a statement of mockery and a means of blindfolding, but perhaps given the cruciality of "the face," it means more. If so, it suggests that in contrast to God's hiding God's face, here Jesus is the passive object. His face is denied power and the covering is in fact an act of defiant dethronement. He is denied his freedom to act. The capacity to render others blind is to make them helpless, dependent, and certainly no threat. Thus to cover the face, to prevent Jesus seeing, is the other side of the human desire to see everything.

49. On this way of understanding the act, see Robert McAfee Brown, "The View from Below: Theology in a New Key," *A.D.* 32 (September 1977): 28–31. By contrast, consider Karl Barth's description, in *Protestant Theology in the Nineteenth Century* (London: SCM Press, 1972), 33–136, of the age of absolutism, when everything was settled "from above." On pp. 43 and 47 Barth refers to the "revolution from above." Thus I suggest that the covering of the face of God from above or from below is decisive in understanding the radical theology expressed in the passion of Jesus. The scandal of Jesus' face is that it rejects every "revolution from above." The covering and abuse of the face, that is, its deglorification, establish the dialectic of shame-glory, which is central to Paul's theology. The argument of Paul, however, is not that shame has replaced glory but that shame is now the form of glory. See Douglas J. Hall, *Lighten Our Darkness* (Philadelphia: Fortress Press, 1976). I suggest that the transfiguration/transformation narratives of the Synoptics thus should be more closely linked to Phil. 2:5-11, in which the *form of the king* is emptied with the movement from the form of God to the *form of a servant*, obedient even to death. In this way the crisis of the presence is worked out in terms of glory as crucified presence.

his accusers seeks to "deglorify" this face, unaware that it has taken a new form of glory that the world can neither recognize nor tolerate.

Second, in a quite different idiom, the vision of the end time is presented in terms of the face of Jesus. Now abruptly we turn from *the face in trial* to *the vindicated, ruling face* that is promised. The one who is on his way to death in Jerusalem is the same one who will come again in triumph. The face of the enthroned one is forbidding to fractured, disobedient life. Thus, that face, even in the end time, has a terrible harshness in it:

> Then I saw a great white throne and him who sat upon it; from his presence [*prosōpou*] earth and sky fled away, and no place was found for them. (Rev. 20:11)[50]

But there is more than harshness for those who have the faithful courage to look:

> There shall no more be anything accursed, but the throne of God and of the Lamb shall be in it, and his servants shall worship him; they shall see his face [*prosōpon*], and his name shall be on their foreheads. (Rev. 22:3-4)

The text is deliberately ambiguous. The grammar does not clarify whether the face now to be seen is the face of God or of the Lamb. In the visioning process, however, it does not matter, for the rule is one. The face had been withheld from Moses and from Israel. Nor had it been seen or known by the authorities in Jerusalem, who never knew whom they had tried, even though they were empowered and accustomed to probe all things.[51] The vision of Revelation

---

50. On the lack of place, perhaps the displacement of the other creatures is the antithesis to Matt. 8:20 and Luke 9:58, in which the Son of man has nowhere to lay his head. Though the terminology is different, the two situations are reversed. Now the one with no place is given the primary place. The language is clearly that of enthronement and replacement in power or "exaltation," in the language of Mann, *Divine Presence*. The juxtaposition of no place for Jesus and no place for the others implies radical political criticism and redistribution of power.

51. Knierim has observed that Isa. 6:9 presents the matter of seeing/knowing in its strangeness. It is not difficult to see that this text became much used in the early church (Matt. 13:14-15; Mark 4:12; Luke 8:10; John 12:39-41; Acts 28:26-27). The very face that they were permitted to see they did not know. The world's way of knowing cannot come near the mystery of presence. The richness of the metaphor of "face" is evident in the rendering of *prosōpon* in Rev. 20:11; 22:4. The RSV translates the first by "presence" and the second by "face," so that some of the tension in the metaphor is perhaps unfortunately relaxed.

is all in prospect, but the prospect of that literature is not ever for the authorities in Jerusalem. Nor is it ever far from the face set toward Jerusalem. It is, here and always, only for those who trust the face they cannot see and pursue the rest they cannot grasp. This is not a vision of beautiful, mystical quiet. It is a political vision, robust in its claim that the face of the true king will be seen and known and that the distance that was so necessary and so dangerous has been now overcome.[52] The eschatological hope of Israel here articulated is that when the kingdom is fully come, the incongruity of Exod. 33:12-17 and 33:18-23 will be overcome.

The New Testament, of course, struggles with "the already and not yet," with the face unrecognized for its weakness and the face to come triumphant and in glory. These two features are reflected in our two texts: (1) in the *raw historicality of the face spat upon* (Matt. 26:67; Mark 14:65) and seemingly effectively deglorified; and (2) in the *visionary hope of the fully glorified face* (Rev. 20:11; 22:3-4). But they are ages apart and we are always prone to choose. Thus, the tension of our two texts in Exod. 33:12-23 is, in the New Testament, given a present-future scheme. And so "liberals" choose the face of the passion that does not in itself assert too much transcendence, and "conservatives" choose the hope of Revelation 20–22 when the glory is not dimmed by too much of history. Taken alone, Revelation 20–22 may only extend the yearning to see in Exod. 33:18-23, and taken alone, the raggedness of Matt. 26:67 and Mark 14:65 may only reflect the hidden face to trust in Exod. 33:12-17. But as in the canonical form of Exod. 33:12-23, they must be held together both as affirmation and as withholding.

Third, I suggest it is in Paul that these motifs of *the suffering face* and *the glorified face* are held together. In his Second Letter to the Corinthians, Paul offers reflection on the vision of God's glory. He presents the argument as a juxtaposition of Jews who always see through a veil (and therefore never see) and Christians who "turn to the Lord" and may then "with unveiled faces behold the glory of the Lord" (2 Cor. 3:15-18). For that much, Paul seems to affirm rather

---

52. The ground for understanding this transformation in political categories includes (1) the fact that the text appeals to royal imagery, and (2) that apocalyptic is surely to be understood not as escapist literature engaged in fantasy, but as the construction of an alternative political life-world. See especially Paul D. Hanson, *Dawn* (see chap. 5, n. 18). Most tersely, Rev. 22:15 shows the political power of the language: "The kingdom of the world has become the kingdom of our Lord and of his Christ, and he shall reign for ever and ever."

undialectically that those who believe in Jesus and turn to him are
given to see the face, thus apparently relaxing the tension of Exodus
33 and the tension of holding together *the shameful face* of Matt. 26:67
and Mark 14:65 with *the glorified face* of Rev. 20:11 and Rev. 22:3-4.[53]

But Paul will not let it rest in such an undialectical way. We may
observe three ways in which he hedges that sweeping statement:

1. In 2 Cor. 4:6 he asserts that the glory promised in 3:18 is *linked
to Jesus:*

> ... to give knowledge of the glory of God in the face of Christ.

This is not a free-floating, nonhistorical glory of God, but it is precisely the glory of God in the face of the crucified. Thus, our theme is
reaffirmed: that it is none other than the crucified one, the one spat
upon, who is the means by which the hidden glory so long withheld
is now given. Note that in 4:10, the one identified as the focus of
glory is the crucified, for Paul speaks of "always carrying in the body
the death of Jesus." Paul is here surely a theologian of the cross. For
him the glory is always linked to the scandal of suffering, because
that is the form that the glory takes. Others who do not look into the
face of the suffering one will not and cannot see the glory (4:4).

2. It is clear that Paul's discussion of God's glory is addressed to
the concrete *vocation of ministry:*

> Therefore, having this ministry by the mercy of God, we do not lose
> heart. (4:1)

> All this is from God, who through Christ reconciled us to himself and
> gave us the ministry of reconciliation. (5:18)

Paul is not interested in a theoretical or isolated consideration of
God or God's glory or face, not anymore than was Exodus 33. Taken
alone, Exod. 33:18-23 might have conceivably permitted such a consideration. But that unit is now firmly linked to the remainder of
Exodus 33 and set between chapters 32 and 34, so that the issue of

---

53. Already seeing the face, that is, fully realized eschatology without any eschatological reservation, is parallel to the heresy of having "already been raised," on which
see James M. Robinson, "Kerygma and History in the New Testament," in Robinson and Helmut Koester, *Trajectories through Early Christianity* (Philadelphia: Fortress
Press, 1971), 32–36. In both cases, Paul insists that things are not fully given, thus his
opposition to Gnosticism.

Yahweh's presence is enmeshed in the issue of *Moses' vocation*.[54] The glory is shown to the practitioners of faithful suffering. Thus, the linkage of Paul to Exodus 33 suggests, as has been frequently indicated, that Exodus 33 is not about God's face of presence but about the office of mediation whereby covenant is made possible again. The themes in Paul are peculiarly parallel to those of Moses.

3. It is telling that the ones to whom the vision is given are not safe and serene. The vision of God's face/glory here is promised to those in a *vocation of trouble:*

> We are afflicted in every way, but not crushed; perplexed, but not driven to despair; persecuted, but not forsaken; struck down, but not destroyed. (4:8-9)

Paul identifies viewers of God's face/glory in the crucified as those who groan (5:2) and have anxiety (5:4), and finally he concludes that the faithful witnesses to God's glory must walk by faith and not by sight (5:7). Now we have come full circle to the affirmations of Exodus 33. It is both telling and ironic that for Moses as for Paul, the ones who have *seen* do not walk by *sight*. Those very ones must walk by faith. That, I conclude, is the point of Exod. 33:12-23, especially the more evangelical assertion of vv. 12-17. The face has assured Moses, but he may not see it. Moses had asked to see (v. 18). That is the craving of all religion, and Paul asserts that we are not given to see but only to venture in trust. If I have rightly understood these texts, there is a remarkable coming together of themes here, for the courage of faith of being "at home or away" (5:8) is precisely the courage of Moses in sojourn with Israel toward rest, the courage of disciples with Jesus en route to Jerusalem, the courage of the church under Roman persecution, living by the promises of Revelation 20–22. The cluster of texts has remarkably transformed the world's agenda of presence into the gospel gift of courage for ministry. We are led to the strange conclusion that these texts are not at all about their presumed subject, namely, seeing God's face, for the gospel has preempted the agenda and turned it to the faith-

---

54. It is important to recognize that at least vv. 12-17 (though probably not vv. 18-23) are not concerned with the presence of God per se, but with the issue of Mosaic leadership. Thus Muilenburg understands the text as a liturgy concerned with the establishment of a mediator. Cf. Childs, *Exodus*, 599; and Reindl, *Angesicht Gottes*, 61. It is obviously important to see the issue in the entire complex of chapters 32–34, for when taken in isolation, the urgency of this historical question is easily displaced.

ful ministry of the crucified one.[55] To do that, we have found the use of two constructs to represent the tension of our two passages. These are the *present/future*, for *now* we see the face of the crucified and *then* we shall see the glory,[56] and the *suffering/glory* as a way of speaking about the *crucified/exalted* one. Both these constructs, however, are turned to a summons to ministry.

V

Two other texts are drawn into the vortex of Exodus 33, even though they are not as directly linked to the notion of face. The two parts of our text of Exod. 33:12-23 are linked to Moses *yearning to know* and his *yearning to see*. We shall consider two texts from Paul that appear to be related to these two parts and two themes in our text:

First and more obviously, attention must be paid to Romans 9:14-18, for it is directly linked to the second part of our text, the part about seeing. On the surface, Romans 9–11 seems remote from our passage. Whereas Exodus 33 is concerned with the crisis of presence, Paul is here dealing with the problem of historical election and the seeming injustice of the provisional rejection of the Jews. Paul's initial foray is based on the Abraham-Jacob materials (Rom. 9:6-14), which seem more appropriate.

Our interpretation requires that we seek a connection between these texts of Exodus 33 and Romans 9. We may discern two instructive links, one direct, the other less so. While Moses' desire to see the glory and Paul's question of God's justice seem remote, they are alike on a single point, namely, the human hunger to penetrate the mystery of God, to know what God knows, in a word, to be "like God."

---

55. In making such a judgment, obviously very much rests on the word "know." How is Yahweh known or how does Yahweh know? If the term be taken in terms of religious phenomenology, it is easily tilted toward "see," as reflected in the LXX rendering of v. 13, followed by the RSV. Thus knowing is only a variant form of seeing. But clearly that is not intended in vv. 12-17, which resist "see" and turn "know" to "being known." Thus known-know is concerned with historical-covenantal categories. On knowing so understood, see José Miranda, *Marx* (see chap. 7, n. 26), 44–53. See also Muilenburg ("Covenant Mediator," 176–81) on "know" as a covenant term.

56. We shall here not pursue the abundant reflection on that theme in the Johannine literature, for that would require a major study. Obviously the presence of the crucified as the way of knowing and seeing God is crucial to John. On seeing and glory in the Fourth Gospel, see Juan Luis Segundo, *Our Idea of God* (Maryknoll, N.Y.: Orbis Books, 1970), 109. He makes special reference to John 1:18, 46.

The abrupt demand of Moses in Exod. 33:18, as we have noted, is not unlike the tree of Eden (Gen. 3:5) or the tower of Babel (Gen. 11:4-6). The mystery of God, God's face, holds an incredible fascination for humankind. And there are important theological traditions—gnostic, charismatic, apocalyptic, mystical—that seek to penetrate that mystery. The statement of sovereign freedom by God in Exod. 33:19 asserts God's capacity to have God's own reasons, to act in ways that do not fit our rationality, to practice graciousness that falls outside our own lawfulness. Thus, the grace-law theme is not confined to the issues of human sin and forgiveness, but it also speaks to God in relation to our best human rationality. To *understand God's graciousness* in human history is of a piece with wanting to *know God's secret person*. As the one is denied in Exodus 33, so the other is withheld in Roman 9. Paul is here not given to *explaining* God's way, but to *asserting* that God is free from the field of explanation. Thus the assertion of freedom in Rom. 9:15 that refers to our passage is followed in Rom. 9:19 with assertion reminiscent of Job and more directly of Isa. 45:9-13, both of which do not answer or explain but exclude the question.

The second linkage with our passage is less direct, by way of Rom. 9:17, in which Paul quotes Exod. 9:16:

> ... but for this purpose have I let you live, to show you my power, so that my name may be declared throughout all the earth.

Paul quickly changes themes from *mercy and compassion* in 9:15 to *power* in 9:17, but the power theme is the other side of mercy and compassion.[57] The linkage to the exodus event shows that what is mercy and compassion to Israel is power to pharaoh. We have already seen that in Exod. 33:16 the text uses the term *pālâ*, which has important connections to Exod. 9:4. So we see that Exodus 33 and Romans 9 are both informed by this remarkable collage of themes in Exodus 9, of which we may observe three:

1. v. 4, the *distinction* without explanation or cause,

---

57. For a summary of the movement and shifts in the argument of the text, see Paul Ellingworth, "Translation and Exegesis: A Case Study (Rom. 9:22ff.)," *Bib* 59 (1978): 396–402.

2. v. 14, the claim of Yahweh's *incomparability*,[58] so that Yahweh may be discerned as free of the system and not subject to it, and

3. v. 16, the assertion of *power* against Egypt and for Israel.

The three motifs of *election, uniqueness,* and *power* are all of a piece. They suggest a confession of God and a modeling of society, both of which are underived from and unexplained by imperial (or legal), that is, systemic, definitions and expectations. Thus Paul's argument in Romans 9 is not a careless use of texts but an appeal to the substance of the text from Exod. 33:19. The juxtaposition of compassion and free power in Rom. 9:15-17 is illuminated by the recognition that glory is a political category of authority and sovereignty. That Yahweh must explain Yahweh's action is an attempt to deny the divine freedom to govern. Paul's opponents, like the Mosaic community, wanted to leave nothing to God, wanted to see, wanted to penetrate, wanted to walk finally by sight and not by faith.

Thus, the assertion of God's freedom in both texts, Rom. 9:15 and Exod. 33:19, is an assertion of the distinction between God's way of ruling and our best discerning of it. It is that theme that protects from ideology, from the too close identity of the person of God and human conjurings.[59] Thus, the Pauline argument is not an attempt to explain election and rejection but an assertion that God's glory may not be seen or preempted in any way that denies God's sovereign rule.[60]

The other text that directly falls in this cluster of texts is the expectation of Paul that we shall see "face to face":

---

58. On the theme of incomparability, see C. J. Labuschagne, *Incomparability of Yahweh* (see chap. 7, n. 16); and Friedrich Stolz, "Jahwes Unvergleichlichkeit und Unergründlichkeit," *WD* 14 (1977): 9–24.

59. That danger has been well stated by John Goldingay, "The Man of War and the Suffering Servant," *TynBul* 27 (1976): 106–13. Although he particularly applies it to liberation theology, the same danger is even more acute for so-called objective theology.

60. As might be expected, Karl Barth, in *Church Dogmatics* (see chap. 5, n. 29), finds this text an especially important one for holding together the utter sovereignty and radical graciousness of God. Cf. vol. 3, no. 1, 18-19, 61, 353, 371-72. As we would expect Barth to notice, it is not only God's disclosure that is gracious but also God's hiddenness, for "man cannot see God's face, God's naked objectivity, without exposing himself to the annihilating wrath of God." It is precisely because God's compassion is grounded in nothing other than the heart of God that the election of the Gentiles in Romans 9 is an act of mercy and not of arbitrariness. Thus Stolz's "Unergründlichkeit" is important here.

> For now we see in a mirror dimly, but then face to face [*prosōpon pros prosōpon*]. Now I know in part; then I shall understand fully, even as I have been fully understood. (1 Cor. 13:12)

In his Corinthian correspondence, Paul had especially to deal with the problem of knowledge (cf. 1 Corinthians 1–3 and note in 2 Cor. 4:6, already considered, that he speaks of "knowledge and the glory of God . . . ").[61] That knowledge, to which the church aspired in 1 Corinthians 12–14, is manifested by the claim of special secrets and higher gifts that caused division in the church. It is in response to that claim that Paul offers *agapē* as an alternative to knowledge.[62] The reference to our passage of Exodus 33 is not explicit in v. 12, but it is surely intended. Both the motifs of *seeing* and *knowing* are articulated here.[63]

In Exod. 33:12-13, three times Moses presses to know:

> You have not caused me to *know*. (V. 12)
> Cause me to *know*, I pray, your way, that I may *know* you. (V. 13)

The answer, anticipated in v. 12 and asserted in v. 17, is, "I know you." That is, while Moses wants to *know* and be *agent* of the active verb, he is *known*, and is the *object* of that verb.

That is precisely the situation of the argument in 1 Cor. 13:12, where Paul accepts the status of being known. He is known but does not know. In the end time, when the mediation is overcome, knowing will be as full as being known. In the meantime, that is, for historical existence, the face that is assured (Exod. 33:14) and not seen (Exod. 33:19, 23) is enough, and Paul is content with it.

That the Pauline argument appeals explicitly to this dialectic from Exodus 33 is evidenced in two ways:

1. Although the chapter is concerned with *knowing* (and the argument is that knowing consists of being known), in v. 12 Paul unexpectedly turns to *seeing*. Thus, the flow of the argument seems to follow closely that of Exodus 33 as it moves from "being known" (vv. 12-17) to "seeing the back" (vv. 18-23). The juxtaposition of

---

61. Cf. Ulrich Wilckens, *Weisheit und Torheit* (Tübingen: Mohr [Siebeck], 1959).

62. Thus see the references to knowledge in 1 Cor. 13:2, 8-9. In terms of being known rather than the active knower, see esp. 1 Cor. 8:2-3: "If any one imagines that he knows something, he does not yet know as he ought to know. But if one loves God, one is known by him."

63. Knierim ("Offenbarung," 220) recognizes the extreme complexity of the language.

knowing and seeing in Paul is surely informed by the Moses tradition.

2. Verse 12 also contains the promise of face-to-face, which might easily be derived from Exod. 33:11. That passage lies outside our general discussion, but it is a more primitive theophanic tradition. While it does not protect the divine face with the subtle dialectic of vv. 12-23, it does hedge about the face of Yahweh by insisting that this theophanic directness belongs peculiarly to Moses and is not anticipated generally for Israel. Thus, even though not protected in other ways, it is surely exceptional.

So in making this eschatological claim of face-to-face, Paul looks back to the intimacy enjoyed by Moses and presents that directness as the substance of the promise for all God's people.[64] Thus his vision of the end corresponds to that of Rev. 22:3-4. Even though Paul appeals to Exod. 33:7-11 as a model for the end time, in the meantime, he appeals to Exod. 33:12-23 on knowing and seeing.[65] Knowing for now is being known and in the end there will be knowing equal to being known. Seeing will be direct in the end time, but now it is dim; or, in keeping with Exod. 33:18-23, now it is seeing only the back, but then it will be face-to-face.

Thus, I suggest that Paul appeals to the Mosaic text in schematic fashion:

Moses:	*Paul:*	*present*	*promised*
Exod. 33:12-17, knowing consists in being known		knowing in part	knowing as known
Exod. 33:18-23, seeing only the back		seeing in a mirror dimly	seeing face-to-face

In the future there will be full knowing and full seeing, but for now there is only evangelical being-known and trusting seeing-dimly. That, however, is ground enough for *agapē*.

---

64. Eichrodt, in "The Promises of Grace to David in Isaiah 55:1-5," in *Israel's Prophetic Heritage*, ed. Bernhard Anderson and Walter Harrelson (New York: Harper & Row, 1962), 196–207, has argued that Second Isaiah in Isaiah 55 has democratized the Davidic promise and made it a promise to all of Israel. I suggest that Paul has done the same to the theophany of Moses in Exod. 33:7-11. He has democratized it and made it a promissory possibility for all faithful people.

65. Note the tent-sojourn motif surfacing in Rev. 21:2. Following Clifford on the theme of the tent as a place of assembly, it is clear that the apocalyptic imagery stays with political intentionality. It appears to use this imagery as the only ground on which to stand against the established religio-politics of the time.

I suggest that out of this remarkable, dialectical reflection on God's presence in Exodus 33, in scattered places Paul has constructed three of his most central antitheses:

- in 2 Cor. 5:7, faith/sight,
- in Rom. 9:6-18, mercy/law or promise/flesh, and
- in 1 Cor. 13:12, love/knowledge.

These are all variations on the key Pauline theme that our preferred access to God has been broken and qualified by the reality of the crucifixion; that is, the face is not the triumphant face from above but the suffering face from below. There is no strident exposure to God, either by knowing or by seeing. The *agapē* of the gospel has radically altered the way we know God. The mercy and compassion of the gospel now characterize the way we see God. As a result, all the analogies to the image/face of God in the ancient world that intend to assert power, authority, sovereignty, even stridency, all are rendered irrelevant by this brokenness. Thus, it is a most radical statement of Paul to claim that the "glory of God" is to be found in the "face of Christ" (2 Cor. 4:6), the same face that was spat upon and unrecognized.

I submit that the two claims of Exod. 33:12-23, placed in tension, already anticipate that qualification of crucifixion:

- My face will go with you.
- My face will not be seen.

More than that cannot be had from this God who exercises sovereignty in such a strange, scandalous way.

VI

We began with the claim that how Yahweh is present in Israel and how Israel shall speak of God's presence are both important and difficult. We have seen that Israel made use of a standard theologoumenon of the day, likely appropriated from normal cult practice, probably especially important for making royal, imperial claims. That standard way of speaking and experiencing, however, is in conflict with the evangelical, historical ways in which Yahweh gives God's self to Israel. Although the theme of face may be used, it is clear that it means both more and less than it seems to say and was understood to mean in the religious context of the time.

In the Mosaic tradition, the interface between *standard theologoumenon* and *particularistic affirmation* is accomplished by the juxtaposition of vv. 12-17 and 18-23, a dispute form and a theophanic narrative cast as a divine soliloquy. The two together concede little to Moses, but enough to make renewed covenant and continued pilgrimage possible.

In the New Testament, that interface of *religious habit* and *christological affirmation* is accomplished by reference on the one hand to the historical, despised face of Jesus crucified, and on the other to the face of the anticipated fully ruling one. Thus, it is the language of crucifixion and exaltation, of shame and glory, that reshapes the language of face and of presence.

Clearly, neither the Old Testament nor New Testament references offer any speculative or theoretical consideration of divine presence. In both cases, the issue is linked to matters of obedience, vocation, and ecclesiology. The Mosaic exchange is aimed at the renewal of Israel's obedience after Exodus 32. In the New Testament, in various ways the issue is the faith and practice of the church in the company of the crucified. The Pauline reflection is regularly linked to affirmations of ministry (cf. 2 Cor. 4:1; 5:18).

Methodologically, this chapter has sought to operate within the horizons of canon criticism. It is not argued that one can trace the theme of face historically from Moses to Paul. Rather, this chapter intends to suggest that the Old Testament and New Testament passages, which surely have a kinship if not an intentional link, will both be understood more perceptively if they are seen as impinging upon each other. In our conventional historicism, we assume that the influences flow from older to more recent texts, from Old Testament to New Testament. If we take the claim of canon seriously, we may take more seriously Paul's assertion that when the veil is lifted, we may not only hear a new word but discern the old word with unveiled freedom (2 Cor. 3:12-18). Thus, we dare to say (letting the impact run both ways) that the juxtaposition of Exod. 33:12-17 and 18-23 is illuminated by the themes of *shame/glory* and *crucifixion/resurrection* in the New Testament gospel. I have attempted here to contribute to the question of how we are to do a biblical theology that listens to the texts of the Old and New Testaments as they illuminate each other.

9

A Shattered Transcendence?
Exile and Restoration

THE EXILE AS EVENT, experience, memory, and paradigm looms large over the literature and faith of the Old Testament. Together with the restoration, the exile emerged as the decisive, shaping reference point for the self-understanding of Judaism.[1] Moreover, the power of exile and restoration as an imaginative construct exercised enormous impact on subsequent Christian understandings of faith and life as they were recast in terms of crucifixion and resurrection.

I

I take as foundational for our theological reflection three propositions that are beyond dispute:

1. The exile was indeed a *real historical experience* that can be located and understood in terms of public history.[2] A considerable number of persons were deported by the Babylonians, but different

---

1. J. Maxwell Miller and John H. Hayes, in *A History of Ancient Israel and Judah* (Philadelphia: Westminster Press, 1986), write, "The fall of the city and the exile of its citizens marked a watershed in Judean history and have left fissure marks radiating throughout the Hebrew Scriptures. The 'day of judgment' heralded in prophetic announcements had not just dawned, it had burst on Judah with immense ferocity" (p. 416).

2. See the data summarized by Miller and Hayes, *History*, 416–36, and John Bright, *A History of Israel* (Philadelphia: Westminster Press, 1981), 343–72.

accounts yield different results. In any case, much of the leadership of the community was deported. It is conventional to conclude that the sociopolitical situation of the exiles was not terribly difficult, although Smith has made a strong case for the notion that in fact the deported Jews in exile faced enormous hardship.[3]

2. Even though the actual number of persons exiled must have been relatively modest, the exile as a theological datum became *a governing paradigm* for all successive Jewish faith.[4] The experience, articulation, and memory of the exile came to exercise influence upon the faith, imagination, and self-perception of Judaism quite disproportionate to its factual actuality. As a result, the exile became definitional for all Jews, many of whom were never deported. Part of the reason that a modest historical fact became a dominant paradigm for self-understanding no doubt can be understood in terms of the exercise of social imagination and social power by the Jews who were in exile, who insisted upon and imposed their experience on Judaism as normative for all Jewishness. The community of the deported established ideological, interpretive hegemony in Judaism, insisting that its experience counted the most. Such a sociopolitical explanation, however, does not fully account for this interpretive turn in Judaism.

In addition to the interpretive authority of the exilic community in the political process, the intrinsic power and significance of the exile must be acknowledged. Since the Mosaic articulation of covenantal faith, built as it is around stipulation and blessing and curse, an articulation appropriated in the prophetic tradition, Israel has been subject to the moral seriousness of its own covenantal-ethical enterprise. Thus, the exile required, power-politics notwithstanding, construal in Israel in terms of those covenantal categories. As a result, the exile is an event not only of historical displacement, but of profound moral, theological fracture.

That moral, theological fracture generated two primary responses: On the one hand, the paradigm of exile/restoration is concerned with the moral failure of Israel, so that exile is punishment and judgment from God. This is a dominant stream of *"golah*

---

3. Daniel L. Smith, *The Religion of the Landless: The Social Context of the Babylonian Exile* (Bloomington, Ind.: Meyer Stone, 1989).

4. See Jacob Neusner, *Understanding Seeking Faith: Essays on the Case of Judaism* (Atlanta: Scholars Press, 1986), esp. 137–41; and Paul Joyce, *Divine Initiative and Human Response in Ezekiel*, JSOTSup, no. 51 (Sheffield: Sheffield Academic Press, 1989), 12–17.

theology," voiced especially in the tradition of Deuteronomy. On the other hand, however, the crisis of exile cannot be contained in the categories of covenantal sanctions. Thus, there is also the posing of urgent questions concerning the fidelity of God that are more profound than a simple moral calculus of blessing and curse. These questions are voiced, for example, in the Prophets, in the Priestly tradition, and perhaps in Job. Thus the immediate question of *moral symmetry* and the more subtle question of *theological fidelity* created a large arena for Israel's venturesome theological reflection.[5]

3. The experience and paradigmatic power of the exile evoked in Israel a surge of theological reflection and *a remarkable production of fresh theological literature*.[6] The exile decisively shattered the old, settled categories of Israel's faith. It did not, however, lead either to abandonment of faith or to despair.[7] Indeed, it is the moral claim of covenantal faith that permitted a response to the exile to be something other than abandonment or despair. Israel was driven to reflect on the moral, theological significance of exile. The characteristic tension between acknowledgment of shattering, on the one hand, and the refusal of despair and abandonment, on the other hand, required, permitted, and authorized in Israel daring theological energy that began to probe faith in wholly new categories that are daring and venturesome. Indeed, it is not an overstatement to say that exile became the matrix in which the canonical shape of Old Testament faith is formed and evoked.[8] In that context, the old tradi-

---

5. See the analysis of Richard Elliott Friedman, in *The Exile and Biblical Narrative* (Chico, Calif.: Scholars Press, 1981), on the two great narrative responses to the crisis of exile.

6. See Peter R. Ackroyd, *Exile and Restoration*, OTL (Philadelphia: Westminster Press, 1968); Ralph W. Klein, *Israel in Exile*, OBT (Philadelphia: Fortress Press, 1979); Enno Janssen, *Juda in der Exilszeit* (Göttingen: Vandenhoeck and Ruprecht, 1956); and Joyce, *Divine Initiative*.

7. The reality of exile may have led some to despair, but not in the community that generated the text. Elaine Scarry, in *Body in Pain* (see chap. 3, n. 3), has shown how speech counters the dismantling of personhood. In parallel fashion, I submit that text counters despair, both as text-making and text-reading. The exilic community was intensely engaged in text-making and text-reading as a counter to despair.

8. James A. Sanders, *Torah and Canon* (Philadelphia: Fortress Press, 1972), has argued this case effectively. Canon criticism, he writes, "begins with questions concerning the function of those ancient traditions which were viable in the crucifixion-resurrection experience of the sixth and fifth centuries B.C. and which provided the vehicle for Judaism's birth out of the ashes of what had been.... But if one's interest is rather in the actual history of how the Bible came to be, what events gave rise to the collecting of the materials actually inherited, and why these traditions were chosen and not others, then two main historical watersheds impose themselves. The Bible comes to us out of the ashes of two Temples, the First or Solomonic Tem-

tions are radically revamped and recharacterized,[9] or the theological process strikes out in quite fresh and inventive ways.

These three factors—historical experience, paradigmatic power, and inventive literary imagination—are crucial for recognizing the context of the exile as decisive for shaping Old Testament faith. These three factors, however, in and of themselves do not constitute a theological probe. They are the context for such a probe. My intention here is to push beyond historical-literary issues to theology proper.

II

The literary-historical-cultural aspects of the exile have posed the general, overarching question of *continuity and discontinuity*. This rubric permits us to consider a number of subpoints in relation to the general problematic. The dominant Wellhausen paradigm for Old Testament history and interpretation revolves around the question of continuity and discontinuity.[10] Wellhausen's powerful model insisted upon a significant discontinuity between the earlier faith of Israel and the later development of Judaism. It is not clear to what extent that model was designed to criticize and even depreciate later Judaism, which he found inferior to earlier prophetic faith; nor is it clear to what extent that critique and depreciation either were motivated by or served (unwittingly) a kind of anti-Semitism. In any case, very much critical Christian scholarship has regarded the emergent faith of the Jewish postexilic community as inferior, so that a clear line has been drawn from the earlier prophetic faith to the New Testament.[11]

---

ple, destroyed in 586 B.C., and the Second or Herodian Temple, destroyed in A.D. 70" (pp. xix, 6). See the discerning statement by Donn P. Morgan, *Between Text and Community: The "Writings" on Canonical Interpretation* (Minneapolis: Fortress Press, 1990), on the canonical power of the exilic experience.

9. This is the essential dynamic of Gerhard von Rad's two-volume Old Testament theology. See von Rad, *Old Testament Theology II* (see chap. 3, n. 9), 263–77, and Paul D. Hanson, "Israelite Religion in the Early Postexilic Period," in *Ancient Israelite Religion*, ed. Patrick D. Miller et al. (Philadelphia: Fortress Press, 1987), 485–508.

10. For a careful review and assessment of the contribution of Wellhausen and his dominant paradigm, see Douglas A. Knight, ed., "Julius Wellhausen and His *Prolegomena to the History of Israel*," *Semeia* 25 (1983).

11. It should be possible to acknowledge some crucial discontinuity between ancient Israel and emergent Judaism without a judgment of inferiority, but to assert discontinuity without "bootlegging" inferiority requires an important break with

Distinct from Wellhausen's powerful paradigm, none has thought more carefully and perceptively about the question of continuity and discontinuity than has Peter Ackroyd. In a series of four articles, Ackroyd has carefully and judiciously reflected on the crises of history and culture and the powerful drive for continuity in the midst of the cultural, historical break.[12] Ackroyd has considered the ways in which cult objects (temple vessels), theological constructs, and reutilization of textual formulations have served the concern for continuity.[13] It does not surprise us that, in the end, Ackroyd concludes that continuity is the overriding reality for Judaism: "The restoration and the destruction are all of a piece; discontinuity is resolved in the discovery of a continuity within it."[14]

There are two very different reasons why Ackroyd comes down on the side of continuity: First, there was, in and through the exile, a surviving continuity of vibrant Judaism as a community. As a historical fact, the Jews did indeed have continuity, and they claimed that continuity for themselves. Second, Ackroyd poses questions of social history; he is concerned with the community over time and through time. Ackroyd is interested in institutional sociology and, therefore, is attentive to the gestures, textual and otherwise, that sustain continuity. A historical critic could hardly entertain the notion of deep discontinuity, so there is an inevitable bias toward continuity in our common work of criticism.

I do not at all suggest that Ackroyd has misconstrued the data, for his historical methods serve well to understand the community that lives in and through an ongoing tradition. I suggest, however, that Ackroyd's analysis has not in fact penetrated beyond cultural, institutional, community-generated continuities to the more difficult theological question, namely: *What happened to God in the process of the*

---

the assumptions of the Wellhausen paradigm. Hanson, in "Israelite Religion," has enunciated that discontinuity without suggesting inferiority.

12. See Ackroyd: "Continuity: A Contribution to the Study of the Old Testament Religious Tradition" (original book at Oxford: Blackwell, 1962), reprinted in *Studies in the Religious Tradition of the Old Testament* (London: SCM Press, 1987), 3–16; "Continuity and Discontinuity: Rehabilitation and Authentication," in *Tradition and Theology* (see chap. 7, n. 46), 215–34, reprinted in *Studies in the Religious Tradition*, 31–45; "The Temple Vessels: A Continuity Theme," VTSup, no. 23 (1972): 166–81, reprinted in *Studies in the Religious Tradition*, 46–60; and "The Theology of Tradition: An Approach to Old Testament Theological Problems," *Bangalore Theological Forum* 3 (1971): 49–64, reprinted in *Studies in the Religious Tradition*, 17–30.

13. Intertextuality, as reflected in the work of Michael Fishbane, provides a powerful way to maintain a flexible continuity in contexts of discontinuity.

14. Ackroyd, "Continuity: A Contribution," 15.

exile? Or to put the question more critically: What does the text say happened to God?

In putting the question in this way, a methodological acknowledgment is required. To do biblical theology, I suggest, requires us to leave off the kind of critical observation that stands outside the text and to enter into the dynamic that operates inside the text and its claims. Or to put it differently, biblical theology, unlike historical criticism, requires us to approach the text more *realistically*, as though this were indeed a word about God and about God's life, very often a word from God about God's life.[15] Such an approach may appear critically to be naive, but it is the only way we have to penetrate the difficulty of God's own life in the exile.[16]

When we ask a theological question of the text—as distinct from a literary, historical, or sociological question—the issue of continuity and discontinuity takes on a different configuration. Whereas concerning literary, historical, and sociological questions, one can point to evident continuities that override discontinuities (as Ackroyd has done so well), a theological focus on the rendering of God's own person as a character in Israel's large drama of faith is not so unambiguously on the side of continuity. The texts attest that the exile constituted a significant crisis in God's own life. As a character rendered in Israel's "covenantal discourse," as a character central to the plot of Israel's self-presentation, God is deeply impinged upon by the crisis of the exile.[17] The theme of continuity asks whether the character of Yahweh continues to be the same character in, through, and beyond the exile. The theme of discontinuity asks whether (and to what extent) the character of God is decisively changed by the crisis of exile, that is, if God ceases to be in some crucial way who this God was heretofore.

The evidence is not clear and consistent. The articulation of the text, nonetheless, makes clear that the displacement and suffering

---

15. Such a statement makes no assumptions about inspiration, revelation, or authority. I refer to such theological realism in terms of the claims made by the text itself. The ground for such a claim is of course theological, but in the first instant, it can be heeded on the grounds of the text as a classic that requires our attendance.

16. On such an understanding of the text, see Dale Patrick, *Rendering of God* (see chap. 2, n. 17). This approach understands theology as dramatic rendering and proceeds by bracketing out metaphysical questions.

17. On the notion of covenantal discourse, see Harold Fisch, *Poetry with a Purpose: Biblical Poetics and Interpretation* (Bloomington: Indiana University Press, 1988), 118–31. The gain of Fisch's assertion is that it takes seriously the claim of the text itself without excessive historical-critical reservation. See also Fisch's theological realism concerning the Psalms, pp. 108–14.

of exile break something of God's own self, both permitting and requiring Yahweh to be presented in a different way. Clearly, such a substantive theological argument depends upon the texts being taken as "realistic" speech about God and the metaphor of personhood being taken as the governing image, both being taken so that a rendering of the person of God in this drama is what is available to Israel (and derivatively, available to us). Clearly, there are in the exile literary continuities through reused speech formulae, historical continuities through genealogy, and sociological continuities through cultic acts and gestures. These continuities, however, all appear to be organized to cope with the peculiar reality of discontinuity with which God struggles.

In putting the theological question in this way, I note two implications that directly relate to the work and writing of J. Christiaan Beker. First, the continuity/discontinuity of Israel's God in exile is a theological counterpart to the christological problematic in the New Testament concerning the relation of the "Jesus of history" to "the risen Christ."[18] The New Testament church struggles to assert continuity in the person of Jesus through the events of Good Friday and Easter, but it also must assert that in those events there is a decisive, transformative discontinuity in the person of Jesus. So it is as well concerning the God of Israel in the exile.

Second, Beker's poignant and remarkable discussion of suffering and hope is a reflection on the power of hope in the midst of suffering.[19] Beker's mode of expression asserts that hope confronts and overrides suffering. An alternative model might be that hope arises precisely in and through suffering. In either case, the life of the God of Israel in the midst of exile, a life of suffering in solidarity and of powerful resolve against displacement, is a life that struggles for continuity in the brokenness. I mention this connection to Beker's work in order to suggest that the question I pose is an intensely practical issue, for Israel sees through this crisis of God how real suffering is,

---

18. On that question of continuity and discontinuity, see Ernst Käsemann, "Blind Alleys in the 'Jesus of History' Controversy," in *New Testament Questions Today* (London: SCM Press, 1969), 23–65; Ernst Fuchs, *Studies of the Historical Jesus*, SBT (Naperville, Ill.: Alec R. Allenson, 1964), 11–31; and James D. G. Dunn, *Unity and Diversity in the New Testament:: An Enquiry into the Character of Earliest Christianity* (Philadelphia: Westminster Press, 1977). Cf. Beker's theological discussion of the question, *Paul the Apostle: The Triumph of God in Life and Thought* (Philadelphia: Fortress Press, 1980), 192–208.

19. Beker, *Suffering and Hope: The Biblical Vision and the Human Predicament* (Philadelphia: Fortress Press, 1987).

how seriously suffering is taken, and how suffering impinges even
upon the life of God, both to shatter something old in God's own life
and to evoke something utterly new in God's life.[20]

I have selected three texts from different exilic sources that explore different dimensions of the way in which God is voiced.[21] One
can certainly understand the different voices in these texts critically,
that is, explaining their different theological claims by referring to
the literary, historical sources. But if one is theologically "realistic,"
the diverse voicings evidence the struggle in God's life over the way
God will be God in the face of such a crisis.

III

Our first text is Deut. 4:23-31. The critical problems concerning
the history and unity of this text are considerable. They are made
more complex by the dominant judgment of two redactions by the
Deuteronomic tradition. Specifically, vv. 29-31 are widely judged to
be a secondary redaction.[22] Thus, the text may be composite. In any
case, the entire passage as it stands reflects a concern about the exile.
Verse 26 speaks of "utterly perish from the land," and v. 27 of "scatter." The phrase "from there" (v. 29) no doubt refers to exile, so the
text as we have it advances from a warning about exile (vv. 23-28)
to a situation in exile and an anticipation after exile (vv. 29-31). And
if vv. 29-31 are indeed an intrusion, as critical study has concluded,
then they are an intrusion reflective of God's new exilic situation.

In this sustained and extended speech, Moses traces a remarkable

---

20. For the purposes of my argument, it cannot be insisted upon too strongly that
the mode of God's self-presentation is dramatic and that we are witnessing the character of God through a drama. The warrant for such a mode of discourse is that the
text itself proceeds in this way.

21. On the several theological resources from the exile that give different voice to
God, see the works of Ackroyd and Klein (n. 6) and Friedman (n. 5).

22. Andrew D. H. Mayes, in "Deuteronomy 4 and the Literary Criticism of
Deuteronomy," *JBL* 100 (1981): 23–51, supported by the argument of Georg Braulik,
has made a strong case for the literary unity and coherence of the passage. See Nor-
bert Lohfink, *Höre Israel! Auslegung von Texten aus dem Buch Deuteronomium* (Düsseldorf:
Patmos Verlag, 1965), 87–120; and Braulik, *Die Mittel deuteromischer Rhetorik*, AnBib,
no. 68 (Rome: Biblical Institute Press, 1978). On the two redactions, see Frank M.
Cross, *Canaanite Myth* (see chap. 7, n. 7), 274–89; and Richard D. Nelson, *The Double
Redaction of the Deuteronomistic History*, JSOTSup, no. 18 (Sheffield: JSOT Press, 1981).
On vv. 29-31, see Hans Walter Wolff, "The Kerygma of the Deuteronomic Histori-
cal Work," in Walter Brueggemann and Wolff, *The Vitality of Old Testament Traditions*
(Atlanta: John Knox Press, 1975), 96–97.

move in the character of Yahweh. Put concisely, Moses voices Yahweh *before* exile and *after* exile around the geographical/temporal reference to "from there" (v. 29). Prior to "from there," Israel is not yet "there," not yet in exile, nor is Yahweh yet addressed "from there." Prior to exile, Mosaic Israel is defined by the demands, sanctions, and warnings of Sinai. The burden of the speech of Moses is that attentiveness to the Torah is the condition for remaining in the land (vv. 25-26). The theological dimension of this pre-exilic warning is that Yahweh is "a devouring fire, a jealous God" (v. 24), a God who will brook no rival and tolerate no disobedience. The entire warning and urgency of Moses grow out of the character of Yahweh, a God who is uncompromising about demand. Thus the ominous warning of Moses is appropriate to pre-exilic Israel and grows from the jealousy of Yahweh.

Were the character of Yahweh sustained into exile in continuity, we would expect Israel in exile and beyond exile to continue to deal with a jealous, uncompromising God. The God who is available "from there," however, is not the devouring God from pre-exile. In the middle of the text, in the middle of Israel's experience, and we may believe, in the middle of God's life with Israel, there is a new "there," that is, exile. When Moses continues his testimony about the God with whom Israel has to do, everything is changed. One may say that this change reflects layers in the redactional process and, therefore, different theological perspectives. Or the change may reflect only the pastoral emergency of the exile when the producers of theological literature said something different to meet new needs. If, however, we are to do theology, what emerges in the text is a real break in God's way with Israel, that is, a real break in God's way of being God. Now there is no more talk of devouring fire and jealous God. Now Moses speaks of a "merciful God" (v. 31). The *'ēl qannā'* (v. 24) has become the *'ēl raḥûm* (v. 31); the one who scattered in anger is the one who will not forget covenant.

There is continuity in this God to whom Moses bears witness. If one follows the rhetorical pattern of the text, however, there is also a discernible discontinuity in the move from *'ēl qannā'* to *'ēl raḥûm*. This God who keeps the same name has ceased, so far as the text is concerned, to be a jealous, devouring God and has now become a God of compassion. Of course one may conclude simply that one need not say everything about God in every sentence and that the God of Israel has all along been *'ēl qannā'* and *'ēl raḥûm*. That, however, is not the way the text works. I submit, rather, that in this one text, the voice of Moses expresses a profound break in the character of God and that that break makes visible the emergence of a God of compassion whom Yahweh has not been before in this text, an emergence evoked by the exile.

Thus, we may provisionally suggest that as hope arises in the midst of suffering, hope that did not heretofore exist, so the mercy of God is evoked, formed, and articulated just here. The formal reality of discontinuity permits a substantive assertion of compassion. And if one follows Phyllis Trible's notion of compassion as "womb-like mother love," then the exile becomes the place where the character of God turns in a quite fresh direction.[23]

IV

Perhaps the most remarkable text for our theme is Isa. 54:7-10. Having just utilized the metaphor of a wife deserted (Israel) by her husband (Yahweh, vv. 4-6), the poem asserts the restoration of the relationship when the husband takes a fresh initiative to restore the relation. Within this metaphor, the husband makes two quite distinct assertions, each reiterated in a parallelism. First, "I forsook you" (*'zb*), "I hid my face" (*str*). Second, "I will gather you" (*qbṣ*), "I will have compassion" (*rḥm*).[24] The contrast of the husband's two moves are *abandon/gather* and *hide/have compassion*.

Three interpretive questions may be posed about these assertions:

First, was the abandonment a real abandonment and the absence a real absence? Did God in truth abandon covenant partner Israel? The wording of the poem is candid and unambiguous. The abandonment is real and complete, without qualification.

Such an assertion is difficult when there is a felt need to claim that God's resolve is unbreakable, that is, when continuity is stressed in

---

23. Trible, *God and Rhetoric* (see chap. 4, n. 16), 31–59.

24. On the double movement, see Zech. 1:15-17 and Isa. 60:10-14. The former text has important parallels to our text. On the hidden face of God, see Samuel E. Balentine, *The Hidden God: The Hiding of the Face of God in the Old Testament* (New York: Oxford University Press, 1983), esp. 148; and Lothar Perlitt, "Die Verborgenheit Gottes," in *Probleme* (see chap. 3, n. 4), 367–82. On the double theme in Jeremiah, see Johan Lust, " 'Gathering and Return' in Jeremiah and Ezekiel," in *Le Livre de Jeremaie*, ed. Pierre M. Bogaert (Leuven: Leuven University Press, 1981), 119–42; and Thomas M. Raitt, *A Theology of Exile: Judgment and Deliverance in Jeremiah and Ezekiel* (Philadelphia: Fortress Press, 1977).

every circumstance.[25] Thus John Calvin seeks to find a way around the clear statement of the text in the interest of continuity:

> When he says that he *forsook* his people, it is a sort of admission of the fact. . . . What the prophet says in this passage must therefore refer to our feelings and to outward appearance, because we seem to be rejected by God when we do not perceive his presence and protection. And it is necessary that we should thus feel God's wrath, even as a wife divorced by her husband deplores her condition, that we may know that we are justly chastised. But we must also perceive his mercy; and because it is infinite and eternal, we shall find that all afflictions in comparison are light and momentary.[26]

Such a reading, however, clearly goes against the wording of the text itself. Serious theology is placed in jeopardy when texts are in this way explained away. Calvin's comment is an example of the way in which a concern for theological continuity (transcendence) wants to outflank and override the text.

In the face of postwar tragedy in Europe, Kornelius H. Miskotte voices a much more sober reading of the text, directed against an interpretive posture like that of Calvin:

> The very first thing that is said here makes it clear that this situation actually cannot be understood on the two-dimensional level of experience and its interpretation [so Calvin]. It is a real abandonment. And those who did not recognize and understand it as an actual abandonment by God are now compelled to hear it proclaimed as God's own word. It was an actual abandonment by God. Without this proclamation of the (partially recognized and partially unrecognized) abandonment by God, the prophetic word is not in the full sense the word of God. He scattered the people, he hid his face from them. The

---

25. Hans Frei, *The Identity of Jesus Christ: The Hermeneutical Bases of Dogmatic Theology* (Philadelphia: Fortress Press, 1975), holds a magisterial view of the single story of God focused on Jesus Christ. That single and magisterial story necessarily asserts a profound and universal continuity. Against such a claim of any "great story," see the protest of Jean François Lyotard, *The Postmodern Condition: A Report on Knowledge* (Minneapolis: University of Minnesota Press, 1984). See the judicious comments of William C. Placher, *Unapologetic Theology: A Christian Voice in a Pluralistic Conversation* (Louisville: Westminster/John Knox Press, 1989), esp. 156, concerning a universal story and the Christian narrative.

26. Calvin, *Commentary on the Book of the Prophet Isaiah* (Grand Rapids: Baker Book House, 1979), 140.

fact is that we have actually lived under the condition of this act; but
it is only the Word that reveals to us that it is an act of God.[27]

Miskotte's reading poses much more difficult theological questions
than does the reading of Calvin, but it surely is more faithful to the
text. The poem asserts that Israel's condition vis-à-vis God is one
of profound discontinuity without qualification. All transcendental
guarantees about God are shattered; God's goodness in Israel is
decisively broken. It is instructive that it is Miskotte's European experience of discontinuity that both permitted and required a radical
rereading of the text.

Second, because the break in abandonment and anger is "for a
brief moment" (*rega'*; vv. 7-8), we may ask, as Israel must have asked:
How long is a *rega'*? The word suggests that while the abandonment
by God was total and without qualification, it was only for an instant.
Or we may reverse the proposition: The abandonment was only for
an instant, but long enough for it to be massive, total, and decisive.
The other uses of *rega'* do not tell us very much, because they are
the same appeal to brevity and decisiveness; that is, "a moment" is
long enough for a total inversion or transformation.[28] I suggest that
in this word as it is used here, we are at the crux of the issue of
discontinuity and continuity for Israel in exile. The time span of
the break interests us because we wonder if it was so brief that the
carryover of God's commitment still prevails.

In considering "for a moment," perhaps an analogy will aid us.
The moment of God's abandonment is like the effect the breaking
of an electrical circuit has on a digital clock. The breaking of the
circuit may be only for an instant. To my unscientific observation,
it appears that sometimes the circuit breaks briefly when the power
goes off, but not so long as to disrupt the time reporting of the clock.
The clock continues to function through the brief break in power.
At other times, or with other clocks, the seemingly same disruption
of current does break the functioning of the clock, and it must be
reset. In both cases the break is "for a moment," but in one case
continuity persists, and in the other it does not. Thus the "instant"
of circuit breaking is a delicate one, and one does not know when
a clock (or one clock rather than another) will be disconnected and
cease to function accurately.

---

27. Miskotte, *When the Gods Are Silent* (New York: Harper & Row, 1967), 405. See
also Karl Barth, *Church Dogmatics*, vol. 2, no. 1 (see chap. 5, n. 29 [1957]), 372–73.

28. Cf., e.g., Exod. 33:5; Isa. 26:20; 47:9; Ps. 30:6; Lam. 4:6.

In like manner, this poem, I suggest, intends us to focus our theological attention on the instant of the breaking of God's loyal love. We are left by the poem to ponder whether the breaking of the circuit of God's faithfulness precludes the continued function of the covenantal commitment of God. It is for Israel a close call; whether or not the current leaps the break for Yahweh determines continuity or discontinuity for Israel. This poem deliberately lodges the entire issue of continuity and discontinuity on the freight of one word, a word so delicate we cannot decide precisely. Thus, the hard verb "abandon" is set next to the adverb "for a moment," and there the matter rests. The verb in the end is more decisive than the adverb. The husband did indeed abandon the wife in wrath; but it was only for an instant, "a twinkling of an eye."[29] It was enough of a circuit break to cut the connection, briefly, but decisively.

This double statement of the acknowledgment of real abandonment by God is followed with a countertheme introduced by an adversative conjunction:

> but with great compassion I will gather you....
> but with everlasting love I will have compassion on you,
>   says the Lord, your redeemer. (Vv. 7-8)

Miskotte comments on the "reverse" of the rejection:

> This at the same time reveals that this word is a saving word—by reason of the fact that the event [i.e., the exile] is now past and is no longer the ultimate truth about our condition.... Therefore the church must be all the more aware of the reverse side of this truth, namely, that grace, which is the annulment of judgment, confirms and corroborates the judgment as God's judgment. In the multi-dimensional realm of his freedom, God does not arbitrarily pass from one to the other, from yes to no, from rejection to acceptance. He resists the resistance. He breaks the rebellion by breaking his own heart.[30]

---

29. Cf. 1 Cor. 15:52.

30. Miskotte, *When the Gods Are Silent*, 405. Miskotte understands that the move from abandonment to compassion happens only through God's deep pathos, that is, through "the breaking of his own heart." Claus Westermann, in *Isaiah 40–66: A Commentary*, OTL (Philadelphia: Westminster Press, 1969), is not as explicit; but he alludes to the same reality: "A change has come over God. He ceases from wrath, and again shows Israel mercy" (p. 274). In his comment, however, Westermann speaks of the way Israel's "heart throbbed" but does not draw God's heart into the trouble in the same way.

Abandonment, *wrath*, and *hiddenness* are countered by *steadfast love*, *compassion*, and *redeemer*.

Third, because of the adverb *'ôlam*, we may inquire about the relation of the negative and affirmative triads. When *'ôlam* is rendered "everlasting," we might conclude that God's *ḥesed* was at all times operative, that is, before, during, and after the abandonment. On that reading, the abandonment by the husband does not cut deeply, and an underlying continuity is affirmed in spite of the hiddenness of God's face (so Calvin). An alternative reading, however, does not regard the qualifying *'ôlam* as mercy before and during, but only after the abandonment. Thus, the relation of rejection and embrace is not an ongoing *parallelism* whereby *ḥesed* denies ultimate seriousness to abandonment, but the two are *sequential*. *Ḥesed* arises out of, after, and in response to the rejection, so that *ḥesed* stands on the other side of the discontinuity and not in powerful opposition to the discontinuity. Thus, the "everlastingness" of *'ôlam* is into the future but not through the past of Israel's exile.

Thus, we may answer our three interpretive questions:

1. The abandonment is *real* and not only "seems" so.

2. The abandonment is *for an instant*, but long enough to matter decisively.

3. The promised *ḥesed* is *after and in response to* the abandonment, and not in its midst as an antidote.

The upshot of this reading is that there is discontinuity in God's own resolve for Israel, a discontinuity that evokes, permits, and requires a new response by the compassionate God who is redeemer.

This reading of discontinuity is sustained by the following lines in vv. 9-10: "This [the exile] is like the days of Noah."[31] God swears "from wrath" (*mqṣp*) and from "rebuking" (*g'r*), as Yahweh "swore that waters would not again pass over the earth" (cf. Gen. 8:21-22; 9:11). In the analogue of the flood, it is clear that the promise in Genesis is a promise that it will not happen "again"; that is, it is a promise *after* the flood that precludes its replication.[32] There was a real flood, a real release of chaos, a real abandonment of the earth, which left creation bereft of God's protective care. Thus, in the flood

---

31. Much of the Noah-flood story is from P and, therefore, from the exile. Thus it is not unexpected that that flood narrative should be on the horizon of this exilic poet.

32. The "again" (*'ôd*) of Isa. 54:9 is clearly reminiscent of the same word in Gen. 9:11, with the same intention.

story, the promise and assurance do not persist through the flood but come in sequence after the discontinuity of the flood.[33] The analogue supports our reading vv. 7-8 as a statement of deep discontinuity, with the same "again" implied; that is, the exile of abandonment will not happen *again*, as it manifestly has happened this time.

The sequencing of abandonment and compassion in v. 10 is not a denial of recently experienced discontinuity but an assurance against future discontinuity. Mountains and hills are juxtaposed to God's *ḥesed* and *berîth šālôm*.[34] Now, in light of the promise, God's compassionate resolve is more reliable than the ordering of creation. That assurance is given and received postflood, postexile, postabandonment. Thus out of the massive discontinuity of chaos (flood, exile), God arrives at a new, overriding resolve for fidelity and compassion that wells up out of the discontinuity. The husband who has abandoned now embraces. The God who has been wrathful acts in compassion. The relation that has been breached is now solidified. Out of discontinuity comes a profound decree of continuity, after the discontinuity. The text exhibits no interest in and makes no comment on how it is that the newness arises out of, from, and in the midst of the break. The movement of this sequence is not unlike the sequence we have found in Deut. 4:23-31. In Isa. 54:7-10, it is *from wrath to compassion*; in Deut. 4:23-31, it is *from jealousy to compassion*. The situation of exile features a profound recharacterization of God.

V

The cosmic reference of Isa. 54:10, which contrasts "mountains and hills" with "steadfast love and covenant of peace," leads us to our third text, Jer. 31:35-37. These verses immediately follow after the new covenant passage (vv. 31-34). The announcement of "new covenant" appears to accent the discontinuity between the new covenant and the old covenant, which it is not like (v. 32). Indeed, the

---

33. Bernhard W. Anderson, in "From Analysis to Synthesis: The Interpretation of Genesis 10-11," *JBL* 97 (1978): 23–29, has shown that Gen. 8:1 is the pivot of the flood narrative, that is, when God remembers Noah. In the structure of the narrative, that decisive *remembering* is preceded by God's *forgetting* of Noah. In the same way, in Isaiah 54, God's act of compassion is preceded by a real act of abandonment. Thus the analogy of our text to that of the flood narrative applies to the entire dramatic structure of the narrative.

34. On "covenant of peace," see Bernard P. Batto, "The Covenant of Peace: A Neglected Ancient Near Eastern Motif," *CBQ* 49 (1987): 187–211.

dominant tendency of the Jeremiah tradition is to accent the discontinuity of exile. Oddly, vv. 35-37, immediately following, are a stunning statement of continuity. These verses counter the main tendency of Jeremiah and make a high claim for continuity. Whereas Isa. 54:10 acknowledges that the structures of creation may indeed "depart" (*mûš*) and "be removed" (*môt*), in this text it is assumed that the "fixed order" of creation will not "depart" (*mûš*).[35] In Isa. 54:10, God's *ḥesed* to Israel is more reliable than creation; in this text, God's guarantee of Israel "all the days" is as assured as the fixed order of creation, which is utterly assured. Thus, the argument on the same subject, to make the same claim, is stated very differently. Whereas Isa. 54:10 moves beyond the experience of discontinuity to make its claim, our verses appeal to the experience of continuity to make a similarly large claim.[36]

This assertion of utter continuity is not one we expect in Jeremiah. It is as though the tradition cannot finally settle the matter of continuity and discontinuity. Each time it makes an assertion, it must follow with a counterassertion. As a result, even in the Jeremiah tradition, preoccupied as it is with discontinuity, there is added this countervoice that insists that God's guarantee of Israel is not and cannot be disrupted.[37] The ostensive protasis-apodosis structure of the passage, twice voiced, appears to be governed by a conditional "if"; the rhetoric in fact denies any conditionality (against the grain of Jeremiah) and assumes an unconditional relation between God and Israel. In this text, even the exile allows no disruption in Israel's life with God because of God's steadfast love and fidelity. Unlike Isa. 54:7-8, Israel's partner does not abandon and does not act in wrath.

VI

These three texts—Deut. 4:23-31, Isa. 54:7-10, and Jer. 31:35-37— we may take as representative of the theological reflection evoked by

---

35. For that reason, this text does not need an *'ôd* of reassurance. That is, this text entertains no discontinuity, and, therefore, there is no need for reassertion and new promise.

36. In Isa. 54:9-10, the claim for the future is based on *'ôd*.

37. On the late dating of vv. 35-37, see Robert P. Carroll, *Jeremiah* (see chap. 3, n. 28), 115–16; and William L. Holladay, *Jeremiah 2*, Hermeneia (Minneapolis: Fortress Press, 1989), 199. Holladay dates the text to the time of Nehemiah. My argument, however, is that in doing theology, one must move beyond such a critical judgment to take the realistic assertion of the text. Such a posture, I suppose, is one of second naïveté.

the exile. These three disclosures together suggest that the issue of continuity and discontinuity was for Israel an urgent issue, one that admitted of no simple or settled solution. Four observations arise from this analysis:

1. Even though the historical, sociopolitical dimension of the exile is hardly in doubt, the exile cannot be treated simply as a historical problem concerning the continuity of the community. The exile is *a deep problem for the character of Yahweh* as well as the community of Israel. Thus, exile constitutes a profound theological problem and must be treated theologically as a crisis for God. The texts we have considered are all decrees in the mouth of God, that is, disclosures of a moment in God's own life that cannot be explained simply as a historical or sociological issue.

2. The theological crisis that these texts enunciate and with which they struggle is that *the transcendence of God is placed in deep jeopardy* by the exile. From this it follows that even God's abiding commitment to Israel is at risk, impinged upon by the reality of the exile. It is our common theological propensity, as indicated by Calvin, to exempt God from such jeopardy, to imagine that at bottom, Israel's God is not subject to the terms of the historical process. Such transcendentalism of course offers assurance, but it must necessarily refuse to take either the text or Israel's experience of exile with real seriousness. These texts entertain the thought that God is radically vulnerable to the realities of Israel's life.

In making this affirmation, Israel breaks with magisterial "common theology" that reduces God to a part of a fixed, predictable retribution system.[38] Such a common theology cannot countenance the exile as a crisis for God, and cannot entertain the stunning affirmation concerning God's own life that emerges in the midst of such jeopardized transcendence.

3. The texts assert the jeopardy of transcendence but cannot finally adjudicate the extent or depth of that jeopardy; that is, the texts refuse to come down cleanly either for continuity or discontinuity. In each case, the text tends to *counter the tradition in which it is embedded*. Deuteronomy 4, which ends in compassion "from there," counters the familiar "theology of command" featured in Deuteronomy. Isaiah 54 is embedded in the vibrant affirmation of exilic Isaiah

---

38. Such common theology necessarily interprets exile simply as punishment in a sharper system of retribution. On common theology, see Morton Smith, "Common Theology" (see chap. 1, n. 11), Norman K. Gottwald, *Tribes* (see chap. 1, n. 6), 667–91; and chap. 1 of this volume.

but pauses over God's radical abandonment in the exile (cf. 40:2). The affirmation of continuity in Jer. 31:35-37 lives in tension with the Jeremianic inclination to discontinuity. In this way, the texts keep the question of the jeopardy of God's life with Israel delicately open. Every tilted statement is promptly corrected by a counterstatement, thus permitting no statement to be a final one. Israel's way of doing theology, or more fundamentally, God's act of self-disclosure, bespeaks a profound and ambiguous lack of closure that resists every systematic closure.

4. The texts *move toward God's compassion*. This is true more directly of Deuteronomy 4 and Isaiah 54 than of Jeremiah 31, but see Jer. 30:18; 31:20; 33:26. Indeed, God's compassion seems to be the primary and powerful theological emergent of the exile. The exile evokes new measures and fresh depths of compassion in the character of God. Taken pastorally, the articulation of God's compassion is a humanly needed assurance. Taken theologically, the exile evokes in God a new resolve for fidelity, a resolve that was not operative prior to the hurt and dread of the exile.[39] That resolve on God's part is seeded in old texts (cf. Exod. 34:6-7); the exile, however, provides a rich array of texts voicing this newly central and newly appreciated theological datum. The exile permits God to become toward Israel whom God was not.[40] The fresh characterization of God seems to arise inexplicably but freely in, through, and out of exile. The tone of God's speech toward Israel is dramatically transformed through this terrible jeopardy, a jeopardy that God shares with Israel.

VII

The exile is the moment in the history of Israel and in the life of God when an irreversibly new theological datum is introduced in the horizon of faith. In conclusion, I suggest three dimensions of our interpretive work that are impinged upon by this theological reality emerging in exile:

1. The *paradigm of exile and restoration*, which has its theological counterpart in God's abandonment and God's new compassion,

---

39. The new resolve of God in our texts is not unlike the new resolve of God in the flood narrative (Gen. 8:20-22; 9:8-17). In the flood narrative no reason is given for that new resolve, as none is given here.

40. Critically, the changes can be explained by the identification of distinct literary sources. Such distinctions, however, often violate the intention of the final form of the text, which is the proper material for doing biblical theology.

provides crucial and decisive categories for understanding the crucifixion and resurrection of Jesus and the New Testament "dialectic of reconciliation."[41] While Trinitarian theology has opened a variety of ways of getting from Friday to Sunday, the typology of exile suggests both that the abandonment of God is real and decisive, albeit brief, and that the God who is evidenced in Easter is decisively different from the God who abandons and is abandoned on Friday.[42] The theological reality of the exile warns against any protective tran-

---

41. Jürgen Moltmann, in *Crucified God* (see chap. 8, n. 29), has most powerfully insisted upon this dialectic of crucifixion and resurrection, refusing to let the resurrection overcome or nullify the centrality of the crucifixion in the story of God's life.

42. On getting from Friday to Sunday, George Steiner, in *Real Presences: Is There Anything in What We Say?* (London: Faber & Faber; Chicago: University of Chicago Press, 1989), concludes with a pathos-filled statement:

> There is one particular day in Western history about which neither historical record nor myth nor Scripture make report. It is a Saturday. And it has become the longest of days. We know of that Good Friday which Christianity holds to have been that of the Cross. But the non-Christian, the atheist, knows of it as well. That is to say that he knows of the injustice, of the interminable suffering, of the waste, of the brute enigma of ending.... We know also about Sunday. To the Christian, that day signifies an intimation, both assured and precarious, both evident and beyond comprehension, of resurrection, of a justice and a love that have conquered death. If we are non-Christians or non-believers, we know of that Sunday in precisely analogous terms.... The lineaments of that Sunday carry the name of hope (there is no word less deconstructible).
>
> But ours is the long day's journey of the Saturday. Between suffering, aloneness, unutterable waste on the one hand and the dream of liberation of rebirth on the other. In the face of the torture of a child, of the death of love which is Friday, even the greatest art and poetry are almost helpless. In the Utopia of the Sunday, the aesthetic will, presumably, no longer have logic or necessity. The apprehensions and figurations ... which tell of pain and of hope, of the flesh which is said to taste of ash and of the spirit which is said to have the savour of fire, are always Sabbatarian. They have risen out of an immensity of waiting which is that of man. Without them, how could we be patient? (Pp. 231–32)

Steiner's poignant statement from outside the Christian faith (as a Jew) is paralleled from inside the Christian community by Nicholas Lash, *Easter in Ordinary: Reflections on Human Experience and the Knowledge of God* (Charlottesville: University Press of Virginia, 1988). Lash writes: "In a fascinating section of *What is Man?*, Buber distinguishes between 'epochs of habitation and epochs of homelessness.' Whether we like it or not, ours is an epoch of homelessness.... But homelessness is the truth of our condition, and the 'gifts of the spirit,' gifts of community and relationship, forgiveness and life-giving, are at least as much a matter of promise, of prospect, and of the task that is laid upon us, as they are a matter of past achievement or present reality" (pp. 216, 268). Both Steiner and Lash voice the discontinuity and affirm that our current habitation is in the homelessness between. The Old Testament moment of exile is indeed one long Saturday, which afterward may seem to have been "a moment."

scendentalism in the midst of the failure of God's life with Israel and
Israel's life with God.[43] Thus, New Testament theology might take
more seriously this paradigm that comes to govern the imagination
of Judaism as a way of reflecting upon the abandonment of Jesus
and the rule of the risen Christ.

2. The new theological datum of exile impinges upon *the crisis of modernity and postmodernity in theology*. There is in the exile a
decisive disclosure of God that should warn us against certain theological temptations. Three aspects of our crisis occur to me in this
connection.

a. Much theology has been a search for universals, an attempt to
articulate truth that lies outside the concrete experience and testimony of the confessing community.[44] Against every such universal,
the claims of the biblical God come down to particular moments of
embrace and abandonment, to particular verses of texts, and to particular moments (*rega'*) of crisis. More than anywhere else in the Old
Testament, in the exile Israel faces "the scandal of particularity" in all
its pathos. Such an exilic voicing of God stands powerfully against
any would-be universals.

b. Much of theology, particularly as voiced in conventional confessional traditions, has sought to voice God in transcendental categories that leave God freed from and untouched by the vagaries of
historical discontinuity. The disclosure of God in these exilic texts refuses such a posture and allows no certitudes about God out beyond
the jeopardy of discontinuity.

c. The moral propensity of modernity is ragingly enacted in the
brutality expressed in technological categories, most dramatically
(but not exclusively) in the Holocaust. It may indeed be that the exile
is no adequate paradigm for the technological brutality quintessen-
tially expressed in the Holocaust; nonetheless, we are the generation
that has witnessed massive hurt generated through technological
strategies that bespeak the power of death and the absence of God.
The technological production of massive pain makes all our conven-

---

43. Moltmann, in *Crucified God*, underscores the abandonment that overrides every
claim of transcendence. Thus "The Fatherlessness of the Son is matched by the
Sonlessness of the Father" (p. 243).

44. Lyotard, in *Postmodern Condition*, insists that there are only concrete narratives
and claims in communities of testimony. The reality of Israel's struggle with God
requires the giving up of every universal. See his appeal on p. 40 to a figure from
Wittgenstein, that a town consists of many little houses, squares, and streets (p. 40).
See the remarkable argument by Stephen Toulmin, *Cosmopolis: The Hidden Agenda of
Modernity* (New York: Free Press, 1990), esp. 31–32.

tional theology open to question and drives us to the more elemental categories of God's presence and absence, God's abandonment and reemergence.[45] In the exilic texts, human failure evokes God's absence and abandonment; *mutatis mutandis*, our shameless linkage of brutality and technology may evoke a moral calculus that requires God's absence. It may, however, be that same shameless linkage of brutality and absence that evokes God's reemergence in a fresh posture. In, with, and under the brutality and pain, God emerges anew as the generator of human possibility.[46] The new theological data of exile have much to teach us about our current theological situation, much that we should already have learned but did not.

3. The new theological data of the exile not only offer decisive material for the shaping of New Testament theology but crucial illumination of a substantive kind for our current theological task. Its major offer to us is the suggestion of *new ways of doing theology* in poetic, narrative forms that eschew conventional modes of discourse, that offer God as a speaker in the poetry, a character in the narrative plot, a God who moves in and through terrible disjunctions to newness. Thus, the rhetoric of these texts shapes God's own life with Israel: (*a*) "from there" (Deut. 4:29); (*b*) "but...but" (Isa. 54:7-8); and (*c*) "if...then, if...then" (Jer. 31:35-37). Such a way of theology is concrete, particular, and inherently subversive of every settlement, spilling over from daring rhetoric into public reality, where exiles must live and trust.

---

45. On the Holocaust, see Richard L. Rubenstein, "Job and Auschwitz," *USQR* 25 (Summer 1970): 421–37. Emil Fackenheim, in *To Mend the World* (see chap. 2, n. 6), has most eloquently characterized our new, post-Holocaust theological situation that requires theology to lower its voice back to more concrete claims that are brought to speech only in communities of hurt and risk.

46. Beker concludes: "Finally, a biblical theology of hope allows us to be realistic and honest about the poisonous reality of death and dying in our world....And so the biblical vision still offers a promissory word in the face of suffering due to the power of death" (*Suffering and Hope*, 91). Beker's final affirmation is rooted exactly in the testimony of exiles who discern God making promises to exiles, in exile, beyond exile.

10

Genesis 50:15-21—
A Theological Exploration

THE STUDY OF THE JOSEPH narrative has been dominated by the work of Martin Noth and Gerhard von Rad, but their work has led to a cul-de-sac.[1] Noth has been interested only in the "great themes" of the Pentateuch and so has paid little attention to this narrative. Von Rad, with his "wisdom hypothesis," has also disregarded this narrative in his study of the Hexateuch, and he has treated the internal character of the narrative in something of a vacuum. Neither Noth's concern for external function nor von Rad's attention to internal character has opened a way for a theological understanding of the narrative.

I

Scholarly work since von Rad and Noth includes the following: Donald B. Redford and George W. Coats seek to find the core story that has been subsequently expanded, but both of them are interested in the internal literary character of the narrative and focus on the intent of the present text very little. Rolf Rendtorff seeks to take the text as

---

1. Noth, *A History of Pentateuchal Traditions* (Englewood Cliffs, N.J.: Prentice-Hall, 1972), 208–13. Von Rad has treated the text in a variety of places: *Old Testament Theology I* (see chap. 1, n. 22), 172–75; "The Joseph Narrative and Ancient Wisdom," in *The Problem* (see chap. 4, n. 30), 292–300; *Genesis* (see chap. 8, n. 37), 347ff.; and "The Story of Joseph," in *God at Work in Israel* (Nashville: Abingdon Press, 1980), 19–35.

it stands without dissection. His work has the merit of letting the text be a discrete "cluster," and he has paid attention to the promise motif, thus opening the way for a theological analysis. Brevard S. Childs and David J. A. Clines, from the perspective of canonical criticism, have tried to see the narrative in its present canonical setting. Childs presents the narrative in terms of the promise under threat. Clines suggests that the narrative is a reversal of the disastrous flow of Genesis 1–11. Both see the promise still unresolved and open-ended. It appears that the work of Rendtorff, Childs, and Clines helps in moving our work out of the sharp contrast of internal and external foci left by Noth and von Rad.[2]

One result of this shift in perspective is that von Rad's sapiential interpretation is increasingly disregarded and denied, for it does not seem to take the narrative on its own terms in its present context. The part of von Rad's understanding that likely will endure is the portrayal of the "deep hiddenness" of God and God's plan fulfilled through suffering.[3]

The Joseph story is lodged here not simply as a "formal bridge" (though it may be that) or as a convenient place for a wisdom narrative (other places may have been equally convenient), but because Israel at this point in the narrative needed not so much a great Pentateuchal theme as a reflective moment concerning how the promise could be trusted and kept credible against the reality of nonfulfillment. The inscrutability of Yahweh is not simply a literary technique for bridging (so Noth) nor simply a cultural advance reflective of an enlightenment (so von Rad) but an experiential reality in the faith of Israel, as presented in this literature. From whatever source it may have been taken, the Joseph narrative now serves to meet a religious need in the experiential faith of Israel. The "redescribed" character of Israel's faith is created and made available by this literature.[4]

---

2. Redford, in *A Study of the Biblical Story of Joseph (Genesis 37–50)*, VTSup, no. 20 (Leiden: Brill, 1970), attempts (much more than Coats) to identify the stages through which the story has expanded. Coats, *From Canaan to Egypt* (Washington, D.C.: Catholic Biblical Association of America, 1976); see also his discussions in "The Joseph Story and Ancient Wisdom: A Reappraisal," *CBQ* 35 (1973): 285–97, and in "Redactional Unity in Genesis 37–50," *JBL* 93 (1974): 15–21. Rendtorff, *The Problem of the Process of Transmission in the Pentateuch*, JSOTSup, series 89 (Sheffield: Sheffield Academic Press, 1990); see also his "The 'Yahwist' as Theologian? The Dilemma of Pentateuchal Criticism," *JSOT* 3 (1976): 2–10. Childs, *Introduction* (see chap. 1, n. 6), 150–58. Clines, *Theme* (see chap. 4, n. 22).

3. Von Rad, *Old Testament Theology I*, 172–73.

4. Paul Ricoeur has most helpfully presented the idea of "redescribing" as the work of revelatory literature: "Biblical Hermeneutics" (see chap. 4, n. 47), esp. 31;

My point is that the more recent scholarship may provide a legitimate way to pose again a theological issue that has been prevented by the hardening of scholarly constructs and the rigidity of analytical categories. Thus the theological issues on which the narrative turns are not those of credal theology or sapiential reflection from the Solomonic enlightenment (the issues left for us by Noth and von Rad). Rather, the issues are those of the revelatory character of God and the hiddenness of God, the sense that in the hiddenness God still governs but that the hiddenness opens toward new disclosure that is stunning in its power and yet not unambiguous in its meaning. Posing the question this way permits us to think about theological claims and religious needs, issues that our scholarly constructs have excessively subordinated to matters of cultural history and more analytic questions of date and source.[5] That disclosure, as we shall see, is carried by the character of Joseph in our text, who is both stunning and, up to a point, not unambiguous. It is the ambiguity of the person of Joseph that points to the ambiguity of God in this moment of historical ambiguity.

The part of the narrative to be considered here is the conversation of the brothers with Joseph after the death of their father, Jacob. It is introduced by lamentation and burial of their father (49:28—50:14).[6]

---

and "Imagination in Discourse and in Action," in part 2 of *The Human Being in Action: The Irreducible Element in Man*, ed. Anna-Teresa Tymieniecka (Boston: Reidel Pub. Co., 1978).

5. It is beyond the scope of this chapter to consider the Joseph narrative from the perspective of the New Literary Criticism, although there are important gains to be made through such an approach. For efforts in that direction, see Donald A. Seybold, "Paradox and Symmetry in the Joseph Narrative," in *Literary Interpretations of Biblical Narrative*, ed. Kenneth R. R. Gros Louis, James S. Ackerman, and Thayer S. Warshaw (New York: Abingdon Press, 1974), 59–73; and Mary Savage, "Literary Criticism and Biblical Studies: A Rhetorical Analysis of the Joseph Narrative," in *Scripture in Context: Essays on the Comparative Method*, ed. Carl D. Evans, William W. Hallo, and John B. White (Pittsburgh: Pickwick Press, 1980), 89–100. See also the discerning treatment of Robert Alter, *The Art of Biblical Narrative* (New York: Basic Books, 1981), esp. 157–76. On two points, however, that kind of literary criticism is inadequate for our question. It tends to screen out theological issues and to take the text apart from the community. On both these points, I judge the method to be important, but by itself inadequate.

6. For both Redford (*Study*, 163–64, 186) and Coats ("Redactional Unity," 15, 21), this passage falls outside the principal narrative. Coats does allow that this is a "supporting satellite narrative" that functions as a "recapitulation," so his judgment is not as radical as that of Redford. But neither of them addresses the crucial placement and function of this piece. The judgment of Claus Westermann is not different; see his *Genesis 3* (Neukirchen-Vluyn: Neikirchenen Verlag, 1982), 230–31.

II

In what follows, we consider 50:15-21 as a piece of carefully wrought theology. Our discussion will address itself to two points:

1. This exchange is a theological statement drawing upon those theological motifs that Israel found most useful in contexts of fear and hopelessness, of which exile is a primary example.[7]

2. The Joseph story is now shaped for the primary purpose of staging this speech, which is carefully placed at the seam between Exodus and Genesis. The careful placement is not simply to make a literary or historical linkage, however, but to articulate a theological affirmation. The chapter functions typologically for a religious seam or crisis in Israel's life.

The unit portrays an exchange between Joseph and the other sons of Jacob. Absent now is the third party to the triangle, the father who had always played a decisive, mediating role. When that third party is removed, relations between the two remaining parties must be reconfigured, and not without risk. It is that re-configuration that is now reported.[8] The space between Joseph and the others is ominous and ill-defined, filled with terror for the brothers. All parties know that the absence of their father matters enormously. And no doubt the terror consists largely of un-resolved guilt. At the same time, Joseph is noncommittal. When he is passionate with weeping and not at all cool (for example, Gen. 45:14; 46:29), we are not sure what it means. All parties are now set in a dangerous situation of rawness. Old guarantees, protections, and conventions are removed. Now all parties must face the danger, and none knows beforehand how it will turn out. The risk in the family without the controlling presence of Jacob is not unlike every exile in which old systems of support have been lost.

---

7. Such an argument may appear to support the late dating generally taken by the Toronto School. Cf. John Van Seters, *Abraham in History and Tradition* (New Haven: Yale University Press, 1975). Our concern here, however, is not chronology but a characteristic, if not paradigmatic, response to exile. I mean to beg the question of dating.

8. On "triangling" as a characteristic dynamic of family interaction, see Murray Bowen, *Family Therapy in Clinical Practice* (New York: J. Aronson, 1978). Social "recon-figuring" should be seen as related to the literary act of "redescribing," mentioned above. Literary "redescribing" serves and permits social reconfiguring.

III

The encounter is initiated from the side of the brothers, the admittedly guilty party. The subject is now retribution, the settling of accounts that could not happen while the father lived (v. 15).

1. It is as though retaliation and the settlement of accounts were not clear and present dangers while Jacob was alive. For the brothers, Jacob embodies something of a barrier against retribution, which has now been removed. Now everything is at risk.

2. The device of sending a message (a messenger is not mentioned) in vv. 16-17a is marvelously ambiguous, as everything in this interaction is ambiguous. The commentaries speculate on whether Jacob had in fact commissioned such a message.[9]

We must not speculate, however. We must stay inside the story, and inside the story everything is ambiguous for all parties. Thus, whether Jacob gave such a directive is intended to be uncertain. We are not told. It is likely that the brothers do not know if it is true. We do not know how Joseph will respond. If it is a true word from the father, the brothers do not know if Joseph will remember it or if he will think (with the commentaries) that it is a device. Or if Joseph remembers, we do not know if he will honor it. Thus the literary mode of a message serves to delay the encounter and to heighten the suspense and risk. The situation with Joseph is now quite new, one of discontinuity. The brothers want to cling to their old support, even if it means claiming too much for Jacob. They hope the old support by Jacob still has force. But of course they do not know.

3. But the appeal to Jacob is almost diversionary to the movement of the encounter. In v. 17b, the brothers' initiative moves to the present petition: *wĕʿattâ*. In that moment of confrontation, neither the terror of the brothers nor the injunction of the dead father counts for anything. The brothers must stand helpless before the great ruler who may or may not act like a remembering kinsman. The petition is bold, accompanied only by a definitional term "servants."

The petition is simple and massive: "forgive transgressions." The request is first in the mouth of Jacob and then in the mouths of the brothers. The formula is used in a telling way in Exod. 10:17, where pharaoh petitions Moses and Aaron for forgiveness. Here the situ-

---

9. Von Rad (*Genesis*, 432) takes the trouble to say it is a "false assumption" that the brothers are lying in this act, but we do not know. The narrator does not intend us to know.

ation is exactly reversed. Here it is needy Israel come to the great Egyptian officer. There it is the pharaoh himself come in need to Israel. Perhaps the two uses together attest the general inversion. For our purposes, however, perhaps the most interesting use is that made in a lament psalm. In the petition of Ps. 25:16-18, there is a cluster of terms for seeking relief from a situation of trouble:

> Turn thou to me, and be gracious to me;
> for I am lonely and afflicted.
> Relieve the troubles of my heart,
> and bring me out of my distresses.
> Consider my affliction and my trouble,
> and forgive all my sins.
> (Cf. 1 Sam. 15:25; 25:28)

The language of petition used by the brothers is the standard language of the lament psalm. In the psalm the petition is addressed to God. Here the petition is addressed to Joseph, not to God. In each case it is addressed to the one who has power to act to extricate the guilty, and here that is undoubtedly Joseph.

The way in which the petitioners identify themselves is important. In v. 17, where Jacob said it for them, they are "your brothers." Now they say only "servants of the God of your father." Two times, here and in v. 16, it is "your father," not "our father." So the brothers have moved a distance from brother to servant. They do not yet say directly "your servant," but "servant of God." They are not yet ready for full capitulation, but they are on the way. In their fear, they have abandoned the brother-talk their father thought appropriate. They still want to make a case of family binding, but they dare to do it only by making a general theological reference. Thus far in the narrative, we have no clue about how the petition will be received. We do not know if they act in good faith or deviously. We do not know how the great man will respond, and the brothers do not know either.

IV

The narrative might have moved directly to Joseph's definitive response in v. 19, but it does not. The narrative holds off as long as possible, so in vv. 17b-18 there is an intermediate stage, a parrying between brothers, a dramatic delay. When one comes to such a staggering confrontation, one must not rush to resolve what cannot be resolved in a rush.

1. So first there is Joseph's initial response, which is profoundly ambiguous. Joseph wept when they spoke to him. Joseph's characteristic response to family matters is weeping. The response seems obvious. But we are not told at all what the weeping might mean. We are apparently free to speculate in any way we choose. We are told nothing of Joseph's motives or feelings. The narrative is disciplined in that regard. The action functions to slow the conversation, and we must still wait to find out Joseph's response to his brothers. It could be a mocking. Or it could be that Joseph is deeply moved. Or if our assignment of the petition to a lament form is correct, it could be that Joseph stands in solidarity with their grief, recognizing that he also has transgressions that await forgiveness. It is, in any case, recognized as an occasion proper for weeping.

This situation includes a loss of conventional support, an emergence of questions concerning retribution, and an acknowledgment of fear and displacement. This is the situation in which all parties find themselves, and the narrator invites the listening Israelite into that situation as well. The crying perhaps characterizes not only Joseph but all who participate in the narrative, its actors and its listeners.

2. The other element in this intermediate section is the response of the brothers to the weeping of Joseph in v. 18. They fall before him, a motif we have watched steadily in the entire narrative since the initial dream of chapter 37. So the encounter now has intentional binding with the beginning of the entire family narrative.

What interests us more is the way in which the brothers refer to themselves. They are no longer "brothers," as in v. 17, nor are they "servants of God," as in v. 18. Now it is an act of unambiguous political deference. They say simply "your servants" (v. 18). In two careful moves, the term has gone from "brothers" to "servants of the God of your father" to "your servants," all the way from kinship to political realism and submission.

The speech is not of familial embrace but the working out of power relations. The brothers have acknowledged their guilt. Now they abase themselves completely. They are helpless petitioners, without a bargaining chip. And that perhaps is precisely what is desired by Joseph, as the narrative offers him to us. There is no talk of brothers or of father or of forgiveness, but there is a complete abandonment of every other help, reference, and resource. The narrative has moved carefully to this radical act of self-abasement.

V

Only now are we ready for the third element, Joseph's lordly response (vv. 19-20). The exchange has begun from the side of the brothers with their guilt and fear. The exchange concludes with Joseph's carefully crafted response. Nothing is conceded. The brothers have it right. They are servants. Joseph is lord. No one in the meeting is unclear about that.

1. The speech begins, "Do not fear." We have here the salvation oracle that Begrich has studied in such detail. Taken by itself, it is clear that this is a response directly to the petition "forgive!" We have seen that it is a situation of fear and guilt, in which questions of retribution and retaliation are on the table, a situation of weeping when all old supports have failed and there is utter abasement along with complete helplessness.

In response, the salvation oracle "Do not fear" is perhaps the most appropriate answer available among the formularies of Israel. The salvation oracle marks a radical break, a move from the other side, a beginning again out of radical discontinuity. It is the characteristic way in which Israel experiences the overcoming of fear, the termination of retribution, the eradication of weeping, the raising up after complete abasement. The word uttered by Joseph is the best word Israel has to offer. None of the old modes of relation is pertinent, not the devices of the brother, not the protective oversight of the father, not the calculations of Joseph. The situation is resolved in the only way it can be, by a new generative act permitting life, spoken by the one with all the power.

2. Who is Joseph to speak such a word? The formula is characteristically the speech of God.[10] How dare Joseph speak such a word? So the marvelous announcement is followed by a most curious rhetorical question: "Am I in the place of God?" Again the narrator leaves us with a remarkable ambiguity. What is the intended answer to the rhetorical question? If one answers the question "yes," it suggests that Joseph can speak a "fear not" and, implicitly, that he can forgive sin because he has placed himself in God's place. That may be the

---

10. See the comprehensive analysis of the formula by Thomas M. Raitt, *Theology* (see chap. 9, n. 24), chap. 6.

intention, because all through the narrative the brothers perceive him as acting as though he were God, or as though he thought he was God. Conversely, if one answers "no," then it means that Joseph is not in God's place, cannot really forgive sin, and thus his "fear not" is not ultimately believable.[11] The question may preclude either Joseph's capacity to forgive or his capacity to retaliate.

We do not know which way the narrator intends the question to be answered. We do not even know if an answer is intended. I suggest, rather, that the darkness and ambiguity of the encounter are here maintained and intensified by this enigmatic statement. Joseph's initial response does not alleviate the fear or offer any assurance. The brothers still have the burden of guilt and, therefore, of fear. The brothers are here given no clear assurance of forgiveness even though it appears so on the surface. The petition that seeks forgiveness receives a response "fear not," but it is a response short of resolution. The following rhetorical question places the salvation oracle in a position of jeopardy, and seems immediately to take back what has been so wondrously given.

3. Finally, the delaying tactics of the narrative lead to the well-known formula of v. 20, "You meant it for evil, God meant it for good." The most influential interpretation is that of von Rad, who regards the statement as a summary of wisdom teaching, which he several times relates to Prov. 16:2, 9; 19:21; 20:24; 21:30.[12] Von Rad calls this formulation "a bold mixture of divine activity and guilty human deeds."[13] That is, the plans of God are wrought through the guilty actions of the brothers.

We may suggest three objections to the relation of this statement to wisdom:

a. The verse is often, even by von Rad, taken by itself, without reference to its context. When the statement is taken in its context, we have seen that it is surrounded not by sapiential marks but by characteristics of the Psalms, the petition, the weeping, and the salvation oracle. Thus, we would do better to look at the Psalms for illumination.[14]

b. It is telling that in the set of proverbs regularly cited in this re-

11. The most obvious parallel rhetorical question is that of Jacob in Gen. 3:2, which requires a negative answer.

12. See von Rad: *Old Testament Theology I*, 439–40; *God at Work*, 33; and "Joseph Narrative," 297–98.

13. Von Rad, *Wisdom* (see chap. 1, n. 25), 200.

14. See the comments of Westermann in *Genesis*, 283.

gard (Prov. 16:2, 9; 19:21; 20:24; 21:2; 21:30)[15] never does the word *hāšab* occur twice, as in our formula, and only two times (16:9; 19:21) does it occur even once. I shall suggest that the parallels in the Psalms are much more pertinent.

c. Faithful to the claims of wisdom, von Rad tends to view the "meant" of the brothers and the "meant" of God as somehow continuous, as though the one is wrought out of the other. I suggest that such a reading of the relation of the two elements is not in keeping with the text. In the proverbs cited, the contrast is one of discernment and mystery, but that does not approach the moral crises surfaced in 50:20. Rather, the two "meant" statements here are adversative, and what is asserted is that the plan of God defeats the plan of the brothers, not that it is a mixture of the two or a use of one by the other. If that is correct, then the statement finds a better habitat in the conflictual, adversative language of the Psalms than in the accommodating, embracing language of wisdom.[16]

On all three grounds, I suggest that the resolution of this entire encounter is more likely to be understood in the tradition of the Psalms. This statement about good and evil is not a general statement, but it is the cry of the righteous one who has been or is about to be vindicated against the evil wrought by the wicked. Thus, the context requires that Joseph's speech is not a statement of cool reconciliation, but it is a victory assertion in which the brothers must indeed be servants and not brothers because God gives well-being to God's righteous one. The relation between Joseph and his brothers is not that of family members at a love-feast but of litigants appearing before the throne. No wonder Joseph is not in the place of God. He takes his place before God and claims vindication. Joseph is pictured not as forgiving, for there is no hint of that, but as a righteous man who is vindicated. The wisdom interpretation, I should argue, with its propensity for harmonization, misses the abrasive, threatening tone used here.

I suggest that the double use of *hāšab* here functions in the same way as in the psalms of lament. Note especially Pss. 35:4, 20; 36:5; 40:6, 18; 56:6; but see also 10:2; 21:12; 41:8; 52:3-4; 92:6-7; 140:2-3, 5. The sum of this evidence is that the psalmists trust the plans of God to defeat the plans, schemes, and plots of evil persons.

---

15. See von Rad, *Old Testament Theology I*, 439.

16. See the counter use of *hšb* in Mic. 2:1-3; and cf. Patrick D. Miller, *Sin and Judgment* (see chap. 1, n. 24), 29–31. Miller's entire analysis presumes an adversative relationship, which is what we have in our text.

The language occurs in several genres, but the primary usage is in the complaint psalm that appeals to the plan of God against the destructive plans of the evil.

This contrast is most clearly expressed in Ps. 33:10-11:

> The Lord brings the counsel of the nations to nought;
>   he frustrates the *plans* of the peoples.
> The counsel of the Lord stands for ever,
>   the *thoughts* of his heart to all generations.

This psalm is certainly not without reminiscences of wisdom, but the language is much loser to lament than to any of the proverbs cited by von Rad.

The formula of v. 20 serves as a vindication of Joseph. Conversely, it is an indictment of the brothers, who are rightly not more than servants. Their way of ordering the life of Israel (and the future of Israel) has been defeated. The language of vindication and indictment is a way of appropriate entry into the exodus narrative and a reflection of the tenor of the entire Joseph narrative. The reference to *'am rab* in v. 20 indicates a readiness to move on into the public history of Israel (cf. Exod. 1:9).

4. We come now to the last structural element in the encounter of Joseph and his brothers, who have become his slaves. I have suggested that the text falls into two primary parts, vv. 15-17a, an approach by the brothers, and vv. 19-21, the resolution by Joseph, with a transitional element in vv. 17b-18. The two main parts are structurally complementary, each dominated by an assertion that is reiterated after *wě'attâ*. For the brothers, it is:

> Forgive, I pray their transgressions...
> *wě'attâ* forgive the transgressions...

This is matched in the response of Joseph:

> Fear not...
> *wě'attâ* do not fear...

In each case, the reasserted element after *wě'attâ* is much more forceful. In each case, the preliminary statement seems dramatically less secure. The concluding response of Joseph following the *wě'attâ* consists in three parts:

a. There is the reiterated "do not fear." Now there is no rhetorical question to qualify.

b. This is followed by a self-assertion, governed by the imperfect verb, "I will provide." This formula is in the position of completing the salvation oracle, although the usual particle *kî*, "for," is absent. This statement offers the ground for not fearing. And in this usage, Joseph operates with godlike authority (cf. Gen. 41:38-41).

c. The final element contains two factors of great interest. First, the verb *niḥam* (*pi'el*), "Joseph comforted his brothers." The text still does not say that he forgave or that he felt affection. Perhaps the earlier rhetorical question is honored; that is, only God can forgive. The use of the word *niḥam* cannot be accidental. The *pi'el* usage is widespread and diverse. But in four clusters its use sustains my thesis concerning parallels in the Psalms. The term is used in lament psalms (69:21; 71:21; 86:17; 119:76,82). It is used in the poetry of the book of Lamentations (1:2, 9, 16, 17, 21; 2:13), in the speeches of Job (7:13; 16:2; 21:34; 29:25), and in Second Isaiah (40:1; 49:13; 51:3, 12, 19; 52:9), with which we may associate the following: Jer. 31:13; Ezek. 14:23; 16:54; Isa. 61:2; 66:13. All these usages refer to situations of distress, either hoping for or rejoicing in an act of rescue and intervention that makes all things new.

Dramatically speaking, as related to the lament psalms and Second Isaiah, we may conclude that the salvation oracle is the decisive factor in being comforted. That is, the use of *niḥam* is made possible by the "do not fear" that precedes. As nearly as we can place these various uses, they refer to situations of exile, if not the specific situation of sixth-century exile. Joseph's speech and action are presumably exile-ending acts; he speaks a word that lets the past be past and then moves on to the promises of *'am rab* and the provisions for that future.

Second, the use of the verb *niḥam* is supported by the final statement, "He spoke with words that touched their hearts" (*way yĕ dabbēr 'al-libbām*) (Jerusalem Bible). Again the phrase "speak to the heart" is widely used. It may mean "to remember" (Jer. 3:16; 12:11; Isa. 46:8), "to take seriously" (Isa. 42:25; 57:1; Mal. 2:2), or "to determine" (Dan. 1:8). But the closest parallels would suggest that it is language of intimacy, care, and embrace (Gen. 34:3; Judg. 19:3; Ruth 2:13).[17]

---

17. Hans Walter Wolff, in *Hosea*, Hermeneia (Philadelphia: Fortress Press, 1974), 42, says that it "belongs to the language of courtship."

This last usage in Ruth 2:13 is of special interest for us because the full statement that Ruth speaks to Boaz is:

> You are most gracious to me, my Lord,
> for you have comforted me and spoken kindly.

This speech combines *dibbēr 'al-lēb* with the *pi'el* of *niham*, closely paralleling our passage. Here Boaz has performed an act of inordinate power and kindness that permits a hopeless person to begin a new life.

The phrase of Joseph's statement, however, points especially to Hos. 2:16 and Isa. 40:2. In Hos. 2:16, the speech of Yahweh "to the heart" has the effect of permitting Israel to begin again, again after the death sentence of vv. 4-15. The object of the speech "is to overcome sorrow and resentment (cf. also 2 Chron. 32:6), obstinacy and estrangement."[18] In the decisive passage of Isa. 40:2, the great exile-ending speech that seems to answer to the hopelessness of Lamentations, again *'al lēb* is closely linked to *niham*.

Thus, Joseph's speech after the *wě'attâ* consists of four elements: (*a*) salvation oracle, (*b*) promise of provision, (*c*) comfort, and (*d*) speaking to the heart. All together, they are about ending the terror and guilt expressed in vv. 15-17a.

VI

Our analysis may yield these conclusions:

The theological motifs used are those regularly used by Israel in *situations of fear and hopelessness*. More specifically, this piece reflects the motifs used in the theological crisis of Lamentations and Second Isaiah:

1. The *loss of the support and safeguard* of a father is not unlike the loss of all conventional social props in 587 B.C.E., which are grieved for in the book of Lamentations.

2. The overriding *response of Israel* to the situation of 587 B.C.E. is one of guilt and fear (cf. Lam. 1:8-9, 14, 18, 20, and esp. 22). The brothers are here portrayed in a like situation, in dread because they are justly subject to retaliation.

3. The *response of Joseph* with a salvation oracle is not unlike salvation oracles generally in response to laments. Specifically, Second

---

18. Ibid.

Isaiah has used the form to provide hope and comfort to the exiles (cf. Isa. 41:10, 13, 14; 43:1; 54:1; cf. Jer. 30:10-11; Lam. 3:57). In both cases the speech is exile-ending.

4. The decisive statement of v. 20 in which the *plans of Yahweh* override the destructive plans of the brothers is parallel to two exile-ending assertions in Jer. 29:11 and Isa. 55:6-9.[19]

5. The final formulation of "comfort/speak to the heart" functions as an *anticipation of "homecoming"* when illuminated by the intimacy of Ruth 2:13 and the proclamation of Isa. 40:2.

Thus, the piece draws primarily from the language used in laments and oracles in the Psalter and not from that of the wisdom literature. The language is that which comes closest to exilic speech of despair and new possibility. In both senses, our text is paradigmatic for what Israel characteristically says in such contexts. The Joseph narrative, featuring the brothers as desperate Israel and Joseph as a giver of the future, is not linked to the Pentateuch artificially but integrally, an entry point to the book of Exodus.[20] We meet Israel in the book of Exodus precisely at the point of despair. In Gen. 50:15-21 (22-26), important promises have been made that have not yet been fulfilled. This moment of the brothers before pharaonic Joseph presents Israel in its utter helplessness, waiting for a new word, a word spoken in Egypt by Moses and in Babylon by Second Isaiah. The culmination of the Joseph narrative shows that the promise of Genesis has its own life. It still may be fulfilled, but it has not yet been fulfilled. We may thus find a way beyond that method-

---

19. The *šālôm/ra'* contrast here is not unlike the *ṭôb/ra'* contrast in our text. Indeed, the Deuteronomic tradition of Jeremiah plays with the motif. Cf. Jer. 44:27; 39:16; 24:6. The claims of our text sound very different when set in the abrasive context of exile.

20. Cf. Rendtorff, *Das Problem*, 75. He notes especially the use of *pāqad*, which is used in Exod. 3:16; 4:31. Note the same word in Jer. 29:10, with reference to return from exile. Miller, in *Psalms and Inscriptions*, VTSup, no. 32 (Leiden: Brill, 1980), 330–32, observes that *pqd* is a word used in prayer of petition in time of distress. This fact is yet another small point that links our text (cf. vv. 22-26) to the Psalms and to the exilic situation. Hartmut Gese, in *Essays on Biblical Theology* (Minneapolis: Augsburg Pub. House, 1981), appeals to the entire scene of the death of Jacob: "In Genesis 50 we read about how the great funeral of Jacob, the eponymous hero of Israel, was performed in reverse analogy to the exodus. All the Egyptian court and the army of chariots and horsemen accompanied the deceased to the Holy Land. This becomes a symbol in reverse of the exodus, but in an anticipation that corresponds to the truth. Life in the land first became possible through a grave; through a grave the group put down roots in the land" (p. 37). Although Gese's interpretation is correct, he does not comment upon the decisive role played by the speech-exchange of Joseph and his brothers. It is the speech that turns the history of Israel toward the land.

ological impasse to see that the intimate conflict of Joseph's family
and the larger sweep of Israel's tradition are not two separated phenomena. They partake of the same continuing interaction of lament
and assurance. The substantive theological judgment is that this
exchange foreshadows the exodus and indeed offers a succinct articulation of the main theological paradigm for Israel's faith. It is
placed here just as the saving narrative of Israel begins. Scholarly
treatment of the Joseph narrative has tended to split the external
function of the narrative (so Noth) from a study of its internal character (so von Rad). I suggest that attention to the issue of helplessness
(expressed as lament) and to response of assurance (expressed as
salvation oracle) releases us from the impasse; that is, appeal to a
primary formulary pattern of Israel's faith lets us see the character
and function of the narrative in a new way. The resolution of the
relation of the brothers given in the narrative may use sapiential
motifs, but its main appeal is to forms found in the psalms that place
it at the center of Israel's faith. Life begins again for the guilty and
hopeless when a word is spoken by the one who can forgive the guilt
and make provision for the future. The family of Joseph is indeed a
bearer of this understanding of historical vocation, always troubled,
regularly addressed in exile-ending ways.

11

1 Samuel 1—A Sense
of a Beginning

THE FRAMERS OF THE canonical books of 1 and 2 Samuel
have a lively, daring "sense of a beginning."[1] Their subject is the
new narrative of Israel's new social possibility of monarchy. They
wish to assert that the monarchy did not appear in Israel either because of the initiative of dazzling personalities or because of large
concentrations of socioeconomic, military power, but because of the
inscrutable, inexplicable initiative of Yahweh. This particular insistence, which shapes the account of 1 and 2 Samuel, requires a
narrative beginning that bespeaks fragility, surprise, and fidelity, and
that does not too quickly permit the account to be routinized as a
standard political narrative. In a delicate and playful way, 1 Samuel 1
functions to articulate this beginning that is freighted with wonder, which in turn relativizes all conventional political claims. In
this chapter, I shall consider in turn the internal dynamic of chapter 1 and the canonical futures of 1 and 2 Samuel that this narrative
generates.

I

First Samuel 1 is framed as a problem in vv. 1-2 and a resolution in
v. 28b, with four scenes that trace the movement from problem to

---

1. With this phrase, I intend to parallel the phrasing of Frank Kermode, *The Sense
of an Ending: Studies of the Theory of Fiction* (New York: Oxford University Press, 1967).

resolution. The ostensible subject of the narrative is a birth granted to a barren woman, so we have as structure for the narrative a type scene reflective of a birth narrative.[2] In itself, the narrative stays completely contained in the crisis of Hannah's barrenness, and it shows no explicit awareness of the larger public issues of political power that are to follow in the books of Samuel. The framers thus have found a subtle and shrewd way to initiate us into subsequent public questions by this intimate tale of fragility, surprise, and fidelity.

The problem of the narrative is stated directly and carefully in vv. 1-2. We are led quickly and intentionally from Elkanah with his social pedigree and location to his two wives and to the contrast of "children/no children." The problem is simply stated by the narrator, without value judgment. *The solution of the narrative* is tersely given in v. 28b: "They worshiped the Lord there." This odd conclusion ill fits the problem: Barrenness ends in worship. Yahweh, who is no part of the stated problem of vv. 1-2, is clearly decisive for the solution. The narrator has transformed the barrenness of Hannah into a Yahwistic issue that depends solely upon Yahweh for a resolution.

The movement from problem to solution, from barrenness to worship, is narrated in four scenes:

The first scene (vv. 3-8) is an assertion of barrenness. The central actors are Elkanah and Hannah. (Peninnah, Elkanah's other wife, is silent in the scene but powerfully present in the background.) Elkanah is a pious man. He "goes up" yearly to Shiloh (v. 3). In this scene, we have the first journey to Shiloh in this narrative; although Hannah is subsequently in Shiloh, we are told only that Elkanah "went up." Hannah is taken for granted in the journey, but she is not noticed or mentioned. Almost as an aside, the centrality of Shiloh and the priestly family of Eli are introduced, foreshadowing the narratives still to come.[3] In this scene, Shiloh serves only as the context for Elkanah's "inequity" whereby Hannah receives only one portion while Peninnah receives more portions for her children.[4]

---

2. On the type-scenes in general, see Robert Alter, *Biblical Narrative* (see chap. 10, n. 5), 17–26; on our particular text, see 81–87. On the pattern of birth and annunciation narratives, see Robert Neff, "The Birth and Election of Isaac in the Priestly Tradition," *BR* 15 (1970): 5–18, and "The Annunciation in the Birth Narrative of Ishmael," *BR* 17 (1972): 51–60.

3. On the significance of Eli and Shiloh in this extended narrative, see John T. Willis, "Samuel versus Eli: 1 Samuel 1–7," *TZ* 35 (1979): 201, 212; and Martin Cohen, "The Role of the Shilonite Priesthood in the United Monarchy of Ancient Israel," *HUCA* 36 (1965): 59–88.

4. P. Kyle McCarter, Jr., in *1 Samuel*, AB, no. 8 (New York: Doubleday & Co., 1990),

Three dramatic elements in the scene make the problem of barrenness more poignant for the narrative:

First, we are told twice that "the Lord had closed her womb" (vv. 5, 6). This statement is an advance upon v. 2 where no such affirmation about cause is made. By this verdict, the story is decisively made into a Yahwistic account, but even here, the narrative is laconic.

Second, although it is Yahweh who has created Hannah's problem, Hannah's response is not against Yahweh but against Peninnah (vv. 6-7). It is because of Peninnah that Hannah is provoked and irritated. It is because of Peninnah that Hannah weeps and does not eat (v. 7). The narrator's reference to Yahweh does not in fact nullify the social dynamics of family rivalry so crucial to the scene.

Third, the scene ends with Elkanah's fourfold question, three times *lameh*, "why," plus a concluding question about his own value to Hannah (v. 8). Elkanah's questions are voiced in pathos. He does not understand Hannah's response; moreover, he is helpless to change Hannah's situation. Elkanah is helpless about the problem of barrenness caused by Yahweh, and he is helpless in the destructive interaction between his wives. Hannah is deeply needy and immobilized, and her husband is helpless. The family system seems desperately closed. The only opening is that every year Elkanah goes up to sacrifice to Yahweh, the very one who has closed Hannah's womb.

The second scene (vv. 9-18) is an enactment of lament and priestly response. Hannah is in Shiloh and she "arose" (v. 9). In the first scene, we were not told that Hannah went to Shiloh. In this scene we are not told that Elkanah is still in Shiloh. Elkanah is absent in this longer scene. The problem of barrenness is still the subject of the narrative. Only now the problem is not placed in the tension of family dynamics. Now it is a pastoral problem, enacted in the presence of a priest.

Hannah prays (vv. 10-11). Her prayer is a wholly different response from the one she makes in scene 1 (v. 7). Hannah is distressed, as she was in scene 1, but now her distress can receive speech. Her

---

51–52, discusses the textual and interpretive problems concerning the portion allotted to Hannah. He concludes that the narrative must report on a disproportionately generous share to Hannah, and so he reads that Hannah's portion was a "single portion equal to theirs." This suggestive reading has no bearing on the structural analysis offered here.

speech is addressed to Yahweh in the form of a vow.[5] Hannah prays in her affliction (*'onî*), asking Yahweh to remember and not forget (v. 11). If remembered by Yahweh, she will yield the gift of a son back to Yahweh.

Eli's response shows his instability. Eli misperceives and misunderstands Hannah (v. 14). Eli's weakness is important for his demise in subsequent chapters. Here the narrative quickly ignores Eli's weakness and moves on to the point to be made.

Hannah voices her great trouble to Eli. Hannah is not drunk but praying. She is not base but needful. She is beset by profound anxiety and vexation. While Hannah is forthcoming about her emotional state, she does not tell Eli (as she has told Yahweh) what her need is or what her hope is. She only wants to be positively received and reassured by the priest.

Eli's response, lacking specificity from Hannah, is a characteristic priestly response to such a petition of need (vv. 17-18a). Eli blesses Hannah with "peace."[6] Eli has given Hannah the needed blessing.[7] Hannah's life is immediately transformed by the utterance of a Yahwistic assurance. The woman who wept and could not eat (v. 7) now eats and is not sad (v. 18b).[8]

These first two scenes together present the governing problem of barrenness that dominates the story. Thus, they need to be seen as a deliberate pair of scenes. In the two scenes, however, two very different narrative strategies are employed: In the first, we are offered a standard birth-narrative type scene. We expect it to be resolved by an announcement of birth. In the second scene, however, a quite different strategy is introduced. This scene contains almost no element of the conventions of the move from barrenness to birth. Now the dominant elements are complaint to Yahweh (vv. 10-11), petition to the priest (vv. 15-16), and response from the priest (vv. 17-18a).

---

5. On the role and cruciality of the vow in this scene, see Wolfgang Richter, "Das Gelübde als theologische Rahmung der Jakobsüberlieferung," *BZ* 11 (1967): 23–26.

6. On 1 Samuel 1 in relation to the classic pattern of complaint and thanksgiving, see Patrick D. Miller, *Interpreting* (see chap. 3, n. 6), 56–57; and "In Praise and Thanksgiving," *TToday* 45 (1988): 180–82.

7. The words used by Eli in his priestly response are worth noting. In addition to the word *Shalom*, Eli also uses the term *šā'al* ("grant, petition"). The term is often interpreted with reference to Saul, and that may be correct. In the context of the narrative, however, it is enough that Hannah is the one who "asks," that is, who addresses need to Yahweh and receives a gift from Yahweh. In v. 27, in her last speech, Hannah returns to the same word usage.

8. On the significance of Hannah's eating, see Jacob Weingreen, "A Rabbinic-Type Gloss in the LXX Version of 1 Samuel i 18," *VT* 14 (1964): 225–28.

Not only is this strategy lodged in the sanctuary, but the speech elements are standard liturgic exchanges. The issues now turn not on barrenness and birth but upon submission to Yahweh and trust in Yahweh. Thus, while the two scenes share a common problem, they approach the problem very differently. Scene 1 treats the problem of barrenness as a matter of family struggle. In scene 2 the same problem has been redefined in Yahwistic categories of need, submission, and trust.

The third scene (vv. 19-20) is an announcement of birth. The scene is quick and decisive. Elkanah and Hannah "rose early," worshiped, and went home. It is as though the encounter with Eli in scene 2 has loosened the hopelessness around this family. Elkanah, absent in scene 2, is now necessarily and decisively present. Elkanah knows Hannah (v. 19). We expect the next line to be, "and she conceived." The narrative disrupts that expected sequence, however, to intervene with, "The Lord remembered her." This is what Hannah has prayed in v. 11. Her prayer has been answered. Yahweh has not forgotten.

The report does not move directly from "know" to "conceive" because the narrator is pursuing a more subtle, complex strategy. The typical scene of "birth to barrenness" would resolve scene 1 with scene 3. In this telling, however, scene 2 has changed the intent of the narrative. It is the matters of complaint, petition, and assurance that are decisive. The tale is now utterly Yahwistic.[9] The prayer of Hannah to Yahweh and the response of Eli that gives a Yahwistic assurance are not incidental or marginal to the tale. They are crucial and determinative for the narrative. Yahweh is the key actor in the narrative. Hannah could speak complaint and petition only because she submitted to Yahweh. Eli could give assurance to her only because he spoke on behalf of Yahweh. The son is born only because Yahweh remembered. Everything depends on asking Yahweh and being answered by Yahweh. Thus, scene 3 resolves scene 1, but only by way of the decisive intrusion of Yahweh through scene 2.

The fourth scene (vv. 21-28a) is an enactment of thanksgiving, balancing the *enactment of lament* in scene 2. The beginning of the scene in v. 21 is conventional, as we would expect. Elkanah "went up."

---

9. On "Yahweh remembered" as the decisive turn in many texts and as the literary and theological focus, see Brevard S. Childs, *Memory and Tradition in Israel*, SBT, no. 37 (Naperville, Ill.: Alec R. Allenson, 1962), 31–44. For this same pivotal use of "Yahweh remembered" in the flood narrative, see Bernhard W. Anderson, "From Analysis to Synthesis" (see chap. 0, n. 33).

The line reiterates v. 3. Hannah, however, does not "go up" until
v. 24. The subscene of vv. 21-23 is a strategic narrative delay because Hannah and the boy are not yet ready to travel. That will come
later, when the boy is weaned. In this subscene, two things strike us:
First, Hannah is already aware that the boy is to remain "forever" in
Shiloh. She has only gotten the boy in v. 20, and in v. 22 she is prepared to yield him.[10] Hannah's life consists in receiving and yielding.
Second, Elkanah speaks only for the second time in the entire narrative (v. 23). His first speech was one of helpless bewilderment (v. 8).
Now he speaks a genuinely supportive word that Hannah should do
what is right in her own eyes. He utters a Yahwistic formula: "May
the word of Yahweh be established." Elkanah is fully participatory in
Hannah's new life. His bewilderment in v. 8 has been transformed
in v. 23 into affirmation.

It is Hannah, however, who claims our attention in this scene
as elsewhere. Indeed, the scene really begins only in v. 24 when
Hannah "takes up" the weaned boy with her.[11] Like her husband,
Hannah is pious and careful about appropriate rites of sacrifice
(vv. 24-25). What counts in this scene, however, is Hannah's speech
(vv. 26-28a). Hannah addresses Eli, who does not need to answer
her. Hannah needs no answer here, even as she desperately needed
an answer in scene 2. Hannah identifies herself as the one who had
been so needy and who prayed. She is the one to whom Yahweh has
given her request. She is the one who will keep her vow and give up
the child granted to her.

---

10. The immediate sequence of birth and relinquishment in vv. 20 and 22 is structurally not unlike the birth and near-relinquishment of Isaac in Gen. 21:1-7 and
22:1-14. The circumstance and motivations in the Isaac narrative are very different,
but the requirement of faith is the same in both narratives, whereby God reclaims the
gift of the son almost as soon as it is given.

11. In my analysis of scenes, the exact placement of vv. 21-23 constitutes something of a problem. I have regarded v. 21 as the beginning of scene 4 because of the
conventional beginning, "Elkanah . . . went up." Elkanah, however, does not in fact go
up in v. 21, for Hannah's conversation with him in vv. 22-23 takes place while still at
Ramah. Thus it is plausible to begin scene 4 in v. 24 when Hannah departs for Shiloh.
This division of scenes would have the gain of keeping Elkanah confined to scene 3
and make him absent in scene 4. In what follows, it will be evident that this would
provide a more symmetrical analysis. The issue of where to begin scene 4 is not in any
case crucial for my analysis. I note this only to call attention to my uncertainty about
the placement of vv. 21-23 and to suggest that more than one division is possible.
Elkanah's final speech (v. 23) serves to bind this narrative to its larger context. The
phrase "Do what is right in your own eyes" is reminiscent of the formula in the final
narratives of the book of Judges. The wish "May the Lord establish his word" anticipates the decisive verdict on Samuel and Yahweh's word in 1 Sam. 3:19-21. Thus the
statement of Elkanah looks both backward and forward in its phrasing.

Scenes 3 and 4 are a pair, not unlike the pairing of 1 and 2. They are the two scenes of resolution. Like scenes 1 and 2, however, scenes 3 and 4 are cast very differently. The assertion of birth in scene 3 corresponds to the assertion of barrenness in scene 1. These two scenes are faithful to the genre of "barrenness to birth." The enactment of thanksgiving in scene 4 matches the enactment of complaint and petition in scene 2. These two scenes are concerned not with the birth but with Hannah coming to terms with the reality of Yahweh. She is portrayed as the one who is needy, trustful, submissive, and grateful. She is a model of fidelity. In this second narrative strategy, the dominant place is given not to the crisis of barrenness but to the possibility of faith in Yahweh.

The conclusion of the four scenes is in v. 28b: "And they worshiped the Lord there." The subject of the narrative has been radically changed from the problem of vv. 1-2. Because the problem is barrenness, we expect a conclusion concerning birth. Scenes 1 and 3 stay close to the presenting problem and its resolution. The conclusion of worship, however, is concerned with Hannah's relation to Yahweh and more closely derives from scenes 2 and 4, concerning lament and thanksgiving. Thus the problem (vv. 1-2) and scenes 1 and 3 utilize the conventional strategy of birth narrative. Scenes 2 and 4 and the conclusion (v. 28b), however, reflect a counterstrategy that concerns Yahwism and coming to terms with that reality. The concrete problem of barrenness is thus radically reshaped by the second strategy. It is important that the boy is born, for without the birth there will be no continuing narrative. Clearly the narrative wants us to see more than that, however. The future of the story now to be told in 1 and 2 Samuel concerns not only the newly born son but the rule of Yahweh, to whom laments are addressed and thanksgiving uttered. No wonder the narrative ends with yielding, grateful, trusting worship. The presenting issue has been preempted by a second, more foundational affirmation.

II

This subtle narrative thus employs two quite distinct strategies, both of which are essential to beginning the books of Samuel. The "barrenness to birth" theme is essential to the concreteness of the human story. The "complaint-thanksgiving" construct is necessary to focus the narrative on its Yahwistic intent. The twofold strategy yields two configurations of the narration of problem and resolution.

Considered in one configuration, scenes 1 and 2 belong together as two statements of the problem, and scenes 3 and 4 are two statements of the resolution. Considered in a different configuration, scenes 1 and 3 are paired as are scenes 2 and 4. In this configuration, scenes 1 and 3 concern the direct issue of barrenness and birth, and scene 3 resolves the matter of scene 1. In these two scenes, Elkanah is Hannah's counterpart in the drama. He is a pious man, but he is primarily a concerned husband. In scene 1, Elkanah asks his questions; in scene 3, he impregnates his wife, but he does not speak.

Whereas scenes 1 and 3 feature Elkanah, in scenes 2 and 4, the second set, Hannah's counterpart is Eli, the presence and voice of Yahweh. Because Eli instead of Elkanah is present, priest instead of husband, we are not surprised that these scenes are filled with conventional and extended religious talk.[12] In scene 2, the speech is complaint and priestly response; in scene 4 the primary speech is one of thanksgiving and yielding.[13] Even though the religious speech of scenes 2 and 4 is not surprising in the context of priest and sanctuary, the same speech would be strikingly inappropriate in scenes 1 and 3, which are not primarily concerned with religious categories and in which there is no priest or sanctuary.

Thus, I suggest that the four scenes are arranged in a tightly disciplined quadrilateral with several patternings operating at the same time (see figure 1).

Four other observations may be derived from this analysis:

1. The scenes are clearly delineated by two markers. In each scene Hannah has only one serious partner, but scene 4 has a subscene. Hannah is present and decisive in each scene; her partner is alternatively Elkanah (vv. 3-8), Eli (vv. 8-18), Elkanah (vv. 19-20, 21-23), and Eli (vv. 24-28a). Except for the complication in scene 4, the counterpartner is absent from each of the scenes; that is, Eli does not intrude into Elkanah's scenes, nor Elkanah into Eli's scenes.

---

12. Elkanah is not present in scene 4, except in the preliminary exchange in vv. 21-23. See n. 11 on this matter.

13. Hannah's complaint in scene 2 and thanksgiving in scene 4 are complementary. Claus Westermann, in *The Psalms: Structure, Content, and Message* (Minneapolis: Augsburg Pub. House, 1980), 73–83, has seen that the song of thanksgiving characteristically reiterates the previously voiced complaint and then tells how the situation of complaint was resolved. "The main part is then the *narrative account of God's deed*, almost always divided into a review of the crisis and an account of the rescue" (p. 76).

the problem of *barrenness*

	Scene 1 Hannah's vexation	Scene 2 Hannah's petition and vow	
Elkanah as concerned husband			*Eli* as priestly presence
	Scene 3 resolution as birth	Scene 4 yielding in thanksgiving	

the *resolution* as birth

Figure 1

Moreover, each scene is marked by a verb at its outset, indicating movement and change of location:

- This man used to go up (*'ālâ*) (v. 3).

- Hannah rose (*qûm*) (v. 9).

- They rose early (*šākam*) (v. 19).

- She took him up (*'ālâ*) (v. 24).[14]

This verbal pattern indicates the discipline and intentionality of the narrative construction.

2. Each scene centers around a crucial Yahwistic statement. This is what one would expect in scenes 2 and 4 as the religious counterpoint to scenes 1 and 3, but the Yahwistic accent is also sounded in scenes 1 and 3 where the priest is absent:

- The Lord had closed her womb (vv. 5, 6).

- The God of Israel grant your petition (v. 17).[15]

- The Lord remembered her (v. 19).

- The Lord has granted me my petition (v. 7).

---

14. Here I have listed the verb from v. 24. As indicated in n. 11, the same verb is used in v. 21 with Elkanah as subject.

15. Eli speaks of "the God of Israel." He does not name the name of Yahweh. That name, however, is on Hannah's lips in this scene three times (vv. 11 [twice], 15), and the narrator twice reports that she prays "to the Lord" (vv. 10, 12).

In the end, each scene is dominated by the action of Yahweh. That
action of Yahweh is variously voiced. In scene 2, it is spoken by
Eli; in scene 4, it is Hannah, responding to Eli, who mentions Yahweh. In scenes 1 and 3, which feature only Elkanah and which do
not focus on religious issues but on domestic reality, the Yahwistic
point is scored by the narrator who insists that the point should be
everywhere heard.

3. The decisiveness of Yahweh is matched by the fact that Elkanah and Eli, at least in their speaking parts, are marginal and weak
characters. They are no threat to the centrality of Yahweh in the narrative. Elkanah's speaking part (excluding the incidental wording of
v. 23) is limited to his befogged question in v. 8, in scene 1. Although
Elkanah acts in scene 3, he does not speak. Thus, his speaking is
modest in scene 1. As the narrative advances, he has no voice in
scene 3.

The same pattern is true of Eli. In scene 2, he speaks. Like Elkanah in scene 1, he is not sure of what he is saying and has no clue
about the situation of Hannah to which he is responding. In scene 4
Eli utters not a word. Thus, in both cases, the speech of Hannah's
male partner is diminished and nullified; they speak in each case
only once and without awareness of the real situation. Elkanah does
not understand Hannah's vexation; Eli does not know the source of
Hannah's distress. The two men mean well, but they do not understand. In each case, the speech of the man disappears in his second
scene. One reason the speech disappears is that in scenes 3 and 4,
their well-intended befuddlement and ineptness are overwhelmed
and superseded by the decisiveness of Yahweh. Hannah needs no
human voices to assure her when Yahweh acts decisively.

4. The other reason the speech of Elkanah and Eli disappears is
that this is a narrative that traces the process by which Hannah gains
her voice and her own decisive role in the history of Israel. Through
these scenes, Hannah moves from silence to speech. In scene 1, she
speaks not at all. She is irritated, vexed, weeping, and unable to eat.
She has no power to be present in the story. In scene 2, Hannah
begins to speak. She speaks out of affliction. Her first speech is addressed to God out of her deep need (vv. 10-11). This is followed by
a second articulation of need, this to Eli (vv. 15-16). There is still no
move beyond pitiful need. In the third scene, Hannah is the only
one who speaks. Now she speaks freely, boldly, exultantly, as the
one who has been heard and remembered. Yahweh's remembrance
of her gives her speech, presence, and power. In scene 4, Hannah

speaks a long, buoyant affirmation to Eli. Now she is fully voiced, fully present in Israel's history, full of faith. The process through which Hannah gains her voice is accomplished through the recurrent, decisive work of Yahweh who nowhere speaks but everywhere acts. Because of Yahweh, Hannah is given both life and voice.

The narrative prepares Hannah and us for her full speech in 2:1-10, in which she subversively and dangerously rereads Israel's history in terms of Yahweh's awesome inversions and in which she powerfully voices Israel's long-term royal hope. In the narrative life of Israel, Hannah never speaks again after her song of 2:1-10. She does not need to. She has said it all. She has said enough to push Israel's public life in a new direction. She has made life in Israel possible. The transformation of Hannah from silent affliction to buoyant speech anticipates and prefigures the transformation of Israel from futile marginality to buoyant possibility. It would have been impossible in our first scene for Hannah to have spoken with the boldness of her final song. She would have been "out of character" to assert herself in scene 1, for she has no character in the first scene. A painful process of hurt voiced and gift received permit her to enter Israel's historical arena with authority and speech. Hannah is the voice of the gospel making history possible among the marginal who, through her, receive their voice.[16] The narrative subsequently adds the note that Yahweh visited Hannah and she bore more children (2:21). Hannah's life continues to be an arena for Yahweh's gift of new life in Israel.

III

The narrative of Hannah's barrenness is not simply an idyllic tale. Nor is it an incidental or romantic addendum at the front of the books of Samuel. It is, rather, an expression of "a sense of a beginning." The narrators wanted to tell the story of Israel's rise to power (David's monarchy) in a peculiar way. They must have pondered long how to stage this narrative so that the subversive themes of fragility, surprise, and fidelity would not be lost either in the celebration of personality or in the worldly, impressive forms of power.

---

16. On history-making among the marginal, see Walter Brueggemann, *Hope Within History* (Atlanta: John Knox Press, 1987), 49–71. On the voice of women making history in Israel, see Gail R. O'Day, "Singing Woman's Song: A Hermeneutic of Liberation," *CurTM* 12 (1985): 203–10.

The strategy of the narrators, a complex and imaginative strategy, is to begin the longer Davidic narrative with this tale of "barrenness to birth," this speech of *complaint and assurance*, this voice-acquiring tale that culminates in the yielding of grateful worship.

In its present placement, the account of Samuel's birth functions to introduce the larger canonical literature of Samuel. Brevard S. Childs has taught us, when asking about canonical shape and canonical intentionality, to pay careful attention to beginning and endings. In the case of the books of Samuel, Childs has concluded that the Song of Hannah constitutes "an interpretive key" for all that follows.[17] It is Hannah's song about powerful inversions caused by Yahweh that becomes the perspective from which the rise of David is understood and narrated, for David is indeed one of the "needy" who "sits with princes" (2:8). Moreover, Childs suggests that the poem in 22:1-51 forms a counterpart to 1 Sam. 2:1-10 so that the story of Israel's monarchy is bracketed and bounded by lyrical statements that voice Yahweh's decisive role in the life of Israel.[18] In these poems at the beginning and at the end, the pious assert that the real power in Israel's life and history belongs only to Yahweh, not to the king or any other human agent.

In these arguments, I believe Childs is correct. Without qualifying his major gain in any way, I wish to set alongside Childs's word some suggestions from my study of 1 Samuel 1. Attention to 1 Samuel 1 may support and enhance Childs's suggestion for two reasons: First, the Song of Hannah is not at the beginning of the literature; we are therefore pressed to ask if Childs's insight about chapter 2 can be restated to take account of chapter 1. Second, I have attempted to show that chapter 1 is crucial to chapter 2.[19] It would not do to begin the literature of 1 Samuel with the buoyant, exultant, almost

---

17. See Childs, *Introduction* (see chap. 1, n. 6), esp. 273. Robert P. Gordon, in *1 and 2 Samuel*, Old Testament Guides (Sheffield: JSOT Press, 1984), refers to the Song of Hannah as "the appropriate clef sign for the story of Samuel" (p. 26).

18. Childs, *Introduction*, 272–73, 278.

19. The canonical function of 1 Samuel 1–2 as an introduction to the larger narrative is parallel to the canonical function of Luke 1–2 as an introduction to the narrative of Luke-Acts. Hans Conzelmann, in *The Theology of Saint Luke* (New York: Harper Brothers, 1960), had developed his schematic interpretation of Luke-Acts only by disregarding the role of Luke 1–2. Paul S. Minear, in "Luke's Use of the Birth Stories," in *Studies in Luke Acts*, ed. Leonard E. Kech and J. Louis Martyn (New York: Abingdon Press, 1966), 111–30, has shown that Luke 1–2 cannot be ignored, and that when they are taken seriously, Conzelmann's scheme cannot be sustained. For a detailed analysis of those two chapters, see Raymond E. Brown, *The Birth of the Messiah* (New York: Doubleday & Co./Image Books, 1977), esp. 239–55.

strident voice of the song. The situation of Israel requires a narrative
beginning in affliction and need (2:5). Thus, I submit that the narrative of chapter 1 is crucial for understanding dramatically how it
is that Hannah can have such a dangerous voice, a voice even more
dangerous when we hear it as the voice of one recently vexed, provoked, weeping, and not eating. The interpretive point is not only
Hannah's great faith expressed in the song but the story of inversion, whereby she can leave off her distressed silence and become a
powerful evoker of faithful newness.

Moreover, as Childs has matched the poem of 2:1-10 to the
poems of 22:1-51 and 23:1-5, I suggest a close and intentional correspondence between the first narrative of 1 Samuel 1 and the final
narrative of 2 Samuel 24. In that latter narrative, we watch a transformation of David that corresponds, albeit in reverse order, to the
transformation of Hannah in chapter 1. We have seen Hannah's
transformation from a voiceless woman of distress to a powerful
voice of history-making. She is indeed a low one now exalted (2:7).

In 2 Samuel 24, however, David develops in the opposite direction.[20] The narrative begins with the enigmatic "inciting" of David
by Yahweh (v. 1). The inciting by Yahweh is effective. David is fully,
immediately, and uncritically committed to the census; he will not be
talked out of it by Joab (see vv. 3-4). Then follows a quick account of
royal officers who invade every village (vv. 5-7). We may believe those
royal officers terrorized the little people, those not unlike Elkanah.
David is portrayed as ruthless and full of himself and his royal office.
In the long tale of the book of Samuel, we witness David becoming
"stronger and stronger" (2 Sam. 3:1) and more full of himself. David
is indeed the one "made rich" (2:7).

As the narrative of 2 Samuel 24 unfolds, however, "David's heart
smote him" (v. 10). David confesses his sin in taking the census and
admits that he has done foolishly. We do not know how David came
to this new awareness. There is no agent from God to tell David,
as with Nathan in chapter 12. We are not told how David is reached
anymore than we are told how Hannah came to have child and voice.
We only listen while the change in David happens. David casts him-

---

20. See chap. 12; J. William Whedbee, in "On Divine and Human Bonds: The
Tragedy of the House of David," in *Canon, Theology, and Old Testament Interpretation*,
ed. Gene M. Tucker, David L. Petersen, and Robert R. Wilson (Philadelphia: Fortress
Press, 1988), 162–64, interprets the appendix in a way quite counter to my reading.
He suggests the texts serve to legitimate David rather than to delegitimate, as I have
argued. I suggest my reading serves better the canonical shape of the literature.

self on the mercy of Yahweh (v. 14). As David prays about his sin a second time, he is transformed (v. 17). Now he does not ask to be relieved of punishment but only that his "sheep" should not receive the punishment he rightly deserves for himself. This is a remarkable prayer from one so recently enacting extreme royal power. This narrative exhibits a marked change in David from the one who so recently would not listen to Joab (v. 4).

In the end, David is left with little royal power and no royal arrogance. This narrative surely has "a sense of an ending."[21] The very last verse of 2 Samuel says simply: "So the Lord heeded supplications for the land, and the plague was averted from Israel" (2 Sam. 24:25). In the end, David has no royal arrogance left. He has only prayer and recourse to Yahweh's mercy. He has left to him as a resource only what Hannah had found available in her distress. David is a much weakened ruler who is now dependent and willing to trust Yahweh and petition Yahweh.

The account of Hannah at the beginning and that of David at the end go together.[22] Hannah's story is one of a voiceless, marginal woman being given a voice to cause history. David's story concerns a powerful, ruthless monarch led to the point of yielding, not able to assert but only to trust, wait, and receive. This David, not seen everywhere, but certainly seen here, is like Hannah. David has life only as a gift from Yahweh, which he gratefully acknowledges.[23] I

---

21. There is clearly an unresolved issue between the canonical shape of the books of Samuel and the critical consensus about the succession narrative, which culminates in 1 Kings 1–2. Here we are considering the canonical shape with chapter 24 as the close of the canonical book. The common critical judgment continues the literature into 1 Kings 1–2. We have not yet reached a way of understanding the relation between critical and canonical perspectives, though Childs has addressed the issue.

22. One specific item in this connection is worth noting. In 1 Sam. 1:5-6, it is twice stated, "The Lord had closed her womb" (*rḥm*). In 2 Sam. 24:14, David says, "His mercy (*rḥm*) is great." The use of the same root, *rḥm*, in these two contexts is remarkable, especially when it is recognized that the word is used nowhere else in the Samuel literature. Phyllis Trible, in *God and Rhetoric* (see chap. 4, n. 16), 38–53, has made a compelling case that the root *rḥm*, variously used as "womb" and as "compassion," has a stable meaning that is present in both uses. That stable meaning is something like "womblike mother love." It is likely more than good fortune that the term is used in our two texts and nowhere in between. In 1 Samuel 1, it is an act of Yahweh's graciousness that God should open the womb of Hannah. In 2 Samuel 24, it is confidence in God's "mother-love" that causes David to submit. The use of the word in these ways further substantiates the linkage between Hannah and David, both of whom depend upon and receive the compassion of Yahweh.

23. On Yahweh's gift to David, see David M. Gunn, "David and the Gift of the Kingdom (2 Sam. 2–4, 9–20, 1 Kgs. 1–2)," *Semeia* 3 (1975): 14–45. Gunn shows that for David, his future from God is always given as gift and never grasped.

suggest that the narrators have knowingly positioned this beginning narrative and this ending narrative as the frame for the long account of the emergent monarchy in Israel. That account is peopled with blood, intrigue, fear, and death. As the narrative stands, however, the framers will not give in to that vision of Israel's life. They do not agree that blood, intrigue, fear, and death are how this history is to be discerned. The narrators will insist, at the beginning and at the end, that Israel's historical process is bounded by Yahweh, who gives voice to a silent woman, who empties a full king, who hears and who answers.

Thus 1 Sam. 2:1-10 and its counterparts in 2 Sam. 22:2-51 and 23:1-5 are clues for reading the narrative that occurs between these poems. Those songs, however, need the narratives behind and before them (that is, 1 Samuel 1 and 2 Samuel 24) to assert how one rises to such a song and how one falls from great arrogance.[24] This completed shaping of the story of monarchy is a tale of the fall and rise of many in Israel (cf. Luke 2:34); the beginning and end of the narrative concern the exposition of that rise and fall.[25]

Finally, we are in a position to see how this narrative framing permits us to reread the books of Samuel. Clearly the stories of Samuel are preoccupied with David. David is awaited in 1 Sam. 2:1-10, hinted at in 13:14, and anticipated in 15:38. The wonder of Israel, according to this literature, is the rise of David. If we work backward from David to the origins of this new royal reality, we shall linger briefly over Saul, who finally authorizes David (1 Sam. 24:20; 26:25). Saul provides the royal authorization David clearly needed to show that David is legitimate successor and not a usurper. Behind Saul, of course, is the authorizing power of Samuel, who first identifies David (1 Sam. 16:12-13) and who, even in death, attests David as Yahweh's chosen one (1 Sam. 28:17). The sequence backward from David to Saul to Samuel is clear and known.

In reflecting on this sequence, we are still required to ask: From whence comes Samuel? How did this king-maker and king-breaker appear? Where did Samuel come from and how did it happen that his word is so decisive in Israel (1 Sam. 13:19-21)? The answer is that

---

24. The language of "rise and fall" may be peculiarly appropriate to Hannah and David in this narrative. Hannah is the one who rises from silence to speech, from barrenness to birth. David is a more complex and compelling character. We listen while he rises, and in 2 Samuel 21–24, we watch something of his fall.

25. On the poem in Luke from which comes the phrase, see Brown, *Birth of Messiah*, 460–62.

behind Samuel stands Hannah, frail, distressed, weeping, not eating. It is Hannah who finally dares to pray and to vow, to receive, to
yield, to worship. Israel's monarchy, we are told, begins in this voiceless voice of hopeless hope. Hannah embodies the voicelessness and
hopelessness of Israel's historical beginning. And behind Hannah?
There is only Yahweh, who closes wombs, who remembers, who answers prayers, who gives sons. There is only Yahweh, and Yahweh
has initiated the sequence of Hannah, Samuel, Saul, and David *ex
nihilo*, out of nothing but hurt brought to voice, hope dared, uttered
fidelity, petitions risked, and vows kept. The framers of the canonical
literature have a sense of a beginning. They sense how the literature
had to begin in barrenness and voicelessness. They sense at the same
time how the history of kingship had to begin. In order not to be
misunderstood or misappropriated, Israel's monarchy had to begin
in weakness, barrenness, prayer, and miracle. The literature had to
begin the same way the new history of Judah began.

As we pursue the sustained narrative of 1 and 2 Samuel, we watch
how the literature moves and how Israel's history is shaped. There
intrudes into the faithful history of Israel greed and power and fear
and death, many swords, much vengeance, and great cunning.[26]
In this canonical framing, however, all such intrusions are odd and
under criticism, because such intrusions do not easily find congenial this narrative boundary of fragility, surprise, and fidelity. The
framers of the narrative perhaps did not at the outset see the whole
story that was to come. They had, however, an awed sense of a
beginning. We call this barren woman "mother Hannah." She is indeed the mother of the entire narrative. Hannah did not begin as a
mother, however. She began in a muted voice of despair. In the hidden presence of Yahweh, Hannah fought for and gained her voice.
She sang Israel to power, and she sang David to the throne. Even
now, the singing of Hannah keeps birthing the new history of Israel,
battling against silent despair and against autonomous arrogance
that forgets how to voice and to yield.

---

26. Paul M. van Buren, in part 2 of *Discerning the Way* (see chap. 2, n. 4), 184–94,
has compellingly argued that such terrible ambiguities in the life of Israel are not incidental but belong necessarily and intrinsically to a faith that thrusts a people into the
ambiguous reality of land and therefore political strife. Thus, following van Buren,
we may conclude that the intrusion of greed, power, fear, death, many swords, much
vengeance, and great cunning in the story of the monarchy "goes with the territory."
While that is so, the canonical framers, by placing 1 Samuel 1 and 2 Samuel 24 where
they did, hope for a less ambiguous practice of faith in history.

12

2 Samuel 21–24—An Appendix of Deconstruction?

SINCE THE WORK OF Leonhard Rost in 1926,[1] the David materials in 1 and 2 Samuel have been understood in terms of two extended narratives: "the rise of David" and "the succession narrative." While scholarship continues to criticize this hypothesis, a scholarly consensus still holds roughly to Rost's proposal. Outside these two stories are the miscellaneous materials of 2 Samuel 5–8, which fall between the two great narratives, and 2 Samuel 21–24, commonly regarded as a miscellaneous appendix inserted before the conclusion of the succession narrative in 1 Kings 1–2.

Karl Budde had first seen that the appendix is not simply miscellaneous but a deliberate chiastic arrangement of two narratives, two lists, and two poems.[2] For the most part, scholarship has been content to reiterate this insight about the pattern, but it has not probed beyond that observation.

---

1. Rost, *The Succession to the Throne of David*, Historic Texts and Interpreters in Biblical Scholarship, no. 1 (Sheffield: Almond Press, 1982); this is a translation of the author's *Die Überlieferung von der Thronnachfolge Davids*, BWANT, no. 42, 3d ser., vol. 6 (Stuttgart: Kohlhammer, 1926).
2. Budde, *Die Bücher Samuel*, Kürzer Hand-Kommentar zum Alten Testament, no. 8 (Tübingen: Mohr [Siebeck], 1902), 304.

I

Two studies may be mentioned that propose a closer theological consideration of the appendix: First, R. A. Carlson, in an extended treatment, has suggested that the materials constitute a Deuteronomic critique of royal ideology.[3] Carlson's discussion is of great importance. In my judgment, however, his analysis is impeded by two factors: (*a*) Carlson is preoccupied with his Deuteronomic hypothesis even though evidence of the Deuteronomic editors in these chapters is scant, if present at all; and (*b*) Carlson is excessively attentive to his hypothesis about cycles of seven and the seven years of punishment. On both counts, Carlson operates with quite hypothetical constructions that do not focus on the text itself.

The second helpful discussion is the brief comment of Brevard S. Childs, in which he proposes, predictably, that these chapters provide a canonical clue to the Samuel corpus.[4] He concludes:

> In sum, the final four chapters, far from being a clumsy appendix, offer a highly reflective, theological interpretation of David's whole career adumbrating the messianic hope, which provides a clear hermeneutical guide for its use as sacred scripture.[5]

Childs's comment is suggestive, and I am in agreement with his inclination. His suggestion, however, lacks specificity about the content of that messianism.

I wish to consider the theological intention of the appendix and hope to make positive use of the work of Carlson and Childs. My particular perspective has been triggered by two factors:

First, James Flanagan, in a remarkable study, has proposed that 2 Samuel 5–8 is not a mere miscellaneous collection but is organized into three pairs of literary elements: two lists, two battle narratives, and two narratives of legitimation concerning ark and oracle.[6] This sequence of six elements is arranged chiastically. Moreover, observes Flanagan, in each of the pairs the second element is designed to supersede the first element so that in the lists, the bureaucracy replaces kinship; in the war narratives, imperial wars replace Philistine

3. Carlson, *David: The Chosen King* (Uppsala: Almqvist & Wiksell, 1964), 194–259.

4. Childs, *Introduction* (see chap. 1, n. 6), 273–75.

5. Ibid., 275.

6. Flanagan, "Social Transformation and Ritual in 2 Samuel 6," in *The Word of the Lord Shall Go Forth*, ed. Carol L. Meyers and M. O'Connor (Winona Lake, Ind.: Eisenbrauns, 1983), 361–72.

struggles; and finally, in the narratives of legitimation, royal ideology replaces the tribal ark. In these three pairs, the narrative is arranged to enact the dramatic and decisive transformation of the power of David as it moved from chiefdom to monarchy. Flanagan comments:

> This scene of David and Michal was staged . . . as a period of release from usual constraints and an occasion for creative response. It was here that the structures of the former state no longer held sway and the new state of Davidic dynasty had not yet been fully established. The dialogue between Michal and David made explicit that the issue was the legitimacy of his house as leaders in Israel.[7]

Second, just as I was considering Flanagan's interpretation of chapters 5–8 as designed to exhibit and assert the transformation of ideology toward a high view of kingship, my colleague David M. Gunn offhandedly suggested that 2 Samuel 21–24 intended to serve as a "deconstruction" of David. I understand by this that the literature seeks to dismantle the high royal theology that has been enacted elsewhere in the narrative and, historically, in the Jerusalem establishment. The analysis of Flanagan and the comment of Gunn led me to wonder whether the six elements of 2 Samuel 21–24 are positioned to counter the six elements of 2 Samuel 5–8. Whereas chapters 5–8 trace and enact a move to a higher royal claim, so chapters 21–24 may seek to combat that higher royal claim. This suggestion has close affinities with Carlson's work and asks about canonical arrangement with Childs, but it intends to stay closer to the text.

II

Thus, I propose to consider the six elements of 2 Samuel 21–24 to see to what extent they function to deconstruct and to combat the well-established royal ideology.

1. The first narrative, 2 Sam. 21:1-4, concerns David's slaughter of the seven sons of Saul. The narrative reads in a sequence of bloodguilt–famine–expiation. That is the plain telling of the narrative. The bloodguilt (revealed directly to David from the Lord) is said to be caused by Saul's slaughter of the Gibeonites (v. 1). That, however, is private information. The rest of the narrative argument

---

7. Ibid., 368.

is public data. There is a famine, and there is expiation by the execution of Saul's heirs. The only hidden part is the alleged bloodguilt,
disclosed quite privately only to David.

The historical problem of this sequence is that we have no evidence of Saul's slaughtering of the Gibeonites.[8] Historical investigation suggests that Josh. 9:3-16 contains evidence of an old treaty
with the Gibeonites, so it makes sense that a broken covenant with
them must be "expiated." But what is missing is the sequence of
bloodguilt–famine–expiation; or, alternatively, what is missing in the
sequence of covenant–violation–response is the dimension of bloodguilt or violation on the part of Saul. The connection between old
covenant and David's action depends for credibility on the "Saul-
element," which is missing. It is odd that this element is missing in
the Samuel narrative, which wants to be as dismissive as possible of
Saul and to legitimate David in every way possible.

Because of this glaring gap in narrative evidence, we are permitted for a moment to read the story backward from the expiation-
execution to famine to bloodguilt. In 16:8, Shimei accuses David
of "the blood of the house of Saul." This may refer to the deaths
of Saul, Jonathan, and Eshbaal, or it may refer to the seven in our
narrative. Either way, it attests that there was in Israel powerful suspicion about David's disposal of Saul's family.[9] If we may entertain
the suspicion with Shimei that David is implicated in some Saulide
murders, then our narrative may intend to call attention to the fact
that the Saul-element of a Gibeonite crisis is missing from Israel's
narrative repertoire. What we have, so far as evidence is concerned,
is a famine blamed on Saul only in a private oracle, bloodguilt attributed to Saul only in a private oracle, and expiation-execution by
David, justified by Saul's alleged action. But the blame, attribution,
and justification all rest on a private communication to David, which
at the most came to him through his hired priestly functionaries. The
suspicion thus permits the possibility that David killed Saul's family
but provided a rationale by blaming Saul, a rationale for which there
is no public evidence.

---

8. See Joseph Blenkinsopp, *Gibeon and Israel*, SOTSMS, no. 2 (Cambridge: Cambridge University Press, 1972), 53–64; F. Charles Fensham, "The Treaty between
Israel and the Gibeonites," *BA* 27 (1964): 96–100; and Abraham Malamat, "Doctrines
of Causality in Hittite and Biblical Historiography: A Parallel," *VT* 5 (1955): 1–12.

9. See Leo G. Perdue, "'Is There Anyone Left of the House of Saul . . . ?' Ambiguity and the Characterization of David in the Succession Narrative," *JSOT* 30 (1984):
67–84; and James C. VanderKam, "Davidic Complicity in the Deaths of Abner and
Eshbaal," *JBL* 99 (1980): 521–96.

This suspicious reading of the narrative is not necessary exegetically, but it is possible. Read suspiciously, this narrative presents David as a political killer who hides his actions in religious justification. Read less suspiciously, the categories of bloodguilt and expiation portray David as one who must act in terms of the most elemental religious taboos and constraints, as elemental as anything Samuel ever required of Saul. Even read in that way, the narrative punctures a royal claim that the king is a powerful person who can decree new social reality. The king is portrayed as a modest agent who functions as a priest implementing rites but without power beyond these conventional religious perimeters.

Read more innocently, David is presented as a dutiful king, scrupulous about religious obligation, with ready access to God, one who deals gently with Saul and Saul's body, one who kills only as is necessary, and one who honors the memory of Saul. That surface reading, however, is placed in the context of suspicion or religious primitivism. Carlson has seen that the narrative is now placed next to chapter 20, which discloses northern resistance to David.[10] Thus, we may read suspiciously, ironically, or innocently. Shrewdly, the narrative does not dictate our reading.

2. The first list, 2 Sam. 21:15-22, is of four great warriors in Israel who killed Philistine heroes. In the middle of this list, "David's men" (presumably led by Abishai) pronounce a massive assertion of royal ideology: "You shall no more go out with us to battle, lest you quench the lamp of Israel" (v. 17).[11] This sentiment is paralleled in 2 Sam. 18:3, in which David's men want him safe because "you are worth 10,000 of us." The person of the king has taken on sacral significance. I suggest that the narrative/list of 2 Sam. 21:15-22 cites this royal ideology in order to assault it.

The royal assertion is placed in a telling context. Two matters are of note: First, in v. 15, "David is weary." He is not filled with power and vitality, but is utterly dependent on his men. It is a consummate and daring piece of artistry to place the theme of weariness (v. 15) next to the royal ideology (v. 17). Second, in the list of four heroic killings, David does nothing. Especially in the noted case of Goliath, it is Elhanan the Bethlehemite who kills (v. 19). This

---

10. Carlson, *David*, 194–96.

11. Aubrey R. Johnson, in *Sacral Kingship in Ancient Israel* (Cardiff: University of Wales Press, 1967), 1–2, has seen that this formula is set at the beginning of the course of royal ideology in Israel. Johnson juxtaposes it to Lam. 4:20 at the end of the monarchal period.

great king, who is the "lamp of Israel," accomplishes nothing even
against the Philistines, who are in fact dealt with by other courageous
Israelites. The narrative is arranged to leave the royal slogan sus-
pended without any supportive statement or evidence. The slogan
is deliberately placed in a vacuum where it appears ludicrous. The
high claims for the person of the king are unsupported by any data
of action or achievement. Without this "lamp," Israel does indeed
deal effectively with the Philistines.

3. The first poem is the long psalm of 2 Sam. 22:1-51. No doubt
this is an independent, already existing song now inserted here. The
song falls into three parts; the three-part structure nicely brackets
the central section, which is of primary interest to us.

First, vv. 2-20 are a song of deliverance in which the singer acknowledges that God has rescued him from dire straits. Verses 5-6,
in highly mythic language, report the threat of chaos. In vv. 8-20,
theophanic language is used to characterize the powerful coming
of Yahweh and the rescue. In the midst of such daring mythic language, v. 7 is a rather simply conventional statement: "I called; ... I
called; ... he heard." The structure of the rescue is thus traditionally
expressed, and the speaker is a mere suppliant.[12]

Second, in vv. 29-51 we have a victory song in which the speaker
asserts all he has done by way of defeating his enemies:

> I can crush a troop, ...
>> I can leap over a wall. (V. 30)
>
> I pursued my enemies and destroyed them. ...
>> I consumed them; I thrust them through. (Vv. 38-39)
>
> I beat them fine. ...
>> I crushed them and stamped them down. (V. 43)

All this self-assertion is matched, even overmatched, however, by
"thou" statements, showing that the power and fidelity of Yahweh
are decisive; that is, the power of the speaker (ostensibly the king) is
fully subordinated to and derived from the power of Yahweh.

Third, the claim for the king ends in praise and yielding. The
king dramatically yields to the real governance (vv. 50-51). The king
lives by the steadfast love and triumphs of the Lord.

In between the song of rescue (vv. 2-20) and the song of victory (vv. 29-51) is the middle section of vv. 21-28. This section is

---

12. See 1 Sam. 7:8-9; 12:17, 18, 23.

not doxological but didactic. It speaks of moral symmetry and strict retribution, in which God rewards according to righteousness and wickedness. The speaker dares to say:

> The Lord rewarded (*gml*) me according to my righteousness (*ṣdq*);
> according to the cleanness of my hands he recompensed me (*šwb*).
> For I have kept the ways of the Lord,
> and have not wickedly departed from my God . . .
> I did not turn aside,
> I was blameless (*tmm*), . . .
> and I kept myself from guilt (*'ôn*).
> Therefore the Lord has recompensed me (*šwb*) according to my
> righteousness (*ṣdq*),
> according to my cleanness in his sight. . . .
> With the blameless (*tmm*) you are blameless.

Astonishing! The rescue of vv. 2-20 and the victory of vv. 29-51 are put into the service of the king's innocence. The rescue and victory are the king's just reward from a God who is faithful.

Childs suggests that this is a portrayal of David, the genuinely righteous king, that is, that the picture has been cleaned up.[13] Perhaps. But Israel knew better. In 1 Kings 15:4 (with another reference to a "lamp" in Israel), the Deuteronomist has given a most telling verdict on David: "David did what was right in the eyes of the Lord, and did not turn aside from anything that he commanded him all the days of his life—except in the matter of Uriah the Hittite." Big exception! It is, moreover, an exception known in Israel.

The acknowledgment of 1 Kings 15:5 poses the dilemma of how to relate the high claims of *ṣĕdāqâ* and *tāmîm* in the psalm to the reality of David's life. It may be, as Childs proposes, a purged model for kingship. I prefer to think that this is a critique of David. He is a

---

13. Childs, *Introduction*, 275. Gerald T. Sheppard, in *Wisdom as a Hermeneutical Construct*, BZAW, no. 151 (Berlin: de Gruyter, 1980), 144–58, is also inclined to read this poem (as well as 2 Samuel 22) as a positive statement of the idealized David as righteous. Sheppard concludes: "Therefore, the readers of Scripture are invited to see in David a model of the obedient life in the manner of the biblical wisdom tradition" (p. 158). This may be correct, but my suggestion of a more subtle, more critical reading is warranted by Sheppard's own judgment that this "core assessment of David's righteousness is not a free and independent estimate of David. Rather, it is grounded in the actual interpretation of the preceding narrative" (p. 157). Just so. Israel knew too much about David. I suggest there is more critical irony here than Sheppard is inclined to recognize. Hans Wilhelm Hertzberg, in *I and II Samuel*, OTL (Philadelphia: Westminster Press, 1964), 415–16, makes the same positive rendering of David in this text.

king not marked by *ṣĕdāqâ* and *tāmîm*. The deliverance and victory of the psalm are not due to his royal person but to the incredible fidelity of Yahweh. The juxtaposition of the middle section with the first and third sections serves to remove from the king any claim of legitimacy, merit, or virtue. It shows that the king, like all others in Israel, is a creature of Yahweh's willingness to listen and intervene. The king achieves nothing, deserves nothing, guarantees nothing. It is Yahweh, only Yahweh, who delivers. It is all Yahweh, no one else, surely not the king. Thus, the middle section does not celebrate this king, but in fact indicts him and shows how the life-realities of David require a God who hears and acts freely.

4. The second poem is 23:1-7. Like Luke 22:51, which mentions the king, the anointed, this psalm also alludes to the anointed who has been "raised up high" (v. 1). This psalm also seems to assert high royal theology. At its beginning, it is the "spirit of Yahweh," "the God of Israel," "the rock of Israel" who has authorized kingship (vv. 2-3). A high theological claim is made for kingship. At the end of the psalm (v. 5), the king asserts: "For he has made with me an everlasting covenant, ordered in all things and secure." Surely the *bĕrît 'ôlām* is high royal theology, echoing the decree of 2 Sam. 7:14-16 and reminiscent of Ps. 89:24, 33-36. This theology affirms that God's guarantee of this monarchy is indeed unconditional and therefore perpetual.

In the middle of the psalm, however, is this single line (2 Sam. 23:3) that moves against the ideology:

> When one rules justly (*ṣaddîq*) over people,
> ruling in the fear of God . . .

Then the king is like the morning light, sun, and rain, that is, the source of life. The king is not unreservedly and automatically the source of life. Only the king who is *ṣaddîq*—that is, who governs according to the Torah—can give life.

Verse 3 has a sobering intention in the midst of exaggerated royal theology. Indeed, this single line sounds strangely like the warning of Samuel in 1 Samuel 12:

> If you will fear Yahweh and serve him and hearken to his voice and not rebel against the commandments of the Lord, and if both *you and your king* who reigns over you will follow the Lord your God, it will be well; but if you will not hearken, . . . then the hand of the Lord will be against *you and your king*. . . . But if you still do wickedly, you shall be swept away, both *you and your king*. (Vv. 14-15, 25).

Three times the text asserts "you and your king." The king is like the others and not different from other Israelites. The speech of Samuel and this psalm intend to subordinate the king to the rule of Torah, to the old requirements. This means that the *bĕrît 'ôlām* of v. 5 is considerably placed in jeopardy by the *ṣaddîq* of v. 3. And if the claim is in jeopardy, then the royal ideology must be treated with circumspection. In both psalms, then, the middle section (22:21-28; 23:3) contains a peculiar challenge to the royal theology that the songs purport to articulate.

5. The second list is in 2 Sam. 23:8-39, a list of "the three" and "the thirty." Four comments may be made in relation to our general topic.

a. The list shows that there can be many heroes in Israel. The exploits of many brave people can be recited, and their names known. There is a remarkable democratizing tendency showing that David did not have a monopoly on greatness or public celebration, and David did not need to have such a monopoly.[14] Such a democratizing tendency clearly works against a high royal theology or personality cult in which there are no other heroes and no names can be honored except that of the king. My impression is that in high royal annals, the names of the others have all dropped out. Not here, however. This suggests an ordering of power that is understood as relatively open. Conversely, in this list as in 21:15-22, David does not do anything. He is not celebrated for his prowess or courage.

b. In vv. 9 and 12, the victories are credited to Yahweh: "The Lord wrought a great victory that day." This may be only a convention, but it is a nicely stated convention. In that formula, David is not mentioned. It is not said, as in 8:6, 14, that "Yahweh gave David victory." Nor is it said, as in 8:13, "David won a name for himself." David is absent in this account, which is remarkably theonomous in its casting. The theonomous character of the list, like its democratic inclination, speaks against high royal theology.

c. The last name among "the thirty" is "Uriah the Hittite." It may be routine that his name is included. It cannot be routine, however, that his name is last. Uriah's name is last as a gesture, a reminder, a warning. His name is an assertion against royal propaganda that "we

---

14. If David did not have and did not need such a monopoly of honor, it is possible that the David presented here would not be alarmed by lyrical comparisons of himself with other warriors, as was Saul in 1 Sam. 18:7. Saul is portrayed as not being able to tolerate such a sharing of honor. It is proposed in this text that David could entertain much more of such sharing than could Saul.

have not forgotten." The utterance of his name also evokes the entire scenario of royal hubris, of the limits of pride, and of the price paid for such pride. The presence of Uriah reminds those subscribing to the Jerusalem ideology that there is another Governance that will not be mocked. What may be pleasing in the king's eyes may not be pleasing in the eyes of Yahweh (2 Sam. 11:25, 27).

d. In the middle of this list is an odd narrative account (vv. 13-17). David wishes for water from Bethlehem. His men who adore him secure the water at the risk of their lives. David, in a magnificent gesture of solidarity, in an act of sacramental imagination, pours the water out on the ground, for he says, "Shall I drink the blood of the men who went at the risk of their lives?" (v. 17). His men must have adored him all the more.

No doubt this story is told to enhance the greatness of David, but we should notice the peculiar dimension of greatness that is articulated. David is one who is in the battle with his men, not back in the royal enclosure (contra 18:3; 21:17). He has a longing (a desire, if not a need), and he is intimate with his men so that he is willing to share that desire/need with them. They are his comrades in arms, not his servants. They are willing to be his servants, but he does not treat them so, nor does the story present them so.

Most important, however, David does not drink the water. David does not assume that he is entitled to the benefit of the service and risk of others. David does not monopolize the benefit. In high royal theology, the others exist for the sake of the king, and the king is entitled to a disproportionate share, if not a monopoly, of what is produced by the community. David, however, eschews such preferential treatment and acts in sacramental solidarity. He has an awesome power with his men, but it is the power of magisterial humanness, not ideological priority. Finally, notice that while he is at war, David does not fight, and he wins no battles. His greatness is not in his prowess but in his solidarity, one "among brothers" (cf. Deut. 17:15).

This episode, I suggest, performs a peculiar function in the midst of the lists of "the three" and "the thirty." The other soldiers are the great ones in Israel. David commands respect, but it is respect gained "from below," not insisted upon "from above."

6. The second narrative is 24:1-25. I will deal with the narrative under two groupings of motifs:

First, there are three religiously curious elements that I shall consider. I do not believe they are crucial for my argument, but they are interesting and problematical. First among these, in v. 1 there is a framing comment in which Yahweh is said to "entice David." It was Yahweh who put David up to his unfortunate scheme. As in the manner of Job, or perhaps as in the private oracle of 21:1, this notice stands outside the narrative. It functions to support the claim that there is much more going on in David's life than David himself knows about or initiates. David does not in fact hold the final initiative for his life. Second, there is the curious playfulness in vv. 11-13, in which David is given the choice of punishments, rather like playing Russian roulette. Third, in v. 16, an angel of pestilence is dispatched by Yahweh and then recalled before full destruction. The religious playfulness of all three elements suggests that there is a primitive religious awareness that the high claims of royal theology have not been able to tame or subdue. The king and his learned, legitimated advisers may want to reduce all of life to their plans, but there is more on the loose than they can manage. The God who acts in these three elements may be like the parent of a teenager: The parent is always doing free, embarrassing things, just when the teenager has it all worked out. The freedom of God is maintained by the narrative in the face of ideology that seeks to order life in bureaucratic and rational ways.

It is the second grouping of motifs that concerns us, however. There is a remarkably developed characterization of David offered in this narrative. We watch while David is transformed through the process of this narrative. I note five elements:

a. David proposes a census. "Yahweh enticed," but David proposed the census, and David must answer for his policy. There is a vigorous protest from Joab, who is the voice of the old tradition and knows that the census is wrong (v. 3). David overrides Joab's objections. The characterization of the census in vv. 4-9 bespeaks an administrative flurry: fast horses, ruthless officers, government agents rushing into obscure villages. I suggest that the census is a form of bureaucratic terrorism in which the crown invades villages and tribal life. In v. 9 we learn the formal purpose of the census. It is to number for the sake of the military, for the "valiant men." In the census, David acts the role of the potentate who will mobilize all his power for his own ambitious and oppressive ends. In this act, David is indeed preparing to "take," the very taking anticipated by Samuel in 1 Sam. 8:11-19. The narrative portrays the model of royal policy in all its ugliness.

b. In v. 10, David confesses, "I have sinned greatly." The narrative is laconic about David's awareness. We do not know how or why David came to this awareness. The narrative presents David as having some critical distance from the seductive ideology of kingship. It is David's awareness of sin that leads to the discussion of various punishments. David has already decisively broken with the royal self-description by making his confession.

c. In v. 14, David makes a staggering theological confession. He knows he must be punished. He would rather trust himself to God (that is, the pestilence) than to human agents (through war), for "God's mercy is great." This dramatic move, which transforms David, is stunningly beyond our expectation of David. The king who had said "Go...number the people" (v. 2) had spoken in such unqualified self-assurance. David here has forsaken that mode of royal pretension and now speaks as a child of the covenant.

d. In v. 17, David reiterates his confession. This is in the face of the repentance of Yahweh in v. 16.[15] But the confession of v. 17 goes beyond that of v. 10. In v. 10 David cared about his own iniquity. In v. 17 David cares more about "these sheep," that is, the people. David no longer worries about his person or this throne, but he remembers the community entrusted to him. David anticipates Ezekiel 34 in his awareness that the shepherd exists for the sake of the sheep.

e. Finally, in vv. 18-25, David acts as a religiously submissive and obedient man. He gets land and builds an altar. The outcome of v. 25, which ends the appendix and the book of Samuel, is "Yahweh heeded the supplication." David prayed and Yahweh heard. The initiative is with Yahweh. David, proper David, is an obedient servant of his Lord, a child who cries out in need. David understands that petition, empty-handed petition, is his proper posture before Yahweh, as it is for an Israelite.

III

This literature is highly complex and is not easily summarized. It is indeed the very telling that deconstructs, and when we summarize, we miss the subtlety of deconstruction. We may, nonetheless,

---

15. Yahweh's repentance in order to save the city is reminiscent of Jon. 3:10—4:2. The difference is in the reaction of the human agent. Whereas Jonah is chagrined that Yahweh should have compassion, repent, and save the city, David relies on the compassion of Yahweh, which causes Yahweh to repent and save the city. The same motif of Yahweh's repentance in order not to destroy a city is evident in Jer. 18:1-11.

note some elements that seem obvious concerning our suggestion of deconstruction:

1. In the narratives:

a. In 21:1-14, David either is suspiciously criticized for his realpolitik in the name of religion or is portrayed as a child of extreme religious scruple.[16]

b. In 24:1-25, David is dramatically transformed in the process of the narrative from a self-serving monarch to a repentant, supplicating creature of covenant.

2. In the lists, David does not act but is surrounded by those who act:

a. In 21:17, the high formula of royal theology is surrounded by David's passivity and weariness.

b. In 23:8-39, David is portrayed as democratic and theonomous, and as a genuine comrade in solidarity.

3. In the songs, David is held accountable for *ṣĕdāqâ*, which qualifies *bĕrît 'ôlām* (23:3-5). David's shabby righteousness and blamelessness are set in a context of God's delivering, faithful power.

All of these elements, I submit, intend to dismantle any high royal pretension and invite an understanding of David (or any king) that must be held in the framework of an older, covenantal theology.

Three conclusions may be drawn from this review:

1. It is neither possible nor necessary to date the material. It is conventional to hold that these chapters are early pieces of material subsequently gathered together. It is worth noting that three elements present David at the threshold of Jerusalem power, that is, the first narrative and the two lists.[17] Specifically, the two lists (21:15-22; 23:8-39) are largely set in the days of the Philistine conflict. That is, David's greatness, such as it is, belongs to those earlier days. Conversely, the settlement of the "Saulide problem" and the census reflect David's move to Jerusalem and the accompanying royal pretensions, as David participates in a new form of power and security.

In the poems, the *bĕrît 'ôlām* (23:5) and the mocking of David's *ṣĕdāqâ* (22:21-28) reflect the uneasiness of Israel with the Jerusalem

---

16. The operation of realpolitik in the rise of David is, of course, not in doubt. See Niels Peter Lemche, "David's Rise," *JSOT* 10 (1978): 2–25. What is at issue is whether there are other factors at work along with realpolitik.

17. I use the word "threshold" with intentional reference to the analysis of Flanagan, "Social Transformation," who uses the terms "threshold" and "liminality" on p. 367 and elsewhere.

enterprise. There are hints of arranging the materials so that the Philistine period offers a model that is approved, and the Jerusalem context is regularly criticized as a distortion of David's proper role. This means that dramatically (not chronologically) the "good" David is the early David, the one who lived prior to the seductions of the royal theology. Thus, the deconstruction that operates here is not a deconstruction of everything about David or about kingship, but it is the dismantling of a certain David, a David too certain, a David who believes in, acts on, and is defined by ideological claims that are regarded as alien to the older memory.[18] The narrative is still a celebration and an appreciation of David as a king and a man of faith. The deconstruction asserts that it is possible to be king and a man of faith without the perversion of royal theology. The royal theology (which is here opposed) speaks against democratic and theonomous inclinations and in favor of killings (21:1-14) and countings (24:1-9) that oppress and betray the faith of Israel.

The method and approach of this chapter do not require a chronological dating of the edited texts. The theopolitical perspective of the texts is crucial. This perspective may have arisen at any time when the Jerusalem establishment was under criticism. This could be (*a*) in the immediate wake of Solomon, (*b*) during the period of prophetic criticism, or (*c*) when the monarchy had failed after 587 B.C.E.

2. It is too early in my thinking to correlate this material more closely with that of 2 Samuel 5–8, but I suggest that this set of six elements intends to counter that set of six elements. Both pieces of literature have six elements arranged chiastically, even though the six of the appendix do not seem to have an internal dynamic such as Flanagan has seen in chapters 5–8. I do suggest, however, that as Flanagan has shown chapters 5–8 to be a literary enactment across the threshold from traditional Yahwism toward "centralized supra- and extratribal administration [that] signaled class and social distinctions," so the appendix is a dramatic invitation to go back across that threshold to an egalitarian covenantal mode of life.[19] What chapters 5–8 regard as the great new facts, chapters 21–24 regard as a distortion to be rejected; that is, what is deconstructed is not simply the character of David, but patterns of faith

---

18. On the power of the older claims of Israel as a decisive political force, see Martin Cohen, "The Role" (see chap. 11, n. 3).

19. Flanagan, "Social Transformation," 363.

and modes of power for which David is the literary and sociological vehicle.

The appendix wishes to assert that the new Davidic world of guaranteeing oracle (7:1-17), imperial wars (8:1-14), and bureaucratic power (8:15-18) will lead to death. The appendix urges a return to a more lively faith and simpler modes of power. Put in the parlance of chapters 5–8, a return is urged to kinship relations (5:13-16), wars of defense (5:17-25), and tribal religion (6:1-23). As chapters 5–8 brought Israel dramatically into a new arena, so chapters 21–24 propose going back out of the heady land of "Jerusalem," back to better days. The reduction of Israel's choices to these two options, however, is a gross oversimplification. The actual historical formation of Israel's political structures is less clear, more complex, and more ambivalent. The literature nonetheless works with models that do not linger over complexity and ambiguity. The dramatic act of going back out is not unlike the vision of Hos. 2:14-15 (MT vv. 16-17), which wants to lead Israel back out of the land so that the "Valley of Trouble" may become "the door of hope." To depart from high royal theology back to simple faith is for this literature a "door of hope."[20]

Carlson has seen that 2 Samuel 24 leads to 1 Kings 1–2.[21] In 1 Kings 1–2, the culmination of the Davidic story shows the extreme edge of David's new mode of power, which is bloody and ruthless and which could be topped only by the cynicism of Solomon.[22] At

---

20. Assuming that Flanagan is correct in the "rite of passage" to kingship in 2 Samuel 5–8, I propose that 2 Samuel 21–24 proposes an inverse situation of liminality back to a condition of trust and vulnerability. That inverse liminality is expressed in Hos. 2:14-15:

> Therefore, behold, I will allure her,
> and bring her in to the wilderness,
> and speak tenderly to her.
> And there I will give her her vineyards,
> and make the Valley of Achor a door of hope.

If there is a parallel of deconstruction in our text to that of Hosea, it is not accidental. For Hosea has the most critical view of kingship in the Old Testament and has Yahweh say, "They made kings, but not through me" (Hos. 8:4). This statement, not uncongenial to the Shilonite ideology (see Cohen, "The Role," 64 n. 18), could readily apply to a high ideology of kingship that is "not through me." Such a critical deconstruction might be as appropriate to David and Jerusalem as to the northern kings of whom Hosea speaks.

21. Carlson, *David*, 196–97.

22. Cohen ("The Role," 91–94) observes that the prophetic critique of Solomon in 1 Kings 11:29-39 is in the mouth of Ahijah the Shilonite. Cohen suggests that the

least in the culmination of the succession narrative (1 Kings 1–2), the deconstruction of 2 Samuel 21–24 is disregarded.

3. Finally, I want to comment on one canonical dimension of this study. Childs has observed that the two poems of 2 Samuel 22:1-51 and 23:1-7 stand as a canonical balance to the Song of Hannah (1 Sam. 2:1-10) at the beginning of the Samuel corpus. The Song of Hannah provides a "hermeneutical key" for the entire Samuel literature. Robert P. Gordon has nicely referred to the Song of Hannah as the "clef sign" for the musical score of Samuel.[23]

In the poem, Hannah stands as the extreme counterpoint to royal power. She is empty-handed and full of trust while awaiting God's inversion. Indeed, that inversion of the needy to sit with princes is embodied in David. Hannah's Song, in its present form, ends in v. 10 with reference to "his king" and "his anointed."

I wish to add to Childs's canonical observation one other point. As the poems at the end match the initial poem, I submit that 2 Samuel 24 matches 1 Samuel 1 in its canonical placement. In the initial chapter, Hannah is a barren woman, hopeless, without recourse other than to petition to God. Her petition is heard, God acts to give life and to begin a new history. Her tale ends in glad, submissive worship (1:28). What counts is that the Lord is heard. In 2 Samuel 24, after his confession in vv. 10, 17, David also comes empty-handed, ready to petition. He must come empty-handed, for he has relinquished his census, emblem of royal power. David no longer comes as a king but as a needy suppliant. He intercedes for his people. The conclusion is that Yahweh heard the supplication and gave life to the land (v. 25).

On the one hand, David has now become the true king, the one Samuel envisioned, the one who claimed, presumed, and possessed nothing, but who trusted and cried out to Yahweh, and obeyed. David is indeed deconstructed of royal pretensions. On the other hand, David becomes the approved king because he has become more like Hannah, Samuel's mother. Like her, he is empty-handed, utterly needful, utterly trusting. These narratives of Hannah and David petitioning and being heard provide an *inclusio* for the Samuel narrative about power and the transformation of power. The power approved is empty-handed and waiting for inversions that make

---

most important characteristic of Ahijah is that he is a Shilonite, that is, the voice of the party that most resisted the high ideology of kingship embodied in Solomon.

23. Childs, *Introduction*, 272–73. Gordon, *1 and 2 Samuel* (see chap. 11, n. 17), 26.

full.[24] This is certainly an odd notion of kingship, which is gladly abandoned in the heady moves of chapters 5–8 but now urged again in chapters 21–24. The David proposed in chapters 21–24 is now indeed "a man after God's own heart" (1 Sam. 13:14).

---

24. The theme of "empty-full" as crucial to the dramatic inversion of the story of Ruth has been well explicated by Phyllis Trible, *God and Rhetoric* (see chap. 4, n. 16), esp. 193–94. It is perhaps not incidental that the Ruth narrative ends with a genealogy leading to David (Ruth 4:18-22), the one who is finally taken empty and made full. Notice that in 2 Sam. 15:21, the response of Ittai to David is closely paralleled in Ruth's pledge to Naomi (Ruth 1:16-17). The story of Ruth is a useful heuristic clue to the links between the model of Hannah and the critical portrayal of David offered in these texts. See Carmel McCarthy, "The Davidic Genealogy in the Book of Ruth," *Proceedings of the Irish Biblical Association* 9 (1985): 53–62.

13

Unity and Dynamic in the Isaiah Tradition

As MUCH AS ANYWHERE, the older literary criticism achieved much of a consensus on the book of Isaiah, as it has not on the books of Jeremiah and Ezekiel.[1] As is commonly recognized, that consensus includes a division of Isaiah 1–39 (eighth century), 40–55 (sixth century), and 56–66 (probably fifth century). The articulation of a third Isaiah is much less secure, but at least the "assured results" separate Assyrian and Babylonian Isaiah. Notice that these conclusions concern three distinct literary pieces correlated to three identifiable historical contexts. Very little attention has been given to the interrelation of the parts. Indeed, the accepted tools of historical criticism militate against such a consideration.

I

A new phase of Isaiah scholarship has been initiated by Brevard S. Childs, strengthened in important ways by Ronald E. Clements.[2] In Childs's decisive book on canon criticism, his most spectacular success is with the book of Isaiah. His argument is that even if we

---

1. That consensus is reported in the standard introductions. See the summary Childs, *Introduction* (see chap. 1, n. 6), 216–25.

2. Ibid., 325–38. See Clements, "The Unity of the Book of Isaiah," *Int* 36 (1982): 117–29, and "The Prophecies of Isaiah and the Fall of Jerusalem in 587 BC," *VT* 30 (1980): 421–36.

critically separate the book into various Isaiahs, which he does not doubt, canonical study must ask about the coherence of the whole, in its present form; that is, even if the various elements of the book are separate and distinct in origin and original intention, in the canonical shape of the book a new statement is made that must be taken with primary seriousness.

Childs's argument is that 1–39 from the Assyrian period is essentially a statement of *judgment* and that 40–66 is essentially concerned with *promise* that now supersedes the judgment. In this he agrees with the more general argument of Clements that the final form of prophetic books is regularly redacted around the themes of *judgment and promise*.[3] Four specific elements of Childs's argument may be noted:

1. The purpose of the juxtaposition of 1–39 and 40–66 is to establish that the judgment declared in 1–39 is real and has been implemented. There really is a judgment and Isaiah's message has come to fruition.

2. That judgment, however, is not the last word. The last word is promise. It is the last word theologically; thus, it is the last word canonically. Second Isaiah and, even more, Third Isaiah are in fact eschatological, looking to the full coming of the new age. Second and Third Isaiah come theologically and canonically after First Isaiah, but Childs has no special interest in their *historical* placement.

3. Childs and Clements, in an important break with the critical consensus, have argued that the rubric of old/new in Second Isaiah does not refer to exodus/new exodus but to the *old judgments* of Assyrian Isaiah and the *new promises* of the Babylonian Isaiah. "Former things" are the judgments of Isaiah 1–39. Thus the paradigm of judgment/redemption dominates exegesis here. I am not sure on this point, but it is crucial for the shift proposed by Childs and Clements. A quite similar passage in Jer. 23:7-8 might support the older judgment of Aage Bentzen and Christopher R. North, but in any case, that is the shape of the present argument.[4]

---

3. Clements, "Patterns in the Prophetic Canon," in *Canon and Authority* (see chap. 7, n. 25).

4. Clear presentations of the older hypothesis that "former things" refers to the pre–587 B.C.E. saving events are offered by Bentzen, "On the Ideas of 'the Old' and 'the New' in Deutero-Isaiah," *ST* 1 (1948-49): 183–87, and North, "The 'Former Things' and the 'New Things' in Deutero-Isaiah," in *Studies in Old Testament Prophecy*, ed. Harold H. Rowley (New York: Scribner, 1950), 111–26. From a tradition-critical perspective, see especially Bernhard W. Anderson, "Exodus Typology in Second Isaiah," in *Israel's Prophetic Heritage* (see chap. 8, n. 64), 177–95, and "Exodus and

4. Following Georg Fohrer, both Childs and Clements argue that Isaiah 1 is an important introduction to the canonical book; that is, the chapter is designed to announce and anticipate the themes subsequently to be played out in the entire tradition.[5] That chapter is not the work of Isaiah in the eighth century, but is a carefully wrought, later redactional piece to serve canonical purposes.

All of these elements together show that the book is a unity, permitting Clements to conclude that the basis of unity for the book of Isaiah in its various collection is "the continuity and connectedness of this divine power."[6]

II

The main problem I have with Childs's approach generally, and also with that of Clements in this case, is that their view is essentially static. Childs exhibits little interest in the *social dynamic* behind the text and apparently regards such an interest as a distraction from a proper canonical study. In this regard, I find his work less helpful than that of James A. Sanders, who attends especially to the social dynamics involved in the shaping of the text.[7] Though Childs may be correct, as I hope he is here, I am still left with something like the question: So what? Given his analysis and conclusion, I am left wondering: What do we do next and how does this analysis help us do it?

Covenant in Second Isaiah and Prophetic Tradition," in *Magnalia Dei* (see chap. 4, n. 26), 339–60.

5. Fohrer, "Jesaja 1 als Zusammenfassung der Verkündigung Jesajas," *ZAW* 74 (1962): 251–68.

6. On the basis of unity, see Clements, "The Unity," 129. It is also important to note that the issue is not simply one of continuity, as though a canonical agenda is always tilted that way. It is impossible that discontinuity could also be a programmatic concern of canonical shaping. Peter R. Ackroyd, in "Continuity and Discontinuity" (see chap. 9, n. 12), has stressed the power of continuity for the tradition. But an equally strong emphasis on discontinuity is also made by Walther Zimmerli, "Prophetic Proclamation and Reinterpretation," in *Tradition and Theology* (see chap. 7, n. 46), 69–100. See my comments on the issues, Walter Brueggemann, *The Creative Word* (Philadelphia: Fortress Press, 1982), esp. chap. 3. See the judicious and suggestive statement of Theodore M. Ludwig, "Remember Not Former Things," in *Transitions and Transformations in the History of Religions*, ed. Frank E. Reynolds and Ludwig (Leiden: Brill, 1980), 25–55, which takes the issue in a properly dynamic and dialectical way.

7. See esp. Sanders, "Adaptable for Life" (see chap. 4, n. 26). See also the suggestion of James D. G. Dunn, "Levels of Canonical Authority," *HBT* 4 (1982): 13–60, who proposes that a literature may have levels of canonical authority, each of which must be taken seriously.

I suggest that the work of Norman K. Gottwald may be of special help here. Gottwald has paid primary attention to the creative role of the community in formulating the text as an aid to a *social intentionality*. Here I must tread lightly, for I judge the relation of the work of Childs and Gottwald—that is, a canonical approach and a study of social dynamics in relation to the text—to be the most difficult as well as the most important question facing us in our study of these issues. Childs is wont to let the canonical approach transcend the realities of social interaction, to withdraw the text from such turmoil. Indeed, that may be his interest in the word "canonical." Conversely, Gottwald is inclined to so draw the text into the social operation that it loses its distance, that is, its own claim to authority over against the social interaction. His temptation is no doubt that of Ludwig Andreas Feuerbach.[8]

Nonetheless, I suggest that Gottwald's perspective may complement that of Childs and Clements, for it asks about the dynamic and integral way these texts interact, not simply about a late canonical settlement. Now in posing the question this way, I do not diminish the importance of Childs's canonical question. But we must try to ask: What were the processes and dynamics that caused the literature to reach this particular shaping? And that question cannot be answered on simply literary grounds or on theological grounds but must ask about social processes. So I suggest that in shaping the text in this way, the community was performing specific hermeneutical tasks that attend to the historical reality of the community and to the diachronic reality of the text. I propose, then, in broad sweep, that each of the Isaiahs articulates a specific practice of social transformation. The ministry that is evoked by this canonical text is to engage in the same specific practices of social transformation. The text is more than a text; it is a presentation of a way through to a world of faith.

III

Isaiah 1–39 articulates *a radical sustained critique of the dominant ideology of that culture*. Childs suggests that the matchup of promises and

---

8. See Gottwald, *The Tribes* (see chap. 1, n. 6). In "Sociological Matrix" (see chap. 1, n. 6), Gottwald has explored possible interactions and complementarity between his work and that of Childs; however, his statement does not concede very much to the approach of Childs.

threats in Isaiah 1–39 is itself a redactional device. So here I speak only of the judgments or, in the language of Claus Westermann, of the judgment speeches in all their variation.[9]

To be sure, this can be a historical judgment about Isaiah in the eighth century as well as a literary judgment; that is, that historical Isaiah serves to expose the ideology. Apart from historical placement, however, Clements has identified the redactional outcome so that First Isaiah is *essentially judgment* for a society and regime that are ordered against Yahweh's purposes.

My proposal is not strange to our common assumption, but I wish to transpose the terms so that we deal not with prophetic judgment but with social criticism. All social transformation begins in social criticism. One might consider many different texts. The important thing to note is that this is neither generalized scolding nor righteous indignation. It is, rather, a precise exposé of cultural practice and cultural value that engage in systemic perversion. Take as an example the "woes" of Isa. 5:20-23.[10] Here we can leave out the important question of possible provenance from sapiential circles, and consider only what Isaiah makes of the form. If "woe" refers to "death," then these are statements made in pathos and not in anger, statements that the practices out of which society expects life will surely yield death. Verse 20 speaks about programmatic dishonesty:

> Woe to those who call evil good and good evil,
> who put darkness for light and light for darkness,
> who put bitter for sweet and sweet for bitter!

Social criticism begins by calling things by their right name. Verse 21 speaks of death for the self-sufficient, autonomous ones, who are answerable to none, who act against the fabric of society:

> . . . wise in their own eyes,
> and shrewd in their own sight!

---

9. In speaking of 1–39 as judgment over against 40–66 as promise, Childs and Clements must be somewhat reductionist, for in 1–39, both elements are found. This is simply to acknowledge that I am following their particular reduction in my discussion. I do not know how else the discussion can proceed. On lawsuit speeches, see Westermann, *Basic Forms* (see chap. 1, n. 23).

10. On these texts, see J. William Whedbee, *Isaiah and Wisdom* (New York: Abingdon Press, 1971), chap. 3.

Verse 23 speaks of death wrought by the indulgent who pervert the economic structure for personal well-being:

> . . . acquit the guilty for a bribe,
> and deprive the innocent of his right!

Obviously not every text in 1–39 speaks so, but that is the canonical argument made by Childs and Clements that I presume. Death will come to a society so deeply organized against reality, against God's sovereignty. The judgment anticipated by the prophet is not supernatural. It comes in the very fabric of social experience.[11] For that reason we may speak of social criticism as a mode of prophetic judgment.

This part of canonical Isaiah is a bold distancing between Yahweh's truth and Israel's fraudulently constructed social reality. Such a practice of critique of ideology, which now is a main requirement of ministry, operates on three premises:

1. There is a normative reality (Yahweh's purpose, cf. Isa. 14:24-27) that endures and persists in the face of every systemic perversion and will not be altered by the posturing of the regime. The world is not a subjective construct. That normative reality is borne in Israel by the Torah (cf. 5:24).[12] God and God's truth will not be mocked (37:17-19).

2. The present "world" in which we live is a contrived world, not a given world. This critique is against the positivism that every regime wants to foster, a positivism widely and easily accepted. This analysis urges that the "known world" is a contrivance, and if it is a contrivance, it could have been contrived differently. And we should not imagine that this world is a given.[13]

3. The contrivance is not disinterested or accidental. It is contrived in the service of quite specific and identifiable interests. And

---

11. So Patrick D. Miller, in *Sin and Judgment* (see chap. 1, n. 24), concludes: "The correlation of sin and punishment while effected by Yahweh is not manifest in a capricious and irrational way unconnected to the nexus of events, as if it were an 'act of God' in the sense that insurance companies use such a term. . . . There is no such trivialization of the notion of judgment in the passages studied" (p. 138).

12. On Isaiah's appeal to Torah, see Joseph Jensen, *The Use of Tora by Isaiah*, CBQ Monograph Series, no. 3 (Washington, D.C.: Catholic Biblical Association of America, 1973). Notice, in the summation on pp. 130–31, the juxtaposition of 2:2-4 and 5:24.

13. On alternative worlds, see David J. A. Clines, *I, He, We and They*, JSOTSup, no. 1 (Sheffield: JSOT Press, 1976), 59–65, in which he articulates and evokes an alternative.

those interests are against the general interest.[14] The tradition of
Isaiah thus proceeds in the assurance that

a. the reality of good and evil is not in doubt or debatable;

b. the ones condemned are those who have contrived it differently;

c. they have done so for their own advantage.

The prophet is not driven simply by anger or even by anguish, but
he has made a cold intellectual assessment of the social processes
around him.

Thus, the first task of "redescribing the world," a task the tradition of Isaiah takes up, is critique of ideology. That requires a bold
intellectual act that can be done only by those with a clear sense of
alternative norms. This task is as crucial now as it was in Jerusalem in
the eighth century. Citizens then and now are extraordinarily naive
about the positivistic claims of the rulers of the age. And the first
task, painfully done, is to raise the question of distance, to begin to
see that how reality is *presented* is not in fact *how it is*. And that establishment of critical distance is the first task of canonical Isaiah—to
show that the presumed world does not square with the real world;
that the decreed truth is in fact partisan, self-serving truth out of
which cannot come life; and that those who cling to this presumed
world may be sure that death and judgment will result. To speak so,
as does Isaiah, requires a bold vision of an alternative world.

IV

Now we come to the crucial question in the presentation of Childs
and Clements, the relation of First and Second Isaiah. There are
of course important *theological* linkages between the two parts. Both
Childs and Clements urge that connection in terms of judgment and
promise. I find that convincing, but by itself inadequate. So I pose
the question: Are there elements of social *interaction* that correlate

---

14. On the critique of vested interest as done by the prophets, see Robert B. Coote,
Amos (see chap. 7, n. 23), esp. chap. 2; Bernhard Lang, "The Social Organization of
Peasant Poverty in Biblical Israel," *JSOT* 24 (1982): 47–63; Hans Walter Wolff, "Micah
the Moreshite—The Prophet and His Background," in *Israelite Wisdom: Theological
and Literary Essays in Honor of Samuel Terrien*, ed. John G. Gammie et al. (Missoula,
Mont.: Scholars Press, 1978), 77–84; and James L. Mays, "Justice: Perspectives from
the Prophetic Tradition," *Int* 37 (1983): 5–17.

with and evoke this redactional arrangement? Is there something in the experience of Israel that causes the theological venture of Second Isaiah to emerge out of First Isaiah?

Obviously I will answer yes. And my answer is based on this: The purpose of critique of ideology (which is how I have characterized First Isaiah) is to permit people to become aware of their real situation, to begin to observe the incongruities, ambiguities, and contradictions that are covered over by ideology. If the critique of ideology be addressed only to the managers of that ideology, it will evoke hostility. But if that critique of ideology be heard or even addressed to the victims of that ideology, as Robert R. Wilson suggests, the probable result is that people will get in touch with their victimization, exploitation, and pain.[15] Thus, for example, this ideological practice of wrongly labeling things good/evil, bitter/sweet, is not haphazard. It is done to benefit some at the expense of others, the innocent who are thereby deprived of right. Isaiah does a discerning critique of the power of propaganda. Control of the public media of communication can present a fake world that benefits and denies rather intentionally.

So the argument here is that the ideological critique of 1–33 makes possible the surfacing of, entry into, and embrace of pain, regret, and alienation. And this pain, regret, and alienation are indeed a social fact for the community gathered around this text. So the second dimension of social interaction that correlates with the Isaiah tradition is *the public practice of pain*, which touches both guilt and grief, guilt at being responsible for so much of value that is denied, grief that it is gone and irretrievable. It is Second Isaiah that moves through the embrace of pain.

Now the correlation I make of this in Second Isaiah is threefold:

1. Second Isaiah is the voice of a pastoral poet who profoundly acknowledges the pain and grief of his community, a community that has reflected deeply upon and lived through the social criticism of Isaiah. Much of this action of reflection and living through is presumably lodged in the hiatus between Isaiah 39 and 40.[16] We do not know what happened between the two elements, either historically or theologically. But surely the space between the chapters is a poignant space, not simply a blank passing of two hundred years.

---

15. Wilson, in *Prophecy* (see chap. 3, n. 17), has articulated the social role of "central" and "peripheral" prophets.

16. See the discerning comments of Ackroyd, "Interpretation" (see chap. 8, n. 41).

It is the brooding, doubting, suffering of Israel, not knowing if this is an end of Isaiah or if indeed there is to be "more Isaiah," that is, a second Isaiah. And it is the brooding of God, about what to say next, for what can a God say after chapter 39, after a king as good as Hezekiah is so captured by ideology that he hopes only for peace in his time?[17] Neither Yahweh nor Israel (nor the Isaiah tradition) knows just then if there is to be more, either theologically, historically, or literarily, that is, canonically.

One cannot know. But I suggest that for purposes of dramatic movement, we consider the poetry of the book of Lamentations as lodged just there in the faith and experience of Israel. It is that poetry, closest to the demise of 587 B.C.E., the payoff of the threats of Isaiah, that shows Israel embracing and acknowledging the deep pain of loss, the complete collapse of the contrived world of royal construction that had no contact with reality. If that possibility can be entertained for a moment, we can observe three things that illustrate the deep acknowledgment of pain:

a. The beginning of 40:1, "comfort, comfort," sounds like a deliberate response to the refrain of Lamentations, "there is none to comfort" (1:2, 7, 17, 21). The poetry of comfort arises precisely from a cry of "none to comfort."

b. As Westermann has shown, a key genre of Second Isaiah is the salvation oracle. Following Joachim Begrich, we may suggest that the extensive use of the genre in Second Isaiah is precisely in response to laments that are either those of Lamentations or are very much like them.[18] The move cannot be directly made from 1–39 to 40ff., but only through the abyss between 39 and 40, the gulf between judgment and promise where guilt and grief have their powerful say. And where there is not guilt and grief, there will not be comfort spoken.[19]

c. In 49:14 we are offered one example of a lament that must have been characteristic, a lament imbued with a sense of forgottenness.[20]

---

17. On the theological imagination through which God can say more after God has spoken the last word, see J. Gerald Janzen, "Metaphor" (see chap. 2, n. 24).

18. Westermann, *Isaiah 40–66* (Philadelphia: Westminster Press, 1969), 11–14; and Begrich, "Das priesterliche" (see chap. 4, n. 20). See also Thomas M. Raitt, *Theology of Exile* (see chap. 9, n. 24), esp. chap. 6.

19. Robert J. Lifton, *The Broken Connection* (New York: Simon & Schuster, 1980). Lifton has shrewdly explored the positive role of grief and guilt in permitting people to take new actions that may be redemptive.

20. The lament of Isa. 49:14 attributed to Zion is surely closely linked to Lam. 5:20. See the theological-rhetorical analysis of Lothar Perlitt, "Anklage und Freispruch

This example makes clear that Second Isaiah is a response to such lamentation, which is the public practice of pain. One cannot move from critique (judgment) to promise, as Childs and Clements seem to suggest, without the intervening reality of pain expressed. Second Isaiah presumes the grief and brings it to speech, even as it is evoked by the critique of ideology. Understanding the dynamic preserved in the shape of the canon means to take the embrace of pain into account, and that embrace can be seen as a textual reality.

2. Clearly, Second Isaiah not only embraces and acknowledges pain, but also responds to it, moves through it to hope and promise. Now that point is both a canonical-literary one and a theological one. The promise is not artificially juxtaposed by an editor, but, I suggest, the hope is both permitted and required only by the suffering faced and claimed by the exiles. In Rom. 5:3, Paul shares a key insight of this entire tradition: "Suffering... produces hope." The suffering of exiles, the *embrace of pain* made possible by *critique of ideology*, permits the announcement of newness. The poetry of Second Isaiah, thus, is not lightly offered by someone who stands outside the grief wrought by First Isaiah but by someone who has lived into that trouble and there (and only there) finds a word of hope to speak; that is, the hopeful poetry of Second Isaiah is scarred and is spoken by one who knows.[21] In that way Second Isaiah theologically is seen to be organically derived from First Isaiah.

The response of 49:15 ("Can a woman forget her suckling child?") to the complaint of 49:14 is the most poignant offered. Such an offer of hope through a radical metaphor is not made from the outside, but from within the pain. This speaker of this good news knows about the abandonment, about the utter risk, and about the late discovery of a mark on the hand (v. 16) that shows to whom Israel belongs when all seems lost.[22]

Gottes," *ZTK* 68 (1972): 290–303. Perlitt makes clear that the entire future depends on this free speech of God against the past that is closed and hopeless. Edgar W. Conrad, in "Second Isaiah and the Priestly Oracle of Salvation," *ZAW* 93 (1981): 243, correctly observes that "Second Isaiah's speech as a whole is intimately related to ideas, motifs and expressions exhibited in the Psalms of Lament." Conrad sees the relationship of this to exilic reality.

21. Amos Wilder, in "A Hard Death," *Poetry* 107 (1965–66), writes about death and new life: "Accept no mitigation / but be instructed at the null point; / the zero breeds new algebra" (pp. 168–69).

22. I am indebted to two of my students, Linda Chenowith and Rosalie Berkeley, for helping me understand the radical character of the metaphor here of a nursing mother, a radicalness I would have missed for obvious reasons. Not only does the suckling child need the mother, but the mother needs the suckling. If the mother

I suggest that the enigmatic Servant Song of 52:13—53:12 is structured in the same way. It is not an easy assurance, but it is a "therefore" of assurance (53:12) wrought only through the remainder of the painful poem. We speak readily about Second Isaiah and "the suffering servant" being the high point of Israel's faith. But that point is not reached from the outside. It is reached by the remarkable insight that the suffering, which seemed to be only punishment, turns out to be vocation, that once the cover of ideology has been broken, as it was in the words of Isaiah or in the events of 587 B.C.E., suffering need not be shunned but can be received as a way to live that opens the future.[23]

3. One other factor in Second Isaiah is widely recognized but may be differently understood. More than any other speaker in the exile, Second Isaiah returns to the old traditions.[24] He does that in a variety of ways. On the one hand, he seems to take the exodus as a type and urge that the deliverance now supersedes the old event. I think there is some of that imagery, even if Childs and Clements be followed about "former things/new things." On the other hand, with reference to Abraham (51:2-4), Sarah (54:1-3), Noah (54:9), and David (55:3), he uses the old memory to reread the present and discern power for new life.[25]

Theodore M. Ludwig's comments are helpful in letting us understand what is done here. It would have been possible to decide that exile is evidence that the old tradition had failed. But the tradition is taken by Second Isaiah not to have failed but to be powerful and definitional, only in a new way. Why is that? I suggest it is because the ideology critique destroyed the cover-up so that Israel could return to its real story. Under the pressure of contrivance, Israel had come to believe a false story about itself. And now, in the abandonment of false stories, the real story can be reappropriated with authority and

---

should forget the suckling child for any extended period, the pain of not nursing would be severe and the mother must again have the child nurse. One can hardly imagine a more freighted metaphor to articulate Yahweh's share in the pain of alienation with Israel in exile; that is, the mother cannot forget, even if she wants to and wills to.

23. On the break of suffering that matters decisively, see Emil L. Fackenheim, "New Hearts and the Old Covenant: Some Possibilities of a Fraternal Jewish-Christian Reading of the Jewish Bible Today," in *Divine Helmsman* (see chap. 2, n. 28), 191–205, and more fully his statement, *To Mend the World* (see chap. 2, n. 6).

24. That point has been seen, especially by Gerhard von Rad. See also the works already cited of Anderson (see n. 4) and Ludwig (n. 6).

25. On the shape and function of the flood narrative in Second Isaiah, see David M. Gunn, "Deutero-Isaiah and the Flood," *JBL* 94 (1975): 494–508.

power. In the vulnerability of the exile, the recent phony story was found inadequate and so the old story was reembraced and found to have resilient and surprising power. That discovery, however, depended on (*a*) the exposure of the more recent story as false, (*b*) a social context of vulnerability, and (*c*) a poet enough engaged in the experience to contact the power of the memory.[26]

So I argue that *critique of ideology* permits *embrace of pain* and causes new contact with the long-denied memories that can yield life.[27] This move from critique to ideology to embrace of pain is to be correlated with Childs's "former things" and "new things" and with Clements's "threat and hope," except that I want to insist, much more than they seem to, that the first experience is fundamental to the happening of the second. There is no touch of hopeful pain unless there is a critique of that ideology that cuts us off from memory, requires us to deny hurt, and actively censors every complaint.[28]

If the tradition of Isaiah be taken as *model* as well as *text* (and every authoritative text is a model for reality), we learn important things about ministry.[29] If we are able to do ideology critique well, we shall have our community placed in crisis. People begin to notice the exploitation they had not yet experienced. We shall have a new sense of the incongruity, ambiguity, and contradiction that the ideology covers over. And some of us will be angry, some of us filled with remorse, some of us smitten with grief. It is my judgment that in our generation, as with the generation between chapters 39 and 40, very much is at stake at this point. It could be that we will cling to the ideology, nullify the critique, banish pain, and censor lament. But the pastoral

---

26. Second Isaiah, in that regard, practiced what Paul Ricoeur has called "a hermeneutic of retrieval." But that can only happen after there is "a hermeneutic of suspicion," which Israel had rhetorically experienced in First Isaiah and historically experienced in exile. For a most suggestive statement of Ricoeur's constructs of suspicion and retrieval, see David Tracy, "Religious Values" (see chap. 6, n. 14). Tracy proposes that after the Holocaust, Christians as well as Jews must be engaged with retrieval of the Jewish dimension of their faith. He does not say so, but no doubt that is possible only as there is suspicion about scholastic theology, which has covered over that Jewishness. There may be in this something of an analogy to the situation faced by Second Isaiah, now ready for retrieval.

27. Following Johannes Baptist Metz, Tracy ("Religious Values," 90) calls this "the 'dangerous' prophetic memories" (though in that statement he refers to stories of Jesus). But the point can be made with Israel's newness as well. It is because they are dangerous that ideology has covered them over, and only pain embraced can release that waiting danger.

28. Childs, *Introduction*, 329; and Clements, "The Unity," 126–27.

29. On the function of a text in modeling a new world, see the comments of Clines, *I, He, We*, 59–65.

task of the community of faith, if this is a model for pastoral action, is to articulate the grief, respond in hope wrought precisely out of the grief, and enter again the stories that have power for life. Suspicion and retrieval offer a way not only into the tradition of Isaiah, but through Isaiah into our own cultural crisis of faith.

After First Isaiah, we tend to take Second Isaiah so much for granted. But it may not have turned out that way. That Second Isaiah is the next thing after First Isaiah, that *retrieval* follows *suspicion*, that *promise* follows *judgment*, is by no means sure in advance. Thus, the words of Second Isaiah in their place are as unexpected and nearly as subversive as those of First Isaiah, for he argues that in suffering, only in suffering, comes hope. Isa. 45:9-13 is evidence that Second Isaiah had opponents. Very likely they were the proponents of the old ideology who did not believe that suffering is a mode into hope, who did not believe that contrived reality had failed, and who did not discern that the public embrace of pain could lead anywhere. So Second Isaiah is not a natural or obvious next step. It emerged out of conflict, and it established the linkage that is always to be in dispute. Thus, the linkage of First and Second Isaiah is wrought by a powerful intellectual act, an act of enormous faith, and a full embrace of painful vulnerability. The astonishing voice of comfort comes in the midst of a long season of "none to comfort."

V

That leaves us with Third Isaiah (56–66). The issues around those chapters are more problematic and scholars are less sure. Clements is concerned primarily with 40–55 and really does not substantively address the canonical position of 56–66. Childs suggests that Third Isaiah in its canonical placement functions in relation to 1–39 just as does 40–55, as eschatological promise. Thus, neither Childs nor Clements in fact splits Third Isaiah from Second Isaiah. I do agree with Childs, against Walther Zimmerli, that 56–66 is not "spiritualizing," which will be evident in what follows.[30] But I explore what might be discerned if it is treated as a discrete element.

The most thorough analysis we have of Third Isaiah is that of Paul D. Hanson, more recently followed closely by Elizabeth Achtemeier.[31] Hanson's construct is that this literature is the voice of

---

30. Childs, *Introduction*, 333–34.
31. Hanson, *Dawn* (see chap. 5, n. 18). His proposal has been subjected to vigorous

the have-not visionaries, who are "world-weary" against the pragmatic claims of the priestly aristocracy, who are mostly in control (cf.
Ezekiel 40–48). That is, the literature reflects those who present an
alternative scenario of a new world, alternative to the present ordering that leaves this group disadvantaged and marginalized. That
much I find helpful in Hanson. But unfortunately, his analysis is not
helpful for the canonical question we are addressing, namely, the
relation of this material to Isaiah 1–55. On the one hand, Hanson
does not address the connection at all. On the other hand, Childs
lumps this material with 40–55. Neither faces the *canonical* question
in light of the *critical* issues before us.

So I suggest that 56–66 has a very different linkage to 40–55. It
is Second Isaiah that makes Third Isaiah possible. If Second Isaiah
is about the public embrace of pain as the way to return to the old
stories, then Third Isaiah may reflect the results of this. The *public
embrace of pain releases social imagination*, that is, gives the community
freedom, energy, and courage to envision the world alternatively
arranged. Hanson has seen that this is indeed an envisioning literature, an act of social imagination about how the world could be.
But, beyond Hanson, I suggest it is the very act of exile, lamentation,
guilt, and grief that now is overcome by the act of embrace. This is
indeed the payoff of "the new algebra" that has emerged from "the
zero" of Amos Wilder.

One cannot move directly from 1–39 to 56–66, as though 56–66
were just an alternative form of 40–55, as Childs seems to suggest.
The literature is very different and quite clearly serves a different
rhetorical agenda. One cannot move directly from an *assault on ideology* to an *alternative imagination*. One can move there only through
the embrace of pain that unlooses the old givens and lets the maps
be redrawn. The purpose of managed ideology is to be oriented toward "one-world," to insist that "the present system is the solution,"
to insist that the world is presently organized in the only way it could
be organized. Every totalitarian regime makes this claim. And when
we are satiated, we are inclined to believe it, uncritically. It is only the
reality of pain that enables one to look again, to think an alternative
thought, to notice that not everything is accounted for, and to see
that alternative ways could be radically different.[32]

---

criticism by Ackroyd, "Apocalyptic in Its Social Setting," *Int* 30 (1976): 412–15. See
also Elizabeth Achtemeier, *The Community and Message of Isaiah 56–66* (Minneapolis:
Augsburg Pub. House, 1982).
    32. It is liberated imagination that permits a new world. On the function of such

When pain is embraced, the old stories can power new visions, and that is what is happening in Third Isaiah. Israel is created a new people with remarkable imaginative energy. But the royal ideology effectively suppressed that imagination as an engine for social alternatives, and it took the pain of exile to once again permit and legitimate that imagination.

These examples of released social imagination in Third Isaiah may be noted:

56:3-8   This passage envisions the gathering of the foreigners, eunuchs, and outcasts—a remarkable alternative vision when the counterthemes of narrowness, purity, and ritual acceptability were strongly under way in the same period.[33] But in the face of such censorship, this community dreamed its dream and recited its poetry.

58:6-7   This passage offers an unthinkable, unutterable thought. It translates the ritual act of fasting into feeding the hungry and giving the homeless a home. Both the notions of new fasting and hospitality are visions of a quite alternative kind.[34]

61:1-4   This passage is best known for its citation in Luke 4:16-17. But here as well as in Luke, it is a vision of an alternative world that apparently is linked to the Jubilee year, a return into Israel's most radical memory of release and redemption.[35]

Note well that these are not social programs or specific proposals. Rather, they are acts of public imagination that still need to be shaped for implementation. Positively, they are acts that push back the frontiers so that things not before thought are now legitimately

---

imagination, Ricoeur, in *The Philosophy of Paul Ricoeur*, ed. Charles E. Reagan and David Steward (Boston: Beacon Press, 1978), writes: "It is in the heart of our imagination that we let the Event happen, before we may convert our heart and tighten our will" (p. 245); cf. pp. 231, 237–38. See Frederick Herzog, "Liberation and Imagination," *Int* 32 (1978): 227–41, on imagination as a dimension of liberation.

33. This is the main import of Hanson's analysis.

34. On a departure from the norms of social purity, see Fernando Belo, *Materialist* (see chap. 4, n. 34), chap. 1. This motif of home for the homeless is greatly illuminated in sociological concreteness by John Elliott, *A Home for the Homeless: A Sociological Exegesis of 1 Peter* (Philadelphia: Fortress Press, 1981).

35. On a postexilic return to the vision of the early federation concerning social organization, see William J. Dumbrell, "In Those Days There Was No King in Israel; Every Man Did What Was Right in His Own Eyes," *JSOT* 25 (1983): 23–33. On the function of this vision in the Gospel of Luke, see Sanders, "Isaiah in Luke," *Int* 36 (1982): 144–55, and the work of Sharon H. Ringe, which he cites in n. 13.

in view. Critically, they are an assault on all controlled thinking that insists that the world is presently organized in the only way that it could be.

No doubt the most powerful such anticipation of an alternative world is in 65:17-25. That poem bespeaks an alternative earth, an alternative heaven, an alternative Jerusalem. But the vision does not spiritualize. The theme of an alternative Jerusalem is sounded already in 1:26-27. The alternative city for which this poem waits is not that of whoring economics and exploitative politics, but it is a city of equitable advisers and fair judges, of righteousness and faithfulness, of justice. It is a city where there will be disarmament (2:2-4), and there will be an end to hostility (11:6-9). The poem imagines a city free of "weeping and distress" (65:19), no more violence and terror, no more the kind of poverty that leads to high infant mortality rate (65:20). In vv. 21-22, we are offered a "futility curse," but now the genre is used for social reconstruction.[36] Another eats the fruit or another inhabits the house not because of a "sinister force" or because of social chaos but because of a rapacious, confiscatory government policy. Thus, the dream is for a government that does not oppress, precisely the opposite social reality to that presented by First Isaiah. So the new age will be one of longevity (65:22-23), harmony (v. 25), and the presence of God upon the earth (v. 24). Clearly, this poetic act of social imagination is not a prediction or a "futuring," as modern social sciences are wont to do. For these scenarios from the poets are not extrapolations. Rather, they come out of a discontinuity of pain and exile in which an underived newness is entertained as social possibility.

There is much more of such imagination offered, but I wish to make only three points about it:

1. This social imagination is *this-worldly, earthly, and political.* It anticipates a thoroughly transformed organization of social power. The images are characteristically social, political, and economic. This corresponds to the social criticism of First Isaiah.

2. This social imagination is *no substitute for policy implementation* (which is left to such as Nehemiah).[37] But it is my urging that social

---

36. On "futility curses," see Delbert R. Hillers, *Treaty-Curses* (see chap. 3, n. 10). Hillers does not raise in any sustained way the question of the social function of these curses, which is the pertinent question for my analysis.

37. See my discussion of Nehemiah 5 as an example of programmatic implementation of an envisioned alternative social possibility, Brueggemann, "Reflections

policy depends on social imagination and will never go beyond it.[38] Social imagination—the freedom, energy, and courage to envision an alternative arrangement—is the arena, framework, warrant, and engine for specific social policy. Indeed, where there is no vision, the people might not perish, but they will simply be administered in a contrived world.

3. Social imagination of the kind done in Third Isaiah is *possible only because of the embrace of pain* done in Second Isaiah. I think that is experientially the case. As long as we are embodiments of success, prosperity, and self-sufficiency, we cannot entertain alternatives. Social criticism can lead to contact with pain that destabilizes enough to be amazed, and what is evident experientially is also presented canonically.

VI

I have tried to reflect on a *canonical* understanding of Isaiah in relation to the *social dynamics* that might be correlated with elements of the text. So far as I know, I have stayed within the lines of the canonical proposal of Childs and Clements. But I have tried to see what kinds of social dynamics might match this canonical shape, although perhaps Childs and Clements would resist such a matching. What I have in mind is that the tradition of Isaiah, in the words of Paul Ricoeur, may be "limit-expression," to be matched by the "limit-experience" I have suggested here.[39] If the canonical shape is matched to social experience, I suggest these elements of correlation:

Isaiah 1–39:   *a critique of ideology*;

Isaiah 40–55:   *a public embrace of pain that leads to hope*;

Isaiah 56–66:   *a release of social imagination.*

Thus, the parts of the Isaiah tradition are dynamically related to each other. Each is thus better understood out of the preceding,

---

of Biblical Understandings of Property," *International Review of Missions* 54 (1975): 354–61.

38. On the "gift of imagination" in relation to policies for war and peace, see the statement of Leonard Bernstein, "War Is Not Inevitable," *Fellowship* 47 (1981): 3–4. The absence of imagination makes present policies always seem "inevitable."

39. For the constructs "limit-expression" and "limit-experience," see Ricoeur, "Biblical Hermeneutics" (see chap. 4, n. 47), 122–43.

which permitted it and/or the following element permitted by it. I do not suggest, however, that each Isaiah is fully slotted this way. Childs and Clements are not unaware that some elements of social imagination are present in 1–39, so my utilization of such a broad sweep applies only in the sense that their own canonical shaping applies.[40]

Along with a dynamic sense of canonical shape, I have proposed that this canonical structure provides a model for the ongoing life of the community of faith; that is, the situation of ministry out of such texts has not changed. Out of this analysis may come an awareness that there is still need for the socially strategic moves of *critique of ideology, embrace of pain,* and *release of social imagination*. Each step along the way is an act that intends to subvert the present ordering of the world. The first subverts ideology that does not want to be exposed. The second subverts a denial of pain that keeps people hopeless. The third subverts a worldview that denies any alternative is possible. So I offer this statement as a heuristic suggestion of how subversive are the book of Isaiah and the community that may take the text canonically.[41]

---

40. Childs, *Introduction*, 331; Clements, "The Unity," 121.

41. Following Ricoeur, the literary act is *redescription,* the political result is *subversion,* and the theological intent is *destruction of the idols,* which then permits the true God to speak.

14

The Epistemological Crisis of Israel's Two Histories (Jeremiah 9:22-23)

I

TWO DEVELOPMENTS IN recent Old Testament scholarship, when brought together, may illuminate the words and ministry of Jeremiah:

First, recent emphasis on wisdom studies has shown that the sapiential tradition is not at all peripheral to the reflective life of Israel.[1] Wisdom studies are vexed by difficult questions, largely definitional in character. Depending on definitions, we may broadly locate wisdom influence at many points in the Old Testament, or with James L. Crenshaw, we may take a narrow view and resist the notion that sapiential influences can be identified outside conventional wisdom literature.[2]

This chapter does not intend to engage those sticky debates in relation to Jeremiah. Although attention has been given to the possibility of wisdom influences in Amos and Isaiah,[3] only the most

---

1. The literature of wisdom studies is extensive and well known. See the bibliography by Crenshaw, *Studies* (see chap. 5, n. 23), 46–60. Special note should be taken of the work of Crenshaw, Roland E. Murphy, Gerhard von Rad, and Walther Zimmerli, and of the phrase of R. Norman Whybray, "the intellectual tradition of Israel."

2. Crenshaw, "Method in Determining Wisdom Influence upon 'Historical' Literature," *JBL* 88 (1969): 129–42, reprinted in *Studies*, 481–94.

3. See Samuel Terrien, "Amos and Wisdom," in *Israel's Prophetic Heritage* (see chap. 8, n. 64), 108–15; Hans Walter Wolff, *Amos the Prophet* (Philadelphia: Fortress Press, 1973); and J. William Whedbee, *Isaiah* (see chap. 13, n. 10).

superficial attention has thus far been given to Jeremiah.[4] It seems likely that Jeremiah himself utilized the style and imagery of the wisdom teachers.[5] But lacking definitions, that will not be insisted upon here.

More important is the awareness that the appearance of wisdom influences (wherever they appear), of necessity, raises important epistemological issues. When the conventions of a society seem to function, when life is coherent and manageable, when all the definers of reality agree on their perception, epistemological questions are screened out and need not even be raised, much less agreed upon.[6] It is likely that most of the wisdom teachers, at least the ones usually stereotyped by that label, function with such an epistemological consensus. Predictably, their teaching need not be very risky or very profound. They could work from "assured results."

It is when the conventions of society collapse, when the consensus disappears, and when life is experienced as incoherent that the community is pressed to reexamine its epistemological presuppositions and deal with the fundamental issues of how the known is known and what is known.[7] I suggest in this chapter that Jeremiah

---

4. See the sparse suggestions of Johannes Lindblom, "Wisdom in the Old Testament Prophets," in *Wisdom in Israel and in the Ancient Near East*, ed. Martin Noth and D. W. Thomas, VTSup, no. 3 (Leiden: Brill, 1955), 193–200.

5. See William McKane, "Jeremiah 13:12-14: A Problematic Proverb," in *Israelite Wisdom* (see chap. 13, n. 14), 107–20. Several matters will require a quite new perspective on the question: (1) James Muilenburg, in "Baruch the Scribe," in *Proclamation and Presence*, ed. John I. Durham and Joshua R. Porter (London: SCM Press, 1970), 215–38, has opened new possibilities in understanding those parts of Jeremiah that may be tilted toward sapiential influences. More radically, Gunther Wanke, in *Untersuchungen zur sogenannten Baruchschrift*, BZAW, no. 122 (Berlin: de Gruyter, 1971), has called into question our usual presuppositions about Baruch. (2) The matter of Jeremiah's relation to Deuteronomic circles of tradition must be rethought in light of the work of Moshe Weinfeld, *Deuteronomy and the Deuteronomic School* (Oxford: Clarendon Press, 1972), with the prospect of wisdom influences. (3) It is now clear that the rigid distinction of categories among various traditions cannot be sustained in the neat manner of Sigmund Mowinckel. For all these reasons, new categories of interpretation will need to be found for Jeremiah studies that, among other things, take wisdom influences into account.

6. In the following references to epistemological issues, I am working with the constructs especially articulated by Peter L. Berger, *Sacred Canopy* (see chap. 2, n. 5); Thomas Luckmann, *The Invisible Religion* (New York: Macmillan Co., 1967); and Berger and Luckmann, *The Social Construction of Reality* (Garden City, N.Y.: Doubleday & Co., 1966). Pertinent also is the notion of "life-world" from Alfred Schutz, *The Structures of the Life-World* (Evanston, Ill.: Northwestern University Press, 1973). The wisdom teachers reflected in the positive teaching of Proverbs presumed a life-world in which there was a major consensus that needed to be neither challenged nor defended.

7. See the discussion of anomie by Robert Merton, *Social Theory and Social Structure*

lived precisely in a time of collapse of the consensus when the epistemological issues were most raw. The wisdom tradition that he
apparently criticizes likely belonged to the royal definers of reality who continued to operate by a now-discredited consensus. And
conversely, Jeremiah (perhaps characteristically for a prophet) insists that epistemological questions must be raised that will seriously
challenge the illusionary regnant consensus and the royal definition
of reality.[8] Thus, I suggest, we may circumvent the problem of an
adequate definition of wisdom if we discern the clash between those
who presume an epistemological consensus (wisdom teachers, perhaps, but surely royal ideologues) and those who press the hard,
unanswered epistemological issues (Jeremiah and, in my view, the
prophets generally).[9]

If wisdom is characterized in some way as the deposit of the best
observations coming from a long history of reflection on experience,
then it is likely that this epistemology will settle for things that enhance continuity.[10] The substance of such a deposit will inevitably be
conservative in its support of things as they are.[11] It is the task of the

---

(Glencoe, Ill.: Free Press, 1957), chaps. 4, 5. Jeremiah clearly spoke in a context of
anomie that was derived from Israel's ineffective ways of knowing. Crenshaw has been
especially sensitive to these matters in his concern for wisdom and theodicy.

8. Kenneth Wilson Underwood, in *The Church, the University, and Social Party*, 2
vols. (Middletown, Conn.: Wesleyan University Press, 1969), has shown how the crucial task of ministry is the raising of epistemological issues. It means to be concerned
with "systems of knowledge and power" (vol. 1, p. 126). It is clear that this was the
crucial task in the time of Jeremiah as in the present time, when the old consensus has
collapsed. It may well be that Hosea and Jeremiah, both of whom stress "knowing,"
are the very ones who have in Israel discerned the depth of the crisis and are aware
that any lesser question is futile.

9. I do not intend to utilize any narrow, precise definition of "wisdom"; nor do
I presume any necessarily close relation between royal court and an identifiable wisdom school. Rather, I am concerned more broadly with the whole way in which an
established community of opinion preserves, discerns, knows, and decides. Wisdom
both affirms and presents a critique of this unexamined intellectual climate. My impression is that scholarship may miss these urgent issues if it focuses on narrow and
precise definitions and misses the epistemological crisis. My approach here addresses
what Crenshaw calls "wisdom thinking." This approach enables us to take seriously
the stress on falseness, so well underscored by Thomas W. Overholt, *The Threat of
Falsehood*, SBT, no. 2/16 (London: SCM Press, 1970). Šqr does not refer to concrete
acts but to a wrong discernment of all of life.

10. Whybray, in *The Intellectual Tradition in the Old Testament*, BZAW, no. 135 (New
York: de Gruyter, 1974), has advanced the discussion by speaking more inclusively
of an "intellectual tradition" rather than a wisdom movement. I urge that wisdom
be recognized as the consensus by which established order sustains and legitimates
itself. Dennis McCarthy has suggested the phrase "intellectual patrimony" (oral
communication).

11. See Robert Gordis, "Social Background" (see chap. 3, n. 17); and Brian W.

prophet, in such a context, not simply to protest such a deposit but to raise fresh epistemological questions that may have been screened out by the not disinterested tradition of perception.[12]

II

Second, in addition to the widespread attention to wisdom in the Old Testament, it is also clear from recent study that we may identify two histories in the community of Israel, each powered by a different memory, each providing a different lens through which life may be experienced. One such history we may characterize as *Mosaic-covenantal*. It focused upon the radical intrusion of Yahweh through saving events on behalf of the historically powerless. That history is of course borne by the great succession of Moses, Joshua, and Samuel, and it continued to inform the prophets. That history experienced and presented the God of Israel as an intruder who was continually calling establishment reality into question. The tradition referred consistently to Yahweh's intention for freedom and justice, which characterized Yahweh's coming to Israel. George E. Mendenhall has articulated this in sociological categories to suggest that this history powered a people's revolt against tyrannical urban government.[13] It represented a radical critique that prevented the absolutizing of the present arrangement. It also yielded a promise that an alternative social arrangement is yet to be given.

The other history we may characterize as *Davidic-royal*. It was shaped by the conviction of Yahweh's abiding, sustaining presence in behalf of legitimated political-cultural institutions, especially the royal house and derivatively the royal temple. Whereas the first history is radically concerned for *justice*, this royal history is more concerned for *order* ("peace and prosperity"), and it relies on the institutions that are designed to create and maintain that order.

Kovacs, "Is There a Class-Ethic in Proverbs?" in *Essays in Old Testament Ethics*, ed. Crenshaw and J. T. Willis (New York: Ktav Pub. House, 1974), 173–89.

12. On the relation of interest and perception in hermeneutics, see Frederick Herzog, "Liberation Hermeneutic as Ideology Critique?" *Int* 28 (1974): 387–403; José Miranda, *Marx* (see chap. 7, n. 26); and Roy Sano, "Neo-Orthodoxy and Ethnic Liberation Theology," *Christianity and Crisis* 35 (1975): 258–64.

13. Mendenhall's programmatic statement is in *Tenth Generation* (see chap. 1, n. 15), but he had indicated the major line of his argument already in "The Hebrew Conquest of Palestine," *BA* 25 (1962): 66–87; reprinted in *BA Reader*, no. 3 (Garden City, N.Y.: Doubleday & Co., 1970), 100–20.

This Davidic-royal history can be assessed in more than one way. Read positively from a political perspective, the development of enduring social institutions enabled Israel to survive and develop as a responsible historical entity. Theologically, it permitted an institution to be a vehicle for a vision of a messianic reality expressed, for example, in Psalm 72. This monarchial reality provided a guarantee of a humane order in a social world of hostility and threat. Such an institutionally self-conscious order of course needed a management mentality to sustain itself and to preside over its resources. It also needed protection (might), resources (riches), and technical skill (wisdom) to accomplish its goals.[14]

This same history can also be assessed negatively. Mendenhall, most critically, has characterized this history as "the paganization of Israel."[15] Bureaucracy, harem, standing army, tax districts, and temple are not only institutions that concretize a social vision. They are also ways by which pagan, that is, noncovenantal, patterns of life were adapted from Israel's neighbors.[16] This radical adaptation caused the abandonment of a certain vision of history, the loss of a covenantal notion of God and humanity, and a forgetting of the messianic vision the monarchy was intended to guarantee. In short, all the epistemological questions were settled in terms of self-serving continuity. Proper protection became a way of authoritarian management. Necessary skill in governance became a way of preventing change. The consensus of the new institution created a context in which human questions could no longer be raised.[17]

Now it may be that Mendenhall has overstated the case. It is likely that this Jerusalem version of history and reality also has a more positive value as the only possibility of cultural continuity and cre-

---

14. That list is not so different from the conclusion of Mendenhall, in "The Monarchy," *Int* 29 (1975): 156, that "in any given culture, ideology, social organization and technology" are both essential and interrelated. The triad of Jer. 9:22 must be understood not in terms of moral virtues but in terms of sociological realities.

15. Mendenhall, "Monarchy," 160, and "Samuel's Broken Rib," in *No Famine in the Land*, ed. James Flanagan and Anita W. Robinson (Missoula, Mont.: Scholars Press, 1975), 67.

16. See the primary evidence and example of Isaac Mendelsohn, "Samuel's Denunciation of Kingship in Light of the Akkadian Documents from Ugarit," *BASOR* 143 (1956): 17–22.

17. See the statement of Norman K. Gottwald, "Biblical Theology or Biblical Sociology?" *Radical Religion* 2 (1975): 42–57, showing the political implications of some forms of religious consensus.

ativity in Israel, but we may not miss the high cost in terms of human freedom and justice.[18]

These two histories, Mosaic-covenantal and Davidic-royal, continue in tension with each other all through Israel's story. During the period of the united monarchy, it is likely that the rival priestly orders carry these rival traditions. Frank M. Cross has indicated that the Aaronite order, perhaps linked to Hebron and Bethel, was in conflict with the Mushite order associated perhaps with Nob and Shiloh.[19]

In the period of the divided monarchy, it seems likely that the same two consciousnesses are in tension, borne by the dynasty and the prophets.[20] The enduring conflict between them surfaces in the unresolved epistemological question of what is known and how it is known. The royal (sapiential)[21] tradition, inevitably conservative, fashions a life-world that is essentially settled. What is valued—that is, true and life-giving—consists in the resources managed by the king and his regime. Alternatively, the Mosaic-covenantal tradition is characteristically in tension, as it finds the core of a legitimate epistemology in the exodus-sojourn-Sinai memories, stories of intervention by Yahweh on behalf of the politically, historically disenfranchised and against the Egyptian royal reality. The royal consciousness developed a consensus that screened out such an unbearable concern. It was unbearable because, on the one hand, it kept raising to consciousness those very elements in society that had been declared nonexistent.[22] On the other hand, it was unbearable because it articulated a freedom and sov-

---

18. The royal consciousness is never primarily concerned about such matters. In that context one might observe the "interest" served in the program of B. F. Skinner, *Beyond Freedom and Dignity* (New York: Alfred A. Knopf, 1971).

19. Cross, *Canaanite Myth* (see chap. 7, n. 7), 195–215. See also the development from Cross's suggestion by Baruch Halpern, "Levitic Participation in the Reform Cult of Jereboam I," *JBL* 95 (1976): 31–42.

20. See Rolf Rendtorff, "Reflections on the Early History of Prophecy in Israel," in *History and Hermeneutic*, ed. Robert Walter Funk, *JTC* 4 (New York: Harper & Row, 1967), 14–34. Rendtorff explores the dialectical relation of king and prophet.

21. It is my judgment and presupposition in this chapter that sapiential tendencies, broadly identified, can best be understood in relation to the royal consciousness. For the purposes of this chapter, I do not regard the more precise and technical issues of definition to be pertinent. Nor do I wish to deny the force of the "clan hypothesis." But it seems clear that so far as Jeremiah is concerned, he deals with a royal phenomenon.

22. On the royal attitude to the peasant, see John Martin Halligan, "The Role of the Peasant in the Amarna Period," in *SBL Seminar Papers* (Missoula, Mont: Scholars Press, 1976), 155–71. The power of the throne is enormous in denying history to the powerless.

ereignty for God that would not be domesticated by the royal apparatus.

This sustained tension between the two histories, as Paul D. Hanson has now shown, continues into Israel's later history.[23] Hanson has labeled the two opinions as "pragmatic" and "visionary." As he characterizes the two, they are radically distinguished by their epistemology. The pragmatists are those who benefit from the way things currently are. They give religious legitimacy to the present arrangement of realized eschatology. The visionaries are the "world-weary" who have been treated unfairly and so dare to risk and hope. They hold together the tragedy of human denial with a conviction of God's sovereign freedom, which will lead to a new future, calling the present into question.

Not in any of these instances is the issue resolved: not in the united monarchy with Zadok and Abiathar, not in the divided monarchy with kings and prophets, not in the later period with the accommodators and hopers. It is always a question of *singular reliance* on Yahweh or a more *prudent* embrace of the gifts of culture that seem more secure and are not always obviously incompatible with Yahweh.[24] The question of *prudence* and *singular reliance* focuses the epistemological issue. It is that issue that is addressed in this discussion of Jeremiah and wisdom in Jer. 9:22-23.

III

Jeremiah is placed at a critical juncture in the ongoing tension between these two histories. The international history of the time suggested radical changes and disappearance of the old certainties. The internal political history of Judah is characterized by vacillation in foreign policy (with unrelieved fascination with Egypt), by an extraordinary sequence of kings who could not develop a sustained policy, and by a peculiar reform movement that impacted at least the king and no doubt his very particular constituency.

Jeremiah's perception of his people and his leaders is that things had gone utterly sour. Or, in our terms, the Davidic-royal history had

---

23. Hanson, *Dawn* (see chap. 5, n. 18).

24. There can be little doubt that prudence is crucial to a sapiential approach to life. What is apparent in the sociological studies cited is that such prudence is never politically or socially disinterested. Prudence is concerned not to disturb the present ordering. Amos 5:13 is characteristic in that regard.

reached a point of irredeemable failure. The very consciousness that appeared dominant and seemed to have co-opted the Mosaic tradition had failed. The prophet is repelled by what he sees. For him, it is a question whether the royal consciousness can be penetrated at all. The royal consciousness, secure in its own illusionary perceptual consensus, continued its risky game of self-deception (cf. 6:14; 8:11), engaging in the traditional royal ploys of purchased justice, denied humanness, and double-tongued diplomacy. In that make-believe world, the royal apparatus could finally overcome or outlast every threat and question. Even though the royal arrangement potentially may have been the vehicle for a peculiar social vision, it had by this time become concerned only for self-securing and self-justification, and, indeed, for survival.

Jeremiah's sense of the history of his people with Yahweh was so different that he could hardly communicate. He raised questions that lay outside the grasp of his royal contemporaries. Informed by a tradition of the freedom and sovereignty of God, who could create and destroy, who could begin things and end things,[25] he took as his program that Yahweh will "build/plant, tear down/pluck up."[26] Kings in Israel seldom recognized that there had been beginnings when God would plant and build—because the royal reality appeared to be ordained forever. The royal perception was that there was no history before it, because it is the source of history. And surely there could be no ending, never plucking up and tearing down, because royal reality will endure. The royal arrangement fully contains history, and things will continue to be as they have been. Jeremiah insists that there are radical turns, pasts to move from, and futures to embrace. Kings know no past or future, but only "now" is to be defended and celebrated.

Jeremiah translated his alternative covenantal vision into an alternative political reality. Babylon is called and ordained by Yahweh to cause an end to a royal history that presumed it would go forever:

> Behold, I will send for all the tribes of the north, says the Lord, and
> for Nebuchadnezzar the king of Babylon, my servant, and I will bring

---

25. There can be little doubt that Jeremiah belongs to the circle of northern tradition fed by Mosaic memories and expressed in the traditions of Hosea and Deuteronomy.

26. Variations on the theme occur in 1:10; 12:14-17; 18:7-9; 24:6; 31:28; 32:10; 42:10; 45:4. Cf. Robert Bach, "Bauen und Pflanzen," in *Studien zur Theologie der alttestamentlichen Überlieferungen*, eds. Rendtorff and Klaus Koch (Neukirchen-Vluyn: Neukirchener Verlag, 1961), 7–32.

them against this land and its inhabitants, and against all these nations round about. (Jer. 25:9)[27]

That is more than kings can take and more than the royal conscious-ness can ever receive. It must be dismissed as a "weakening of the hands" of the king (38:4).

So the issue is joined between the two histories. It is joined visibly, for Jeremiah is in deathly conflict and great danger from those who cannot bear his word (11:21-23).[28] It is also joined internally, for Jeremiah knows in his person the wrenching of the two histories in conflict.[29] In his person, there is anguish over valuing what is, deeper anguish over abandoning it for the sake of Yahweh's freedom and sovereignty. Jeremiah anguishes because he himself is not sure which history is true history. He cannot easily walk away from royal reality that must at times appear to be the only real history; yet, he is deeply sure that that epistemology is based on an unreality.[30] That wisdom is based on a consensus that has no correspondence to reality.

IV

My suggestion in this chapter is that in 9:22-23, these two issues—that is, (1) the problem of wisdom and the epistemological crisis and (2) the two alternative histories in Israel—come together and pro-vide in this text a focal point from which the work of Jeremiah can

27. See also 27:6 and 43:10. Although textual problems may lessen the claim of these particular texts, as Werner E. Lemke has argued, in "Nebuchadnezzar, My Servant," *CBQ* 28 (1966): 45–50, there is little question that this expectation from Babylon is central to Jeremiah's discernment of Yahweh's will for Judah. Cf. Overholt, "King Nebuchadnezzar in the Jeremiah Tradition," *CBQ* 30 (1968): 39–48.

28. In an unpublished paper, "Jeremiah and the 'Men of Anatot,'" S. Dean McBride, Jr., has suggested that the men of Anathoth are not among the villagers of his home community but must be located "within the Jerusalem establishment of the prophet's day, particularly among prominent Temple personnel." Such a judg-ment would strengthen the intensity of the conflict between the two perceptions of reality.

29. It is not necessary to pursue the question of the meaning of Jeremiah's "la-ments" here. See also Henning Graf Reventlow, in *Liturgie* (see chap. 3, n. 8), 205–57. Even if Reventlow is not correct about their being public liturgical pieces, he is surely correct in seeing that the struggle concerns not a private problem but anguish over the course and end of Israel's public life. On that anguish as it reflects an alternative consciousness, see Abraham J. Heschel, *Prophets* (see chap. 2, n. 14), esp. 108–27.

30. That issue is clearest in the encounter with Hananiah, Jer. 27–28. Cf. Hans Joachim Kraus, *Prophetie in der Krisis* (Neukirchen-Vluyn: Neukirchener Verlag, 1964), 82–104.

be discerned.[31] In these verses, Jeremiah voices in sharpest form the hard epistemological questions facing Judah, the royal consciousness notwithstanding. In these verses, the two histories collide and are sorted out, both in a way characteristic for the prophets and in a way quite unacceptable to the royal consciousness.[32]

Only in a most general way can anything be determined about the present placement of the verses in the text. It is possible that the unit is displaced here.[33] In the general movement of 8:4—10:25, we may note the recurrent reference to themes of "know" and "wisdom":

My people *know* not
the ordinance of the Lord. (8:7)

How can you say, "We are *wise* . . . "?
Behold, the *false* pen of the scribes
has made it into a *lie*.[34]
The *wise* men shall be put to shame, . . .
and what *wisdom* is in them? (8:8-9)

They did not *know* how to blush. (8:12b)[35]

They do not *know* me, says the Lord. (9:2b)

They refuse to *know* me, says the Lord. (9:5b)

Who is the man so wise that he can *understand* this? (9:11)

---

31. Bernhard Duhm, *Das Buch Jeremia* (Tübingen: Mohr [Siebeck], 1901), 97, had dismissed the text as "a harmless insignificant saying." On the contrary, I suggest that it may provide a decisive point of entry to understand the tensions and intent of the tradition of Jeremiah.

32. The verses contain no textual problems that need detain us. Perhaps the last negative of v. 22 might have an added conjunction to parallel the second, but it is not necessary. In v. 23, the LXX has a conjunction before the second object of the participle, but that also is unnecessary. The authenticity of the saying has been challenged by Duhm and William L. Holladay, *Jeremiah* (see chap. 2, n. 13), 59. The following, however, retain it: Friedrich Giesebrecht, *Das Buch Jeremia*, Göttinger Handkommentar zum Alten Testament (Göttingen: Vandenhoeck and Ruprecht, 1907), 61–63; Wilhelm Rudolph, *Jeremia*, HAT, no. 12, 2d ed. (Tübingen: Mohr [Siebeck], 1958), 63; John Bright, *Jeremiah*, AB, no. 21 (Garden City, N.Y.: Doubleday & Co., 1965), 75–80. There seems no compelling reason to regard the words as other than those of Jeremiah.

33. So A. S. Peake, ed., *Jeremiah and Lamentations*, 2 vols., New-century Bible (Edinburgh: T. & T. Clark, 1910–11), vol. 1, 169; and Annesley W. Streane, *Jeremiah*, Cambridge Bible (Cambridge: Cambridge University Press, 1913), 68.

34. On *šqr* here and characteristically, see Overholt, *Threat of Falsehood*, 74–82. The lie refers to a fundamental misconception of covenantal reality.

35. On forgetting how to blush, see the remarkable words of Heschel, *Who Is Man?* (Stanford: Stanford University Press, 1965), 112–14. He quotes our verse in making the contrast between self-glorification and "a sense of ultimate embarrassment."

Send for the *wise* women to come. (9:16b)[36]

I *know*, O Lord, that the way of man is not in himself,
that it is not in man who walks to direct his steps.
Correct me, O Lord. (10:23-24a)[37]

Pour out thy wrath upon the nations that *know* thee not. (10:25a)

Two problems must be acknowledged in such a listing. First, it is
likely that this is a collection of various fragments that have no original coherence. Nonetheless, they have been brought together, and
it may well be that our themes of *knowing* and *wisdom* have been
the guide for bringing them together.[38] Second, it is obvious that
the words italicized have a variety of different nuances, exploring a
whole field of meanings. But perhaps even with this recognition, it is
not too much to conclude that in all of them the poetry means to pose
the central epistemological question that Jeremiah discerned at the
end of royal history. The ones who claim to know do not know. There
is no knowledge of the Torah (8:7), nor of how to blush (8:12), nor of
Yahweh (9:2, 5; 10:25). The only positive knowing (10:23-24) is done
by Jeremiah himself in a statement suggesting that he knows what
the others do not know. Thus, even the positive statement is another
way of asserting that the others do not know. Most of all, what they
do not know is that the human creature (= king) is not self-reliant.
Jeremiah's knowledge is contrasted with the noncovenantal foolishness of the royal consciousness.[39] This climactic statement recognizes
that human well-being is not derived from human capacity.

---

36. Clearly the term refers to skill and so is not theologically important. Cf. 4:22
for a similar use. Nonetheless, it adds to the semantic field being explored by the
prophet.

37. This saying clearly echoes sayings in the book of Proverbs. Cf. Gerhard von
Rad, *Old Testament Theology I* (see chap. 1, n. 22), 439, and his comment on Prov.
16:2; 16:9; 19:21; 20:24; 21:2; 21:30-31. Each raises the issue both of this passage
and of our primary text. The plea for correction with the word *yāsar* suggests a
sapiential-educational tradition. Cf. Kraus, "Geschichte als Erziehung," in *Probleme*
(see chap. 3, n. 4), 267–71. Note the importance of the word to Hosea. Whybray
(*Intellectual Tradition*, 128), suggests the term belongs to the sphere of education but
denies it specifically to wisdom.

38. Claus Westermann, in *Jeremia* (Stuttgart: Calwer Verlag, 1967), 36, suggests the
principle of *catchword*.

39. See Donald Gowan, *When Man* (see chap. 7, n. 24), on the problem of hy-
bris as it shapes royal consciousness. See William McKane, *Prophets and Wise Men*,
SBT, no. 44 (Naperville, Ill.: Alec R. Allenson, 1965), 89–90. McKane speaks of "self-
contained . . . sagacity," and helpfully relates our passage to a trajectory of related
passages.

Thus 10:23-24 speaks of true wisdom. But the wisdom of Judah, presumably held by members of the other history in the royal circle, is a joke (cf. 8:8-9), because in all their pretension, they cannot do what must be done. The wise men have failed (9:11) and the only wisdom now valued is that which knows how to weep (9:16), that is, those who do not pursue their self-deception continuously but who have the sensitivity to respond appropriately to death.[40] The real wisdom appropriate to the moment is to recognize the end that surely has come upon this people. There is no other wisdom in Judah that now can make any difference.

The entire "unit" uses images that are at least reminiscent of wisdom teaching. It employs analogy (8:6-7), rhetorical questions (8:4-5, 8-9, 12, 19, 23; 9:11),[41] as well as admonition (9:3-4). Thus, the style of the unit, if it may be regarded now as a unit, raises the question of knowing and wisdom in a context of painful ending and death. True knowing consists in facing Yahweh's remarkable freedom. Real wisdom consists in acknowledging death and responding appropriately (9:20). The foolishness of the so-called wise is to have business as usual. The lie they speak (8:8; 9:2, 4), the deception they practice (9:4-5), is that they continue in the illusion of the royal history, which knows no end or beginning but only cherishes *šālôm* (8:11, 15) and anticipates healing (8:22)[42] but cannot recognize that this history is finished. It is the other history, of planting and building, of plucking up and tearing down, in which Judah must now participate. Kings cannot do that.

So the epistemological issue is joined. It is not a theoretical issue of experience and authority. It is a question of having defined reality in ways that keep what is real from ever surfacing. And Jeremiah must now use his best imagination to show that it is history with a

---

40. Cf. Amos 5:16. Perhaps the same motif is present in Matt. 5:4, surely a sapiential form. The blessed are the ones who are wise enough to know the appropriate response to the proper time. Royal consciousness is likely not attentive to the times, because the establishment believes only in managed time. Cf. Jer. 8:7 on not knowing the times, surely not the time for repentance and death; and von Rad, *Wisdom* (see chap. 1, n. 25), 138–43.

41. See Walter Brueggemann, "Jeremiah's Use of Rhetorical Questions," *JBL* 92 (1973): 358–74. I have shown there that Jeremiah's use of the form serves to call into question conventional presuppositions and conclusions, a very different function from the usual wisdom teaching.

42. See James Muilenburg, "The Terminology of Adversity in Jeremiah," in *Translating and Understanding the Old Testament*, ed. Harry T. Frank and William L. Reed (New York: Abingdon Press, 1970), esp. 46, 50, 57.

covenant-making God that is the only history. Every other history is an illusion and a deception.

V

Thus 9:22-23 is not inappropriate to its present context, which concerns wisdom/foolishness on the way to death. Jeremiah had discerned that while the royal consciousness presumed its own continued well-being, that history was already destined for death. The form of this saying is likely sapiential, but that is difficult to sustain in light of our fuzzy definitions.[43] The messenger formula at the beginning seems inappropriate to its style, but it may be imposed on this saying in order to claim authority in the harsh conflicts of epistemologies. (In chapters 8–10, the messenger formula occurs elsewhere only in 9:6, 16.) The concluding formula, *nĕ'um yahweh*, also occurs in 8:17; 9:2, 5, 8, 21, 24, but seems to recur in various settings without impacting the rhetoric.[44]

Thus, both formulae seem to be extraneous and may be discounted. Without them the saying appears to be a didactic statement consisting in two parts—first, three negative admonitions, then a contrasting positive with three members together with a motivational clause:

> Let not (*'al*)[45] the wise one glory in his wisdom,
> Let not (*'al*) the mighty one glory in his might,

---

43. So Arthur Weiser, *Der Prophet Jeremiah*, ATD, no. 20 (Göttingen: Vandenhoeck and Ruprecht, 1960), 89; von Rad, *Wisdom*, 102–3; and Robert B. Y. Scott, *Proverbs and Ecclesiastes*, AB, no. 18 (Garden City, N.Y.: Doubleday & Co., 1965), xxxv. This saying apparently meets the requirements of Crenshaw as well. Lorenz Dürr, in *Das Erziehungswesen* (Leipzig: J. C. Hinrich, 1983), has not only linked our passage to wisdom but has explicitly related it to Prov. 3:7. Erhard Gerstenberger in turn has found Prov. 3:7 to be a summary and motto for wisdom instruction generally; see Gerstenberger, *Wesen und Herkunft des "Apodiktischen Rechts,"* WMANT, no. 20 (Neukirchen-Vluyn: Neukirchener Verlag, 1965), 49. If both Dürr and Gerstenberger are correct, as seems likely, then our passage may indeed express a central wisdom teaching; however, the teaching is much more concrete than is Prov. 3:7. The warning is not only against "evil," but wisdom, riches, and power. The urging is not only toward fear of Yahweh but also toward very specific covenantal factors.

44. Cf. Rendtorff, "Zum Gebrauch der Formel 'ne'um Jahwe' im Jeremiabuch," *ZAW* 66 (1954): 27–37; and Francis S. North, "The Expression 'The Oracle of Yahweh' as an Aid to Critical Analysis," *JBL* 71 (1952): x. The form is apparently not integral to this unit, as is also the case in a number of passages in Jeremiah.

45. It is worth noting that the negative is not *lo*, as might be expected, but *'al*, which might also stress the sapiential connection, as Gerstenberger would argue.

> Let not (*'al*) the rich one glory in his riches;
> But (*kî 'im*) let him who glories glory in this,
>   that he understands and knows me.
> Surely (*kî*) I am Yahweh who does kindness,
>   justice, and
>   righteousness in the land.
> Surely (*kî*) in them I delight.

The three negatives, all modifying *yithallēl*,[46] introduce a triad. The reflexive verb serves here to turn the subject back on himself.[47] What is prohibited by the negative plus the reflexive is preoccupation with self and self's resources.[48] The alternative is sharply presented by the abrupt *kî 'im*. The same verb is used, but the object now is not self-resources. The boast now concerns Yahweh.

The two motivational clauses, both introduced by *kî*, serve to delineate further this recommended choice so sharply contrasted with the previous objects of wisdom, might, and riches. Yahweh is not to be confused with or associated with wisdom, might, or riches. He is differently characterized, again by a triad, *hesed, mišpāṭ,* and *ṣĕdāqâ*. That triad is surely deliberately cast in parallel form but radically contrasted in substance. The second *kî* clause further identifies what is legitimate for approval and celebration.

The form is clearly didactic, but not strenuously hortatory.[49] The *kî 'im* is too common a form to be identified as sapiential. But we may note a peculiarly close parallel in Prov. 23:17-18a:

> Let not (*'al*) your heart envy sinners,
> But (*kî 'im*) continue in the fear of the Lord all the day.

---

46. The hithpael form of *hll* is not used often. In Proverbs it is used three times negatively (25:14; 27:1; 30:14) and once positively (31:30). Elsewhere, it is used for praise to Yahweh (Pss. 34:3; 63:12; 64:11; 105:3; 106:5; 1 Chron. 16:10; Isa. 41:16; 45:25; and especially to be noted, Jer. 4:2). It is used negatively in Pss. 49:7; 52:3; 97:7. Outside of these poetic passages, it is used only in 1 Kings 20:11, on which comment will be made below.

47. Too much should not be made of the grammatical form in claiming this. Its usage simply shows two primary functions: (1) praise of Yahweh and (2) inordinate celebration of something else, often implying pride and self-preoccupation. Mendenhall suggests the form means "saying hallelu to self" (oral communication).

48. In such uses it is the very opposite of the affirmation of Jer. 10:23-24, also a wisdom saying.

49. The tone is not unlike the "summary-appraisal form" identified by Brevard S. Childs, *Isaiah and the Assyrian Crisis,* SBT, no. 2/3 (Naperville, Ill.: Alec R. Allenson, 1967), 128–36. Our form contains a number of conclusions not dissimilar to the climactic conclusion of Childs's form. Similarly, these conclusions do not urge a specific action but simply make a nondiscussable judgment about conduct and consequences.

> Surely (*kî 'im*) there is a future,
> and your hope is not cut off.[50]

The parallel in form is close, but not total in the three parts: *'al,
kî 'im, kî 'im*. The second *kî 'im* in the proverb does not, however,
function as a disjunctive, as does the first, but serves as a motivational clause. With that provision, the form is a striking parallel to
the passage under consideration, which has *'al, kî 'im, kî*. The rhetorical stress of our unit falls on *kî 'im*, which serves to contrast the two
triads. The *kî 'im* is used broadly and is not the monopoly of any
circle of tradition. While it serves to contrast, it may also serve to
introduce a radical call to a certain kind of behavior:

> And now, Israel, what does the Lord require of you,
> but (*kî 'im*) to fear, . . . to walk, . . . to love, . . .
> to serve, . . . to keep . . . ? (Deut. 10:12-13)

> And what does the Lord require of you
> but (*kî 'im*) to do justice, and to love kindness,
> and to walk humbly with your God? (Mic. 6:8)[51]

It may be used to introduce a new teaching that replaces the old:

> In those days they shall no longer say:
> "The fathers have eaten sour grapes,
> and the children's teeth are set on edge."
> But (*kî 'im*) every one shall die for his own sin;
> each man who eats sour grapes,
> his teeth shall be set on edge.
>   (Jer. 31:29-30)[52]

It may be used to contrast what is in quantity but of indifferent value
and what is rare but precious:

---

50. The form with this particle serves to make a sharp, unqualified distinction between sinners and fearers of the Lord. Characteristically in such parallelisms, it serves
to contrast.

51. While this teaching is now set in a prophetic context, it also echoes a sapiential
concern. Note the more general address to human beings, in contrast to Deut. 10:12,
where the same address is to Israel. Note also that the items urged are similar to those
urged in our verses.

52. In a way similar to the rhetorical question, the particle challenges conventional
wisdom expressed in the proverb and sets out an alternative.

> But (*kî 'im*) the poor man had nothing but one little ewe lamb,
> which he had bought. (2 Sam. 12:3)[53]

It serves to create an opening for new behavior:

> The Lord made a covenant with them, and commanded them,
> "You shall not fear other gods or bow yourselves to them
>   or serve them or sacrifice to them;
> But (*kî 'im*) you shall fear the Lord. . . .
>   You shall not fear other gods,
> But (*kî 'im*) you shall fear the Lord your God."
> (2 Kings 17:35-36, 38-39)[54]

These parallel uses make clear the radical contrast Jeremiah draws between the two triads, which are not simply lists of virtues and vices but embody the core of the two histories and which provide the parameters of contrasting epistemologies. The form itself would suggest there is a deathly way and a life-giving way for Israel. Jeremiah's context is one in which the death-choosers think their way will lead to life. His anguish is that he has discerned its sure end in death.

VI

The first triad—*wisdom, might, riches*—characterizes one history in Israel, the royal history. These three terms occur nowhere else together. The prophet has constructed a new triad, which intends to summarize the whole royal history that has continually reassured and deceived its key actors but that has now brought Judah to the point of death. One could not imagine a more radical critique of the royal consciousness, for in one stroke Jeremiah disposes of all the sources of security and well-being upon which the royal establishment is built.

His critique is more radical than the older proverbial wisdom. That reflective tradition had been aware of the temptation of riches

---

53. It is not necessary to insist that this parabolic form is sapiential, but its structure and intent do make a contrast in what is to be valued in a way that is surely congenial to wisdom teaching.

54. The contrast set forth by the Deuteronomistic Historian is surely didactic. Given the suggestions of Moshe Weinfeld, we may suggest that the contrast here between service to Yahweh and to the other gods is not unlike the sharp sapiential contrast of Prov. 8:32-36, which presents ways to life and death.

(Prov. 11:28; 23:4; 28:20). It saw the positive good of riches but believed they are gifts that will be given and are not to be pursued for
themselves (Prov. 3:16; 8:18; 10:4, 22; 22:4; 28:25).

Even that tradition is radical enough to see that riches deceive
and are finally linked to foolishness that will destroy:

> A rich man is wise in his own eyes,
>> but a poor man who has understanding (*bîn*) will find him out.
>>   (Prov. 28:11)[55]

We are, however, still in the area of relatively simple virtue in a
quid-pro-quo world. In that world there is little reflection upon the
problem of might. It is not particularly celebrated and other things
are better (Prov. 16:32), but it is scarcely an item of interest. And
certainly wisdom receives no critique, except, as noted, when one is
"wise in his own eyes." In that world, *might* is of little concern, *wisdom*
is to be valued, and only *riches* are seen as a danger.

Thus, Jeremiah's polemic does not grow out of that tradition
in any direct sense. It is only when these matters are discerned in
royal history that they are a threat. That history, beginning with
Solomon, has turned these three matters into a way of life that is
self-securing and finally numbing, both toward human need and divine purpose.[56] While Jeremiah may draw upon wisdom teaching,
he fashions this negative summary out of a direct response to royal
history that seemed utterly secure and yet now had led to death.
That he adds wisdom and might to the sapiential warning on riches
indicates how he has deepened the critique to an epistemological
level:

1. Riches are a royal prerogative. They are the gift to the king
(1 Kings 3:11, 13; 2 Chron. 1:12; Dan. 11:2; Esther 1:41; 5:11). They
are an identifying mark of a good king (of David: 1 Chron. 29:12, 28;
of Solomon: 1 Kings 10:23; 2 Chron. 9:22; of Jehoshaphat: 2 Chron.

---

55. McKane, in *Proverbs* (Philadelphia: Westminster Press, 1970), 621, has observed
that this saying equates wealth and impiety, poverty and piety. The fool is one who will
not submit to Yahweh and to Torah. McKane observes that the question of theodicy
has surfaced, surely an issue that came to full expression in the pathos of Jeremiah.
This saying on wisdom is more radical than most in Proverbs and reflects the tradition
to which Jeremiah appeals.

56. Mendenhall (*Tenth Generation*, 121) refers to our saying in identifying the meaning of Solomon. There can be little doubt that in Solomon's regime, this alien ideology
that Jeremiah resists became legitimated in Israel.

17:5; 18:1; of Hezekiah: 2 Chron. 32:27). They are the king's to give (1 Sam. 17:25). Riches belong precisely to royal awareness.

2. Might does not refer here simply to the fullness of manhood as it sometimes does. Here it refers to the capacity of the royal establishment to work its will by human power before which none may issue a challenge. Might in its various forms (*gbr*) is the peculiar claim of the king (2 Sam. 10:7; 16:6; 20:7; 23:9-22). The regime managed to order its own universe and combine the mythic power of virility together with the hardware of a war machine.[57]

3. And wisdom in such a context is no longer the power to discern but the capacity to manage and control, to reduce everything to royal proportions. By placing wisdom in the context of this triad, Jeremiah has defined and nuanced it in a harshly critical way. Wisdom is presented as self-serving. The form itself makes wisdom negative.

The triad as a whole speaks of placing trust in places from which can come no health, but the king never knows it. The critique of Jeremiah thus may be related to several other passages:

a. Psalm 49, often associated with the sapiential tradition of Israel, reflects on those who trust in their wealth and who boast of the abundance of their riches.[58]

> Yes, he shall see that even the wise die...
> and leave their wealth to others.
> Man cannot abide in this pomp (*yqr*)....
> This is the fate of those who have foolish confidence.
> (Vv. 11, 13, 14a; cf. 17-18, 21 [Engl. 10-13a; cf. 16-17, 20])

The psalm discerns the boundary of self-securing. These apparent sources of long life and well-being can promise nothing.[59]

---

57. Lewis Mumford, in *The Myth of the Machine* (New York: Harcourt, Brace & Co., 1970), has in a general way shown the dialectical development of technology and mythic claims. More specifically related to Israel, see Mendenhall and Gottwald in the works cited.

58. There can be little doubt that this psalm is informed by wisdom traditions. Cf. Mowinckel, "Psalms and Wisdom," in *Wisdom in Israel* (see n. 4), 213–15; and Ronald E. Murphy, "A Consideration of the Classification 'Wisdom Psalms,'" in *Congress Volume, Bonn 1962*, VTSup, no. 9 (Leiden: Brill, 1963), 161–63.

59. These verses have much in common with the general tenor of Ecclesiastes. Cf. Jay Williams, "What Does It Profit a Man?" in *Studies* (see n. 1), 375–89. Jeremiah seems to refer to such a tradition. The difference is that he has, as they do not, a positive alternative to urge. On the triad, see esp. Qoh. 9:11. Ecclesiastes asserts that might, riches, and wisdom—the very items named in our passage—finally have no significance.

b. Psalm 52, not inappropriately assigned in the superscription against royal power, begins with an attack on a mighty man who boasts (*tithallēl*, v. 3), who trusts in the abundance of his riches, and who seeks refuge in his wealth (v. 9). The psalm concludes with a contrast of the well-being of the one who eschews might and riches and trusts the goodness of God. Thus David and Saul are presented as models of the two histories, David being the one who trusts and Saul the one who secures his own way and must surely come to ruin.

c. Isa. 5:21-23 in turn presents a radical critique of those who are

> *wise* in their own eyes (cf. Prov. 28:11), . . .
> *mighty* in drinking, and . . .
> takers of *bribes*.

Even though the third member of the triad is not quite "riches," the triad is very close to that of our verse in Jeremiah.[60] The criticism of Isaiah turns each element so that it must be negative: not wise, but wise *in their own eyes*, not mighty, but mighty *in drinking*, not rich, but only *in bribes*.

None of these texts—Psalms 49 and 52 or Isa. 5:21-23—contains our triad. But the various configurations suggest a pattern of critique against the most elemental values of the royal-urban consciousness that, by the time of Josiah, was bringing Judah to death. Each of these texts has affinities with what is commonly thought to be a wisdom teaching. Jeremiah challenges the foundations of the establishment credo.[61] In 5:27-28 he appears to appeal to a tradition of such criticism that likely is rooted in and derived from sapiential circles, but he has recast it in more radical ways. His critique characteristically is not interested either in inner attitudes or in conduct per se but in the inevitable price paid in terms of human injustice. Thus, he links deceit and oppression to refusal to know Yahweh

---

60. See Whedbee, *Isaiah and Wisdom*, 81–110, for a full discussion.

61. His radical critique is apparent in many places, but note especially 5:27-28. The prophet describes: (1) their self-deluding prosperity, (2) the disregard of order and boundary, and (3) the social consequences. On the political implications of the epistemology, see Abraham Katsh, "The Religious Tradition or Traditions in a Traditionless Age," in *Christian Action and Openness to the World*, ed. Joseph Papen (Villanova, Pa.: Villanova University Press, 1970), 213–17. Katsh shows how this tradition leads to democratic society and its absence to oppressive class society.

(9:5).[62] The practice of self-deception expresses itself in terms of oppression. That brings death, and Jeremiah had seen it clearly even though the royal mentality continued to deny it.

VII

The alternative history is expressed in two ways:

First, to "know Yahweh." We have already noted the references in chapters 8–10 on this theme. See also 2:8; 4:22; 5:4, 28-29; 7:5-6; 22:3, 16; 24:7; 31:34. The theme of knowing Yahweh has been well explored and requires no additional comment here. Hans Walter Wolff has established that it means a knowledge of the mighty deeds and the Torah claims.[63] Herbert B. Huffmon has shown that it refers to acknowledgment of covenantal sovereignty and required allegiance.[64] Thus the "refusal to know" is the fundamental critique against the royal consciousness because it could not embrace the serious impact of covenantal reality without giving up its claims and pretensions. Thus, in contrast to the first triad, Jeremiah announces his primary theme that serves to discredit and dismantle the epistemology of the regime.

Jeremiah asserts that if Judah will have something of legitimate pride, it must terminate the royal history that leads to death and embrace the history of the covenant. That history is always precarious, never yields stately mansions, but in inscrutable ways brings life.[65]

The prophet tersely inquires about national priorities in relation to national well-being. As in the more expansive statement of 22:13-17,[66] he lays out the life/death issues:

---

62. The text is difficult, but cf. Bright, *Jeremiah*, 66–72.

63. See Wolff, " 'Wissen um Gott' bei Hosea als Urform von Theologie," *EvT* 12 (1952 53): 533, 554, reprinted in *Gesammelte* (see chap. 4, n. 20), TBü, no. 22, 182–205.

64. Huffmon, "The Treaty Background of Hebrew *Yada*," *BASOR* 181 (1966): 31–37; and Huffmon and Simon B. Parker, "A Further Note on the Treaty Background of Hebrew *Yada*," *BASOR* 184 (1966): 36–38.

65. On the inscrutable source of life as it relates to wisdom teaching, see Murphy, "The Kerygma of Proverbs," *Int* 20 (1966): 3–14, and Prov. 8:32-36 on the gift of life from wisdom.

66. On this text as a central one for our hypothesis of two histories, see Wolff, *Anthropology of the Old Testament* (Philadelphia: Fortress Press, 1974), 195–96.

The anguish of the prophet is that he knows, cognitively and cove-nantally, what the royal community in its congenital stupidity could not learn.

Second, this alternative history is summarized in an equally powerful triad, *ḥesed, mišpāṭ, ṣĕdāqâ*. As in the first triad, the prophet has shrewdly expressed the central issue, namely, solidarity not only between person (king) and God, but in the community, the very solidarity against which wisdom/riches/might militate.[67]

This second triad occurs, to my knowledge, only in one other text, Hos. 2:21-22, upon which Jeremiah is likely dependent.[68] It occurs only in these two prophets most deeply sensitive to the pathos of God as articulated in covenant and most knowing about the deathly course of Israel.[69] Only these two dare to entertain the alternative "knowing Yahweh," which will bring new life. Jeremiah has recited the entire history of death (riches, wisdom, might). Hosea has, in parallel fashion, reviewed the history of fickleness and betrayal. Incredibly, both of them can now use this triad to speak of an alter-native history with the radically faithful one who can bring newness where death seemed final.[70] It is not very helpful to try to identify

---

67. Radical liberation theology is helping us discover that these phenomena are in-herently against solidarity. This is the insight of the prophet—that riches, might, and that kind of wisdom belong inevitably to the consciousness that practices domination and oppression and so destroys community.

68. On the relation of Hosea and Jeremiah, see Hans Wildberger, *Jahwes Eigen-tumsvolk* (Zürich: Swingli, 1960), 112; and Kurt Gross, "Hoseas Einfluss auf Jeremias Anschauungen," *NKZ* 42 (1931): 241–56, 327–43. More recent tradition-critical study confirms this connection. More than any other they sensed the depth of the tragedy of Israel's royal consciousness. On "knowing" in Hosea, cf. 4:1, 6; 5:4; 6:4; 8:2.

69. On the pathos of God into which the prophets entered, see Heschel, *Prophets*. On the ways in which the other consciousness leads to apathy, see Jürgen Moltmann, *The Experiment Hope* (Philadelphia: Fortress Press, 1975), 69–84; and Dorothee Sölle, *Suffering* (Philadelphia: Fortress Press, 1975).

70. Yahweh is not only in favor of these things but *does* them. Yahweh's doing them makes clear that Yahweh has freedom to act against and in spite of the royal manage-ment that attempted to circumscribe Yahweh's action. The saying asserts that Yahweh will work the divine will in spite of all the ideological commitment to wisdom, riches, and power that try to prevent it. This is in contrast to the mood of the time expressed

what in this comes from the traditions of wisdom or covenant or prophets. The epistemological crisis does not concern simply circles of tradition but the change made in all perceptions (of every tradition) by radical Yahwistic faith. Every epistemology is called into question when knowing begins in the faithfulness of Yahweh, which requires and evokes a responding faithfulness from Israel. Hosea and Jeremiah believed that a new history was possible, but on quite different grounds.

VIII

The two triads set the choice Israel must make. These triads, contrasted by the emphatic *kî 'im*, set in juxtaposition the two histories, the one of self-glorification, the other of vulnerable fidelity. By setting the two histories together as indeed they had finally collided in his time, Jeremiah sets the choice Israel must now make. We may learn more of the prophet's intent by noting the two envelope words, *hithallēl* and *ḥāpēṣ*. The crisis in Israel's history concerns a cause for glorification. Since Solomon, Israel had sought a cause for glory and, since Solomon, had been glorying in deathly things.

The act of boasting in and of itself is not bad. When it is addressed away from self toward God, it is of course approved and we may call it "praise" (Ps. 34:3; cf. Jer. 4:2; Ps. 64:11). The problem for Jeremiah is not boasting, but it is boasting turned toward self, that is, toward royal history as the generator of its own life, meaning, and security. Again we may note the affinities with the psalms already cited:

> ... men who trust (*bāṭaḥ*) in their wealth
> and *boast* of the abundance of their riches. (Ps. 49:7)

> Why do you *boast*, O mighty man ... ?
> See the man who would not make God his refuge,
> but trusted (*bāṭaḥ*) in the abundance of his riches,
> and sought refuge in his wealth. (Ps. 52:3, 9)

---

in Zeph. 1:12. On Yahweh as doer, cf. Paul Volz, *Der Prophet Jeremia*, KAT, no. 10 (Leipzig and Erlangen: Deichert, 1922), 118; as well as Isa. 9:6. On the participial form, see Job 9:9-12 with the double verb plus the concluding rhetorical question, and Amos 4:8. Thus the form is likely sapiential. The substance concerns his royal authority in the face of those who deny or circumscribe it. On the royal motif, see Jer. 23:5; and Pss. 99:4; 103:7. On wisdom formulation, Exod. 34:7, see Robert C. Dentan, "The Literary Affinities of Exodus XXXIV 6f," *VT* 18 (1963): 34–51. See also Giesebrecht, *Buch Jeremia*, 62.

In both texts the term *tithallēl* is parallel to *bāṭaḥ*. Boasting thus is understood as misplaced trust. The word *bāṭaḥ* occurs in various contexts, 5:17; 7:4; 8:13; 9:3; 13:25; and Isa. 31:1. See especially the harsh declaration of Jer. 2:37b:

> Surely the Lord has rejected those in whom you *trust*.

Note the contrast in 17:5a, 7:

> Cursed is the man who *trusts* in man. . . .
> Blessed is the man who *trusts* in the Lord,
>   whose *trust* is the Lord.

Again the two histories are clearly contrasted.

Concerning the formula used in our text, we may learn from the defiant statement of the king of Israel to the taunting Ben-Hadad:

> Let not him that girds on his armor boast himself (*yithallēl*)[71] as he that puts it off. (1 Kings 20:11)

Probably this was a sapiential saying that warned against claiming too much in prospect, in contrast to legitimate claims in retrospect.[72] Thus it is a warning against presuming too much for one's own powers in a situation likely to be beyond one's control. But it is now used in this narrative as a defiant affirmation of trust in Yahweh against enormous odds. On the basis of this parallel, Jeremiah may be understood as throwing down the gauntlet of radical faith against enormous odds, that is, of trusting and obeying Yahweh's covenantal gifts and demands in the face of external threat and internal collapse. In the same defiant manner as 1 Kings 20:11, Jeremiah asserts that the power of riches, wisdom, and might, the substance of royal history, is a poor match against *ḥesed*, *mišpāṭ*, and *ṣĕdāqâ* in determining what will finally shape history.

---

71. This is the only text in the *narrative* traditions of the Old Testament in which the hithpael occurs. It is a remarkable passage that contrasts the boasting of Syria and the confidence of Yahweh expressed by Israel. On the formulae of the chapter as assertions of faith, see Zimmerli, "Das Wort des Göttlichen Selbsterweises," in *Gottes Offenbarung* (see chap. 8, n. 21), 129.

72. Cf. John Gray, *I and II Kings* (Philadelphia: Westminster Press, 1963), 376; and Hans Jürgen Hermisson, *Studien zur israelitischen Spruchweisheit*, WMANT, no. 28 (Neukirchen-Vluyn: Neukirchener Verlag, 1968), 43.

Attention may also be called to David's defiance of Goliath.[73] Although not a wisdom saying, it also makes a defiant contrast in the face of the enemy. The two-part assertion is not unlike that of our text:

> You come to me with a sword and
> > with a spear and
> > with a javelin;[74]
> but I come to you in the name of the Lord of hosts,
> > the God of the armies of Israel,
> > whom you have defied. (1 Sam. 17:45)[75]

Again we are offered an assertion of the power of Yahweh against the apparent power of Goliath. The giant is mismatched because David's presuppositions lie outside Philistine awareness and call into question that entire understanding of reality.

In both 1 Kings 20:11 and 1 Sam. 17:45, sharply contrasting views of reality are presented in the context of war and in the face of a major threat. In both cases, reliance on Yahweh calls into question the presuppositions of the other party. In a similar way, Jeremiah uses what appears to be a sapiential form, perhaps honed by usage in a context of defiance against a stronger military power, to call Judah to a new history in covenant.[76] The Israelites whom Jeremiah addresses are as misinformed about reality as are Goliath and Ben-Hadad. A wisdom teacher might declare what is proper for boasting and what is not. A war story might turn this against an arrogant enemy. But the form has been radicalized by Jeremiah to carry the fundamental challenge to royal presuppositions, and this against his own king. If that is a correct way of understanding the text, we may

---

73. See the comment of Hermisson, *Studien*, 43.

74. Note the triad. Too much should not be made of the triad, but perhaps it illuminates the pair of triads in our passage. The same historical consciousness is reflected in the triad sword/spear/javelin as in the triad riches/might/wisdom.

75. Attention might be drawn in this connection to 1 Sam. 16:18, where David is presented as the one with the true wisdom and capacity to cope with the boaster. In that text he may well be a paradigm of the way in which wisdom and faith are held together. The critique of Jeremiah is that wisdom and its companion properties have displaced faith. Cf. Hermisson, *Studien*, 125.

76. See the analysis of Jeremianic texts by William J. Holladay, *The Architecture of Jeremiah 1–20* (London: Associated University Press, 1976). In his analysis of Jeremiah 4–6, 8, Holladay suggests that "there is a steady movement in each of these sections from battle scenes to wisdom preoccupations. . . . The battle is a *lesson* to the people" (pp. 67, 85). See pp. 110–13 for a parallel comment on 8:14—9:8. What Holladay discerns in a larger structural analysis is indicated also concerning our verses.

better understand the promise to Jeremiah (1:17-19) that he will be a safe man of war against the odds, for the risky proposition of Jeremiah against his contemporaries is at least as bold and risky as David against Goliath or Ahab against Ben-Hadad.[77]

The term of self-congratulations, *tithallēl*, is balanced by the concluding use of *ḥāpēṣ* in our text.[78] Its climatic position gives it stress; so the entire saying contrasts the self-congratulations of the royal managers and the unfailing desires of Yahweh. The prophet clearly means to assert that the history of Israel and its risky future will not be determined by self-securing but by Yahweh's purposes. *Ḥāpēṣ* cannot be assigned to any circle of tradition in particular. It is used for acceptance of cultic offerings, in wisdom instruction, and in interpersonal relations.

Applied to Yahweh, several stresses are important: (1) The term is used to assert Yahweh's radical freedom to do what Yahweh wills (Pss. 115:3; 135:6; Jon. 1:14). (2) In radical freedom, Yahweh may reject (Pss. 65:12; 66:4; 5:5) and even will death (Judg. 12:23; 1 Sam. 2:24; Ezek. 18:23). (3) Yahweh's characteristic action is willing life and not death (Ezek. 18:32; 33:11), but the gift of life requires radical turning. Thus, the word bears the good news that Yahweh wills covenanted living. (In this regard as in so many, Jeremiah has affinities with Ezekiel and holds out the promise of life.) (4) The substance of Yahweh's desiring of life is the triad of the alternative history of *ḥesed, mišpāṭ, ṣĕdāqâ*. When this is practiced, life comes. When it is not, death comes. This understanding of the will of Yahweh is twice articulated:

> Surely I desire *ḥesed* and not sacrifice,
> > *knowledge of God* rather than burnt offerings.
> > > (Hos. 6:6; cf. 1 Sam. 15:22-23)[79]

> He does not retain his anger for ever
> > because he delights in *ḥesed*. (Mic. 7:18)

The dramatic teaching thus presents a good news/bad news pattern that surely will lead to life or death.

---

77. On war themes in Jeremiah, see Bach, *Die Aufforderungen zur Flucht und zum Kampf im Alttestamentlichen Prophetenspruch* (Neukirchen: Moers, 1962); and Patrick D. Miller, "The Divine Council and the Prophetic Call to War," *VT* 18 (1968): 100–7.

78. Holladay (*Architecture*, 123) comments on *ḥpṣ* in this text by observing the structural link to 6:10, which is the only previous occurrence.

79. Note that in 1 Sam. 15:22-23, along with delight, there is also rejection, a point worth noting in the context of Jeremiah's crisis.

IX

It is not too much to suggest that 9:22-23 might provide a screen through which Jeremiah can be understood more generally. It is not at all, as Bernhard Duhm suggested, "a harmless, meaningless text." Rather, it articulates the basic issues that finally cannot be avoided in Judah, especially in the seventh to the sixth centuries. Our analysis suggests that Jeremiah spoke out of a complex relation with Israel's sapiential tradition. On the one hand, he utilizes a speech form and manner of instruction that is likely sapiential. On the other hand, he polemicizes against a self-contained wisdom that will bring death. The presumed wisdom of Israel has turned out to be a foolishness to death. Conversely, the foolishness of the fragile purposes of Yahweh,[80] which seems of little note, finally will bring life.

In categories of Christian faith, Jeremiah here presents a theology of the cross in protest against a theology of glory. In that way, the use of this saying by Paul in 1 Cor. 1:26-31 is seen not to be casually or incidentally related. Rather, in dealing with the scandal of the gospel, Paul has discerned that Jeremiah rightly presented the scandal, which violates royal history.[81] The wisdom of kings is foolishness. The strength of kings is weakness. The riches of kings are poverty (cf. 2 Cor. 8:9). What Paul discerned in Jesus of Nazareth, Jeremiah has seen about Judah's death gasp in his time.[82] Things are not as they seem, especially to kings (cf. Prov. 25:2). That is what wisdom always sought, to find out how things are. God's capacity to hide things outdistances the capacity of the kings to find out.

---

80. Cf. Isa. 55:8-9. In what is likely a sapiential motif, the poet insists God's purposes are different from those of the people. That contrast is fundamental to faithful wisdom but never honored by kings who wish to monopolize wisdom and identify the regime with the purposes of God.

81. See the analysis of Kenneth E. Bailey, "Poetic Structure of 1 Cor. 1:17-2:2," *NovT* 17 (1975): 268–96.

82. Volz (*Prophet Jeremia*, 118–19) notes a derivative motif also in James 1:9-10; see also 2 Cor. 10:27.

15

The "Uncared For" Now Cared For (Jeremiah 30:12-17): A Methodological Consideration

THE PASSAGE UNDER CONSIDERATION is placed in the promissory poems of Jeremiah 30–31, called by scholars the "Book of Comfort." As with many issues concerning Jeremiah, there is no critical consensus concerning the provenance of these passages.[1] It is sufficient to say that these texts surely reflect both an authentic reference to Jeremiah and substantial editorial activity. How that balance operates in any given text is a matter of considerable uncertainty.

With reference to method, the distance we have come (whether progress or not is a different question) in recent years is evidenced in the critical questions concerning the Book of Comfort. The older criticism, under the rubric of "authenticity," was preoccupied with what is genuine and what is gloss. A characteristic decision was to assign vv. 12-15 to Jeremiah but to view vv. 16-17 as a later addition made so that the text would be positive. The reasonable ground for such an opinion is not hard to see. What is evident is that the data have not shifted at all. Scholars still talk about the same texts, but the questions of method have changed. New methodological considerations permit us to notice some things afresh, but we also tend not

---

1. See the quite different judgments made by John Skinner, *Prophecy and Religion* (Cambridge: Cambridge University Press, 1922); largely followed by John Bright, *Jeremiah* (see chap. 14, n. 32); and, in contrast, Ernest W. Nicholson, *Preaching in the Exiles* (Oxford: Blackwell, 1970). See especially Robert P. Carroll, *From Chaos to Covenant* (New York: Crossroad, 1981). On the status of scholarship, see the review articles of James L. Crenshaw, "A Living Tradition," *Int* 27 (1982): 117–29; and William L. Holladay, "The Year of Jeremiah's Preaching," *Int* 27 (1982): 46–59.

to notice things that once were of primary interest.[2] Method is not only determinative of conclusions but also determinative of what is noticed and not noticed on the way to a conclusion.

I

The first part of this unit, vv. 12-15, is more easily assigned to Jeremiah.[3] The metaphor of sickness and healing is one of the more powerful and more radical in the tradition of Jeremiah.[4] Here I will not explore the full range of uses. It is enough to note that the metaphor is rooted in the older traditions to which Jeremiah has important connections.[5] In the extended portions of the curse recital of Deut. 28:27-29, 58-68, the "diseases of Egypt" are offered as the consequence for covenantal disobedience. And in the preaching of Deuteronomy (7:15), which is not unrelated to the Jeremian tradition, the same reference to the "diseases of Egypt" is made. Indeed, the conclusion of the exodus narration (Exod. 15:26) understands the liberation from Egypt as a healing. Israel is rescued from the situation that makes it vulnerable to the "illnesses of the empire."

In using this metaphor, Jeremiah seems to appeal to a very old tradition. In its use, he may perhaps be suggesting that Israel has now come full circle, having finally succumbed to the "diseases of Egypt." Israel's condition, as understood by Jeremiah, is as helpless and hopeless as it is in the curses of Deuteronomy 28 or as it is in the pre-exodus period of Egyptian enslavement. Thus, the metaphor may be directly linked as the end point of the metaphorical trajectory that has its beginning in exodus. Or it may be only a usage intended to speak most radically about the present situation, without a particular reference to the exodus.

The poetic announcement begins with the end; the verdict is announced with finality in v. 12. The sickness of Israel is terminal. The rest of the poem derives from that unquestioned premise. That is

2. The clearest example of this that I know of is the drastic change made in our understanding of "new things" in Second Isaiah under the influence of canon criticism. See chap. 13.

3. Even Carroll inclines to this judgment; see *From Chaos*, 207.

4. See James Muilenburg, "The Terminology of Adversity in Jeremiah," in *Translating* (see chap. 14, n. 42), 42–63.

5. See also Holladay, *Jeremiah* (see chap. 2, n. 13), chap. 2, and especially "The Background of Jeremiah's Self-Understanding: Moses, Samuel, and Psalm 22," *JBL* 83 (1964): 153–64.

not negotiable; nor is reason for it given. The vocabulary of sickness is rich and diverse. The opening phrase, *'ānûš lĕšibrēk*, is answered with the same words in v. 15a, but there they do not constitute a single phrase. Verse 15a does return to the verdict of the first line. In v. 15 the verdict is announced again, only now Israel is chided for crying out in pain or protest. The verdict is sure. The situation is hopeless and it is futile to protest it.

In v. 12, the actual situation of terminal illness is intensified with the double use of *'ên*[6] to strengthen the absolute negation; Israel is left utterly alone, and v. 14 matches that by moving the metaphor of sickness into the political arena. In language reminiscent of Hosea, the former lovers are now cited. But here, in contrast to Hosea, Israel is not rebuked for having lovers. It is too late for that. Now Israel is only pitied for having selected fickle lovers who abandon it in time of trouble. The final phrase of v. 14a is terse and powerful: "You they do not seek."[7]

The linkage to the tradition of exodus should not be pressed. But the entire northern, covenantal tradition of the Elohist, Deuteronomy, Hosea, and Jeremiah is preoccupied with syncretism, with the desire to "be like the nations."[8] Perhaps the linkage here is direct. As Israel has pursued the nations, it has arrived finally at the "diseases of Egypt," which are fatal. In the poetic moves of the prophet, it is no difficult matter to take Egypt as a cipher for the imperial power and threat of Babylon. Thus, the Babylonian exile is indeed a period of "Egyptian disease."[9] When smitten with such a disease, the collaborators (allies, lovers) are not able to help at all. So the sick one (using the medical metaphor) is also the abandoned one (referring to the actual political situation).

The second half of v. 14 draws the metaphor closer to the form of the lawsuit. The *kî* here gives the basis. This is not a "natural"

---

6. The RSV rendering suggests a third negative, but it is not in the text.

7. The characteristic translation "care for" for *dāraš* is undoubtedly on target. See especially the use of Ezek. 34:6, 8, 10–11, where *dāraš* is used with the metaphor of shepherd, but in v. 4 it is used with images for healing. Thus, *dāraš* comprehends both the image of seeking for the lost and that of attending to the sick. "Care for" catches such a range of meanings!

8. The centrality and power of this tradition in shaping our understanding of prophetic faith are made clear by Robert R. Wilson, in *Prophecy* (see chap. 3, n. 17), esp. chaps. 4 and 6.

9. On Egypt in Deuteronomistic theology, which is closely related to Jeremiah, see Richard Elliott Friedmon, "From Egypt to Egypt: Dtr[1] and Dtr[2]," in *Traditions in Transformation*, ed. Baruch Halpern and Jon D. Levenson (Winona Lake, Ind.: Eisenbrauns, 1981), 167–92.

disease; it is a smiting caused precisely by Yahweh. The covenantal claims of Yahweh are not honored. The illness is indeed a curse, but it is not a gratuitous punishment. It is warranted in terms of the violation of the relationship.

This remarkable poetry is able to combine three matters most skillfully: First, the finished form of vv. 12-14 is a lawsuit that appeals to the structure of disobedience-curse. Second, the historical reference is clearly to the practice of syncretism in communal behavior, carried by the cipher "lovers," which alludes to the play of power-politics against which Jeremiah warned. But, third, the carrier of the covenantal agenda and the social realism is the intimate, devastating metaphor of terminal illness. The convergence of covenantal perspective, social analysis, and imaginative metaphor makes this a remarkable poetic achievement.

As vv. 12-14 make the initial statement of the case, v. 15 functions as a kind of reprise that sounds the same themes only to intensify the hopelessness and helplessness of Israel. Now the point is not only to characterize the situation but also to rebuke Israel for thinking either that it is unfair or that it can be altered. The argument of v. 15 is, first, that there is no use in crying, because the illness is terminal. The metaphor implies that the trouble has reached the point beyond recall. Pressure on Yahweh will not matter, because the disease now will take its own course and the doctor is helpless. Second, there is no use crying, because the illness is warranted and completely justified. The indicting formula in v. 15 is a repetition. No new evidence is offered or needed; however, the intensity of v. 15 is weakened in its function as reprise if the last line of v. 14 is removed, as is suggested by some scholars. It is the resounding, powerful repetition that makes the point.

This part of the poem is surely complete in the climatic statement, "I have done these things to you." Yahweh is indeed the enemy. Yahweh's act of enmity is not arbitrary, but the sure outcome of a wasted relationship.

II

We are not prepared for vv. 16-17. We are not prepared because a negative statement after v. 15 would hardly advance beyond the climax we have already reached in v. 15. And we are not prepared for a positive statement because anything except more negativity seems

impossible after the climax. Thus, we rightly expect the poem to
end with v. 15.

But vv. 16-17 are there, and they are introduced by *lākēn*, "therefore." We are teased into expecting another harsh statement, and
we are completely taken by surprise by the context of vv. 16-17. The
lākēn has been handled in a variety of ways. John Bright, following
Wilhelm Rudolph, regards it as logically unsuitable and takes the
first two letters, *lk*, as dittography from v. 15.[10] He reads the remaining *nun* as *waw*, a conjunction, reading "and all." Thus, he simply
dissolves the problem. Robert P. Carroll simply rejects vv. 16-17 as
coming from a different time and place,[11] and in this Carroll joins an
extended company of scholars. But Theodore M. Ludwig observes a
number of instances in which *lākēn* serves to introduce a declaration
of hope immediately following a statement of judgment. Of these,
Hos. 2:16 is the best known.[12] I shall return to this later.

Without resolving the problem of sequence and continuity, vv. 16-
17 offer a marvelous assurance. In these four phrases, three make
use of a wordplay so that the punishment is precisely correlated to
what had been perpetrated against Israel.[13] Thus, v. 16 is a curse
against the enemies, surely the very ones who had been authorized
to punish Israel.[14]

Verse 16 is mainly negative against the nations and does not
closely relate to vv. 12-15, for in those verses the nations are not
sent against Israel. Verse 17 is positive and of more interest to us. It
begins with a strong asseveration, *kî*, "surely." Yahweh then promises, "I will bring up health to you." The verb *'ālâ* corresponds to the
same verb in v. 13 used negatively, "None of the nations comes up to
you." What the nations will not do, Yahweh is willing to do. And the

---

10. Bright, *Jeremiah*, 271.

11. Carroll, *From Chaos*, 207.

12. Ludwig, "The Shape of Hope: Jeremiah's Book of Consolation," *CTM* 39
(1968): 534–35. The other uses Ludwig cites are Jer. 16:14; Ezek. 36:2-7, 13-15;
37:11-12; Isa. 25:3; 30:18; Mic. 5:2; Jer. 15:19.

13. Cf. Patrick D. Miller, *Sin and Judgment* (see chap. 1, n. 24), 69, and his specific translation. Miller has provided many examples of this way of constructing the
prophetic argument.

14. The Old Testament regularly seems to play out this drama. A nation is authorized by Yahweh to move against Israel as Yahweh's agent in judgment; but in doing
so, that nation goes beyond its mandate (or Yahweh's secret intent) and, therefore,
is in turn punished by Yahweh. This dramatic movement is somewhat odd because
the result is that nations are punished for what Yahweh sent them to do. That is perhaps the case in our passage in v. 16. Other examples include Isa. 47:6-7 and Ezekiel
38–39.

action of Yahweh is to heal, which in v. 13 is what the lovers refused
to do. The links to the preceding are expressed not only in the parallel words "go up," "heal," and "smite" (*ālâ, rāpā'*, and *makkat*), but
likely also in the introductory *kî*. The usage in v. 17 seems to answer
the use in v. 14. Both announce an action of Yahweh: The first is a
smiting to death; the second is a healing to new life. Each in its own
case is decisive.

The last line of v. 17 intensifies the helplessness yet one more time
in order to appreciate the stunning help of Yahweh. Israel is called
"outcast," that is, exiled, banished, driven out. And the final word
echoes again v. 14a, "no one cares for" (or seeks out).

Thus, vv. 16-17 are constructed to make a detailed and deliberate counterpart to the preceding. In the uses of "smite," "heal,"
and "go up," contrast is made between what lovers will not do and
what Yahweh will do. But in the last point on *dāraš*, the negative
line is repeated, not contrasted. It is implied that Yahweh does seek
and does care, so the intent is again contrasted with the preceding.
Special rhetorical power, however, is sustained by leaving the actual
statement in the negative. And so the shocking outcome is more
shocking: The one uncared for and unsought, until the very end
of the poem, is now sought and cared for by Yahweh.

We might puzzle over the second *kî* in v. 17.[15] The first one, as
we have seen, is a strong asseveration, "surely," in correspondence
to v. 14b. But the second is likely causative. It is because Israel is an
outcast for whom no one seeks that Yahweh is moved to intervene
in caring ways.

III

Obviously the most interesting and difficult problem of the text is
the relation between vv. 12-15 and vv. 16-17. It cannot be doubted
that the rhetorical move here offers a decisive shift. I suggest three
ways in which this could be handled, not of course counting a textual
emendation, which would not in fact face the rhetorical problem:

1. It was the conventional practice of the older literary criticism to
regard vv. 16-17 as a later gloss from another hand. Such a view fol-

---

15. On the remarkable range of functions for the particle, see Muilenburg, "The
Linguistic and Rhetorical Uses of the Particle in the Old Testament," *HUCA* 32 (1961):
135–60. On pp. 148ff., Muilenburg indicates the various ways in which the particle
functions in a causative or explanatory way. See also Ronald J. Williams, *Hebrew Syntax*,
2d ed. (Toronto: University of Toronto Press, 1980), secs. 444–52.

lows the general practice of resolving any substantive incongruity in the text by positing a redactional move. Such an approach confines its attention to the content of the text and completely disregards the rhetorical intention of the form, which may be aimed at just such a juxtaposition.[16] Such a decision about this text reflects the general assumption that the harsh words of a prophet would not have been followed by positive words from the same person, certainly not in the same poem. The effect is to make almost all positive speech late.[17]

2. A second approach is that taken by Patrick D. Miller, whose general hypothesis is that the prophets offer a "talonic" approach to their social criticism.[18] The things for which a subject is indicted as guilty are the very things they will suffer as punishment and sentence. Miller comments concerning our passage only on v. 16, where the precise correlations are offered: devour/devour, despoil/despoil, prey/prey. But Miller also makes the more general comment that "the judgment of exile upon Judah's enemies is also meant to correlate with the exile inflicted on her." There are two reasons why Miller's analysis (which I regard as shrewd and persuasive) does not help us with this passage. First, he begs the question about whether these verses are an original unit by saying only: "This rather detailed diagnosis . . . turns into a promise of healing." I suspect that he refers to this as an original unit, but he does not say so. Thus, his comment could mean that a redactor "turns" it into a promise. Second, Miller's general hypothesis concerns guilt and judgment, which leads him not to focus here on the two different stances taken toward Israel. In v. 16 (and v. 17), Miller's concern is judgment on the other nations, whereas it is in fact the new, surprising attitude toward Israel, one of healing, that is of interest for our purpose. It is the contrast of attitude and inclination toward Israel that is of

---

16. One example of handling such a literary construction by division into "editions" is the theory of two editions of the Deuteronomist, championed by Frank M. Cross, *Canaanite Myth* (see chap. 7, n. 7), chap. 10. See the same argument in more detail, in Richard D. Nelson, *Double Redaction* (see chap. 9, n. 22). It appears to me that in this hypothesis, where the literature deliberately states an ironic claim, the matter is dissolved by literary dissection; and our present passage is regularly treated in this way.

17. Against such a tendency, see the effort of Gerhard von Rad to retain the promise in Amos 9, in *Old Testament Theology II* (see chap. 3, n. 9), 138. Henning Graf Reventlow has proposed a more dynamic way to retain both judgment and promise speeches by a cultic hypothesis, *Amt des Propheten* (see chap. 3, n. 8), and *Wächter über Israel: Ezechiel und seine Tradition*, BZAW, no. 82 (Berlin: Töpelmann, 1962); but in this he has not been widely followed.

18. See Miller, *Sin and Judgment*.

interest. Attention to the other nations is of secondary importance. Nonetheless, Miller's general hypothesis indicates a sharp turn away from the older dissecting criticism in an attempt to see the passage as it stands.

3. A full appreciation of the text, however, requires a fuller assessment of its present unity. The newer literary criticism accepts incongruities, such as the one between v. 15 and v. 16, not as a problem to be solved by dissolution but as a freighted juncture in the text—the likely point of intentional meaning, likely to be an aesthetic achievement worth noting, and likely also to be a point of theological intentionality.

If we take this text in that way, we begin with the awareness that the two parts are correlated with considerable deliberateness. Our premise now is that this correlation is done by one speaker as an intentional rhetorical move; that is, the abrasion between v. 15 and v. 16 marked by *lākēn* ("therefore") is an intentional construction to make a special point. This correlation includes the theme of no healing/healing, the use of the term *rāpā'* ("heal") in both elements, the double use of *'ālâ* ("go up"), and the placement of *kî* as an introduction of Yahweh's two decisive actions in v. 14 and v. 17. But the most important parallel, I submit, is the two phrases with *dāraš*: "You they do not seek (care for)" (v. 14); and "For whom no one seeks (cares)" (v. 17). It is crucial that the contrast has not changed the second phrase to a positive, as in the other correlations. It is left in the negative, and that is possible because the last line is a quotation; that is, the poet does not say that Israel is an outcast or that Israel is not cared for, but that *the nations* say that Israel is an outcast and not cared for. In this single line the poet quotes others but does not describe Israel. He reports not what is extant, but what is said. As we shall see, the saying of the situation makes an important difference.

I propose that the last line of v. 17 is offered as a causative statement about why Yahweh has moved decisively in attitude from v. 15 to v. 16. In terms of the announced good news, the poem might have ended with v. 16 or at least with the first line of v. 17. It is enough to announce healing and restoration, and that would have completed the contrast. Indeed, we note that the *ne' um* yhwh comes at this point. This does not suggest that v. 17b is added but that, rhetorically, v. 17a does complete a point. But if the unit ended with 17a and the *ne' um* yhwh, then the shift made in vv. 16-17a would have been left unexplained. We would have known that Yahweh is now differently inclined, but we would have had no clue as to why.

Thus, v. 17b serves to disclose the theological ground on which the staggering move has been made.

Yahweh is moved to a wholly new action toward Israel by the contemptuous speech of the nations, quoted in v. 17b. In the speech attributed to the nations, they do not say anything that Yahweh has not already acknowledged in v. 14. Yahweh already knows that Israel is uncared for, but the point of the movement is that the nations now articulate this. Yahweh is moved to healing graciousness by such a contemptuous speech of the nations, even if what they say is true and echoes this statement of Yahweh.

That strange reaction on the part of Yahweh would seem to be so for two reasons:

The first is that the nations who say this seem to think they have put Israel in such a situation; that is, it is a statement presuming too much from their own autonomous initiative. Yahweh will not tolerate that self-serving opinion, because in v. 14 it is clear that Yahweh, and not the nations, has done it (see v. 15 for the climactic statement claiming this). Yahweh's new action of graciousness in vv. 16-17a seems to be in order to recover Yahweh's own initiative over against the false claim of the nations. Or to use Ezekiel's language, both the judgment and the healing are that "the nations may know I am Yahweh."[19] The healing is thus the reassertion of Yahweh's sovereign authority in the face of the nations, a point offered characteristically in the psalms of lamentations.[20] Yahweh acts for the sake of Yahweh's own name, for the sake of Yahweh's reputation among the nations. This judgment follows from taking the final *kî* as causative.

Second, we might suggest, in more homely fashion, that what Yahweh will say in v. 14 about Israel, the covenant partner, Yahweh finds intolerable on the lips of anybody else, such as the nations in v. 17. It is the same point of pride. Such a concern suggests that the punishment may be severe within the family, but a common front is made against the nations, who do not understand. The healing and restoration now given are to close that access to slander and misunderstanding by outsiders. Thus, the motivation given for Yah-

---

19. See the summary of the data by Walther Zimmerli, in *I Am Yahweh* (see chap. 7, n. 8), 1–28. Although that particular idiom is distinctively Ezekiel's and not Jeremiah's, the point of both parts of our text is that Yahweh be known as sovereign. In the first part, it is violation of Yahweh's sovereignty that causes the judgment. In the second part, it is the disrespect of the nations that causes Yahweh to make a harsh judgment that permits the rescue of Israel. In neither case does the cause lie elsewhere than with Yahweh in an assertion of Yahweh's rule.

20. E.g., Pss. 13:4; 74:10; 79:10.

weh's new action concerns the assessment made by nations. That may be to protect Yahweh's honor, but it could also be undertaken because the comment of the nations moves Yahweh to new compassion and attentiveness. Either way, Yahweh's new action toward Israel depends on this statement by a third party.

IV

Out of this analysis, I suggest that the poem as it now stands provides a theological structure that presents to us the main elements of Jeremiah's thought—and indeed a clear structure of biblical faith. In this tradition, biblical faith characteristically includes two moves:[21] The first move is "plucking up" and "tearing down." This is the substance of vv. 12-15. The second move is "planting" and "building," articulated in vv. 16-17. But the crucial point is that this poetic unit affirms that it is the *same God* who governs both moves, toward the *same people*. And if the same God with the same people, then surely our method must allow for these two moves by the *same poet* and in the *same poem*. For to deny them to the same poet and poem implies such a discontinuity in the literature that the moves cannot be made by the same God. Thus, one cannot hold to the same God doing both if one argues that v. 15 and v. 16 cannot belong to the same poem. The literary methods of the poet cannot be kept apart from the theological moves of the poem as it stands. The old redactional methods of criticism are regularly allied with liberal theological opinions about what the God of ethical liberalism would and would not do.

Thus, the newer critical methods, especially rhetorical criticism, have important theological implications. As a poet has enough imagination, courage, and subtlety to make a drastic move within the poem, the poet disclosed the imagination, courage, and subtlety known to be in the heart of God. This poem thus evidences the interiority of God, that God exercises freedom, explores options, makes

---

21. Jer. 1:10 is an excellent model for the two moves; see Prescott H. Williams, Jr., "Living toward the Acts of the Savior-Judge: A Study of Eschatology in the Book of Jeremiah," *Austin Seminary Bulletin* (1979): 13–39. Williams is interested primarily in exegetical matters, and he does not raise larger hermeneutical issues. His analysis, however, is ready grist for making use of Paul Ricoeur, *The Conflict of Interpretations* (Evanston, Ill.: Northwestern University Press, 1974), where he explores hermeneutical postures of "suspicion" and "retrieval." In this context, I suggest that our passage shows an act of suspicion in vv. 12-15 and an act of retrieval in vv. 16-17. Both moves must be made.

new initiatives, and is moved by the hurt of the covenant partner and the cynical abuse of the nations.[22]

None of this detracts from the "finality" of vv. 12-15. Israel is indeed one for whom no one cares, and in v. 17, Israel is still perceived as one for whom no one cares. The theological claim is that Yahweh is moved by and finally will not tolerate the status of beloved Israel as outcast and uncared for. Such a historical reality plays upon the heart of God and motivates (thus *kî* introduces a motivational statement) God to a new move. God cares precisely for the uncared for, and out of that caring in the face of rejection comes new life for Israel. But the new move, so far as we know, is wrought utterly and completely in God's heart and nowhere else. It is not evoked by Israel. It is not forced by the nations. The newness comes solely from God, who is touched by and implicated in the harshness of vv. 12-15.

V

The purpose of this discussion is twofold. First, it means to provide an example of the shift in method that has taken place, to evidence how current method seeks to take the text whole, and to bracket out those redactional possibilities that have preoccupied an older method. The change of method has been under way for a long time, but more practically we may say that the change has come in fact only in the last decade. Second, my purpose is to suggest that this methodological shift has important theological implications. Texts may not be assessed any longer "from the outside," according to our critical control, but must be appreciated for their fullness, filled as they

---

22. Abraham J. Heschel has poignant comments on the theological motifs in both parts of our text, *Prophets* (see chap. 2, n. 14). Concerning vv. 12-15 he writes: "The anger of God may bring misery and distress. Nevertheless, there is an agony more excruciating, more loathsome: the state of being forsaken by God. The punishment of being discarded, abandoned, rejected, is worse than the punishment of exile. Anger, too, is a form of His presence in history. Anger, too, is an expression of His concern" (p. 296). And with explicit reference to v. 17, he writes: "The prophets proclaimed that the heart of God is on the side of the weaker. God's special concern is not for the mighty and the successful, but for the lowly and the downtrodden, for the stranger and the poor, for the widow and the orphan. The heart of God goes out to the humble, to the vanquished, to those not cared for" (p. 167). Thus, the theological reality that God is moved by the fact that Israel is uncared for becomes the clue to understanding the literary construction of the text.

are with irony, subtlety, incongruity.[23] Such fresh critical method opens up ways to observe something creative and interior about the character of God, a theological point mostly denied in the older "reasonable" method.[24]

Newer method is informed by good literary theory, but it is equally clear that the theological claim of the text cannot be bracketed out methodologically. The theological point about God's new decision may guide our literary judgment.

---

23. Reference can still most helpfully be made to the work of Edwin M. Good, *Irony in the Old Testament* (Philadelphia: Westminster Press, 1965), for the ways in which literary finesse articulates the vitality of God.

24. On the dynamic power of the tradition in presenting and probing the creative and interior life of God, see the methodological statement of Dale Patrick, *Rendering of God* (see chap. 2, n. 17). The evocative power of the text is well articulated by Sallie McFague, in *Metaphorical Theology* (see chap. 2, n. 16). Our text may be read in terms of her analysis of the tension "is/is not," that is, cared for/not cared for.

Credits

Permission is gratefully acknowledged for republication of the following chapters of this book:

Chapter 1: *The Catholic Biblical Quarterly* 47 (1985), pp. 28–46.

Chapter 2: *The Catholic Biblical Quarterly* 47 (1985), pp. 395–415.

Chapter 3: *The Annual of the Society of Christian Ethics* (1989), pp. 73–92. Copyright © 1989 the Society of Christian Ethics. Reprinted with the permission of the Society of Christian Ethics, publisher of *The Annual of the Society of Christian Ethics.*

Chapter 5: *Journal for the Study of the Old Testament* 18 (1980), pp. 2–18.

Chapter 6: *Horizons in Biblical Theology* 6 (1984), pp. 1–11.

Chapter 7: *Theology Digest* 32 (1985), pp. 303–25.

Chapter 8: *Horizons in Biblical Theology* 1 (1979), pp. 47–86.

Chapter 9: *Biblical Theology: Problems and Prospects* (J. C. Beker Festschrift), edited by Steven Kraftchick and Ben Ollenburger. Copyright © 1993 Abingdon Press.

Chapter 10: *Vetus Testamentum Supplement* 36 (1984), pp. 40–53. Reprinted by permission of E. J. Brill, Publishers.

Chapter 11: *Zeitschrift für Alttestamentliche Wissenschaft* 102 (1990), pp. 33–48.

Chapter 12: *Catholic Biblical Quarterly* 50 (1988), pp. 383–97.

Chapter 13: *Journal for the Study of the Old Testament* 29 (1984), pp. 889–907.

Chapter 14: *Israelite Wisdom: Theological and Literary Essays in Honor of Samuel Terrien*, edited by John G. Gammie et al., pp. 85–105. Copyright © 1978 Scholars Press, Missoula, Mont.

Chapter 15: *Journal of Biblical Literature* 104 (1985), pp. 419–29.

Scripture Index

OLD TESTAMENT